Writing FOR THE ELECTRONIC MEDIA

SECOND EDITION

PETER E. MAYEUX
UNIVERSITY OF NEBRASKA-LINCOLN

WCB Brown & Benchmark
PUBLISHERS

Madison, Wisconsin•Dubuque, Iowa•Indianapolis, Indiana
Melbourne, Australia•Oxford, England

Book Team

Executive Editor *Stan Stoga*
Developmental Editor *Mary E. Rossa*
Production Editor *Debra DeBord*
Visuals/Design Developmental Consultant *Marilyn A. Phelps*
Visuals/Design Freelance Specialist *Mary L. Christianson*
Publishing Services Specialist *Sherry Padden*
Marketing Manager *Carla J. Aspelmeier*
Advertising Manager *Jodi Rymer*

WCB Brown & Benchmark

A Division of Wm. C. Brown Communications, Inc.

Executive Vice President/General Manager *Thomas E. Doran*
Vice President/Editor in Chief *Edgar J. Laube*
Vice President/Sales and Marketing *Eric Ziegler*
Director of Production *Vickie Putman Caughron*
Director of Custom and Electronic Publishing *Chris Rogers*

Wm. C. Brown Communications, Inc.

President and Chief Executive Officer *G. Franklin Lewis*
Corporate Senior Vice President and Chief Financial Officer *Robert Chesterman*
Corporate Senior Vice President and President of Manufacturing *Roger Meyer*

Cover and interior design by Carol S. Joslin. Cover image ©, 1993, Comstock, Inc.

Library of Congress Catalog Card Number: 92–75883

ISBN 0–697–14399–6

Printed in the United States of America by Wm. C. Brown Communications, Inc.,
2460 Kerper Boulevard, Dubuque, IA 52001

10 9 8 7 6 5 4 3 2 1

T his book is dedicated to the many writers who attempt to improve the human condition through their work in the electronic media. It is hoped that this book serves as a useful guide and an inspiration for those who strive to develop sound standards of professionalism and craftsmanship, a renewed sense of ethics and responsibility, and an enhanced spirit of creativity, inquisitiveness, and determination to serve better the challenging demands of today's electronic media audiences.

P. M.

Contents

3

Basic Writing Styles, Formats, and Techniques 45

4

Commercials and Announcements 93

5

News and Sports 149

6

Editorials and Commentaries 187

7

Documentaries and Investigative Reports 203

8

Interviews and Talk Programs 221

9

Music and Variety Programs 249

10

Special Writing Situations 281

11

Instructional and Corporate Presentations 325

12

Dramas and Comedies 357

13

Professional Writing Opportunities in the Electronic Media   399

Preface

T he importance and impact of the electronic media continue to increase. Today's listeners and viewers demand more than ever from mass media outlets: variety, sophistication, and availability on demand. Increasing competition for audience attention and loyalty creates new challenges for those who manage these delivery systems. This environment has also intensified and expanded the demand for those who can design, create, write, and produce program material that not only attracts a large target audience but also holds their attention and delivers the information or entertainment desired. Emerging technologies continue to intensify the demands that program material be flexible in design and use, as well as commercially viable.

From networks to local stations, major studios to small corporate production units, commercial copywriters to news reporters, dramatists to editorialists, effective and professional writing skills are essential for the continued success and strong impact of the electronic media. Effective writing skills contribute noticeably to the overall efforts of virtually every facet of the electronic media, and that is the subject of this book.

This book is intended to be a concise but thorough introduction to the basic approaches and techniques used to design and write material for the electronic media. It presents the essentials; however, it also explores less routine, more intricate writing situations to provide additional layers of writing information and practice and to explore new, emerging writing opportunities.

Throughout the book, attention is given to the role and responsibility of the writer and to the ways in which they influence the content and impact of what the writer creates. Essential production techniques and processes are presented so that writers will know how to indicate what they want and will be assured that what they want is the best that is available from production crews. Realistic business concerns and practices are also included to show how they relate to the success of the writer's work. Professional writing practices are described directly by writers and then illustrated by their actual scripts to show the reader how the writer's material was developed, refined, and then presented to clients for production.

Minor adjustments have been made to a limited number of scripts to accommodate book design considerations. Generally, however, scripts are shown as originally presented to the author by writers and production companies.

A variety of sources provided the scripts used in this book: stations, networks, syndication companies, institutional organizations, production houses, advertising agencies, reporters and on-air talent, producers, and many others. The result is an interesting array of material, displaying some of the best work possible by writers in the electronic media.

Notice that this book uses the word *electronic* rather than *broadcast* in its title. This designation acknowledges the evolution of the telecommunications systems now available. This evolution has merged into one industry— radio and television networks and stations, computers, satellites, cable channels, videocassette and videodisc outlets, home electronics industries, and many other electronic media delivery and operating systems—to provide various kinds of programs and presentations for today's audiences.

There are several noteworthy features of this book. Special chapters and sections of chapters examine topics and writing activities not fully explored or illustrated in similar books. These include promotional announcements and advertising campaigns, editorials and commentaries, investigative reporting, magazine programs, compilations, animation projects, children's programs, game shows, and techniques writers use to pitch story ideas and projects. Script material has been integrated *into* the chapters in authentic form to illustrate, in a meaningful way, professional writing styles and techniques. Professional writing practices and processes are described and illustrated by script material from electronic media professionals representing a variety of media sources. Appendices A–C provide extensive listings of books, publications, and professional and trade organizations related to various writing specialties; Appendix D shows complete sets of standards and guidelines used by three commercial networks to evaluate script material for network distribution. A wide range of realistic writing situations is used to explain the work of writers in small markets, as well as in major production centers. Common production *processes* are related directly to the writer's work and responsibilities. Hybrid jobs are identified and explained fully to illustrate that writers often tackle additional responsibilities not traditionally associated with writing. For easy reference, principal scripting formats are found in one place (chapter 3), and the techniques writers use to pitch ideas and projects are all in chapter 13. Each chapter is a self-contained presentation of a particular writing activity, but the interrelationships between the contents of each chapter are also noted so that the reader can begin to see the connections between different kinds of writing work. Each chapter concludes with a summary of chapter contents and a wide range of challenging writing exercises keyed to the various levels of writing work explored in that chapter.

Several adjustments have been made from an earlier edition of this book. Whereas the structure and the arrangement of the book have not changed, the content of every chapter has been updated and reorganized.

The revisions are based on the evolution of the nature of a writer's work in the electronic media, on comments by students who have used the earlier edition in classrooms around the country, and on the results of a questionnaire sent to current and prospective users of the book.

Throughout the book, script examples, exercises, and suggested readings have been updated to reflect current practices. Chapter 1 updates the regulations that influence the writer's work and contains an expanded section on how interviews and research can help writers gather material they need. Chapter 2 now traces a full array of standard production practices and techniques writers routinely encounter. Chapter 3 features an expanded writing style and language usage section and additional information on how computers and storyboards are used to develop and refine scriptwriting projects. Chapter 4 now includes an illustration of how copywriting techniques are applied to public service announcements and multimedia advertising efforts. Chapter 5 has been rewritten completely to illustrate contemporary, computer-driven television news scripting formats and to provide additional details needed to gather, write, and produce effective stories and newscasts; specialized reporting, features, and live broadcasts of sports events have also been added. Chapter 8 now traces the processes and procedures used to prepare script material for interactive talk programs, as well as single-person interviews; research notes, rundown sheets, and other script material have been included to trace a contemporary profile of these popular program forms. A discussion of music videos has been consolidated into chapter 9, which also traces the preparation process followed for two radio music program series and a television variety program special. Teleconferences and video news releases are now included in chapter 11 to update the profile of writing and production practices used for instructional and corporate presentations. The discussion of effective comedy writing techniques has been expanded in both chapters 11 and 12. Chapter 13 now includes an expanded description of techniques writers use to pitch ideas and projects; job options and Writers Guild of America (WGA) membership requirements have also been updated. Suggested readings are now placed in an appendix instead of at the ends of chapters. Other appendices provide current listings of professional publications and organizations, as well as program standards and practices that can influence a scriptwriter's work.

Although this book was designed to be used in a one-semester college- or university-level course, it could also be used in a two-semester course sequence. If two courses are planned in tandem, the first course could examine essential writing techniques and approaches covered in the first three chapters. This first course could also cover the shorter writing forms, such as commercials and announcements, news and sports copy, editorials and commentaries, talk programs, and music and variety programs. The second course could study the longer and more intricate writing forms—for instance, documentaries and investigative reports, instructional and corporate presentations, dramas, and comedies.

This two-layer approach is also useful when planning the sequence of material in a single course. Essential techniques and basic writing assignments could be presented first, and then more sophisticated approaches could be explored later. This approach would help students establish essential writing skills before tackling more intricate writing assignments.

This book would also be useful for specialized or advanced coursework. Here are a few examples: multimedia writing courses that illustrate basic styles, formats, and techniques for print *and* electronic media; advertising courses that explore production and copy techniques used by the electronic media; broadcast public affairs courses that cover a wide range of topics, such as news and sports writing, editorials and commentaries, documentaries and investigative reports, talk programs, magazine programs, and special events; and instructional or corporate communications courses that include not only the design and production of electronic media material but also basic formats and writing styles, spot announcements, news coverage, commentaries, documentaries, talk and magazine programs, special events, and even the use of music videos in an institutional setting.

Special educational strategies are often useful when trying to learn electronic media writing techniques. Here are a few that instructors have found beneficial: each student keeps an idea journal to document inspirations, impressions, and concerns as a writer; each student assignment is provided to each other student in the group to enhance the quality of critiques received; and instructors use audiocassette tapes to provide individual comments and/or suggestions about a particular scripting assignment. There are many ways instructors can help students write better scripts.

This book illustrates and examines the principal forms of writing for the electronic media. It displays the range and diversity of material now used. It describes and analyzes the processes and techniques used by successful writers. It introduces basic concepts and provides opportunities to polish writing techniques that will make beginning writers good and good writers even better. It will help them sharpen their skills and broaden their writing potential as they examine and practice techniques used in writing for the electronic media.

This book provides only basic information about a wide variety of writing situations. One cannot expect to become an accomplished writer after simply reading the chapters and end-of-chapter exercises. Writers need to continue to improve their skills through constant practice and thoughtful critique.

Acknowledgments

The quality and scope of this book would have been seriously limited without the advice, cooperation, and assistance of many individuals and organizations. Their help was invaluable in providing the best possible information and illustrations of effective techniques and approaches for writing for the electronic media. Obviously, none of these individuals and organizations is responsible for errors, omissions, or opinions expressed by the author, and not all of them necessarily agree with everything contained in this book.

Some of the people who helped provide material have since changed jobs. Here, and where I have mentioned them elsewhere, I have chosen to list the positions they held when they supplied the material used in this book.

My continued thanks and appreciation are extended to my colleagues in the Broadcasting Department and in the College of Journalism at the University of Nebraska–Lincoln. Their encouragement and advice were very helpful for this project. My sincere thanks go to Linda Shipley, Clancy Strock, and Chuck Piper for their guidance on the development of chapter 4, "Commercials and Announcements."

Current and former students have generously shared their insights and energy. They were very helpful in supplying guidance, script material, and the necessary permissions. Special recognition is extended to Sharon Roesler, Axis Productions, who provided an eleventh-hour effort when script examples were needed; Keri Benell; John Holden; Rick Alloway; Sandra Cowley; James M. Vojtech, Cable News Network; Barbara Simon and Gary Shapiro, KUSA-TV; Ann Pedersen Gleeson, WCCO-TV; Don Browers, KMTV; Dennis Wilden, WOWT; and Dave Madsen, KTIV-TV.

Although the contributions of specific individuals and companies are indicated throughout the book, several should receive particular recognition: *Nan Siemer* and Joe Gillespie, WTOP Radio; Kevin Cerenza, WHYI FM; Mike Beardsley, KPNX-TV; Lester M. Smith, Broadcast Programming, Inc.; Dave Scott Blyth, TM Century, Inc.; Marty Pasetta; Beth Schenker; Don Lee, National Public Radio; Kent Takano and R. M. Montgomery, KXTV; Marjorie Arons-Barron, Elizabeth Cheng, and Curtis Poole, WCVB-TV; Dale R. Woolery, KRNT Radio; Woody Fraser, Cece Caldwell, Marty Tenney, Richard R. Camp, and James E. Witte, "Home"; Michael J. Greene, Mutual of Omaha Companies; Richard V. Ducey, National Association of Broadcasters; Gene Fogel, WJR; Dr. Bernarr Cooper; Bruce Davis, Academy of Motion Pictures Arts and Sciences; John Lippman, KIRO TV; Mark DeVitre, Hanna-Barbera; Blake Hunter, Martin Cohan, Michael Hanel, and Marcia Durand, Columbia Pictures Television and "Who's the Boss?"; Bob Noonan, WLOX-TV; William R. Buccalo, SnowBird Software; Steve Murphy and Marilyn Konigsberg, WOWT; Ken Fearnow, WOW Radio; Katherine Bulwin, Comprehensive Video Supply Corporation; Cheryl Rhoden, Writers Guild of America, west, Inc.; Fred Rothenberg, "Later . . . with Bob Costas"; Leslie Crawford, "The Tonight Show with Jay Leno"; Bettie Denney and Debbie Rodgers, KETV; John Sullivan, KMTV; Bryan Brosamle, KTIV-TV; George Woods, KFAB; Joe Silberman, Kimberly J. Smith, and Mande Moore, Leo Burnett Co., Inc.; Patrick diNatale, Dena Bridgeman, Mike Schreiber, and Bill Musgrave, Bernstein Rein; Richard P. Gitter, Iris Gelt, Gene Shalit, and John Chancellor, NBC-TV; Robin J. Schwartz and Alfred C. Carosi, Jr., NBC Entertainment; Lee Brooks Rivera, Cable News Network; Carol A. Altieri and Susan J. Holliday, CBS Broadcast Group; Alfred A. Schneider and Christine Hikawa, Capital Cities/ABC Inc.; Kim Fleary, ABC Entertainment; Marsha Myers, ABC Children's Programs; Merrilee Cox, ABC News; Jim Bohannon and F. Gifford, Mutual Broadcasting

System; Al E. Smith, Westwood One Companies; Riley Fields, Raycom Sports; Nancy J. Masano and Margaret Cowan, American Physical Therapy Association; Malin Jennings, Investment Company Institute; Sue Edelman, Action for Children's Television; Cora B. Everett, National Broadcast Editorial Association; Gary Taylor, Broadcast Promotion and Marketing Executives; Debbie Palm, International Interactive Communications Society; Inez Wehrli, International Television Association; Sandi Robles, Society of Professional Journalists; David Bartlett and Kathleen Hilburn, Radio-Television News Directors Association; John Spain, WBRZ-TV; Carol D. Knutson, KERO-TV; Lew Hunter; Dale Baglo; Allen E. Hall and Rick Rosenthal, WGN-TV; Rachel Powell; David E. Kelley; Peter S. Fischer; Fred Bergendorff, KNX Radio; Dan Enright, Barry and Enright Productions; Brad R. Moore and Ira Stolzer, Hallmark Cards, Inc.; Lennart S. Carlson, Saatchi & Saatchi Wegener; Wayne Lindberg; David Haselkorn, Recruiting New Teachers, Inc.; Lynn Ross, American Association of Retired Persons; Ed Hinshaw, WTMJ; Sharon Geer and Patti Gorsky, WITI-TV; J. M. Goldstein, Merck & Co., Inc.; Frank Hoffman, Nebraska Public Radio Network; Gene Bunge, Nebraska ETV Network; and Brian R. Glaze.

My thanks go to the following for their insight and advice offered when the manuscript was reviewed for publication: William R. Buccalo, Northern Michigan University; W. Joseph Oliver, Stephen F. Austin State University; Larry N. Phillips, Arizona State University; and Lynda Wahl-Wilson and David Sedman, University of Arkansas at Little Rock. Lynne S. Gross assisted greatly with advice about script acquisitions.

A very special thank-you is extended to my wife Sue and my son Ben for their amazing patience and encouragement during this challenging project.

Peter E. Mayeux
Harold A. and Ethel Bash Soderlund Professor of Broadcasting
University of Nebraska–Lincoln

Introduction to Writing for the Electronic Media

A writer shapes ideas and concepts into words and sentences that eventually will be shared by an immense audience. Writing is a challenging profession that requires a special kind of person and a unique set of skills. Nothing matches the satisfaction and exhilaration a writer experiences when ideas come together on paper and, eventually, are transformed into a presentation that directly touches thousands of lives. That is the challenge offered to you as you read this book—to develop the insights, skills, and techniques you need to write effective script material for the electronic media. This includes radio, television, cable, satellite-delivered interactive video, and taped presentations.

This first chapter will help you understand and appreciate the role, responsibility, and activities of the writer in today's media. The essential qualifications needed to become a writer are discussed so that you can assess your abilities and interests. Next, the role and function of the writer are examined to emphasize the impact an electronic media writer can have. Then, the resources needed by a writer are outlined. Finally, laws, regulations, and concerns of the electronic media are examined to stress the need for the writer to develop a deep, professional sense of ethics and responsibility and to help him or her avoid common legal and ethical problems. The principal purpose of this chapter is to help you understand and appreciate the work and concerns of the professional writer in the electronic media.

Qualifications

Formal training in developing effective electronic media writing skills is not necessarily a prerequisite for success but is highly recommended. Interests that you may have acquired earlier in life can be developed with supervision and direction to sharpen your skills and techniques. Such formal instruction may not give you a passion for writing but could develop and expand your writing talent.

Diverse experience in the telecommunications media, as well as in life, provides a solid knowledge base for the aspiring writer. Internship or part-time experience in a broadcast facility usually provides an interesting perspective on the internal workings of the mass media. At the same time, your life experiences—part-time jobs in school, the loss of a close friend or relative, your hopes and disappointments, the first time you drove a car, your first date—all combine to provide you with a unique perspective from which to write. The more you know about various life experiences, the better your writing will be.

Become a conscious observer. Develop a sense of curiosity, inquisitiveness, and sensitivity to people and events outside your own world. Develop the ability to project yourself into the lives of those around you. Learn to observe, retain, and then creatively use the gestures, mannerisms, and language habits of others, so that you can write in a personal, conversational style. Never stop seeing, listening, feeling, questioning, and probing to explore the wonders and intricacies of the human experience in your writing. This insatiable desire to know, understand, and experience the human spirit is a lifelong learning commitment and adventure.

Become a lover of words—their meanings, innuendos, emotional impact, and nuances. Examine carefully the use of words in great literature. Experience the satisfaction of finding the right combination of words to inform clearly, to entertain creatively, and to influence, with purpose and emotion, the attitudes and behavior of others. Careful word selection begins the process of crafting effective sentences and, eventually, entire scripts that display your love for language.

Be creative. Continually develop the ability to communicate—visually and aurally, as well as on paper. Try to reexperience human emotions and situations with clarity and inventiveness. In short, cultivate a creative spirit that enriches reality with imagination and presents it in an especially effective manner. Several techniques can invigorate your creative spirit. Keep a journal in which you note ideas, record your experiences and impressions, and describe the people and situations you encounter. Read a variety of material written from divergent viewpoints. Try to see and experience familiar situations as though you were encountering them for the first time—for example, riding a bicycle, entering your room, or eating a favorite food. Love and honor your creative force, and nurture your creative ideas. Let them emerge, incubate, crystallize, inspire, and sustain your writing efforts.

Creativity is essential, but you must also be realistic and practical. Although it is admirable to reach for lofty, creative goals, this effort must be tempered with the reality and practicality of the situation. Understand and appreciate the constraints of budgets, deadlines, and technical limitations and know how they influence the writer's work.

An effective writer knows the intricacies and requirements of the electronic media. It is essential for you to cultivate a thorough sense of what is acceptable now and what might be possible in the future. Evaluate critically the current products of the media for form, style, conceptualization, visualization, communicative effectiveness, and language use.

Writing is work. Good writing is hard work. An unidentified but experienced writer said: "The art of writing is the art of applying the seat of the pants to the seat of the chair.'' A writer does not suddenly create material because of a flash of inspiration. A good writer works at it every day. Writing, both for the electronic media and in general, is a self-motivating profession. Discipline your mind and body to the rigors of writing. Establish a writing routine or schedule. You must motivate yourself and invigorate your work to achieve success.

In the electronic media, deadlines are demanding and exacting. Audio and video material is consumed quickly and with little regard for the time and care given to a script or to production. You need rigorous discipline to meet unforgiving deadlines with consistent, quality material. You must be creative and imaginative every hour of every work day, and, if you are a good writer, your work never stops. It becomes a significant part of your life.

Become flexible in your attitudes, work habits, and writing skills. Many successful writers now working in the electronic media began their writing careers in other media—poetry, playwriting, newspapers, or magazines. The basics of effective writing are essential and applicable to all media. The demands of the electronic media often require a commercial copywriter, for example, to create an award-winning announcement in less than thirty minutes. The outline for an interview with an important government official may have to be written at 6 A.M. for use on an early-morning telecast. Often the best writing is done under pressure, something the industry has accepted as reality. It is also important to work well with others, since your work is meant to be used by other people to create the final presentation. It is possible to be persuasive without being abrasive and to work in a team, sharing ideas and insights that will enhance rather than erode your writing efforts. ''People skills'' are very important to any writer.

You must have confidence in your ability to write. You must be determined to succeed despite the likelihood of criticism and rejection of your work. Others will criticize your writing, some with malice and others in a sincere effort to make your creative work even better. The amount and degree of criticism and rejection that you receive often hinge on what you expect of yourself. Give yourself and your audience only your best, now and in the future. Writing demands not only a belief in your ability, but also the courage to deal with uncertainties and the confidence to continue working steadily, with no immediate reward in sight. It is a tough job. Only the tough, and confident, should apply.

Establish goals and objectives—a game plan. What kind of writing work do you want to be doing three years from now? Five years from now? How will you get there from here? What path of professional development will you follow? Without a specific career goal, you cannot develop a sense of direction and purpose or measure your success and progress. Since so much of your success as a writer depends on your own efforts, realistic and challenging goals (both personal and professional) are essential. This is discussed further in chapter 13.

Be organized. It is often necessary to create order out of chaos, to take a large volume of information and condense it into a short, informative, effective announcement or program. A sense of orderliness about life-style, goals, and ambitions will help you produce quality work and to remain alert to the business aspects of the writing profession.

Good writing requires commitment—to yourself and to your audience. You must want to write. The urgent need to express yourself through writing must already be in place. The desire and willingness to share and express, in a meaningful way, your knowledge, observations, feelings, and discoveries must be important to you and to those for whom you write. Without this total commitment and the resultant discipline, your measure of success and satisfaction as a writer will be limited. This commitment—coupled with a measure of talent, a fascination for words, discipline, persistence, flexibility, knowledge of the media, maturity, integrity, energy, and unshakable confidence in your ability to touch other lives in a special, interesting, and meaningful way—provides a unique, challenging, and rewarding life.

Role and Function

Perhaps the words of an unidentified writer spoken some time ago best express the nature of writing:

> I'm only a writer. . . . I deal in the politics of words . . . of human experiences . . . of dreams . . . of sadness. When I am at my best my pages laugh and sing and they also cry. When I'm at my worst my pages wait impatiently for me to make them come alive . . . to add layers of texture and shading until my pages become dimensional. . . . I'm a painter. I'm a composer. I'm a rabble rouser . . . a provocateur. I'm a patriot. I'm the enemy. I wave the flag. And sometimes I hide from it. I'm a tender lover. . . . I'm a hard bargainer. I'm sweet and innocent. I'm hardened and brutal.
>
> I'm a writer. This is my world. Welcome to it. It's a world filled with the unpredictable . . . with blind spots and dead ends . . . with straight lines which out of nowhere, it seems, suddenly change direction. It's a world of ethics and erotica . . . pathos and pleasure . . . and the writer sits in the middle of all this confusion like a sponge being soaked and squeezed . . . and if you really want to write you face a constant dilemma of values . . . yours and everyone else's.
>
> This is the writer's world . . . this is our world.

The writer is a prime mover. An effective radio or television program or announcement begins with the writer—thinking, dreaming, imagining, creating. Although many processes and priorities interplay in the presentation of a program or announcement, it is the writer who first generates an idea and then prepares material in a form that can be used by many others to finish the production.

It is important to maintain standards of excellence. Pride in your work means caring about what you do and how you do it. The pursuit and attainment of excellence bring with them the confidence and reassurance necessary to accept new challenges. Writers often face pressures to compromise their standards. Such situations are best resolved from a position of strength and confidence gained through the writing of quality scripts for a variety of audiences. See Appendix D for sample program and presentation standards and guidelines.

Good writing has an impact—on both the writer and the audience. Each time you write, you should grow and develop as a writer and as a person. Writing can and should be a source of personal satisfaction, as well as a contribution to the improvement of your world. If done well, your writing can also have a significant impact on the attitudes, habits, and behavior of the audience. It can make them more aware of the world around them, establish or support social values and trends, and even help standardize the use of language. Writing is a powerful tool that, when used ethically, professionally, and responsibly through the influential telecommunications media, can inform, influence, and persuade large numbers of people.

Resources

Get to know the tools, or resources, that can help make writing more efficient, more productive, and more effective. Language and writing aids, such as reference books and supplies, can help enhance and refine your expressiveness. Professional organizations and publications can inform you of developments in your profession and help you better understand and appreciate the intricacies of the electronic media. Research can help you uncover the information you will need to write your scripts.

Language and Writing Aids

Two language aids that should be beside the writer at all times are a dictionary and a thesaurus. A dictionary identifies the spelling and meaning of words. A thesaurus helps you find synonyms for words you have used several times in the same script or helps you choose a specific word to use. An excellent dictionary is the latest *Webster's International* (or *Collegiate) Dictionary,* and the latest edition of *Roget's Thesaurus of the English Language* is recommended.

Another item that should be added to your writing library is a reference book on English language grammar and writing style. There are several excellent general reference works; these are recommended: *The Chicago Manual of Style,* 13th ed. (Chicago: The University of Chicago Press, 1982); Lauren Kessler and Duncan McDonald's *When Words Collide: A Media Writer's Guide to Grammar and Style,* 3d ed. (Belmont, CA: Wadsworth, 1992); and William Strunk, Jr., and E. B. White's *The Elements of Style,* 3d ed. (New York: Macmillan Publishing Company, 1979). These reference works provide excellent information on the correct use of language in any medium. Chapter 3 will illustrate specific writing styles and formats unique to the electronic media.

A few tabletop items should be kept nearby: scratch pads, index cards, and inexpensive newsprint or a similar item for making quick notes to yourself as you formulate your writing strategy. Ballpoint pens and sharpened pencils with heavy lead complete your tabletop accessories, except as personal preference dictates.

It is essential to have access to a typewriter or word processor. Although you may sketch out your thoughts or outline your ideas with a pencil and pad as you begin the creative process, your final product must be in typewritten form. It is an industrywide requirement. If you cannot type or if you use the tedious "hunt-and-peck" method, your work as a professional writer is limited. Clean, typewritten scripts are a mark of your professionalism. Your scripts represent you to those who read them.

Microcomputers or personal computers (PCs) are commonly used to generate scripts. A variety of software programs are available and can be used with major brand computer systems to produce scripts in standard form. Writers who have used such systems find that word processing streamlines the writing, revision, and copying of scripts; increases efficiency; and cuts costs. Some writers lease several different computer units before deciding on the brand they want to purchase. The features of computer-generated scriptwriting systems are described and illustrated in chapter 3.

Some writers still prefer to use a typewriter, an acceptable practice in limited situations. The IBM Selectric is the typewriter used most often in professional scriptwriting. It features a wide carriage and the Courier 72, 10-pitch element, which produces 10 characters per inch. Although this is the ideal typewriter to use, any sturdy and reliable machine would be fine.

Computers and typewriters do not substitute for your creativity. That is still up to you. However, machines *can* help you present your work in a strong, professional manner.

Professional Organizations and Publications

Professionals normally associate with other professionals, both in and out of their field. Such associations keep them in tune with the current attitudes and developments of those with similar interests and concerns. Membership in professional organizations enhances their skills and provides perspective on the constantly changing situations affecting all professionals in that field. Often such membership is a means of formulating positions on issues and events.

One way to form a professional attitude is to participate in the activities of professional associations or organizations that relate directly to your work. Many groups publish periodical material that serves both as an internal organ for the membership and as a means of fulfilling some of the objectives indicated earlier. Many professional writers find that the benefits and services provided by such memberships far outweigh any costs or inconveniences involved.

Because the telecommunications industry changes and adjusts rapidly to contemporary demands, many professional writers find it essential to subscribe to one or more periodicals that keep them informed about industry developments, in addition to the publications provided as part of membership in a professional organization. You must also read the industry news and trade press. It is part of the job. Often it is the source for writing assignments.

Appendix B is a list of media publications; Appendix C is a compilation of professional organizations related to writing for the electronic media. Review and use both lists to strengthen your commitment to professionalism as a writer.

Research

This brief discussion will stress the importance of research and outline the primary approaches to gathering information to complete writing assignments for the electronic media.

Importance

Research is vital to good writing. Without research, you cannot present information that is accurate and applicable to the audience being addressed. Research helps you uncover information that can provide depth and texture to your work, as well as fuel for inspiration and creativity.

Approaches

Let the kind of information you need determine the nature and scope of your research. For example, if you are writing a television drama about an older widow who faces the problems of making ends meet, you certainly would want to read material on that topic; however, you would also want to talk to women in that situation, observe their habits and mannerisms, listen to their concerns, and then formulate a gripping plot that features lifelike characters in realistic situations, facing problems you now know and share intimately. The effectiveness of the script hinges on the way you use the information you gather.

The way in which you complete your research—the approaches you take—depends on the nature of the script you are writing, as well as on your time frame, your personal preferences, and your work skills. Approach your research in three phases: (1) determine what you need to know, (2) identify where to find what you need, and (3) handle what you find. What do you have now and *exactly* what do you need to obtain? Who and what are the best sources to provide what you need? Evaluate and organize the material you collect to determine its quality, as well as your need to pursue additional sources.

Some writers organize their research efforts very carefully and in a formal manner. They begin by listing the people they want to contact. This list can be in the form of a "source chart," which indicates the name, title, organization or affiliation, telephone number, complete address, and results of the contact made. Each source can be further identified according to the information or comment the writer will be seeking, the perspective or angle needed for the script, and the urgency to contact that source. If a writer uses a laptop computer, this source chart can be updated easily, and can be a handy reference when each source is contacted. Such planning efforts make research strong, efficient, and consistent.

There are several ways to gather information. These include reading, observing, and interviewing.

Reading   Reading involves finding, digesting, organizing, and retaining information from written sources, such as books, magazines, catalogs, and collections. Learn how to find such information and how to collect and organize it once you have found it. Take a course in basic research methods or seek the help or advice of a research librarian. Many writers use databases for their research needs. Once computers are linked via a modem, information can be retrieved over telephone lines. Databases can locate background information, identify experts, and even retrieve script material from various archives and files.

Observing   As a writer you need a keen sense of observation. You can learn a great deal about people by watching and listening to what they do and say. The method(s) you use to gather the necessary information depend on your preferences as a writer, the topic(s) involved, and the writing assignment.

Interviewing   An expert or resource person can respond to questions during an interview. This can be accomplished in a face-to-face meeting, by telephone, or by written responses in a letter or FAX communication. The next section of this chapter explains how to handle research interviews.

Suggestions

In gathering information, organize your efforts to make the results worthwhile. Each piece of information you gather should lead you to successive ideas, facts, and sources. The more you know, the more you should want to know. Explore all possible leads.

Reading   If necessary, ask a librarian for help. Learn how to use the basic as well as the supplementary services of a good library. Get to know the available services that could be helpful for current as well as future writing projects. Carefully read and clip articles from a reputable daily newspaper or weekly news magazine to tap into an excellent source of ideas and information. Remember to date and file these clippings in a way that helps you organize the material for future use. You should research a subject sufficiently to be able to write accurately and intelligently.

Observing   Become sensitive to your surroundings. Scan what's available—sights, sounds, smells, and impressions. Begin to record what you observe and what it means to you. Your observations will prove valuable when you write various kinds of scripts in the future.

Look beyond the obvious. Notice the details that most people overlook. Observe what people do and say, as well as how they speak, and even how they stand or sit. Notice attitude as well as content.

Careful and consistent observation can provide almost unlimited material for future writing opportunities. Observation is a research tool that must be consciously used and consistently applied.

Interviewing   Interviewing an expert or a resource person is one of the best ways to gather information and comments. Conduct an interview when you need opinions and insights as well as information and when you need to explore, discover, reconfirm, investigate, or understand people and issues directly and personally.

Following are eighteen suggestions to help you make research interviews productive and efficient.

    a. *Get the interview.* Write or call to make an appointment. Indicate clearly who you are, what you need, what you hope to accomplish, and why the comments of the person you want to interview are important. Then get a personal interview if at all possible.

    b. *Prepare.* Gather enough information to know and understand the general subject area, but let your resource person provide new ideas and dimensions. Learn as much as possible about your resource person—for example, his or her credentials, background, and career accomplishments—as well as the issues involved and the interview situation you are likely to encounter.

    c. *Plan your strategy.* Know what you need and determine your plan for getting the information and comments you want.

    d. *Plan your questions.* Prepare an outline or list of brief, specific questions before the interview takes place but after you complete some preliminary research on the topic and on the person you will interview.

    e. *Ask to record the interview.* Your effectiveness as an interviewer will be improved if you persuade the resource person to allow you to tape record the interview. Explain that the purpose of the recording is not to use it on the air but for accuracy and later reference. What has become an established procedure for most print journalists should be acceptable to your expert or resource person. Be certain your equipment is inconspicuous and in good working condition.

    f. *Demonstrate that you are prepared.* Indicate by your organization and confidence that you have done your homework, that you have evaluated the available sources of information, and that you have come to the interview prepared to gather information and insights unique to this source.

    g. *Listen.* Be attentive during your source's responses. React to what the person says. Ask follow-up questions you haven't prepared in advance.

    h. *Observe.* Notice the resource person's words, body language, and moods. This will help you gauge the person's priorities, attitudes, emotions, and point of view.

i. *Converse.* Try to have an interesting conversation. Build rapport. Do not interrogate or cross-examine. Try to understand the person's point of view.

j. *Do not interrupt unnecessarily.* Let your source talk freely and openly about the topic. Guide the conversation, but do not dominate it.

k. *Do not be afraid of silence.* Just as in an interesting conversation with a friend, an occasional pause is not distracting. In fact, it may even be welcomed. Most sources try to fill the void created by even a short silence with additional comments that may be better than those you've already obtained.

l. *Be yourself.* Be natural, relaxed, and confident. There is no reason to pretend to be someone other than who you are— a person interested in obtaining information and insights.

m. *Determine immediate concerns.* What most bothers, interests, concerns, bores, disturbs, bewilders, or confuses the person you are interviewing?

n. *Probe.* Delve into the attitudes, positions, beliefs, and convictions of this individual. Get to the heart of this person. Determine how these findings relate to the topic being examined.

o. *Be tenacious.* Diplomatically, keep probing with your questions until it is obvious you are not going to obtain any substantial additional information. You may need to make your respondent formulate or commit to a point of view or to a feeling. Carefully guide your source through this process.

p. *Maintain control of the interview.* Avoid letting minor concerns or distractions dominate your interview time. Stay on course. The quality of your preparation, plus your own tenacity, will determine your success.

q. *Handle legal concerns carefully.* Questions concerning invasion of privacy, personal attack, libel, and slander must be considered carefully and judicially. Requests to make off-the-record comments during your interview must be decided quickly and with sound judgment. Be prepared for such situations.

r. *Thank the interview guest.* Express your appreciation for the interviewee's time and effort. It would be best to contact your resource person after the interview, repeat your appreciation, and provide a brief progress report on the project for which you received help.

Regulations, Restraints, and Responsibilities

The misuse or the fear of misuse of the mass media's power often results in regulations and restraints being placed on the media by the government, by other organizations, and by the media directly. To some, regulation is a distasteful restriction on their activities. To others, regulation is a welcome protection of basic rights and responsibilities.

Telecommunications is a heavily regulated industry. It has been since the earliest days of the crystal radio sets and continues today in the era of satellite communications, expanding cable systems, and burgeoning home video entertainment centers. Regulations and pressures placed on the industry filter down to the work of the writer. You need to know the basic rights, privileges, and responsibilities associated with writing material for use in this closely monitored and regulated industry.[1]

This is not intended to be a comprehensive discussion of regulations and restraints. Rather, it is a summary of the major restrictions and concerns that have an impact on the responsibility of writing for the electronic media. Specific legal questions should be directed to appropriate legal counsel. Consult the information in this chapter as you read the rest of the text. Study this material to prepare yourself for future writing assignments and to begin formulating the personal and professional attitudes and standards that will affect your work as a writer.

Audio and video signals enter the home and workplace as trusted friends. Programs provide entertainment, information, and inspiration to all ages, ethnic groups, and social classes. Because of this expectation, those who write for the electronic media need to exercise restraint and display a responsible attitude toward their work. This attitude should prevail for over-the-air presentations, as well as for material received via closed-circuit, cable, and private satellite channels. There are differences between some of the regulations that affect licensed radio and television stations and those that affect closed-circuit program services, such as cable systems. No matter how your work is used in the electronic media, however, always be a responsible professional. Monitor carefully the selection and development of *each* writing assignment.

Offensive Material

The Federal Communications Commission (FCC) continues to affirm that the airwaves belong to the people. Service to the people has been an established principle of broadcasting in the United States since its earliest years. The flick of a switch brings numerous programs, which shape opinions and mold life-styles. The intrusive nature of the electronic media creates additional responsibility for the broadcaster; however, this responsibility is not necessarily shared or embraced by those in the print media, where the material to be read is consciously purchased for consumption and can be more readily controlled. Since language in its broadest interpretation (both words and pictures) is the primary vehicle for any writer working in the electronic media you should know what is allowed under the law and make an informed evaluation of the ethical concerns.

Indecent material generally comprises descriptions of sexual or excretory activities or organs in terms that are offensive by contemporary community standards.

Indecency

In 1990, the FCC concluded that its twenty-four-hour ban on the broadcast of indecent material was constitutional. The Commission decided that, since data show that children (defined as minors, age seventeen and under) are in the broadcast audience at all hours, it would be impossible to protect them at all times from exposure to indecent material, so the FCC banned all indecent material from the airwaves.

In 1991, the U.S. Court of Appeals in the District of Columbia questioned whether the FCC's twenty-four-hour indecency ban would satisfy First Amendment requirements. The appeals court ruled in May 1991 that there could not be a twenty-four-hour-a-day prohibition of indecent broadcasts. The appeals court said there must be a daily "safe-harbor" period when such material is permitted on the airwaves. The FCC, pending the outcome of its challenge of the ruling, did not try to bar indecent material broadcast from 8 P.M. until 6 A.M. daily.

In 1992, the U.S. Supreme Court reviewed the appeals court decision and concluded that an around-the-clock ban on indecent radio and television broadcasts violated free-speech rights.

In 1993, the FCC continued to enforce a "safe harbor" of 8 P.M. until 6 A.M. daily, pending legal challenges to the FCC regulations by media organizations. Whereas material that is merely indecent is protected by the Constitution, legally obscene material has no such protection.

Obscenity

The FCC is authorized, under provisions of the Communications Act of 1934, to revoke a broadcast station license or to impose a fine on the licensee for violation of Section 1464 of the U.S. Criminal Code. This section prohibits the utterance of "any obscene, indecent or profane language by means of radio communications [the term has been interpreted to include television]."

The current standard for determining obscenity was established by the United States Supreme Court in 1973 in the case of *Miller* v. *California* (413 U.S. 15). The Court's test is

> whether the average person, applying contemporary community standards,
> would find that the work, taken as a whole, appeals to the prurient interest;
> whether the work depicts or describes in a patently offensive way, sexual
> conduct specifically defined by the applicable state law; and whether the work
> taken as a whole, lacks serious literary, artistic, political or scientific value.

The Court has not ruled directly whether the terms *indecent* and *obscene* are synonymous. The FCC attempted to define "indecent language" with a declaratory order issued in 1975 (Pacifica Foundation, 56 FCC 2d 94), but the Court held that the Commission's Order violated Section 326 of the Communications Act and was unconstitutionally vague. Instead, the Court said the FCC should continue to trust the licensee to exercise judgment, responsibility, and sensitivity to the community's needs, interests, and tastes.

Many media observers have noted with alarm a growing promiscuity and lack of sensitivity toward traditional human values. Many listeners and viewers are offended by the flippant treatment of such themes as drugs, divorce, and unfettered sexual relationships. They are disturbed by the increasing number of adult scenes, situations, and subjects now shown when impressionable young minds are near the set. For some media observers, titillation of the viewer has become an accepted practice.

Program and Advertising Material

Sponsors and program producers contend that this technique is a viable means of competing with other media, that today's sophisticated audiences demand more programming choices than ever before, and that, to capture the available audience, they must make certain calculated decisions and compromises. Most advertisers and program producers agree that high-quality content and a recognition of significant responsibility are important, but they also admit that the economic realities of the media marketplace often prevent this pursuit of excellence. The writer working in this environment must make difficult, but necessary, personal and professional decisions based on ethical and legal concerns. Appendix D displays examples of the industry's efforts at self-regulation.

The Violence Issue

The amount and effect of violence seen on television in the United States have been perennial concerns for parents, educators and other interested parties. Active citizens and consumer organizations continue to monitor the amount of violent behavior on television and report their findings in hopes of encouraging alternatives to what they regard as a deteriorating situation. Public interest groups have been formed to identify and promote quality television shows.

Some observers note that the mass media simply reflect society and the values it displays, that programming must be based on reality to gain widespread audience acceptance. Others counter that the media have a responsibility to enhance and reinforce worthwhile social values and to present such values in an attractive, effective manner for potential audience acceptance. The dramatic writer, for example, uses conflict as a cornerstone for effective drama. Conflict often leads to violence. Thus, the issue of violence is not easy to resolve, for the writer or for the audience.

In late 1992, in response to a federal law two years earlier, the three major commercial television networks announced a joint plan for limiting violence depicted in their entertainment shows. Cable programmers were to be consulted later at an industrywide conference. Among the standards announced in 1992 were the following:

a. Gratuitous or excessive depictions of violence, shown solely for its own sake, are not acceptable.
b. Programs should not depict violence as glamorous, nor as an acceptable solution to human conflict.
c. Depictions of violence may not be used to shock or stimulate the audience.

d. Scenes showing excessive gore, pain, or physical suffering are not acceptable.

e. Extreme caution must be exercised in any themes, plots, or scenes that mix sex and violence. Rape and other sexual assaults are violent, not erotic, behavior.

f. Realistic portrayals of violence or other scenes that are unduly frightening to children should not be included in programs aimed at children.

g. Scheduling of programs that contain depictions of violence should take into account the likely composition of the audience.[2]

The 1992 guidelines were enacted after the network program standards, practices, and codes of ethics shown in Appendix D were in place. Television violence will continue to receive careful monitoring by legislators, as well as telecommunications industry executives, parents, teachers, and writers of program material.

Children's Television Programming

Concern for the effects of indecent, obscene, and violent programming on children who maintain a steady diet of television viewing encouraged Congress in 1990 to pass a Children's Television Act. This law limits television commercial time during children's programs to 10.5 minutes per hour on weekends and 12 minutes per hour on weekdays, and it requires the FCC to consider, at license renewal, whether each licensee has provided programming specifically designed to meet the educational and informational needs of preschool and school-age children. The law also requires the FCC to complete a pending inquiry concerning program-length commercials. The implementation of the Children's Television Act rests with the FCC, which must determine the terms and consequences of this law. Television program executives are still assessing its effects.

Pressure Groups

Several types of organizations demand the attention of the telecommunications industry and, ultimately, the attention and response of the writer. These pressure groups may be labeled as activists, advocates, lobbyists, or by some other designation.

Pressure groups operate under two basic assumptions: (1) the electronic media are primary "shapers" of one's personality, next to one's immediate family, and (2) those who attend movies, watch television, and listen to radio should help determine the kinds of programs shown which exert such a powerful influence on all of our lives. These groups try to influence the kinds of material presented on radio and television and the types of films shown in movie theaters. Their active campaigns against what they perceive as the violence and obscenity on television, for example, have been noticed by network and station executives. Although it is difficult to point to these pressure groups as the sole reason, there appears to be a noticeable trend toward better, perhaps more conscientious, children's television programming. Also, programs featuring minorities, women, and special interest groups are receiving more attention from these groups, as well as from program executives.

Be aware that such pressure groups exist. Understand the kinds of concerns and priorities each group represents, and be prepared to respond to their pressure. You may not have to deal directly with such groups, but you will be expected to respond to their concerns when preparing script material for the electronic media.

Censorship

Section 326 of the Communications Act of 1934 prohibits the FCC from censoring programs and from promulgating rules that interfere with the right of free speech. The FCC does have an affirmative obligation to take appropriate action against a station that does not follow regulations, but only after the fact. However, unofficial censorship of program content exists because of the biases of networks, stations, production companies, and sponsors.

Sponsors tend to disassociate themselves from programs that they believe will alienate even a portion of the potential customers for their products and services or that run counter to entrenched corporate images and sales policies. The sponsor's objective is to become identified with quality programming that meshes with overall sales and corporate philosophy and that impresses a large audience, who then purchase or use the sponsor's products or services.

Those responsible for producing programs for mass audiences prefer to work with established writers, themes, and topics. Often fear of controversy or adverse audience reaction to a character, theme, or setting compels program producers to discard experimentation and exploration of contemporary issues. Program producers and sponsors generally do not want to offend anyone at any time. This philosophy often results in mediocre, self-serving, and safe scripts and programs that lack sparkle and durable quality. It is becoming more difficult for new writers to sell their work and for established writers to provide new, perhaps controversial, perspectives on contemporary themes and topics.

Political Broadcasts

Broadcasters have a number of obligations and responsibilities with regard to political broadcasts. These requirements stem from certain sections of the Communications and Federal Election Campaign acts and various FCC rulings on the subject. Writers preparing news copy, documentaries, investigative reports, editorials, and commentaries must be aware of these regulations, since they affect those who write such material. The importance and complexity of these regulations cannot be overemphasized.[3]

Broadcasts by Candidates

Section 315(a) of the Communications Act indicates that

> no station licensee is required to permit the use of its facilities by any legally qualified candidate for public office [except for federal elective office], but if any licensee shall permit any such candidate to use its facilities, it shall afford equal opportunities to all other candidates for that office to use such facilities. Such licensee shall have no power of censorship over the material broadcast

by any such candidate. Appearance by a legally qualified candidate on any (i) bona fide newscast, (ii) bona fide news interview, (iii) bona fide news documentary (if the appearance of the candidate is incidental to the presentation of the subject covered by the news documentary), or (iv) on-the-spot coverage of bona fide news events (including, but not limited to political conventions and activities incidental thereto) shall not be deemed to be use of a broadcast station.

Political Editorials

Section 73.123(c) of the Commission's Rules requires that, when a station editorial endorses or opposes a political candidate, the licensee (station owner) is required to notify the other candidate(s) for that office within twenty-four hours, give the date and time of the editorial, and offer *free* time but not necessarily *equal* time for the candidate(s) or a spokesperson to respond. If the editorial is broadcast within seventy-two hours of election day, sufficient notice must be provided to prepare and present a response in timely fashion.

Even when a station editorial makes no direct reference to an election but takes a partisan position on a politically significant issue, clearly and readily identified with a legally qualified candidate, the FCC has ruled that this gives rise to the affirmative obligations previously noted.

The Fairness Doctrine

Any writer working on programming involving potentially controversial issues—for example, in talk programs, dramas, and editorials—must know the applicable regulations and requirements and how these affect the material written for various purposes.

In August 1987, the FCC repealed the fairness doctrine, an FCC policy that had required broadcasters to present some programming on "controversial issues of public importance" in their communities and to provide reasonable response time to parties with significant contrasting viewpoints. The FCC also eliminated requirements concerning response time for issue advertising *unrelated* to ballot proposals.

The FCC's action, however, did not eliminate the fairness doctrine as it applies to election-related programming involving candidates or ballot issues, especially those that appear on election ballots. Stations still have an obligation to air programming about community issues. Every three months, every radio and TV station must document its issue-related programming. That programming report is available for citizens' inspection during a station's regular business hours.

Defamation

Defamation is a false statement spoken (slander) or written (libel) that damages the character or reputation of a person or group. Defamation is one of the oldest issues affecting both print and electronic media. A number of cases have been prosecuted on the basis of the inaccurate use of names in news stories or a striking resemblance between a real-life person or situation and a purportedly fictional character or situation in a play, story, broadcast, or novel. You should keep in mind the basic definition and essential elements of defamation, as well as some precautions to take to minimize the risk of a law suit.

States, which generally combine their slander and libel laws, determine whether a particular statement is defamatory and what penalties are involved. Most libel claims will fail unless five elements are present: "publication," identification, false statement, damage, and fault. Someone must see or hear the offending material. Libel suits have been won even though the plaintiff, or the person making the charge, is not identified or named specifically; only a clear reference to the plaintiff has to be established. Although true statements are not libelous, public disclosure of private facts may give rise to a charge of invasion of privacy. Plaintiffs must show that a libelous statement has damaged their reputations. In most cases, a plaintiff must prove that the defendant was negligent; public officials and such public figures as notable entertainers, sports stars, and community leaders must prove not only that a statement was false but also that malice was intended, that the defendant knew it was false or proceeded with reckless disregard about the truth of the statement.

Take the following precautions to minimize the risk of a libel suit:

a. *Be attentive* when processing potentially sensitive information, such as health, race, and age information.
b. *Verify all the facts and comments you use,* especially in news stories, editorials, commentaries, documentaries, and investigative reports.
c. *Be able to prove the accuracy of what you have written.* Keep files and records up-to-date. Verify the truth of every statement and not merely that the statement was made.
d. *Get another opinion about scripts that* might *lead to libel suits.*
e. *If in doubt, talk to your writing supervisor or a qualified attorney.* Learn the basic defenses used in libel actions and the damages awarded by the courts in such cases.

Invasion of Privacy and Release Forms

Although the particulars of invasion of privacy laws vary greatly from state to state, it is possible to say that invasion of privacy most often occurs when you use someone for commercial purposes, such as a product endorsement in a commercial, or when you use someone's name or picture in such a manner as to cause that person embarrassment, as in a documentary or an investigative report.[4] These uses may be considered invasion of privacy only if a person has not consented to your use of his or her name, face, or performance. In legal terms, such consent is called a release or, more specifically, a talent consent release form.

When you want a producer or other prospective employer to review material that you have written on speculation, most often you will be asked to sign a program material release form. The signing of this document should precede a full and formal writing contract offer from the individual responsible for developing such properties. As you can see in the sample provided in figure 1.1, the form protects the parties to the contract from potential legal entanglements.

Figure 1.1
Television program
material release form.

Title and/or Theme of Material Submitted Hereunder:

_____

_____

I am submitting to you today certain program material, the title and/or theme of which is indicated above (which material is herein after referred to as the program material), upon the following express understanding and conditions.

1. I acknowledge that I have requested permission to disclose to you and to carry on certain discussions and negotiations with you in connection with such program material.

2. I agree that I am voluntarily disclosing such program material to you at my request. I understand that you shall have no obligation to me in any respect whatsoever with regard to such material until each of us has executed a written agreement which, by its terms and provisions, will be the only contract between us.

3. I agree that any discussions we may have with respect to such program material shall not constitute any agreement expressed or implied as to the purchase or use of such program material which I am hereby disclosing to you either orally or in writing.

4. If such material submitted hereunder is not new or novel, or was not originated by me, or has not been reduced to concrete form, or if because other persons including your employees have heretofore submitted or hereafter submit similar or identical program material which you have the right to use, then I agree that you shall not be liable to me for the use of such program material and you shall not be obligated in any respect whatsoever to compensate me for such use by you.

5. I further agree that if you hereafter produce or distribute a television program or programs based upon the same general idea, theme or situation and/or having the same setting or background and/or taking place in the same geographical area or period of history as the said program material, then unless you have substantially copied the expression and development of such idea, theme or situation, including the characters and story line thereof, as herewith or hereafter submitted to you by me in writing, you shall have no obligation or liability to me of any kind or character by reason of the production or distribution of such program(s), nor shall you be obligated to compensate me in connection therewith.

I acknowledge that but for my agreement to the above terms and conditions, you would not accede to my request to receive and consider the said program material which I am submitting to you herewith.

_____
(signature)

If you work in a broadcast newsroom preparing routine newscasts, special documentaries, or news-related features, you should be aware of Section 73.1206 of the FCC Rules:

Telephone Conversations

> *Before* recording a telephone conversation for broadcast, or broadcasting such a conversation simultaneously with its occurrence, a licensee shall inform any party to the call of the licensee's intention to broadcast the conversation, except where such party is aware, or may be presumed to be aware from the circumstances of the conversation, that it is being or likely will be broadcast. Such awareness is presumed to exist only when the other party to the call is associated with the station (such as an employee or part-time reporter), or where the other party originates the call and it is obvious that it is in connection with a program in which the station customarily broadcasts telephone conversations.

The FCC has ruled that a conversation begins whenever a party answers the telephone. The prior notification requirement is strictly enforced. Giving such notice to a caller during or after the time a conversation is recorded from the telephone, even before any part of it is used on the air, is not allowed under this regulation. The use of beep tones while recording telephone conversations does not eliminate the requirement that you give specific *prior* notice to a party on the telephone that you are recording or broadcasting the conversation.

Copyright

As a writer, you should know the proper use of copyrighted material. You may need a particular photograph for the opening shot in a television program, or you may want to suggest the use of a specific piece of music in a commercial announcement or dramatic script. All of these situations require a review of copyright regulations and the proper application of procedures to obtain permission to use the copyrighted material.

The current copyright law, in effect since 1 January 1978, protects artistic and literary efforts, recognizes ownership, and grants to the creator of a work all rights, benefits, and privileges that ownership entails. The copyright owner has exclusive rights to print, duplicate, distribute, adapt (i.e., allow "derivative works"), perform, record, sell, or display literary, dramatic, or musical works publicly. To be valid, transfer or assignment of these rights must be in writing and must be made voluntarily by the owner of the copyrighted material. The invasion of any of these rights is termed infringement, the remedies for which include actions for damages and injunctions.

Whether published or unpublished, works fixed in tangible form—for example, a script, record, videotape, film, or photograph—are provided statutory protection from the moment of creation. This protection lasts through the life of the author plus fifty years after the author's death. Exceptions are made-for-hire works, which include work done as a regular employee of a company, such as a broadcast station or cable company, and anonymous and pseudonymous (fictional) works whose copyright protection lasts from 75 to 100 years after creation of the work.

Writers and creators of artistic material have raised concerns about alterations made in protected works by users and purchasers of those works. For example, the "colorizing" of black-and-white films helped ignite a moral rights debate in Congress. At this writing, U.S. copyright law does not include moral rights or "material alterations" provisions. In copyright law, this term would enable artists, writers, or creators to protect a work from "alteration, mutilation or destruction." If this provision were added, it could limit or eliminate the ability of television programmers to edit a movie or other programs. There is also a question about how Congress would decide who possesses moral rights and who does not. The issue becomes even more complex when one tries to identify the contributions of several people, including writers, to the production of a motion picture or television program.

Previously released material can be used in any of three situations:

a. *The material is in the public domain.* This means either that the material was never protected by copyright or that copyright protection has expired. For a fee, the copyright office will determine the copyright status of any previously released or published work.[5]

b. *You have obtained written permission to use copyrighted material from the copyright owner,* who may be the creator of the work, a publisher, a television producer, or any number of people.

c. *The legal doctrine of fair use can be applied,* even though the material is copyrighted—in which case, prior permission is not required. This is a complex, intricate legal alternative. Essentially you need to determine the amount of the original, copyrighted material you will use, its importance, and the impact your use of this material will have on the original, copyrighted work.

Chapter 13 outlines the process and forms used to complete copyright registration at the Copyright Office in Washington, DC.

Music licensing organizations, such as the American Society of Composers, Authors and Publishers (ASCAP) and Broadcast Music, Incorporated (BMI), collect blanket license fees from stations, networks, and production companies. Payment of these fees entitles users to have access to ASCAP and/or BMI artists, composers, and publishers for a specific time period, usually one year.

Recorded music used in commercials, films, or any other type of audiovisual message requires written permission from both the music copyright owner, or publisher, and the record company that issues the recording. The music copyright owner must grant a synchronization license whenever music is used in a timed relationship with a commercial message or other subject. The use of original music may avoid the need for this additional license.

The federal Freedom of Information (FOI) Act establishes a procedure for obtaining access to government documents and restricts the government's right to withhold documents from the public. The FOI Act allows the government to restrict access to certain kinds of information, including properly classified documents, files from ongoing criminal investigations, and personnel and medical files. Disputes are settled in court.

Freedom of Information (FOI) Act

If you write news stories, editorials, and commentaries or prepare interviews, documentaries, or investigative reports, you should know about the FOI Act; it is a valuable resource. To learn how to file FOI Act requests, contact The Superintendent of Documents, U.S. Government Printing Office, Washington, DC 20402.

Broadcasting, like many other industries, has made an effort to regulate itself over the years, perhaps because of government regulations or pressures from special interest groups, but one hopes because of a continuing sense of responsibility. These self-regulation efforts have received mixed reactions.

Self-regulation Efforts

Supporters of such efforts contend that self-regulation in such areas as programming and advertising becomes essential if programmers are to maintain control over what they make available to their audience. Supporters add that self-regulation efforts help anticipate problems, issues, and concerns that ultimately might require lengthy and potentially severe regulations and restraints.

Opponents counter that such efforts are of little value and impact, probably call attention to issues and concerns unnoticed by the FCC and other regulatory agencies, and generally produce vague minimal standards for the diverse subscribers to such codes or standards of good practice. Since enforcement of and adherence to these codes or standards are questionable, one could legitimately speculate about their effectiveness.

At one time, the National Association of Broadcasters (NAB) provided voluntary codes of good practice guiding various activities of its member stations and networks throughout the industry. These codes were discontinued in 1983, after courts ruled they were illegal. In 1990, under political pressure to clean up the airwaves, the NAB adopted programming guidelines that were purely advisory. The guidelines urged the responsible depiction of physical or psychological violence, encouraged creativity and diversity in programming dealing with human sexuality, and cautioned that the use of illegal drugs or other substances should not be shown as socially desirable.

Networks, stations, and professional media organizations have formulated and attempt to adhere to guidelines and policies to meet the exacting demands of individual circumstances. Cutbacks in standards and practices departments have weakened network and local station review of commercial and program material and, consequently, could also weaken self-regulation efforts. Also, written guidelines for self-regulation vary in range and detail. For example, ABC at one time had a commercial standards book approximately one inch thick, covering sixty-four topics, including children's television, endorsements, and nutrition claims. ESPN, meanwhile, had its standards on one page, and other cable program suppliers had no standards written specifically for that program service. Much of the monitoring once done by network standards and practices departments is now handled by programming executives assigned to the production of individual programs. Appendix D contains the codes of ethics of national news-related organizations and the program standards and practices of major broadcasting networks.

Effects of Regulations and Restraints

After reviewing major regulations and restraints that affect the work of the electronic media writer, one might conclude that the situation appears hopeless. However, a more optimistic viewpoint is that things could be worse and have been worse in the past. Whereas some controls have been removed, others continue to challenge writers and others involved in the media.

To avoid controversy and to achieve higher ratings that result in increased profits, networks, stations, and program producers have maintained a safe middle ground. This philosophy in turn has produced programming that often lacks innovation, responsiveness, and sparkle. The imitation of successful formats and styles continues. For regular television viewers, selection of "the least objectionable program" is a daily chore.

The cumulative effect of these regulations and restraints has been to make writers and media executives more responsive to audience demands and tastes. The law requires some of this responsiveness, but a large share of it should be attributed to the desire to provide better programs, which eventually result in higher ratings and more profits. Since telecommunications is a profit-motivated industry, it will most likely continue to aim to please as much of the audience as possible.

Certain types of program material are no longer automatically rejected or discarded. For example, in television dramas, sensitive contemporary themes and situations, such as child abuse, homosexuality, abortion, drug use, and child pornography, are presented in an effort to attract a large audience concerned with these issues and problems.

The criteria of acceptability and appropriateness evolve constantly to match the capabilities of the media and the demands of the audience. Your challenge as a writer is to provide quality work that addresses contemporary needs within the realistic framework of established restraints and regulations, both within and outside the telecommunications industry.

Summary

This chapter focused on the work and concerns of the writer. The section devoted to examining the qualifications, role, and function of the writer should enable you to assess your goals and interests. The impact and influence of the electronic media should motivate you to cultivate a personal and professional sense of pride, ethics, and responsibility toward your work and toward the audience for whom you write. Learn to use the resources available to make your work efficient, productive, and effective. As a writer, you must also be aware of the various laws, regulations, and concerns that influence your writing and take steps to avoid ethical and legal problems that might develop during the creative writing process.

Once you have assessed the work of the writer and developed an appreciation for the impact of such work and the pressures that influence the final product, you can determine your place in this challenging field and take the steps necessary to acquire the skills and insights to become the best writer for the electronic media that you can be.

Suggested Exercises and Projects

1. Based on the characteristics listed in this chapter, take a personal inventory of yourself to determine your qualifications and interests as a writer.
2. Schedule a personal or group visit to a nearby broadcast facility. Determine its organizational structure and management system and the role of the writer within the facility.
3. At a nearby library, look up the research aids available for future writing assignments. While there, locate one of the periodicals listed in Appendix B. Read one of the major articles in one issue of the publication, and then provide a brief summary of the article.
4. Discuss the impact of current broadcast programming trends, policies, and strategies on the work, role, and function of the writer.
5. Observe a particular situation—for instance, a park, a busy street corner, or a checkout stand at a supermarket. Report your observations and indicate the possible future use of these observations in a writing situation.
6. Keep a personal journal for at least six weeks. Record your daily impressions and experiences. Describe the people you meet. Capture bits of dialogue heard in passing. Write yourself notes about script ideas. At the end of the six-week period, assess your journal and note how it has contributed to your work as a writer.
7. Follow the guidelines suggested in this chapter, and formulate a source chart for a research project.
8. Review basic usage styles, using one of the reference works on English grammar and writing style listed in this chapter.
9. For another class project or a publication, interview someone, using the suggestions offered in this chapter.
10. Discuss the impact of censorship and pressure groups on the work of the writer.
11. Discuss your observations of violence and offensive material in the media today. What is the impact of these developments on electronic media writing and programming efforts?
12. Describe a recent situation in which a local broadcast station was faced with the exigencies of complying with the requirements of Section 315 of the 1934 Communications Act, the Children's Television Act, or libel/slander regulations.

Notes

1. See National Association of Broadcasters (NAB), *Legal Guide to Broadcast Law and Regulation,* 3d ed. (Washington, DC: National Association of Broadcasters, 1988).
2. Summary of Cox News Service story issued 12 December 1992.
3. A detailed study of the rules regarding broadcasts by candidates for federal and nonfederal public office is available in the FCC public notice of 20 July 1978, ''The Law of Political Broadcasting and Cablecasting.'' Copies of this public notice may be obtained from the FCC in Washington, DC. Another publication, which provides a comprehensive treatment of this subject, is the latest edition of *Political Broadcast Catechism* available from the National Association of Broadcasters, 1771 N Street, N.W., Washington, DC 20036.
4. This section is summarized from Legal Department, National Association of Broadcasters, ''A Broadcaster's Guide to Releases,'' L-910, June 1979.
5. The Copyright Office, Library of Congress, Washington, DC 20559 can provide an information kit on several copyright-related topics: *Registration Procedures* (Circular R1D), *Radio and TV Programs* (Circular 47e), and *How to Investigate Copyright Status of a Work* (Circular R 22). To speed requests and deliveries of forms for registration of a claim to copyright, call the Copyright Office at 202–287–8700 or 202–287–9100.

Basic Production Techniques

P roduction converts the written script into the flesh-and-bones realism of an audio or a video presentation. It is the crucial final step in the creative process. A writer's concepts and ideas, as scripted on paper, are transformed into a finished, polished presentation through the use of production tools and processes.

You need to know the technical potential and limits of the production tools, so that, when you write a script, you will know what is possible and what is not. You need to know the capability of available facilities and personnel *before* writing even the first draft of a script.

You also need to use standard production terms and be aware of production processes so that you can communicate creatively with production personnel. You need the assurance that what you visualize on the script page can be transferred into an effective production.

New technology continues to broaden and enhance the writer's creative opportunities in the electronic media; however, the essential production elements and techniques generally remain constant. For example, the writing and production of a newscast is the same whether the newscast is seen or heard via cable systems or it is offered via fiber optics, over-the-air stations, or direct broadcast satellite. The more you know about and understand the intricacies of production, the more depth, flexibility, and refinement you will display in your writing for the electronic media. This chapter will not make you an expert in production, however; that can be achieved only with specialized training and instruction.

This chapter will describe the characteristics of radio, television, and motion pictures to help you understand and use the creative and technical capabilities available. The chapter will also examine basic production methods and techniques so that you can better understand the production alternatives that writers face. For both audio and video productions, the chapter will describe the basic facilities, equipment, procedures, and techniques used by the production team so that you can understand what happens when a script is transformed into a finished presentation. There will also be a description of the basic production terms found most often in audio and video scripts. Motion picture production will be examined briefly.

Selecting the Medium

As you formulate ideas as a writer, consider the medium in which you intend to display your work. Your thought process, writing style and technique, and manner of presentation will differ if you are working on a biographical novel rather than a teleplay for national distribution. As a writer, you function differently if preparing a radio commercial than if designing an instructional television program series. You will need to analyze the capabilities of the medium to be used.

Usually, because of employment requirements and constraints, you must create a particular type of message for a specific medium—for example, a commercial for radio. Sometimes the seasoned writer is responsible for more than writing the script. Writers can also serve as producer, director, or marketing manager for the finished production. Such hybrid, or combined, responsibilities allow the writer to select the medium to be used to reach a target audience most effectively with a particular kind of program or announcement.

Each available medium should be analyzed on two bases: (1) the suitability of the medium to present a particular kind of message effectively and (2) the capability of the medium to deliver the right kind of audience.

Shared Attributes

Several attributes are common to the electronic media:

    a. *Universality.* They are readily available throughout the country and are enjoyed by a large number of people on a regular basis.
    b. *Diversity.* They offer a variety of program material appealing to a wide range of audiences.
    c. *Immediacy.* They can present topical, contemporary material for audience needs. Often this is done live.
    d. *Flexibility.* Material can be recorded, edited, and duplicated for multiple playbacks.
    e. *Impermanence.* They are but fleeting, perishable images and sounds in the audience's minds.
    f. *Researched.* They are being studied and evaluated continually by companies that analyze specific audience tastes and characteristics.

Attributes of Radio

The principal characteristics of radio include the following:

    a. A "theater of the mind" can be created for the listener, using only sound.
    b. It is generally regarded as a friendly, personal medium.
    c. It is not conducive to the presentation of detailed information—for instance, prices at a food store in a radio commercial.
    d. Messages must be presented often to reach radio's fragmented audiences.
    e. Radio must compete with the listener's inattention and distractions caused by the way in which the medium is consumed.

f. It is not particularly suitable for reaching young children in the audience because of current programming.

g. It is a portable, mobile medium, going where the listener goes.

h. The profile and size of the radio audience are relatively stable.

i. Production costs are less than in most other media.

The principal characteristics of television include the following:

Attributes of Television

a. The potential for the combination of sight, sound, motion, and color offers exciting creative possibilities.

b. Special effects, such as animation, slow motion, picture enlargement or reduction, freeze frames, or "frozen action," are accomplished easily and effectively.

c. The audience is not as fragmented as in radio, although it may be in the future.

d. Nationally audiences spend more time with television than with other media.

e. Production costs almost always are higher than for radio.

f. Production tends to be complex, with sophisticated equipment and technical crews working as a team to produce the finished product.

Motion pictures share many of the characteristics listed for television. They offer several production advantages and disadvantages:

Attributes of Motion Pictures

a. A specific audience will see the finished motion picture because of the G, PG, PG-13, R, and NC-17 ratings placed on practically all films released in the United States today and because the theme, situation, or characters displayed in a particular film will attract an identifiable target group.

b. Subject matter is not as restricted as in open-circuit broadcasting; closed-circuit alternatives, through cable systems, are available for presenting sensitive, controversial, and stylized material to appropriate audiences.

c. The length of a film presentation can vary according to the topic to be covered and its target audience; for example, a presentation tracing the history of the nation's Capitol may be any length appropriate to the subject and to those who will view the final product.

d. Production of theatrical motion pictures generally requires more time and money than for similar kinds of radio and television programs.

e. It is difficult to transfer effectively the large-screen cinematic experience of the darkened movie theater to the bright, small-screen format required to reach the television viewer.

f. Many of the primary advantages once offered by motion picture production—for example, special effects, precision editing, image sharpness, and equipment portability—are now incorporated into the growing sophistication of television and videotape equipment, facilities, and personnel.

Production Methods

Adjusting to the medium to be used is only the first step. You must also adjust to the method or means of production. Will the program be done live, recorded, or use a combination of recorded segments blended into the spontaneity of a live broadcast? Will all of the production be done in the field, on location, in the studio, through a combination of studio and remote locations?

Before writing even the first draft of a script, be sure to find out the production method(s) that will be used, as well as the technical capabilities of available facilities and the preferences of those who will eventually evaluate the quality of your writing. Why write a script for a commercial requiring three studio cameras when the commercial will be shot with one motion picture camera on location?

You will not usually select the production method(s) used unless you work in a hybrid position, such as writer-producer or writer-director. Regardless, you still must adjust to the production method(s) to be used for a particular script.

The methods used to produce program material for the electronic media depend on several variables: available personnel, equipment, and facilities; the structure and organization of the production staff; the division of production responsibilities; the type of production to be done; and the preferences of the person paying the production costs. Actual production comes only after many steps in the creative process have been completed. Later chapters will sketch, as needed, the techniques and processes used for specific kinds of audio and video production.

Live or Recorded

The nature of production and scheduling demands often dictate whether a program or an announcement will be produced live or recorded in advance and used later. For example, a live broadcast of a football game or parade provides immediacy and spontaneity. However, recorded segments from this same game or parade may also be used in an evening newscast.

Live production is quicker, sometimes easier, and often cheaper than recorded production techniques. Also, live production permits last-minute script and program changes. With live production also comes the risk of production errors or equipment failures. There are no "second chances." It has to be right the first and only time. Your script material must withstand such rigors. This often means preparing stand-by script material to handle situations in which a production goes a different direction than originally scripted and planned.

Recorded productions permit the close control and supervision of overall quality. Often this method is combined with editing and post-production enhancements to further refine production quality and value.

Live and recorded production methods can be combined. Portions or segments of a program can be recorded, edited, and processed in advance and incorporated into a studio production using live talent. For instance, the pregame show for a live sports event could be produced in this manner.

The elements or requirements of a script generally determine whether it is produced within the controlled environment of an indoor studio or at a temporary remote location. A radio commercial featuring multiple voices and musical sequences is best produced in a studio; however, a musical special featuring the exotic beauty of Hawaii would be enhanced if produced on location.

Studio or Remote

Generally it is easier to accomplish production objectives in an indoor facility, which offers temperature control, sufficient electrical power, access to supplementary production personnel, equipment spare parts, and even telephones and rest rooms. The studio setting generally offers comfort, control, security, and predictability.

Thoughtful selection, planning, and full use of a remote production site can provide a unique setting or environment, plus the realism and detail required for the quality and success of a production. Some production requirements, such as elaborate sets or extensive lighting, are eliminated when a remote location is used.

It is possible to combine studio and remote production elements into a finished production. Most newscasts combine anchors in the studio with reporters in the field. The anchor introduces a story and the reporter provides the details. An interactive, satellite-fed corporate video presentation could involve a live studio segment from a company official, followed by comments or questions from employees at sites around the world.

A clear understanding of the personnel, facilities, and equipment involved in audio production will help you write effective scripts for radio applications.

Audio Production

Personnel

The writer is only one member of a team of individuals working together to produce audio program material. The responsibilities and scope of the work done by each individual may be limited or expansive, depending on the project to be produced and the size and operating philosophy of the production facility. Networks and large production companies have larger staffs with more specialized production responsibilities than smaller radio operations, in which one person may be assigned several production jobs. For practical purposes, in this section, the production team will be outlined for the typical small to medium-size radio station.

The major components involved in producing various types of radio program material follow:

a. *Music and sound effects.* This part of the production process involves having access to the list or catalog of music and sound effects available for commercials, promotional announcements, introductions to news and sports programs, talk shows, and documentaries, as well as the music played regularly on the station. Radio stations may designate a music librarian or music director for this work.

b. *Writing.* Generally the writing for certain types of radio program material is done after the sales staff sells air time to clients or after the news director decides on the opening, closing, and format for a regularly scheduled talk program series. Often the writer works with other station personnel to develop script ideas and complete research to meld the elements of the finished, on-the-air program. Some stations complete the writing and production phases as part of other responsibilities—for example, for station promotions and community projects. For instance, news department personnel generally write their own copy for newscasts, as well as many of the public affairs programs. The station manager may work with a committee within the station to develop effective editorials and then assign someone to write the editorials the manager reads on the air. The continuity or copywriting personnel in the station are responsible for the regular writing assignments within the facility. Generally this involves writing spot announcements.

c. *Announcing.* At small and medium-size radio stations, announcers are assigned to a regular on-the-air shift and, in addition, announce or voice the other kinds of program material needed for the station. In most cases, this consists of reading the copy written by the continuity writer and merging the various elements to produce an effective commercial announcement. Announcers at most stations, however, are expected to perform many other announcing functions—for instance, such special events as parades or sports play-by-play broadcasts—depending on the demands and programming format of the station.

d. *Engineering.* In nonunion markets and production facilities, the announcer performs the necessary technical function of mixing voice, music, and sound effects to produce the finished announcement or program. With a unionized engineering staff, the announcer only reads the copy and an engineer operates the audio console. Separation of this production responsibility permits careful attention to specific production details.

The primary tools available to produce audio program material include the following items:

    a. *Control board or console.* Located in the control room or central control point, the control board or console processes the voices and sounds during recording, editing, and dubbing.

    b. *Microphone.* There are several types of microphones, with audio pickup pattern characteristics designed to meet various recording requirements and situations.

    c. *Turntable.* A turntable picks up information recorded on a disc or record and sends this information to the control board for amplification, mixing, processing, and integration with other sound elements.

    d. *Compact disc (CD).* In most production facilities, high-quality digital recordings (especially music recordings) made on compact disc have replaced vinyl records or LPs. CDs are used in audio production as previously described for turntables.

    e. *Audiotape.* Sounds can be recorded in the studio or in the field onto audiotape at standard speeds. Quarter-inch audiotape is used, except in portable audiocassette recorders. The audiotape may be in the form of continuous loop cartridges, or carts, with inaudible stop tones, or cues, placed between the various segments, or the material may be recorded on standard reel-to-reel audiotape machines and edited later.

    f. *Music and sound effects.* Both may be produced and recorded on CD or audiotape in the studio or on location. Both may also be prerecorded on disc or audiotape and integrated into the program material using the control board or console.

Audio Terminology

In production, certain terms and abbreviations have become accepted methods of shorthand, allowing all those involved to understand quickly what is meant and what is needed. Your precise use of terms and abbreviations will ensure that your script is produced almost exactly as you have envisioned. A careless use of terminology will lead to confusion, frustration, and ineffective production value.

Voice Terms

Indicate the voice to be heard by using an easily understood designation—for instance, Voice 1, Billy, or Announcer #2.

    Several terms describe the placement and quality of voices used in audio production. Unless otherwise specified in your script, a voice or character is heard at a normal distance from a microphone—that is, the voice is "on mike" (or "on mic"). If you want the voice to be heard as though speaking from the back of the room or from a distance, you would indicate "off mike." If the voice needs to sound as though it is approaching the center of action in the mind's eye of the listener, then write "fading on" or "fades on." The reverse process, where the voice starts at a normal distance from the microphone and then slowly moves away, could be noted by writing "fading off" or "fades off." To create suspense or to heighten a mysterious mood, you might want the voice to be heard with a slight echo or reverberation; after the talent's designation, you would note "reverb," indicating the need for a slight or controlled use of echo. To create the illusion of a telephone conversation, the notations "filtered" or "behind barrier" can be used, or simply write "as heard through a telephone." As illustrated in chapter 3, the terms used to describe the quality and placement of the voices are written immediately after the name of the specific talent affected.

Music and Sound Effects Terms

Choose from several terms to denote the manner in which to use music and sound effects. As chapter 3 will show, music and sound effects notations are written as separate lines in the script. The common abbreviation for sound effects is "SFX." "CD" is an abbreviation often used to indicate that audio material comes from a compact disc rather than from a cart or reel-to-reel tape. Scripts often note the *source* rather than the *nature* of the audio material used. Thus, a poorly written script might indicate only "CD" or "CART." It would be better to indicate *both* the source and the nature of the material—for example, "CD: MUSIC UP FULL FOR TWO SECONDS AND THEN UNDER."

Do not simply indicate that music or sound effects will be used in a script. Note *how* each is to be used. You might want music or a sound effect to "fade in" (or "up") at the beginning of a program or an announcement. You could note that it "fades out" at the end of a program segment. Various notations indicate that the music or sound effect should be heard at full volume and then the volume brought down so another production element—a voice or another piece of music—can be heard more prominently. Generally these terms are interchangeable: "up full and then under," "feature (establish) briefly and then under," "up for (number of) seconds and then under." If you wish to have either music or sound effects begin under a voice—for example, near the end of the final program segment or closing of a music show—you could note either "music [or SFX] under" or "sneak under." The last term is used when the music or sound effect is heard in the "background" ("b.g.") and then is heard at full volume after a character finishes a particular word.

The transition between two pieces of music or sound effects may be accomplished by writing "segue" (pronounced seg-way), in which one selection ends and the next selection begins immediately, or "cross-fade," in which one selection gradually fades out and the next selection gradually comes in to replace it. Be as specific as possible in writing music and sound effects notations to ensure that your script is produced in the manner you have envisioned.

Other Terms

Other terms often used in audio scripts include the following: "ad-lib," which allows characters or voices momentarily to create their own words, but always in keeping with the general tone, mood, and purpose of the script—for example, spectators in a crowd at a football game or patrons seated at nearby tables in a restaurant; "bridge," which is a general term applied to a transition between sound elements—for instance, "MUSIC: UP FULL AND THEN BRIDGE TO SFX OF FROG UNDER VOICE #3"; "montage" or "collage," which is a collection of related voices or music/sound effects segments, often overlapping, used in quick, uninterrupted succession—for instance, "collage of sounds of subway stop, crowd and street noises"; "Anncr" or "Ann," which are common abbreviations for the designation "announcer." Be certain to add a number or letter after this designation or after the other common term, "Voice," if you anticipate the multiple use of either term—for example, Anncr #1, Anncr #2 or Voice A, Voice B.

Essentially, coordinating the audio portion of a television production makes use of the same components as outlined for radio.

Video Production Personnel

As in radio, the responsibilities and scope of the work done by television production personnel can be isolated into specific job descriptions. Such variables, however, as personnel capabilities, budget, type of production, organizational structure, available facilities and equipment, and philosophy of the production facility may cause two or more jobs to be assigned to one individual or may require an adjustment in production responsibilities. Generally the larger the television production facility and the more complex the television production project to be completed, the more delineated the job descriptions and responsibilities. For practical considerations, only the essential television production components in the typical small to medium-size facility will be outlined in this section.

Producer

The producer assumes responsibility for the entire television production, single program, or series. This includes such essentials as planning, budgeting, scripting, production, coordinating, scheduling, and editing. Depending on the type of production and the facility involved, these responsibilities often are combined with those of the director, the writer, or both.

Director

The director coordinates the efforts of the technical crew members and the performance of the television talent. The director must creatively execute the production designed by the producer, conceptualized by the writer, and envisioned by other creative personnel.

Writer

It is difficult to describe the precise role the writer plays in the television production process. Often the writer works in close cooperation and shares some responsibilities with the producer, the director, or both. The type of program or announcement affects the kind of work and amount of participation by the writer. Basically the writer must conceptualize and formulate the essential television elements into proper script form to accomplish specific objectives.

Technical Personnel

The technical director (T.D.) operates the equipment used to make video changes during the production. The audio engineer supervises all audio components. The engineering staff is crucial for the proper installation, maintenance, and operation of all the television production equipment. The floor manager, who is sometimes called the stage manager, coordinates the director's commands to the talent and production personnel. The floor manager supervises the floor crew, who position the sets, lighting instruments, and cameras used in the production.

Talent

During production, the director and producer supervise the efforts of the on-camera talent—announcers, narrators, and performers, who read the words and perform the actions required.

Special production situations or larger, more expansive production facilities may require more specialized production personnel. For example, an executive producer may coordinate the efforts of several producers and directors working on individual programs in a multi-part series. A unit manager may handle budgeting, equipment, and scheduling details. An art director or scenic designer may plan the physical setting. A graphic artist may prepare the artwork and graphics. A lighting director may plan the lighting. Perhaps assistance is needed for the makeup, wardrobe, or music. In smaller production facilities, these special responsibilities are handled by the technical personnel already mentioned.

Facilities and Equipment

All the tools used to produce audio program material are also used in video production. Just as in radio, the television control room serves as the central control point, where the many production elements are combined to produce the finished program or announcement. It is not uncommon for the control room to be found on location, at a remote site using portable production equipment, rather than in an indoor setting.

Besides those already listed for radio, the primary production tools available to produce television program material include the following items:

a. *Studio.* Generally a studio is an indoor setting where talent perform or execute scripted material. The term "studio" has been broadened to include remote or on-location production sites that provide studiolike settings. This is often labeled EFP, or electronic field production.

b. *Video switcher.* The video switcher allows the operator to select a picture or combination of pictures from various live and recorded sources. The manner of selecting and changing the visual elements determines the pace, tempo, and look of the program, announcement, or segment. Essentially the video switcher controls the visual elements in television production, much as the audio control board or console controls the auditory elements in radio production. Video terms described later in this chapter indicate various ways in which visual transitions can be made using the video switcher.

c. *Cameras.* Studio, or field (outdoor) cameras capture pictures continuously for later processing into the finished program or announcement.

d. *Lenses.* Zoom lenses, used on field and studio cameras, can smoothly adjust the apparent distance between viewer and object, and they can focus on items as close as three feet and as far away as infinity. Excellent pictures can be produced, even in low-light situations. Macro lens features can fill a television screen with objects as small as postage stamps.

e. *Lights.* Various types of lighting instruments provide illumination for studio and field production. Specialized lighting techniques and equipment make it possible to produce some special effects.

f. *Videotape.* This magnetic material permits the recording of sound and picture for later editing and processing or rebroadcast. Most television program material is recorded, edited, and replayed on a videotape recorder (VTR). "SOT" or "SOC" can be used to indicate that both sound and picture are on the same videotape or videocassette recording. The abbreviation SOC is also used for Standard Out Cue, the last sentence given as a news reporter finishes a story—for example, "Chris Moore, Channel 8 News."

g. *Motion picture film.* The standard film gauge, or size, used in local station applications is 16mm. Networks and large production companies use 35mm, the theatrical film gauge, for specialized applications. Common abbreviations indicating television films are "SIL" (silent film, no sound track) and "SOF" (sound-on-film, picture and sound on the same piece of film stock).

h. *Character generator (CG).* Except for photographs, most of the graphic material needed for television production can be created with the use of a character generator, or "CG." These typewriter/television screen systems make it possible to load, store, and retrieve various types and sizes of letters and printed characters. In scripts, instead of simply "CG," you may see an abbreviation for the manufacturer of a particular CG system, such as "ADDA," "DVE," "Chyron," "Vidifont," or "VF."

i. *Slides.* Illustrations, graphics, sketches, and pictures may be photographed on 35mm slide film, placed in slide mounts, and then inserted into the television production as needed. Rather than slides, many production facilities use an ESS system.

j. *Electronic still storer (ESS).* This computer-driven electronic graphics system captures, stores, retrieves, and displays incoming video material from a variety of sources. When combined with electronic paint and CG systems, ESS units can provide a diversity of visual material, including photographs, maps, charts, symbols and logos, and preproduced graphics packages. Composite graphics, in which several visual elements are creatively combined into one graphic, are popular in television production today and are usually accomplished in-house rather than by independent production companies. Writers work with professional graphics specialists to create the graphics material scripted.

k. *Studio or flip cards.* An alternative to 35mm slides and ESS units is the use of in-studio cards, which are made of stiff-backed material. The television camera captures the picture of the card or graphic at the studio or field location.

Video Terminology

You can use the audio terms described earlier to write the audio portion of television and motion picture scripts. The video terms that will be described for use in both television and motion picture scripts are more complex because of the nature of video production.

The precise use of production terminology in scripts ensures the correct application in the resultant production. Provide enough production information in a video script to indicate to production personnel what is to be seen and heard. Production personnel, however, must have an opportunity to contribute their skills and creative talents to the finished production. Thus, you need to know how to use essential video terms in scripts to permit a full and creative experience, but be prepared to curtail the extensive use of such terms as circumstances dictate. Do not plan to use all the terms described in every video script you write. Find out how precise you need to be and then provide only that amount of production detail in the script. The amount of detail needed depends on program, production, personnel, and contractual demands and preferences.

The essential video terms and abbreviations needed for you to function fully and creatively are grouped into four categories: composition, camera adjustment, visual transition, and other useful terms. Script examples in chapter 3 will illustrate how video terms can be used to communicate creatively with production personnel.

Composition Terms

Several terms describe what is seen by the camera, the perspective of the scene offered to the viewer. The description of the composition of a shot involves such elements as the distance between the camera and the subject, the amount of the subject shown, and the position or angle of the camera in relation to the subject.

The principal composition terms are as follows:

a. *Cover shot (CS)/full shot (FS)/establishing shot (ES)*. The major area of action is to be seen. These interchangeable terms can be used at the beginning of a dramatic scene or at the beginning or ending of a studio production. This type of shot helps establish or reestablish the setting for the viewer.

b. *Long shot (LS)*. The widest possible view of the scene is to be shown. This general term is often imprecise; for example, if your script indicates the use of a LS of a building, production personnel could interpret a LS of the building to include all of the building and its surroundings or only a portion of the building. Despite its imprecision, LS is used often in video scripts.

c. *Medium shot (MS)*. A smaller portion of the scene is to be shown than might be in a LS. In effect, a long shot comprises several medium shots.

d. *Close-up (CU)/tight shot (TS)*. A smaller portion of the scene is to be shown than might be in a MS. Several close-ups make up a medium shot.

Some hybrid television composition terms indicate intermediate designations. Common examples are "medium-long shot" (MLS), a camera shot showing more than a MS but less than a LS; "medium-close up" (MCU), a camera shot showing more than a CU but less than a MS; and "extreme-close-up" (ECU or XCU), a camera shot showing only a very limited or small portion of an object or talent—for example, the face of a clock or the eyes of a villain.

If the script specifies a LS of a building, then a MS of the same building would show perhaps a few windows or one side of the building. A CU of that same building would then become one window on one side of the building. Because the terms LS, MS, and CU often lead to imprecise interpretations, it would be better to indicate exactly what is to be seen. For example, instead of writing "MS of building," it would be better to write "MS of building to show a few windows." Even this is not precise enough, but it is better than using only LS, MS, or CU. The interpretation of such terms is generally left up to the director of the production, although the writer is certainly free to suggest what should be shown.

There are other terms available to help add precision to video composition notations in scripts:

a. *Anatomical designations*. These describe the portion of a person to be shown on camera. These types of descriptions indicate that a person is to be shown from the head to the anatomical part listed. For example, you could write "FS of Bill," which would indicate that the camera would show Bill from his head to his feet. Other common designations of this type are "knee-shot" (from the knee to the head of the person), "waist-shot" (WS), and "head-and-shoulder shot" (H&S). Use of these terms will ensure precision when describing how much of one talent to show on camera.

b. *Grouping designations.* These terms describe how groups of individuals or items are to be shown. For example, a "two-shot" indicates that two people or items are shown, a "three-shot" includes three people or items, and so on. Grouping designations could be combined with anatomical designations to produce precise visual descriptions in scripts. For example, it is common to write "two-shot of Bill and Mary." It would be more precise to write "two-shot of Bill and Mary (WS)." Now the camera operator can be instructed to take a shot of Bill and Mary together, showing both from the waist up.

c. *Perspective designations.* These describe the relationship between the subject and the viewer. If the viewer is simply to observe what is happening in a detached manner, *objective* camera terms are used. The video terms described so far generally are considered objective camera terms. However, to offer the viewer a specific viewpoint, usually from the character's perspective, *subjective* camera terms can be used.

Following are some of the common subjective camera terms used in scripts:

a. *POV (point-of-view).* The camera shows the viewer the scene from the subject's viewpoint. For example, write "POV" when you want the viewer to see out of a car window, from the driver's perspective.

b. *Over-the-shoulder (OS).* The camera is placed over the shoulder of one of the characters to show what that character sees. For example, the use of "OS" is effective during an interview or a dramatic scene as one character talks to another.

c. *High angle/low angle.* Here size and dimension can be emphasized. The camera could look down from a high angle on a child to stress his or her diminutive size; you could write "high angle on Bobby," which would show Bobby looking up into the camera lens, emphasizing his short stature. The low-angle notation could be used when showing an adult talking to a child; thus, "low angle on Jane" would indicate that Jane would be shown from a low angle, emphasizing her size and height, as a child would see her.

d. *Canted shot.* If the camera shows a scene or character out of the normal horizontal and vertical orientations, this could emphasize unreality, distortion, or disorientation; the canted shot can illustrate the effects of drunkenness, drug use, or a severe head injury.

You may want to indicate that a change is needed in the composition of a camera shot but may not wish to be specific, allowing production personnel more leeway. One term that can be used in this instance is "angle on," most often used in dramatic scripts to indicate that the character should be shown from a slightly different perspective than in earlier shots. The new camera angle would be selected by the director at the time of production.

Often it is desirable to remain with the shot seen from a particular camera but to adjust the picture composition or to make a transition to another shot. This permits the viewer to see more than the camera is showing at present, provides subtle visual emphases and perspectives, or controls and directs the viewer's attention to a particular aspect of the character or setting. Each camera adjustment specified in a script must be used purposefully and with proper motivation for a specific desired effect.

Camera Adjustment Terms

The principal camera adjustment terms are the following:

a. *Follow.* The camera can be instructed to follow the character's actions while maintaining approximately the same image size and perspective.

b. *Zoom in/out.* Use of a standard Zoomar lens permits the camera to present shots ranging from a CU to a LS and any designation in between. The camera mount remains stationary while the lens performs the visual transition.

c. *Dolly in/out.* A similar effect can be achieved by having the entire camera move toward (dolly in) or away from (dolly out) the character or scene. Technically a dolly is more difficult to execute than a zoom shot but produces essentially the same results. A fast zoom or dolly shot produces a much different effect than a slow zoom or dolly shot. If you think it is appropriate, note how fast the perspective should change and at what point the zoom or dolly should stop. Dolly and zoom shots often are used to follow action, heighten dramatic effects, and orient the viewer. At the beginning of a dramatic scene, the audience could see a CU of a telephone ringing as the camera pulls back (dollies or zooms out) to a LS of the room, as the performer enters to answer the phone and begin the scene.

d. *Pan right/left.* The panorama of the scene can be shown by having the camera mount remain stationary but pointing the lens of the camera to cover the scene. "Pan right" indicates that the camera is to cover or show the scene beginning at the left and continuing to the right. "Pan left" provides the opposite perspective. Pans can be scripted for many reasons, including following action, offering a new visual perspective, making transitions in locales, or heightening dramatic moments—for instance, panning from the face of a frightened victim to a knife poised to strike.

e. *Tilt up/down.* The camera can show a setting or character going from a low to a high angle and vice versa. For example, if you wrote "tilt up to the top of the stairs," the viewer would see a continuous shot from the bottom to the top of the stairs. "Tilt down" provides the opposite perspective. Tilts are used for many of the same reasons noted for the use of pans.

f. *Truck right/left.* The term "truck" is used when you want to follow the action but maintain the same distance between camera and subject. Examples of this technique are showing a character walking down a busy street or items placed on a display table, but always keeping the same distance between the camera and subjects. A trucking shot could also be used to make a visual transition from one locale or setting to another.

g. *Arc right/left.* An "arc" shot is a combination of a dolly and a truck shot. To illustrate the dimension, size, and beauty of an automobile, for example, the camera could arc either right or left around the automobile.

h. *Pedestal/boom/crane up or down.* The camera can show a scene or character from an extremely high or low angle to provide extra visual perspectives for the viewer. The camera shot would be continuous from a normal angle to an unusually high or low angle. A feeling of upward movement could be achieved, for example, if the camera "boomed up" as a helicopter lifted off the ground.

Visual Transition Terms

Writers use specific terms to describe the visual adjustments between each carefully composed shot. As with camera adjustments, select visual transitions to help the viewer move easily from one shot to another with appropriate motivation and a predetermined effect.

The principal visual transition terms follow:

a. *Fade in/out.* At the beginning of a scene, for example, you would write "Fade in to _____." The viewer would see a blank screen, and then gradually the first picture would come into view. "Fade out" would be used at the end of a scene, an act, or a major division of a production.

b. *Cut.* Because it is the most common type of transition between shots, "cut" is not written in the script. It is understood that an instantaneous change is to be made from one shot to another unless otherwise specified in the script.

c. *Dissolve (diss. or dis.).* In a dissolve, one shot gradually fades out as another gradually fades in to take its place. The two images overlap momentarily. You can specify a "quick dissolve" or a "slow dissolve" to indicate the speed of the transition. There are special kinds of dissolves: a "matched dissolve" is made from one shot to another that is closely related in picture size and appearance—for instance, a matched dissolve from a CU of a clock face to a CU of a tire wheel—and a "ripple dissolve," in which a standard dissolve is achieved, but the picture "ripples," or wavers, as the shots change.

d. *Super (superimposition)*. One image is superimposed on another. Essentially a super is produced by stopping a dissolve midway so that both images overlap and are seen simultaneously. The clarity and intensity of each image are diminished because of this overlap.

e. *Key*. The special effects equipment available on most video switchers makes it possible to electronically "key," or place, one image into a background picture. Often the graphics used in "keys" can be colorized to produce a pleasing effect and to blend with other production elements. Name identifications during television interviews and graphics appearing in small boxes over the shoulders of newscasters are generally marked as a key in television scripts—for example, "key in graphic of auto sales stats." A "chroma key" is an electronic effect that eliminates a specific color in a picture and replaces that color with another visual; chroma key is used routinely to show weather maps on television.

f. *Defocus/refocus*. One alternative to the use of a dissolve or fade to make a transition between scenes or segments is to have the camera operator turn the focus knob on the camera so the shot gradually goes out of focus ("defocus"). After changing to another camera location, the shot can begin out of focus, and the camera operator can be instructed to focus (or "refocus") the new shot.

g. *Rack focus*. Various camera lens controls can be adjusted so only a small portion of the scene is in focus. This characteristic of the camera lens allows the camera operator and the writer to control the viewer's attention within a shot. A common application of this technique occurs in commercials in which a performer demonstrates the use of a particular product. At the end of the commercial, when the brand name is displayed, the camera "rack focuses" to the box, can, or bag in the foreground so only the product is in sharp focus, while the background and other parts of the screen are slightly out of focus, thus directing the viewers' attention one last time to the advertised product.

h. *Wipe*. A "wipe" is a visual transition made by gradually replacing portions of one picture with the corresponding portions of a new picture. During a wipe, a new picture moves the current picture off the screen. A wipe can be accomplished in a variety of ways—vertically, horizontally, in a circular pattern, or from any corner of the picture.

i. *Split screen.* When two shots occupy approximately the same amount of screen space simultaneously, it is considered a "split screen." If four images are seen simultaneously in approximately equal portions of the screen, it is considered a "quad split."

j. *Whip or swish pan.* An extremely quick pan by the camera appears as a momentary blur on the screen. This technique can be used, for example, to move the viewer rapidly from one location to another and then instantly into the new setting.

Other Useful Visual Terms and Abbreviations

Other terms can help describe a desired effect more exactly or enhance a particular production:

a. *B.G./F.G.* The abbreviations "B.G." and "F.G." indicate a specific visual element in the background (B.G.) or foreground (F.G.) of a shot.

b. *VO.* This stands for "voice-over," indicating that the provided words are to be read by an unseen character while various images are shown.

c. *OC.* This stands for "off-camera" and means essentially the same as VO.

d. *B-Roll.* "B-Roll" indicates that a film or videotape segment is to be inserted into the main piece of video. The B-Roll material can contain only picture, only sound, or both picture and sound. For example, during a live broadcast of a parade, the script can indicate that a B-Roll be shown at one point. This B-Roll may show the floats being prepared or perhaps one particular float in various stages of preparation. The talent for this broadcast then ad-libs or perhaps reads from a prepared full script information that matches what is seen on the preproduced and edited B-Roll segment.

e. *Stock shot.* When it is not convenient for production personnel to record a particular shot, "stock shots" or footage may be used. For example, this can include shots of a busy downtown street or an aerial view of a forested area. Before this term can be included in a script, you must know what stock footage is available. Stock shots can be used as part of a B-Roll.

f. *Freeze frame.* The term "freeze frame" indicates that the action or motion of a shot is stopped or frozen suddenly.

g. *Montage or collage.* This is a rapid series of shots used to produce a particular mood or image to heighten the tempo of a production. It is the visual equivalent of an audio montage or collage.

h. *Reverse motion.* "Reverse motion" indicates that the sequence of images is seen in reverse of the normal order.

i. *Slow/fast motion.* "Slow motion" or "fast motion" indicates that the images appear at a reduced or an accelerated pace.

The use of motion picture film in television production is diminishing and is being replaced by more sophisticated videotape systems. Still, many television commercials as well as dramatic and comedy programs are produced on film. Of course, motion picture film can be used to produce presentations— if not for television, then for theaters, schools, hospitals, and businesses. This trend away from film production for television applications is likely to continue as more versatile videotape systems are designed to provide the same kinds of visual effects once offered only through film production. Other factors have contributed to an escalated use of videotape, such as improved videotape picture quality, the increased portability of camera and recording gear, reasonable set-up and maintenance costs, and the growing acceptability of video production within the electronic media. You should continue to monitor this shift in emphasis in production methods because of its impact on the kinds of scripts being written.

Generally the information provided for video production (tools, terminology, procedures, and techniques) applies to motion picture production as well. Some differences, however, should be noted; for example, in motion picture production, there is no control room, no video switcher, no videotape, no ESS, and no character generator. Practically all of the other television production terms can be used in motion picture scripts; if anything, a limited number of terms and descriptive phrases are used in most motion picture scripts. There is no technical director (T.D.), but there are other, more specialized personnel involved in film production.

Large-budget motion picture production makes use of 35mm film stock, using traditional film-style, one-camera production techniques rather than the in-studio, three-camera process common in videotape television production. The single-camera process is used, even in videotape production, when out-of-doors or location shooting is involved.

A large production crew, with diverse production specialties, working in a studio or on location, will spend a long time with a single film project. The film may be a theatrical release, a made-for-TV movie, or perhaps the pilot program for a prospective television series. Careful planning and coordination are needed to produce a quality product on time and within the specified budget.

Film Production

This chapter explained basic audio and video production information needed by the writer. Remember that the writer is but one member of a team of people collectively and creatively working together. Know the tools of production that help bring a script to life as it moves from the typewriter or word processor to the radio, television set, or motion picture screen. Remember to use production terminology in your scripts to clarify what is seen or heard, but not so much that it distracts the reader of a script or interferes with the creativity of production personnel.

Summary

Knowledge of these basic production tools, terms, and techniques should help you anticipate the technical limits and expand your creative potential. Such knowledge should be an integral part of your work as a writer. It should lead you to a more satisfying sense of participation in the creative process of writing and producing material for the electronic media.

Suggested Exercises and Projects

1. Compare and contrast the advantages and disadvantages of various mass media (radio, television, motion pictures) from the writer's viewpoint. What kinds of writing challenges do the characteristics of each medium offer?
2. Watch a thirty-minute television program. Chart the length of each major program segment. Note the use of the various camera composition designations, visual transitions, special effects, and camera positions. Report on the production value of the program and the effectiveness of its visual elements.
3. Schedule a personal or group visit to a production facility. Determine its production procedures and processes and how these affect the role of the writer.
4. Record a radio commercial off the air. Note the use of voices, music, and sound effects. List the production terms, described in this chapter, needed to note how these audio elements were to be used to produce the radio commercial.
5. Watch and, if possible, record a television commercial off the air. Note the use of sound and picture. List the production terms, described in this chapter, needed to accomplish these audio and video effects.
6. Do the same as in exercise 5 but for a current motion picture. Comment on the effectiveness of the production elements used and how they interrelate with the writer's work for the film.

Basic Writing Styles, Formats, and Techniques

S cripts are the blueprints used by writers and production personnel to communicate with each other. You need to prepare written material in proper script form to ensure that your work will not be rejected outright. Using standard scripting formats will help you communicate essential scripting and production information clearly and succinctly. Once you have mastered the mechanics of putting script information on a page you can use the various standard presentations to express ideas and concepts easily and effectively.

The purpose of this chapter is twofold: (1) to present the basic concepts and techniques for writing effective aural and visual script material and (2) to show the basic scripting styles and formats to help you provide script material in a standard and effective manner. There will be a discussion of essential aural writing styles and techniques: how to select words, organize sentences, and creatively incorporate music and sound effects into a script. The discussion of visual writing styles and techniques will indicate how to select and use various visual elements. The rest of the chapter will explain standard scripting approaches, styles and formats to show how aural and visual script material is developed and presented on paper by the professional writer. This discussion will cover such writing mechanics as the use of punctuation, abbreviations, timing considerations, and the standard scripting formats. Full-script formats will receive more attention because of their complexity and constant use in many writing situations and applications. Finally computer use and the development of storyboards will be examined to show how they can help generate various kinds of scripts.

The scripting styles and formats presented in this chapter reflect those used throughout the electronic media. This does not imply that everyone will use these styles or formats exactly as presented here. There are variations. This chapter describes the general scripting guidelines, practices, and approaches commonly accepted throughout the industry. Master these basic script forms. You will acquire the insight and flexibility necessary to adjust to a variety of script presentation requirements. Once you know the "rules" of writing for the electronic media, you can either use them or break them— not out of ignorance but from knowledge and practice of the basic methods.

All basic script formats will be explained in this chapter to show the progression of forms available and to serve as a reference for the discussions in later chapters. Several kinds of script material are presented to help you understand how to apply the various script forms to practical writing situations. In this chapter, you should focus on the *form,* not necessarily on the content, of the script examples. It is important to note that margin, spacing, and size adjustments have been made in the material, due to book design considerations. It should also be noted that the application of basic scripting techniques and formats to the complexities of electronic news gathering and writing requirements will be illustrated fully in chapter 5, "News and Sports."

Aural Writing Styles

The use of sound in scripts is an important technique for the writer. It is important in television presentations, even though visual elements tend to dominate. Sound is the entire means of communication in radio.

Sounds have the unique capability of creating an environment for the listener or viewer. Sounds help create and enhance mental images. Creating an environment or a setting is important for the writer, since often this determines the acceptability of future messages and the ultimate success of the communication process.

Imagination is the only limit imposed on the writer's ability to create environment effectively—the imagination of the writer and of the audience, which is willingly stretched to accept altered or enhanced reality. The success of aural messages hinges on this tenuous, although important, human characteristic. Imagination is the key to creating an effective environment through sound.

Radio's often-criticized disadvantage of no pictures actually is its greatest advantage, since the absence of tangible pictures provides no visual or mental restraints on the imagination of the writer and, ultimately, the listener. Through the creative use of various writing and production techniques, entire worlds can be created in the human mind. Actions, emotions, characters, and even words take on new dimensions when they are presented effectively by the writer and accepted by the audience. Persons and objects can project uncharacteristic or unreal qualities. Your creative sensitivities and appreciation for the beauty and functional cohesiveness among the various elements of sound are important determinants of the effectiveness and acceptability of sound in messages prepared for the electronic media.

There are many techniques available to create an environment with sound: language (words and sentences), music, and sound effects. Each will be examined to provide insight into the writer's creative options.

Language

The primary goal of language is to communicate ideas and information to be easily understood. Only after a message has been understood can it entertain, inspire, or persuade the audience.

A writer needs a solid foundation in the basic use of language, especially in the selection and use of words and the combining of words into meaningful sentences. This discussion can touch on only a few of the elements necessary for a writer to use the English language effectively. A solid education in English grammar is highly recommended. Each time you learn something new about the use of language, you bring that knowledge to all future writing assignments. In effect, you become a better writer.

As a writer working in the electronic media, you will face the predictable conflict between the acceptable rules of grammar and the reality of conversation. It is a conflict that pits grammar's precision, form, and style against conversation's clarity, reality, contemporary vitality, and flexibility. Resolve this conflict by relying on your best judgment and writing experience. Apply the essential rules of grammar to the naturalness required in scriptwriting. In your scripts, reflect the changes and reality that occur continuously in conversation. Exercise 7 at the end of this chapter can help you achieve this objective.

Words

Words are the writer's primary tool for expressing thoughts, ideas, and emotions, regardless of the medium. Words have meaning and power. They can explain the most complicated reality and express the subtlest emotions.

Select and use words carefully. Calculate the impact of the words you write. Always think not just of your ideas but also of what you are saying—not just of what effect you *hope* to create but also of what effect you are actually creating.

Remember the audience—their interests, preferences, likes, and dislikes. Use words that are familiar. Directly touch the lives of your audience, create immediate and lasting attention, and have strong personal impact.

Use words that are tied to reality. Thus, informal, rather than formal, language is preferred. There is no second chance for an audience to reread what they hear, so your words must make a clear, easy-to-understand impression the *first* and only time.

Write for the ear, not the eye, of the audience. This applies to video as well as audio scripts. Be sensitive to how individual words sound when spoken and how they blend synergistically with music and sound.

Listen carefully to the ways people talk to capture in your scripts the conversational style you hear. The more you observe and retain about language habits, the more realistic your word choices will be.

Use a conversational *framework*. Structure your scripts like a conversation, but avoid the elements of conversations that make them verbose, redundant, imprecise, rambling, and incomplete. Adopt the *best* of conversational style. Use contractions to make dramatic dialogue natural and familiar; however, avoid clichés, words or phrases used too often to have significant impact on the audience. The use of clichés shows that a writer lacks creativity and the initiative to find words that offer a fresh approach.

Remember that words offer a wide range of meanings and nuances that continue to evolve. Study the context and placement of words. *How* words are placed in a sentence is the final determiner of meaning, or intended meaning. Be a lifelong student of language to expand your word selections and form links in meaning that you may have forgotten or never sensed.

Write clearly. Avoid using complex, technical terms unless absolutely necessary. If you use such terms in a script, explain them in common, ordinary words that will be understood by most people.

Learn the basic elements of language and word usage. Here are a few to keep in mind. *Nouns and pronouns* designate a person, place, or thing; they attach a label to something and specify the perspective for the audience. *Adjectives* identify a distinctive feature of a noun; they add dimension and color to the language and should be chosen carefully to describe in an accurate and enriching manner. *Verbs* provide the power or action in a sentence; they can help express ideas accurately when they are selected thoughtfully and verb tenses are used appropriately. *Adverbs* modify or complement verbs and adjectives; they provide an extra dimension or description for verbs, telling how much, how fast, how tall, and so on. Other elements of language usage are discussed fully in books listed in Appendix A.

Sentences

Sentences are the principal units of organized thought. The way in which you carefully arrange words to form phrases, clauses, and sentences extends your creative potential as a writer. Use these keys to construct effective sentences in scripts: clarity, simplicity, conversational style, and conciseness.

Make clarity your first concern. Clear writing does not have to mean sterile writing. It is possible to write strong, meaningful, expressive sentences with clarity and simplicity. Clarity of expression leads to understanding. Understanding leads to other objectives. Once an audience understands what you have written, then you can inform, persuade, inspire, entertain, and so on.

Simple sentence structure is best—subject followed by verb followed by object. Simple sentence construction ensures clarity, makes your message attractive and interesting, and sets your writing apart from the daily barrage of words and images that inundates your audience. Do not separate the subject from the verb in a sentence; these two units form a logical arrangement. Avoid interjections or explanatory clauses, which can be confusing and do not reflect a conversational style. Carefully insert phrases and clauses into sentences.

Vary your sentence length. This will add variety to your writing, reflect conversational language usage, and better control the pace, rhythm, and flow of ideas. Longer sentences are acceptable if appropriate pauses are marked in the script and if the performer follows such directions and punctuation notations. Too many short sentences sound disjointed and disturb the normal flow and rhythm of a conversational style.

Sentence fragments and incomplete sentences that do not display the usual subject-verb-object arrangement can be used in scripts. This kind of sentence construction can capture the essence of an idea and, thus, promote clarity. These less traditional expressions reflect contemporary usage, save words, and add vigor and variety to language and sentence structure.

Concise writing is "lean" writing. Use only the words necessary to express an idea or emotion. Critically examine each sentence you write, and discard words that do not help move forward the idea or emotion you want to express. Express only one idea in each sentence. It is better to use a few short sentences than one complex sentence.

Read your scripts aloud; *listen* to the sentences you write. Notice the pace, rhythm, and flow of each sentence, each piece of dialogue. Determine *each* sentence's clarity of expression and richness of meaning, and arrange your ideas into a smooth-flowing pattern that creates momentum and adds interest. You have not tested the effectiveness of your writing until you *hear* how the words *sound* when they are combined into a sentence and how each sentence works with the previous sentence, the following sentence, the one after that, and so on. You must *hear* the words, the meanings they convey, the emotions they evoke, and the impact they have.

Music and Sound Effects

A writer can also use music and sound effects in a script. It is important to understand why they are used and how they can enhance the quality of a script.

Uses

Both music and sound effects can be used in scripts to produce the following effects:

a. Attract and hold the attention of the audience
b. Enhance but not overpower the script by adding reality and authenticity
c. Create a mood or environment
d. Establish a locale or setting by helping the audience visualize the scene
e. Direct attention to a specific portion of the setting, such as a character, an action, or an object, by emphasizing that particular element with a short music excerpt or sound effect
f. Make transitions between program segments or to indicate changes in time, place, locale, or mood. It is even possible to create a mental image of two distinct places using a specific sound for each location and then accomplishing, with sound, the equivalent of a motion picture or television "cut."
g. Note entrances and exits
h. Move the action of the script forward
i. Heighten or punctuate a climactic moment in a script
j. Enliven something that is normally silent—for example, providing a musical or sound effect identification for an automobile
k. Counterpoint the mood or tone of the words—for example, a sound effect of a noisy jet plane or a street scene used as counterpoint to a quiet, narrative delivery style

As a separate element, music can be used as the principal program content—for instance, in a radio music program, as the theme or identification for many types of programs and entertainment personalities, or as a substitute for a sound effect—for example, as a musical instrument or phrase used to characterize a person, a character, an animal, or an event.

Often it is the careful *blend* of music and sound effects that produces the most realistic and effective results in the *soundtrack*. For example, to make a transition in time and location, from a quiet rural setting to a noisy urban environment, you could cross-fade from a lush symphonic music excerpt to a soulful saxophone excerpt to a strong rock instrumental. While the music progresses from classical to rock, location or ambient sound could be mixed in. The restive sound of birds chirping can overlap into the regular rhythm of railroad crossing signals blinking and then into the crowd and vehicular congestion associated with city life. By creatively *blending* music and ambient sound, a transition in mood or location can be made more convincing and effective than if only sound or music were used.

Suggestions and Techniques

When inserting either music or sound effects into a script, you should do the following:

a. Relate the music or sound effects to your overall script goal or purpose.

b. Make certain either or both elements integrate well with the other script elements in style, content, tone, quality, tempo, and pace and that there is an effective blend of audio elements.

c. Find the relevant, prominent, representative, or key sound effects or music to create mood, atmosphere, locale, or setting. For example, to create a restaurant locale, do not specify in the script all of the possible sounds heard in a restaurant. Instead, select the one or two key sounds that will suggest the locale to the listener. The rest of the picture will be created in the mind and imagination of the audience.

d. Be sure the audience can identify the sound effects used. For example, it is possible to mistake a car backfire with a shotgun blast. Consider adding a reference to the sound effect in the dialogue or narration.

e. Be specific in your music or sound effects notations. Always identify the exact sound effect or type or title of music to be used. As suggested in chapter 2, indicate how each is to be heard—for example, up full, under announcer, or up for a few seconds and then under—and how each is to be disposed of—for instance, fades out or under and then out.

f. Be certain to note that the music or sound effect is "under" or "in the background" when a voice is to be heard over either. Suggest the use of an instrumental when a voice is to be heard over the music. Song lyrics tend to distract the audience from narration or dialogue.

g. Use familiar music cautiously; it may evoke connotations and images that you do not intend. An additional danger is copyright infringement. Consider using selections from a music library, which offers a variety of melody lines, theme variations, bridges, stings, and other musical forms that can provide the continuity you might need and still meet copyright fee requirements.

Visual Writing Styles

When writing for the primarily visual media of television and motion pictures, you must be able to envision images that convey the mood, purpose, and direction of the situation. You must also envision the *development* of the script—shot by shot, scene by scene, sequence by sequence. Use your imagination to see and hear all the elements in the script—objects, people, action, dialogue, continuity—before writing words on paper. Thinking must precede writing. Idea and image must develop side-by-side so that one reinforces and strengthens the impact of the other. The usual script development pattern is thinking, then seeing, and finally writing. Visualization and sequencing are the processes that can help you select and use the appropriate visual elements to reinforce the audio portion of your scripts.

Visualization

Visualization is the process of translating concepts and ideas into individual images. The writer imagines perfectly composed pictures of the scenes, backgrounds, locales, settings, and characters that best portray what is to be communicated.

Objectives

When using visualization for nondramatic presentations, you should attempt to show objects, performers, and actions as clearly as possible. This is the objective for such programs as newscasts, talk and informational programs, game shows, and instructional and documentary programs.

When using visualization for dramatic presentations, however, you should try to show objects, settings, locales, and performers in such a way as to convey a particular meaning, idea, or perspective. The next time you watch a television or film drama, notice how the position of the camera relates to the performers and the objects in the picture. A change in camera or performer positions can alter the viewer's perspective and interpretation of a scene or sequence or change the viewer's reaction to a particular character.

Limitations

Several factors influence the visualization process:

a. Television is an intimate medium because of screen size. Thus, more close shots should be used to show material in more detail.

b. The vertical and horizontal dimensions of the television screen are in a ratio of approximately 3 to 4. The shape of the medium must be part of visualizing settings and planning sequences so that most of the shots are horizontally rather than vertically oriented. Motion picture screens are also horizontally oriented.

c. Television and motion picture screens are two-dimensional. Thus, to create an illusion of depth, you should suggest the emphasis of foregrounds and backgrounds in the composition of individual shots.

d. Objects, performers, and cameras are constantly moving, yet to the viewer they may appear static because the screen itself does not move. This, of course, is not the case when the writer and director visualize characters and settings for a stage presentation, for example. Keep in mind the audience's visual perceptions of each medium.

e. Because of the severe time limitations involved in television and motion picture production, you will have to limit the number of sets or shooting locations as well as the diversity and difficulty of shots suggested in a script.

Whoever ultimately directs the acting and production personnel using your completed script will have to make crucial decisions about visualization and will be most concerned with the best techniques for accomplishing your visual scripting goals. If you know some of the considerations involved in determining the staging and framing of individual shots, however, you can improve the quality of your visualization and ultimately the script from which the director will work.

Visualization, then, is the first major step toward completing the writing process for the visually oriented media of television and motion pictures. If the visualization process is done conscientiously, competently, and with some foresight, the process of sequencing will follow naturally and provide the final step for the visual portion of the writing process.

Sequencing

Sequencing is the process of placing individual images in a certain sequence to convey a particular message or meaning. A specific idea or perspective can be communicated by changing the order of these individual images and by using continuous motion to bridge the gap between individual shots. Sequencing is the process of creating a *succession* of images devised through the process of visualization.

Visual sequencing can be accomplished by using one technique or a combination of several techniques: movement of performers in front of the camera, camera adjustments, and visual transitions between shots. Each technique, when used carefully and purposefully, helps produce an effective succession of images.

The processes of visualization and sequencing are perhaps the most difficult to master. At first glance, the terminology and specific justifications for the use of certain techniques and procedures may seem bewildering and unimportant. The skillful use of these processes, however, will determine the acceptability, production value, and ultimate success of the script. Without the creative application of the principles of visualization and sequencing, you cannot hope to prepare effective, meaningful, and visually stimulating script material.

Storyboards can help illustrate the sequencing you envision. The development and usefulness of storyboards are discussed later in this chapter, and examples appear in chapters 4 and 10.

Several important writing style considerations apply equally to audio and video scripts. Master these techniques before trying to use this information in later scripting format and writing style applications.

Mechanics of Electronic Media Writing Style

Preparing Script Pages

Lengthy scripts, such as drama and comedy scripts and program series proposals, require a cover page. A cover page should contain the title of the series or program; complete information about the writer (name, address, telephone number); the date the script was submitted; the sections of the script, designated by acts, scenes, or segments; and the appropriate page numbers for each section. Cover pages are not used, however, for short script formats—for example, commercials, talk shows, and interview outlines.

For short scripts or for segments within longer programs, provide identification information at the top left corner of each script page: the program series or client for spot announcements; the program or announcement title, which is a phrase indicating the central theme or concept used; the program or script number, which is assigned by the production company, advertising agency, or station; the estimated length and production setting; your name; and the date. This information readily identifies your work and provides an efficient means of processing your script material. Following is an example of how you could provide identification information for two typical script presentations: the one on the left for a talk program, the one on the right for a commercial:

In Perspective	First National Bank
Mayoral Candidates	"We've Got Your Interest"
IP—#43	FNB 4182-A
30 minutes LIVE	30 second VTR
Wolterstein 2/10	Hillards 9/10

Several routine script preparation guidelines should be remembered:

a. Use a machine that produces at least pica type. In some situations, it is helpful to use extra-large pica type, such as great primer, executive size, or orator, particularly when a script is to be used directly by on-camera television talent from a through-the-camera-lens prompting device. Keep the type clean and change the ribbon frequently. Dark black ribbons are always preferred.

b. Use standard-size sheets of paper (8 1/2 by 11 inches). Use a soft grade of bond paper. If the script is to be used or seen on the air, select paper that does not reflect studio lights and that makes a minimum of sound when handled near a microphone. A special continuous paper roll is used for some through-the-camera-lens prompting situations. Computers can provide fully electronic prompting systems.

c. Write on one side of the paper only.

d. Double-space all script material. There are situations when triple-spacing may be required. Never single-space script material.

e. Determine marginal settings for each writing situation. Leave approximately a 1 1/4-inch border around all edges of each script page. This provides space for content and production notations.

f. Do not hyphenate any word at the end of a line. In an on-air situation, breaking a word at the end of a line makes it difficult to read the script smoothly. It is much better to correct this simple mechanical deficiency earlier in the scripting stage rather than allowing this distraction to cause unnecessary production problems.

g. Conclude each page with a complete sentence. The on-air reader or performer will not have to flip to the next page in the middle of a sentence and disrupt the flow of the script.

h. If it is necessary to provide more than one page to complete a particular writing assignment, one of several scripting techniques may be used: number each page in the script consecutively—for example, p. 2, p. 3 or 2-2-2, 3-3-3; indicate the total length of the script as well as the specific page number—for example, p. 2 of 8, p. 3 of 8; place the notation "add 1," "add 2," and so on at the top of consecutive pages; or draw a conspicuous, heavy black arrow (⟶) in the lower right-hand corner of each page except the last. This last technique is required only in news-related work. Use the page numbering system specified by your writing supervisor.

i. If at all possible, rekey scripts that contain marginal notations, numerous corrections, and errors. Remember that your scripts represent your ideas, concepts, and standards of professionalism.

Guidelines for preparing a variety of script material will be presented later in this chapter.

It may not seem important to spell words correctly, but consistent misspellings detract from the overall quality of a script, distract on-air readers or performers, and serve as another measure of your grasp of the basics of effective writing. The efficient and frequent use of a standard dictionary is an essential technique for a writer. The 30 seconds required to look up a word in the dictionary pays dividends by producing a more readable script. Spelling correctly is mandatory at all times.

Spelling

Since scripts often are read live, on-the-air, you may need to provide pronunciation assistance for the presenter or reader. This is done to avoid embarrassment and to provide a smoother flow for the script. This pronunciation assistance is provided for difficult-to-pronounce names, places, and objects, especially those available locally. If in doubt, it is better to include pronunciation assistance in the script.

Pronunciation

Although the International Phonetic Alphabet (IPA) is the most precise and universal system for transcribing speech sounds, it is not widely used by media professionals. The most useful method for communicating pronunciation is a commonsense approach, using capitalization to indicate syllables to be stressed. Enclose the phonetic spelling in parentheses just after the difficult-to-pronounce word.

```
Our guest today is Harry Schizas (SHY-suss), candidate
for Mayor.

Be sure to shop at Finkleheimer's (FINKLE-high-
murrs) Department Store in the Roca (ROW-ka) Mall.
```

Eliminate most abbreviations from scripts. Scripts can be read more smoothly, without on-air hesitations, if words are written in full exactly as they are to be read. However, it is acceptable to abbreviate commonly recognized titles of personal address—Mr., Mrs., Ms., Dr.—rather than create odd phonetic spellings, such as ''mister'' and ''missus.''

Abbreviations

Use abbreviations or alphabetical designations that are to be read as such if the general audience is familiar with them. It is acceptable, for example, to write ''C-I-O'' instead of ''Congress of Industrial Organizations'' and to write ''Y-M-C-A'' instead of ''Young Men's Christian Association.'' Hyphens are used to separate the letters to be read individually. Use the full name the first time it appears in the script if there is reason to believe that the audience will not understand the abbreviation. Thereafter, once the audience has adjusted mentally to the name of the organization in full, it is permissible to use the abbreviation.

Well-known acronyms, such as NATO, UNICEF, and OPEC, should not be hyphenated or spelled out when placed in a script. The letters are not meant to be read individually.

Do not use symbols in lieu of words. For example, do not write ''&'' for ''and,'' ''#'' for ''number,'' or ''%'' for ''percent.'' Shorthand now will cause confusion later.

Capitalization

Unless otherwise instructed, use standard capitalization. FULL CAPS, or all uppercase letters, are reserved to note character designations, video and audio production details, and special production and interpretation information. Use of this system helps differentiate between the words spoken by the talent and all other script information.

Numbers

Good judgment and consistency must be used when handling numerals. Eliminate as much statistical information as possible. Generalize and simplify intelligently; however, in the interest of accurate and complete communication, do not omit or distort highly important numerical information, particularly in situations such as a documentary or news story.

Use numbers sparingly. When spoken aloud, numbers are often difficult for the talent to read, difficult for the listener or viewer to understand, and, more important, difficult for them to remember. Even numerical information displayed on a television screen may become difficult to understand and absorb as the numbers flash on and off the screen quickly.

Convert figures, especially large ones, into round numbers whenever feasible. ''1,605'' may be rounded to ''16-hundred'' and ''227,523'' may be expressed as ''a quarter-million.'' Identify rounded numbers with such general terms as ''about,'' ''almost,'' ''nearly,'' or ''approximately.'' Strive for as much variation as possible. To avoid repetition and to facilitate understanding, translate trends or changes expressed in figures into such terminology as ''doubled,'' ''cut in half,'' ''dropped 50 percent,'' or ''dipped sharply.''

Indicate the significance of the numbers used. Relate them directly to the audience's interests, concerns, and life-styles. ''The increase in property tax rates means that if you own a home valued at 70-thousand dollars, your tax bill will increase xxx dollars.''

Spell out numbers one through eleven—''three,'' ''six,'' ''ten,'' and so on. Use numerals for numbers from 12 to 999—''85,'' ''118,'' ''865.'' Years can be written as numerals—''1986,'' ''1492,'' ''1776,'' and so on.

Spell out ordinal numbers under twelve—''first,'' ''eighth,'' ''tenth,'' and so on. Use ''st,'' ''rd,'' ''th,'' and ''nd'' after dates, addresses, and streets numbered over 12—''February 13th,'' ''22nd and 43rd Avenue.''

Use a hyphenated combination of numerals and words to express large numbers—''17-million,'' ''15-hundred.'' Express fractions in words, not numerals. Hyphenate the words in a fraction—''three-fourths,'' ''one-half of one percent.''

Avoid use of the dollar sign and cent sign. Write ''ten dollars'' and not ''$10.'' Write ''75-cents'' and not ''75¢.'' This same guideline applies to other terms or symbols—inches, feet, miles, seconds, minutes, hours, and all metric terms; for example, write ''85 kilometers'' instead of ''85 km.''

When writing license numbers, telephone numbers, addresses, and similar series of numerals, use a hyphen to break the numbers as they ordinarily would be read most effectively—"H-14-21," "4-7-2-17-76," "6-21 Lake View Road," and so on.

Punctuation

The appropriate use of standard punctuation marks in scriptwriting is essential if you hope to make full use of all available language tools. Only with systematic use of punctuation will you ensure that you are communicating a feeling or an idea correctly.

As a scriptwriter, you are trying to simulate, with words on a page, the pacing, pauses, lilts, rhythms, and naturalness of human speech and interaction. Punctuation helps the combination of words make sense and sound natural.

Use short, simple sentences. This will remove the need for much punctuation. Still there is a need to assist the performer or talent in phrasing or reading the script more intelligently and to communicate an idea more clearly. In most instances, traditional punctuation rules can be followed. The punctuation marks described are not used in every scriptwriting situation. Exercise good judgment and common sense when using punctuation marks in your scripts. If a mark does not have a clear purpose on a page, it should not be there. The fewer marks used, the easier it will be to read the copy aloud.

Period

A period indicates the end of a complete thought. Scripts often are not written in grammatically complete sentence form, since a conversational style is stressed. In conversation, most people do not speak in complete sentences that contain a subject and predicate. Even then, a period is used to indicate the end of an idea. The period also indicates that a pause should be inserted when the script is read aloud. As in most conversation, we stop at the end of a thought. The period signals both the end of a single thought and the need for a pause, the length of which is determined by the nature of the script and the pacing or rhythm desired.

Exclamation Point

If an entire phrase or sentence should be emphasized, rather than only one word, use an exclamation point. This will help ensure that the entire sentence is more emphatic than if only a period were used. Unfortunately, like many other useful punctuation marks, the exclamation point is overused, thus dampening its effectiveness and the sense of urgency it can convey.

Question Mark

Question marks cause a rising vocal inflection at the end of a sentence or phrase. Help the talent who has to make such rising vocal inflections sound natural. Keep sentences that end with question marks relatively short.

Comma

Commas have many uses in electronic media writing situations. Most often they separate words, phrases, or clauses that are part of a single thought unit or sentence—for example, "trains, rain, and body sprains. Only some of the features on tonight's ten o'clock magazine report." Commas are used for parenthetical phrases inserted into a sentence—for example, "The full impact of unemployment, on the other hand, remains unknown.'' This punctuation mark is also used for short interjections or for directly naming a person—for example, ''Ah, Sarah, how well you look today.'' A comma is used to emphasize a particular phrase or to avoid ambiguity—for example, ''To Harry, Leo was someone special, really special.'' Just as a period indicates a full stop, a comma suggests a slight pause in the reading. In scriptwriting, use a comma when it helps group words and phrases together to produce a more effective and understandable presentation. This guideline does not coincide with the conventional punctuation rules for the use of commas.

Dash

This punctuation mark (--) suggests a more exaggerated response than other related punctuation marks. For example, if you write

```
The unemployed factory worker returned home --
to an unknown future.
```

the dash would indicate that a fairly long pause was needed at that point in the sentence. The use of a comma instead of a dash would shorten the length of the pause. Although this is a fine point of punctuation, carefully consider each punctuation mark, since it guides the interpretation of the words in each sentence.

The dash is also used to indicate a break in a sentence or portion of dialogue. For example, if you write

```
PAT: Now is the time to --
CHRIS: Shop at Petersen's.
```

the dash notes that one character interrupts the other to complete the sentence or thought.

The dash is often used after a series of words or phrases to bridge into a summary statement. For example,

```
Balance, strength, and determination -- all are
needed for athletic success.
```

Most typewriters and many computer keyboards do not have dashes, so, to simulate a dash, type a space, two hyphens, and another space (--).

Ellipsis

Some writers use the dash and ellipsis interchangeably; however, each should suggest a subtle difference in interpretation.

An ellipsis (. . .) can be used to add an extra thought or to clarify an idea—for example,

```
He went back home...to start a new life.
```

An ellipsis could also be used to intensify a dramatic effect by indicating a brief pause or hesitation in delivery—for example,

```
He stepped into the car, touched the starter,
and...a blinding flash!
```

Although the only grammatical function of an ellipsis is to indicate that words or phrases have been omitted from a direct quotation, you can use this same punctuation mark to clarify and intensify scripts and to provide a new shade of meaning. (For scriptwriting purposes, the ellipsis generally has its "dots" set tight, not spaced out as in a more general type of writing.) Although officially the ellipsis has only three "dots," the longer you make the ellipsis—for example, ...—the longer the pause.

Hyphen

As mentioned previously, use the hyphen to connect closely related letters, numerals, or words ("A-F-of-L," "125-thousand," "president-elect"). Hyphens may be used as unspoken substitutes for the words "(up) to and including" or simply "to" ("The years 1970-78 were crucial to the company's development" and "The New York-Chicago train was delayed"). It is best to provide the *exact* word you want to be said rather than use a hyphen as a word substitute.

Emphasis

There are two ways to indicate that a key word or short phrase is to be stressed in a sentence—underlining or writing the word(s) in FULL CAPS. Indicating those words or phrases to be stressed in your scripts will ensure a more precise interpretation of your work. Notice the difference in emphasis and meaning between these two sentences, each with a different word stressed:

```
Now is the time to act.
Now is the time to act.
```

Apostrophe

Use an apostrophe (') to indicate possession—for example, "Frank's car" or "Neil Diamond's songs"; to form contractions to enhance the conversational style used in scripts—for example, "couldn't," "that's"; and to form plurals of letters, numbers, and words—for example, "He has trouble with his r's, 8's and the's."

Colon

Use a colon (:) to separate the name of a character or a music and sound effects notation from the words or description to follow—for example,

```
MARY: Now is the time to buy that new car
      you've always wanted.
MUSIC: (UP FOR 2 SECONDS AND THEN UNDER)
MARY: Yes, they're selling them as fast as
      they come in....
```

Although a dash would also work, a colon could be used to set up an explanatory word or phrase ("She had only one thought: to survive"), to introduce a series of words ("Major interest groups were represented: students, teachers, administrators, and parents"), and to prepare the audience for a direct quotation ("On the president's economic plan, the senator's remark was this: it's the best it can be").

Parentheses

Use parentheses [( )] to suggest the style of delivery, as well as to note any necessary technical instructions.

```
MAN #1: (PLEADING) I KNOW it's my turn to drive
        today.
MAN #2: (MOVING AWAY) Fine. Have it YOUR way.
```

Other Punctuation Marks

Several other punctuation marks are available but are not commonly used in scripts prepared for the electronic media: brackets ([ ]), quotation marks (" "), and the semicolon (;). Both grammatical requirements and performer needs can be accomplished with the punctuation marks already described.

Correct punctuation adds clarity to your writing. Since your written words are meant to be read aloud, the proper and effective use of these notations provide yet another means of indicating variations in meaning, emphasis, tone, pauses, and interpretation.

Editing Marks

Standard editing marks should be used only in emergency situations. They should be used sparingly and only as time constraints and common sense dictate. When these marks are used, they should be used boldly, but neatly, so that they are clearly understood. They should never deter the performer or on-air talent from making interpretation marks on the script or from reading the script smoothly and accurately. Even if proper editing marks are used, if there are too many of them, the script will not be acceptable. In most cases, it is best to retype the entire page and avoid using any script editing marks. The use of computers to edit or change scripts is described later in this chapter.

Most of the more complicated copyreading symbols used in the print media should never be used for scripts written for the electronic media. Following are the basic editing marks to use if necessary:

a. To separate words run together, use a single slanted line, or virgule:

```
The decade was of great/concern to the
American people.
```

b. To close up space between letters in the *same* word, use curved lines *both* above *and* below the gap:

```
The de‿cade was of great concern to the
American people.
```

c. To delete an entire word or a phrase that is not needed, black out the unwanted material *completely* and bridge the gap with a *single* line above the connecting words in the sentence:

```
The decade was of great ⌢most‿ concern to the
American people.
```

d. To insert a word or phrase, print it boldly or type it clearly above the line and funnel it into the proper place in the sentence:

> The decade was ~~of~~ *great* concern to the American people.

e. To correct a misspelled word, black it out *completely* and then print boldly or type clearly the correct version of the *entire word* above the line and funnel the correction into the proper place in the sentence:

> The decade was of great ~~conncorn~~ *concern* to the American people.

f. To close up space when a word, a phrase, or an entire sentence is deleted, use a curved line to connect the two parts of the finished sentence:

> The decade was of great ~~significance to politicians and of course of~~ concern to the American people.

g. To insert a missing punctuation mark, simply provide the missing notation neatly but conspicuously at the proper place in the script:

> The decade was of great concern to the American people.

h. To insert script material at the beginning of a paragraph, use an extended indentation mark:

> The decade was of great concern to the American people.

Timing

The precise timing of complete programs, program segments, and announcements is essential. Unfortunately, highly dramatic and effective scripts have had to be trimmed because the writer used poor judgment when estimating the amount of time needed to present the script. Full-length programs end approximately two to three minutes before the scheduled start of the next program. This allows time to insert announcements as well as network and station identifications.

Several variables prevent precise word and time equivalencies: the script format used—for instance, a one-page semi-script could provide the same amount of program time as several pages of a full-script for the same program; the number and duration of elements other than spoken words, such as music bridges, sound effects inserts, and bits of dramatic "business" by performers; and the inconsistent delivery style and speed of the reader or performer.

With the basic tools of a studio clock to time an entire program and a stop watch to time particular segments and entire announcements, you can design scripts for longer programs using the front timing approach or the back timing approach. When using *front timing,* time each segment of the presentation as it is to be broadcast, starting from 0 seconds to the end. When using *back timing,* the last two to four minutes of the program are timed. Back timing allows the director and talent to pace the show to the end by timing the material needed to complete the crucial last segment of the program. When this point is reached during a live broadcast, the pretimed final segment is begun, allowing the show to leave the air on time.

The best way to approximate the running time of each page of a script is to have the reader or performer who will deliver it read the script aloud and walk through the actions required. After some experience writing material for the same acting and production situations, you can better judge how much playing time each page of a script will occupy. It is helpful to have the reader or performer actually vocalize or read the words out loud several times to fine-tune the timing of the script.

Scripting Formats

Several basic formats, or layout forms, can be used to write script material. Later chapters will illustrate the application of these basic formats in specific kinds of writing situations.

Although the information presented here reflects acceptable industry standards, each scripting format and approach can be modified to meet the specific requirements of each writing project. Find out the standard scripting format needed in each situation and incorporate the format modifications preferred by your employer or writing supervisor.

Proposals

Before writing a script, it is often necessary to provide a proposal for the development of the project. Sometimes this document is called a premise or a concept. Whatever the label attached to this preliminary scripting document, the same kind of information is supplied for review, authorization, and funding by the appropriate officer or executive of the funding organization or company.

A proposal is a written plan for how the script and eventual production will proceed. This document provides information on the working title of the project, its basic premise or objective, the target audience, the project's length, its production cost, the approximate timetable or production schedule, and specific attractive features of the project.

Proposals for regular program series generally are six to ten pages long. The first page indicates the series title, program length, name and address of the series creator, and the writer's agent if there is one. The second page is a brief description of the series and what makes it unique and saleable. The third page is a more detailed description of the series—the situations, locales, and settings. The fourth and subsequent pages are concise, one-paragraph descriptions of principal characters. The last few pages are one-page story summaries or premise statements for three or four episodes in the prospective series.

Most proposals are presented orally in a ''pitch'' rather than in written form. A written proposal either is never done or is prepared as a matter of contract after initial approval has been received for the project. See chapter 13 for a description of the verbal presentation techniques used by writers, especially dramatic scriptwriters, to pitch story ideas. Proposals for special scripting projects, such as made-for-TV movies, miniseries, and anthologies, are in the form of a treatment, step outline, or sequence outline.

Essentially a treatment is a short story or narrative, written in the present tense, that describes the progressive development of a program or story idea from the beginning to the last segment. Writers of dramatic scripts use the term *story outline* to indicate the kind of treatment generally approved before a full-script is written.

Treatments

A treatment is *not* a finished script, only a preliminary indication of how the finished script will be written. A treatment can be sometimes as few as four, but often as many as forty, pages. A lengthy final script requires a lengthy treatment. After the treatment has been accepted, you can begin to prepare the appropriate type of script for the production.

It is best to prepare a treatment when the various developmental stages of a scripting project must be reviewed and approved by several individuals and groups—for instance, when developing documentaries and investigative reports, animation projects, or dramatic scripts. See figure 3.1 on page 65. It is easier to make adjustments at the treatment stage than after a full-script has been written. Also, generating a treatment makes you critically examine the progression of key segments or portions of a presentation before writing the full-script. A carefully prepared treatment makes the scriptwriting task even more creatively fulfilling.

The treatment should indicate a tentative point of view, which you and the production staff will explore and adjust later. Additionally it should describe the style, mood, emphasis, structure, and shape of the presentation—whether dialogue, commentary, narration, or music will be used or whether the presentation style will be factual, dramatized, stylized, serious, or light. The treatment should also indicate the approximate length of the final presentation, the organizational approach, and the content or "action" in each major sequence. The organizational schemes suggested should be based on the nature and purpose of the project. The possibilities are limited only by your imagination and ingenuity.

In the treatment, focus on the action and mood of the presentation. Do not detail other production elements that are not essential to explain the forward movement and progression of the script.

Depending on the type of program to be written, the treatment could supply essential information about program objectives, the main and supporting characters, the locations, the themes, and the action anticipated. Some treatments include information about the crucial camera shots, graphics, short pieces of narration, or dialogue to be used. Some treatments also include a tentative development budget, production timetable, and description of how the finished program could be used beyond the initial broadcast.

In all cases, the treatment should provide a vivid picture, through words, of the essential elements of the production-to-be. The treatment needs to be a positive, accurate, and abbreviated statement about your "vision" of the production.

In writing the treatment, many writers place information on index cards or slips of paper and then adjust the contents and shuffle the order to devise the most effective program structure. The process used to write the treatment is left to the discretion of the writer, who should devise a planning system that works best for the kind of writing project underway.

Some of the many ways to structure or present the treatment document are the following: a simulated magazine or newspaper article, an outline of the program segments with only brief phrases to indicate the continuity and flow of ideas, a condensed script in which the opening and closing segments are fully scripted and the rest of the presentation is only outlined, and a complete storyboard of major sequences. You could use a combination of approaches. The treatment structure must present your ideas in a style that enables others to understand and experience the content, characters, situations, and settings as the audience will.

Once the treatment has been written, it is reviewed and modified, either by written or oral exchanges between the writer and employer, until the project is approved and funded or abandoned. Once the treatment document has been accepted, you can then elaborate on the treatment to begin to prepare the appropriate type of script for the program or presentation.

Some projects require an intermediate planning document to bridge from the treatment to the full-script. A *sequence, or step, outline* provides a detailed sequential description of the content of a presentation. For each sequence or scene, the writer describes exactly what will be seen and heard and, if necessary, how a transition will be made to the next sequence. A step outline should indicate clearly how the content in each sequence will be structured and presented visually and aurally, how one sequence will lead logically and naturally to the next sequence, and how each sequence will integrate smoothly into the overall development and presentation of the content. Sequence, or step, outlines are useful for complicated productions and elaborate dramas.

Developing a treatment or step outline requires hard work, thought, imagination, ingenuity, and creative energy. In the process of evolving new ideas and revising, testing, discarding, and restructuring them, you will experience a creative "high" that is difficult to top as the pieces of the scripting puzzle begin to lock into place.

Show Formats

The show format script provides only a skeletal outline of a program. There are two types of show formats.

The *rundown, or fact sheet,* indicates only the order and length of each program segment. See figure 3.2 on page 66.

TIME CUT TO:

INT. JOHN EDMUNDS' OFFICE - DAY

It is the following day. Madeline, briefcase in hand,
is accompanied by Brian as they enter the reception are of
John Edmunds' office. She walks over and knocks on Edmunds'
door. No answer. She calls out to her broker. Again,
nothing. She then reaches for the door knob and pushes it
open. She freezes, then gasps.

Brain rushes over and peers inside the office. There,
lying motionless on the ground is the dead body of John
Edmunds. A large gaping hole, covered with blood can be
seen on his back. Madeline and Brian exchange looks of
panic. A beat. Then the SOUND OF A POLICE SIREN can be
heard emanating from the street. Madeline runs over and
looks out the window. A police car has just driven up to
the front of the building.

"We've got to get out of here," Madeline says with
urgency.

"We haven't done anything," Brian remarks.

"We're standing over the dead body of a man who does
illegal trading. And I've got seventy-five grand in my
briefcase. Do you want to explain this to the police?"

Enough said. Madeline and Brian make a beeline out of
the office. Madeline motions that they take the stairs.

INT. OFFICE BUILDING - STAIRWELL - DAY

We TRACK with both Madeline and Brian as they dash down
a flight of stairs. As they pass a small trash dumpster,
Madeline stops and hides the briefcase deep into the refuse.
She remarks to Brian that they can return for the money
later that night.

EXT. OFFICE BUILDING - DAY

Madeline and Brian emerge from the building.

"I'll call you later," she tells him as they begin to
walk their separate ways.

Figure 3.1
Portion of the
treatment/story outline
for a "Matlock"
episode entitled "The
Con Man." See figure
3.7 for the correspond-
ing script pages from
the final draft of this
same teleplay.
*Courtesy of Gerald
Sanoff, Dean Hargrove
Productions, and
Universal Studios.*

Figure 3.2
Rundown sheet show
format for the
regularly scheduled
children's program
series, "The Bozo
Show," seen on cable
systems nationwide.
*Courtesy of Allen Hall,
WGN Television,
Chicago.*

```
                              THE  BOZO  SHOW
                           PROGRAM  RUNDOWN      TAPE#  816111
          WALT  DISNEY  WORLD  SHOW #1           BACK UP: M2

     SHOW #  01-111  PRODUCTION DATE  01/21/91  AIR DATE:  02/18/91

     SEG#   CONTENT                       EST LENGTH         ACTUAL

     1.     BILLBOARD: BOZO, COOKY, ANDY, AUDIENCE
            BOZO BIT:  SOUVENIRS FOR A SUCKER
            ISO OUT                          5:00             6:16
                                            (5:00)

     2.     ISO IN
            DISNEY ACT: CHINESE MAGICIAN     7:00
            BOZO BIT: THE HONEY BEE          5:00
            ISO OUT                         11:00             7:24
                                           (16:00)

     3.     ISO IN
            GRAND PRIZE GAME
            BOZO BIT: PRIME TIME CAFE
            ISO OUT                          8:00             9:33
                                           (24:00)

     4.     ISO IN
            FAMILIES                         4:30
            BOZO BIT: STAR FOR TODAY         6:00
            ISO OUT                         13:30             7:22
                                           (37:30)

     5.     ISO IN
            BOZO BIT: BUYER BEWARE           3:00
            DISNEY ACT:  HOLLYWOOD HIT MEN   3:00
            BOZO BIT:  FIREWORKS
            ISO OUT                          6:00            11:47
                                           (43:30)

     6.     ISO IN
            BOZO BIT: STAR STRUCK
            ISO OUT                          3:00             2:58
                                           (46:30)

     7.     ISO IN
            GRAND MARCH                      1:20             1:44
                                           (47:50)

                                       TOTAL:               47:04
```

The *routine sheet* incorporates rundown sheet information but also supplies additional program content and some of the exact wording to be used in a few segments of the program—for instance, the opening and closing, transitions between program segments, and cue-aways to commercials. See figure 3.3.

The show format is a "bare bones" script form. It is written to be used for most regularly scheduled programs—for example, newscasts and sportscasts, interview and talk programs, and some magazine program series. Since these types of programs are produced regularly and the nature and length of the segments remain fairly constant, a more detailed script form is not necessary.

```
:59:10   INTO HEADLINES
GOOD MORNING/AFTERNOON/EVENING!   IT'S _____ DEGREES UNDER _____ SKIES AT
(time) IN THE MORNING/AFTERNOON/EVENING ON (day), THE (date) OF (month).   I'M
_____.   Here are the TOP stories from W-T-O-P NEWSRADIO 15....

((headlines: 5 news + business +  sports + weather))


:59:50   LEGAL ID INTO CBS
WTOP WASHINGTON COVERS THE TOP STORIES FROM AROUND THE NATION AND THE WORLD
WITH CBS.  WTOP NEWSTIME _____.


:05:00   OUT OF CBS
WTOP NEWSTIME _____, IT'S _____ DEGREES UNDER _____ SKIES.   GOOD
MORNING/AFTERNOON/EVENING.

HERE'S THE WTOP 3-DAY WEATHER FORECAST...


:13:00   WEATHER MENTION INTO SECTION 2
WTOP NEWSTIME _____.   _____ SKIES, IT'S (temp) GOING UP/DOWN TO A HIGH
OF/LOW OF (high/low).


:20:10   INTO HEADLINES
GOOD MORNING/AFTERNOON/EVENING!   IT'S _____ DEGREES UNDER _____ SKIES AT
(time :20) IN THE MORNING/AFTERNOON/EVENING ON THIS (day), THE (date) OF
(month).   I'M _____.   Here are the TOP stories from W-T-O-P NEWSRADIO
15....

((headlines: 5 news + business +  sports -WTOP SPORTS AT :46- + weather))
```

Figure 3.3
Computer-generated routine sheet show format for regularly scheduled radio newscasts.
Courtesy of WTOP NEWSRADIO 15.

Semi-Scripts

The semi-script is a more complete scripting format than the show format. In a semi-script, opening and closing segments, transitions between program segments, and commercial cue-aways are fully scripted, but the rest of the program is indicated only in outline form—for example, interview questions or topics or a demonstration segment breakdown. See figure 3.4.

Full-Scripts

The full-script is the most complete and exacting scripting format. It contains every word to be spoken, together with specific audio and/or video instructions. A full-script ensures precise pacing, sequencing, and development from both a writing and a production standpoint.

This scripting format is used often. For example, a full-script is used to produce spot announcements, news and sports stories, editorials and commentaries, dramas, and comedies. News and sports full-scripts are examined in detail in chapter 5.

Figure 3.4

Portion of the semi-script for a program segment of "Home."

Courtesy of Woody Fraser, Cece Caldwell, Marty Tenney, Richard Camp, and James E. Witte.

```
SHOW #953                                        SEG. TIME:
AIRS: JUNE 20, 1991                                  (7:30)
ACT #5
"FILL IN WITH WIL"

TALENT:                                         SEG. PROD:
GARY, DANA, WIL                           (BERNARD GRINBERG)

HOMEBASE                            GARY

                         Joining us now is Wil Shriner...

*APPLAUSE*                (AD LIB GREETINGS)

                         Wil, the requests just keep pouring in.
                         How did you choose today's lucky winner...
                         and I use the term "winner" loosely?

CHYRON:                  (WIL:
WIL SHRINER              *THE FILL-IN OFFICE IS ALWAYS ON
                         THE LOOK-OUT FOR CHALLENGING, IMPORTANT
                         JOBS, AND OUR "RELATIVES" BRANCH GOT 2
                         VERY INTERESTING LETTERS FROM VERONICA
                         DOUGLASS OF VIA WENDOVER, UTAH...

PROPS:                   WIL READS PORTION OF BOTH LETTERS:
2 LETTERS                "DEAR WIL, I'D LIKE YOU TO FILL IN FOR MY
                         DAUGHTER SUSIE'S JOB. SHE LIVES ON A SMALL
VTPB/MOS: "A"            FARM IN A REMOTE PART OF WESTERN UTAH"...
PAN LETTER #1            AND...
RT:_____

                         "DEAR WIL, I'D LIKE YOU TO FILL IN FOR MY
VTPB/MOS: "B"            DAUGHTER SUSIE'S JOB. SHE IS A SHORT ORDER
PAN LETTER #2            COOK AT AN ISOLATED CAFE ON THE LONELIEST
RT:_____                 HIGHWAY IN AMERICA")

                                 DANA

                         It sounds like daughter Susie's a pretty busy
                         woman. Wil, you spent the other day trying
                         to keep up with her. How did it go?

                         (WIL: AD LIB REPONSE. I HEADED OUT FOR BAKER,
                         NEVADA, TO SEE IF I COULD FILL IN FOR NOT
                         ONE, BUT 2, COUNT EM 2 JOBS IN ONE DAY.)
------------------------------------------------------------------
VTPB/SOT:"A" FILL IN-FARM/SHORT ORDER COOK          RT:_____

IN CUE:_____

OUT CUE:_____
------------------------------------------------------------------
                         (AD LIB REACT TO TAPE)
```

AIRS: JUNE 20, 1991
ACT #5
"FILL IN WITH WIL"

Figure 3.4 (*continued*)

<u>GARY</u>

Wil, did you actually learn anything?

(WIL:
*AD LIB REPONSE. MAINLY, HE LEARNED HOW HARD
IT IS TO WORK 2 JOBS)

<u>DANA</u>

What can we look forward to for future
fill-ins?

(WIL:
*THE FILL-IN PRODUCTION CREW IS HEADED
TO THE GREAT SOUTHWEST, WHERE WIL WIL FILL IN
AS A LITTLE LEAGUE COACH, AND AS A FLIGHT
ATTENDANT.)

<u>GARY/DANA</u>

(AD LIB THANKS)

(INTO: BUMPER #5/CMX #4)

Figure 3.4 (*continued*)   MUSIC PLAYOFF
                                 CART:__41 (:11)
                                 B/U = 12

<u>GARY</u>

NEXT, LEARN HOW BLOOD DEVELOPED FROM PIGS CAN
SAVE MILLIONS OF HUMAN LIVES...

* *

BUMPER #5: LIFE BLOOD

(VTR: "A" - BLOODY PIG)

ADO #2

(VTR: "B" - NEXT NO SHUTTERS BG)

IRIS #A60 -- NEXT BG

COMMERCIAL BREAK #4   (2:01)

(INTO ACT #6: "PIG BLOOD")

A full-script is an exact blueprint, the ultimate guideline or framework for a program or presentation.[1] Each element in a full-script should be clearly identified, properly positioned, and carefully punctuated to permit skilled professionals to interpret and to act on the information provided.

The scripting style for both audio and video full-scripts will be described and then illustrated. Efforts have been made to provide a *complete* discussion of each scripting format without unnecessary repetition between format descriptions. You should read carefully the detailed description of each scripting format, with pencil, paper, ruler, and keyboard nearby. Construct your own personal reference guide for each format. Then, examine the script example provided for each format to recheck your notes.

The references that will be given for tab settings on standard typewriters can be easily converted for use on word processing systems. The keyboards for these units generally have a control key, which, when pressed in tandem with standard alphabetical keys that have been designated for special margin settings, allows you to move script information to the proper place on the page. Although it will require careful study of your word processor manual and a little time to set these standard margins, once this task has been accomplished you can focus on writing and not margin settings when it is time to create a script. Each word processing program has its own system for customizing or configuring the keyboard for margin settings, as well as other writing and script filing functions. If your word processor does not have this kind of feature, there are several utility programs available that will allow you to perform this customization. The use of computer software programs in scriptwriting is discussed later in this chapter.

These basic guidelines for full-scripts are presented with the understanding that adjustments will be made to match more closely specified writing and production situations, as well as the preferences and practices of employers. Not every guideline is meant to be used in every scriptwriting situation. The better you understand and remember these basic instructions and the more experience you acquire using them on a regular basis, the more secure and flexible you will be when scripting format adjustments are required.

Also, the examples shown do not always coincide with the *typewritten* margins and spacings of the original script material. Although the original typeface and type styles for *all* scripts used in this book have been retained, book design considerations have caused the size of several scripts to be changed from the original material. Use the resultant space around such scripts to make notes about scripting formats and techniques.

The following are the principal radio script elements with specifications for margin settings, content, capitalization, punctuation, and spacing.

Basic Full-Script Formats

Radio

Scene/Production Descriptions	Beginning at tab setting 20 and ending at tab setting 70, provide general guidelines and information about the mood, tone, pace, and overall interpretation of the script. The notation "SCENE (or PRODUCTION) NOTE:" should be in FULL CAPS followed by a colon. After two spaces, write the description, using regular upper- and lowercase letters, with double-spacing between lines. This kind of scripting notation is used primarily for commercials and announcements and only occasionally for other types of programs.
Talent Designations	Talent or character identifications begin at tab setting 13 and end at tab setting 19. Either generic or specific designations can be used. For example, TALENT #1, TALENT #2 or VOICE #1, VOICE #2 would be acceptable generic designations. The purpose of this script notation is to identify who is speaking. Each talent designation is written in FULL CAPS, underlined and followed by a colon.
Talent Interpretation Instructions	Between tab settings 25 and 70, you can include a brief suggestion about how the talent should interpret certain words, phrases, or sentences in the script. This information is to be included within parentheses after the talent designation, using FULL CAPS. Such notations as (FURIOUS), (CALMLY), (SAD), and the like, placed just ahead of the words to be read by the talent, express the writer's perspective about the interpretation of key phrases and ideas. This type of notation may be helpful for commercials, announcements, and most dramatic and comedic radio productions.
Talent Directions	The same guidelines used for talent interpretation instructions are used to note physical movements by the talent or other, talent-related production information. Such notations as (FADING OFF), (FADING ON), or (AS THOUGH HEARD ON A TELEPHONE) provide additional insight from the writer for production and talent personnel.
Words	Words to be spoken are written across a forty-five-space typewritten line, using pica type, beginning at tab setting 25 and ending at tab setting 70. Regular upper- and lowercase letters are used, with double-spacing between each line of the script.
Music	Music notations are written in FULL CAPS and are underlined to distinguish music from sound effects notations. Music information begins at tab setting 20 and extends to tab setting 70. If music is to be inserted between the words spoken by the talent, the same scripting format guidelines would be followed, except that the entire music notation would be enclosed within parentheses.

The same scripting format guidelines provided for music are used for sound effects notations in radio. The obvious change would be the use of the terms SOUND EFFECT, SOUND, or SFX to alert those involved that a sound effect is to be heard at a particular point in the script. Also, sound effects notations are not underlined.

Sound Effects

Depending on the circumstances and scripting requirements, for longer radio scripts, the rewritten script could include consecutive numbers along the left margin to identify each audio element more clearly. This scripting notation is sometimes used for dramas and documentaries.

Other Radio Script Elements

In addition, a notion about the length or timing of each script segment or page can be included. If this kind of information is required, a consistent, standardized notation system should be used.

To better illustrate the standard style and format used for radio full-scripts, a sample commercial has been prepared in figure 3.5. A radio commercial is used here as an example, since this type of writing often makes use of many of the style and format guidelines just described. Although the script in figure 3.5 may not display all the characteristics of an award-winning radio commercial, it does illustrate standard style for radio full-scripts.

As in radio, the full-script for television and motion picture productions must display standardization in the use of, placement of, and format for essential video and audio elements. The script forms must identify and clearly differentiate between video and audio elements and between talent and production assignments.

Television and Motion Pictures

Full-scripts for video productions are written in either two-column or one-column formats. The two-column format is used for most principal types of video productions and announcements; however, the one-column format is used for feature-length television and motion picture dramas and comedies, action/adventure television programs, most regularly scheduled network television primetime program series, variety and game show series, and other types of television programming requiring large budgets, expansive facilities, and specialized production and talent personnel. The one-column scripting format works well for both live multicamera or taped single-camera production situations, either in the studio or in the field.

In this format, all video information is written in the left column between tab settings 13 and 27, and all audio information is written in the right column between tab settings 30 and 70. When deciding in which column to place script information, simply determine whether the information relates to what is seen or to what is heard and place that information in the appropriate column.

Two-Column Format

All *video information* is written in FULL CAPS with single-spacing between lines. The precision and completeness of the video information or directions depend on the nature of the program script, the production circumstances, and the requirements of your employer.

Figure 3.5
Sample full-script for
a radio commercial.

FIRST NATIONAL BANK
P-T-B System
FNB H-184-A
30 seconds
Jones   10/8

MUSIC: <u>FIRST NATIONAL BANK JINGLE (INSTRUMENTAL-
         CONTEMPORARY BEAT) UP FOR TWO SECONDS AND
         THEN UNDER</u>

<u>ANNCR:</u>   (ENTHUSIASTIC) At the First National
              Bank, we've got a <u>new</u> sound for you!

       (SFX: COMPUTER-TYPE SOUNDS - FEATURE BRIEFLY
              AND THEN OUT)

<u>ANNCR:</u>   It's our new P-T-B System. Anytime, day
              or night, you can call the P-T-B number
              and have your bills paid from your First
              National Bank account...quickly, easily,
              conveniently -- and <u>on time</u>! No more
              hassles with checks, envelopes, stamps,
              and record keeping. It's all done for you
              -- automatically...whenever <u>you</u> want to
              pay your bills, with P-T-B...

       (SFX: TELEPHONE RECEIVER PICKED UP)

<u>ANNCR:</u>   So, call now...5-5-5-21-21...

       (SFX: SEVEN-DIGIT TELEPHONE NUMBER BEING DIALED
              ON PUSH-BUTTON TELEPHONE)

<u>ANNCR:</u>   That's 5-5-5-21-21...Enjoy the savings
              and convenience of First National's P-T-B
              System of bill paying.

       (SFX: ONE TELEPHONE RING)

<u>VOICE:</u>   (AS THOUGH ON A TELEPHONE) P-T-B. May I
              help you?

MUSIC: <u>FIRST NATIONAL BANK JINGLE (VOCAL-
         CONTEMPORARY BEAT) UP FULL TO THE END.</u>

Place all the information for each video entry in the following order: the transition to the camera shot and then the camera shot (i.e., what is to be seen). For example, you could write:

```
FADE TO LS OF OPEN FIELD
```

or

```
DISSOVLE TO WS OF HARRY
```

If the script is for an in-studio production, the information for each video entry would be placed in the following order: the transition to the camera shot, the specific studio camera to be used, and then the camera shot (i.e., what is to be seen). For example, you could write

```
FADE TO C-2 LS OF SET
```

or

```
DISSOLVE TO C-1 WS OF PAUL AND TOM.
```

Each video entry or change in the script must be placed adjacent to the corresponding audio entry. Do not cram all the video information into one long column and then spread the audio column information down the page, using double-spacing. To ensure that video changes are made as scripted, some writers use various markings in the audio column to indicate when the video is to change. Such markings as ⎍, ⎍, and ⊗ at the exact point in the audio where the picture is to be changed can be used by the writer, although most often by the director, to avoid confusion and to ensure appropriate interpretation of the script.

All *audio information* is written with double-spacing between lines, following the same guidelines for capitalization, content, and use of punctuation suggested for radio full-scripts. Because all audio notations must be squeezed into a forty-space line (using pica type), all audio entries for the two-column television full-script format begin at tab setting 30 and end at tab setting 70. The audio information for this scripting form must be just as complete as for radio. Remember that *anything* relating to what is heard in the television announcement or program must be placed in the audio column of the script and not mixed in with video directions described in the left column.

To illustrate the key style and format characteristics of the two-column full-script form, a television commercial has been devised in figure 3.6. The same rationale has been used for the preparation of this script as was used for the radio commercial in figure 3.5.

One-Column Format

This script form is often called the "Hollywood format" because it is the most common script design used in major West Coast production centers and because it evolved out of the silent period of filmmaking, when separate writers wrote the story line while others concentrated on the title cards containing the dialogue. In contrast to a theatrical play, a motion picture tends

```
Beltway Furniture
Clear the Store Sale
BF f-111-B
:30      Jones      10/10
```

VIDEO	AUDIO
QUICK FADE TO	MUSIC: BRIGHT & CONTEMPORARY INSTRUMENTAL-
C-2 (WS OF	UP FOR TWO SECONDS AND THEN UNDER
ANNCR)	ANNCR: (ENTHUSIASTIC)
	They're in a selling mood at Beltway
	Furniture! So they've slashed their prices
FOLLOW ANNCR	to clear the store! (ANNCR WALKS THROUGH
	STORE) You'll find great bargains on every item in
	stock --
SL #1 (SOFAS)	Luxurious occasional chairs and sofas...
SL #2 (LAMPS)	Beautiful lamps and paintings to add
SL #3 (TVs)	sparkle to any room... plus quality R-C-A
	appliances and T-V sets.
C-1 (H&S OF	It's all waiting for you during the
ANNCR)	special "clear-the-store-sale" at --
SL #4	Beltway...River City's finest furniture
	store.
	MUSIC: UP FULL FOR A FEW SECONDS AND THEN
	OUT

Figure 3.6
Sample two-column full-script for a television commercial.

to stress the *actions* of major characters and not necessarily the words they say, to move the plot or story line along. In this case, form follows content. The one-column script format provides more space and attention to such visual elements as scene headings and stage directions and less to dialogue and interpretation of dialogue. Although the emphasis on these visual and auditory elements might shift in some situations, the basic one-column format will continue to emphasize visual over aural script information.

One page of a script written in the one-column format provides a little less than one minute of screen time. The action may be extended or compressed to encompass more than one minute of real time, but actual viewing time is still one minute. Remember this concept when using this format to prepare script material. The script reader anticipates pacing, timing, and length of screen time based on what is written on one page.

Two types of one-column script formats are used for television and motion picture production. The *one-column one-camera format* is used for some television comedy series and for practically all television and motion picture feature-length productions, such as teleplays and screenplays. The *one-column three-camera format* is used for most television situation comedy series and for practically all other television programs produced "live on tape" before a studio audience. There are noticeable differences between the two types of formats. Although both contain the essential script elements necessary to produce a particular program, the placement of, use of, and emphasis given to each element varies to better match the type of program produced. Subsequent rewrites of an original three-camera script are written in a "scene-by-scene" format, whereas a one-camera script is usually rewritten in a "shot-by-shot" format. Consecutive numbers are placed in the left or right margins, or both, of each revised script page by the producer or director when the production or shooting script is prepared. It is best not to use this consecutive numbering system when submitting first-draft script material. It tends to distract the person reading the script for the first time.

There are two additional cautions about writing both types of one-column format scripts. Be sure to insert a new scene heading or description *each* time a new camera set-up is needed or whenever the location of the action changes. Also, provide *minimal* technical directions, even in your full-script. *Briefly* note production considerations, such as sounds and camera angles, that are vital to explain character development and the progression of action. Do not "direct" the production from your script. Allow production personnel an opportunity to enhance the essential production considerations you have noted.

Following are the *specifications for the one-column one-camera script format*.[2]

    a. *Scene headings (descriptions)*. This script information indicates what the audience should see and how they should see it. Scene headings are written in FULL CAPS between margin settings 14 and 73 using pica type and placed in the following order with a hyphen separating each element: INT. or EXT. location - time of day or night - camera angle - what is to be seen. The scene description information is more extensive than in the one-column three-camera format. Also, not every one of these elements is used in each scene heading. Be sure to single-space between lines of the same scene heading, but triple-space between separate scene headings. If a scene continues to the next page, double-space down and write ''(CONTINUED)'' at the bottom of the page at tab setting 61. Then, at the beginning of the next page, write ''CONTINUED:'' at tab setting 14.

b. *Stage directions.* Provide only the information necessary to describe characters, scenes, camera shots, sound cues, and other elements needed to facilitate production of the script. Use regular upper- and lowercase letters to provide these directions between margin settings 14 and 73 using pica type. Single-space between lines of the same stage directions entry, but double-space between the scene heading entry and the start of the stage directions entry. Also double-space between the end of a character's lines and the start of a new stage directions entry.

c. *Camera and sound directions.* Only brief camera and sound cues should be included within stage directions entries placed between margin settings 14 and 73 using pica type. Highlight camera and sound cues by typing the words relating to such directions in FULL CAPS. Use single-spacing, just as for stage directions information. Double-space when separating one camera shot from the next camera shot and when separating the end of a character's lines from the start of a new camera direction notation.

d. *Character designations.* It is important to name each character in the script to whom you have assigned dialogue. This designation may be in the form of a first and/or last name, or it may simply be a role description—for example, police officer, fire fighter, receptionist, clerk. Such designations are typed in FULL CAPS when a particular character is first mentioned in a scene heading or stage directions entry. Character designations are typed in FULL CAPS between margin settings 41 and 54 to indicate the dialogue or lines assigned to that character.

e. *Character interpretation notes.* Suggestions for a particular talent—for instance, stands up, laughs, turns toward door, and depressed—which would enhance the interpretation of specific lines of dialogue, can be written between margin settings 35 and 51 using pica type. Write all words for these personal directions in lowercase letters, enclosed within parentheses, and single-spaced between the character designation and the first line of dialogue.

f. *Dialogue.* The words spoken by each character or talent are displayed exactly in the center of the script page between margin settings 28 and 56 using pica type. Use regular upper- and lowercase letters to write dialogue, with occasional FULL CAPS to indicate stress for specific key words. Use single-spacing between lines of dialogue assigned to one character or talent. Double-space between the end of lines assigned to one character and the next character designation or a camera or stage direction. If one character's lines are interrupted by a stage direction, use "(continuing)," single-spaced down at tab setting 35 just under a repetition of the character's name, to indicate that this particular character continues to deliver lines. If a character's lines continue on the next page, write "(MORE)" at tab setting 41 single-spaced down from the last sentence of dialogue on that page. Then at the beginning of the next page, write "(cont'd)" beside a repeat of the character designation on the same line.

g. *Scene transition notes.* You can choose from many visual transition possibilities to bridge the end of one scene and the beginning of the next. If you wish to indicate a specific technical direction to make such transitions—for example, "CUT TO:" or "DISSOLVE TO:"—write such directions in FULL CAPS followed by a colon placed between margin settings 61 and 76, and double-spaced down from the preceding lines of dialogue. Before starting the next scene heading or description, triple-space down from the scene ending or transition notation.

h. *Beginnings and endings.* To begin the script or a major division of a program, write "FADE IN:" at margin setting 14. After triple-spacing down, write the first scene heading as described earlier. In a teleplay divided into several acts, write "FADE IN:" (FULL CAPS followed by a colon) at the beginning of each act as well as at the beginning of a prologue or teaser segment if this is needed. To indicate the end of the script, write "FADE OUT." (FULL CAPS followed by a period) at margin setting 61 after double-spacing down from the last line of stage directions or dialogue. Then write "THE END" (FULL CAPS and underlined) four spaces down and centered on the page. In a teleplay divided into acts, indicate the end of each act, except the last act, by following the same format guidelines just given, except write, for example, "END OF ACT TWO" (FULL CAPS and underlined) instead of "THE END."

Figure 3.7 illustrates many of the script format guidelines just outlined. Notice the placement, use, and function of each entry in the script pages. Take special note of page numbers, margin settings, capitalization, and spacing used both within and between each item. It is not possible to show in this book how the color of the script page indicates the number of revisions

Figure 3.7

Pages from the final draft of a one-column one-camera full-script written for a "Matlock" episode entitled "The Con Man." See figure 3.1 for the corresponding pages from the treatment/story outline written for this same teleplay.

Courtesy of Gerald Sanoff, Dean Hargrove Productions, and Universal Studios.

14   INT. JASON EDMUNDS' OFFICE - RECEPTION AREA - DAY   14

Madeline, briefcase in hand, enters the reception area accompanied by Brian.

                    MADELINE
          Where's Tina?... the secretary...

                    BRIAN
          Maybe at lunch.

They walk over to Edmunds' office door. Madeline knocks.

                    MADELINE
          Jason? It's me, Maddy.

No answer. She knocks harder. Again, nothing.

                    MADELINE
          Jason?
               (confused, to Brian)
          He knew we were coming.

Madeline tries the knob. The door is unlocked. Both she and Brian enter.

15   INT. JASON EDMUNDS' OFFICE - DAY   15

The pair enter. Expensive office furniture lines the room. Journals sit atop Edmunds' desk as does his computer. The computer is on. Brian remains at the door while Madeline walks around Edmunds' desk. Suddenly, she freezes, then gasps.

                              (CONTINUED)

Figure 3.7 (*continued*)

15   CONTINUED: 15

>   BRIAN
>   What is it?
>
>   MADELINE
>   Oh my God... It's Jason...   *

Brian races over to Madeline, looks down to see

16   JASON EDMUNDS   16   *

>   lying face down on the floor. His body is motionless.
>   A large bloodstain covers much of his back.

17   RESUME SCENE   17

>   Devastated, Madeline kneels by the body. The sound of
>   a police SIREN begins to echo from the street.
>   Madeline pulls away from Brian.
>
>   MADELINE
>   Somebody called the police.
>
>   BRIAN
>   I can't be here.
>
>   MADELINE
>   (distraught)
>   But Jason...   *
>
>   Brian picks up the briefcase, grabs Madeline, tries to
>   move her toward the door.
>
>   BRIAN
>   Madeline, inside trading is
>   illegal. Do you want the police
>   to find you standing over Jason's   *
>   body with seventy-five thousand in
>   cash?
>
>   MADELINE
>   (torn)
>   No.
>
>   CUT TO:

18   INT. HALLWAY OUTSIDE JASON EDMUNDS' OFFICE - DAY   18   *

>   Madeline and Brian bolt from Edmunds' office. As they
>   head for the elevator, they see the elevator doors open
>   and see

Figure 3.7 (*continued*)

19   TWO UNIFORMED POLICEMEN   19

get out. They are engaged in urgent MOS conversation,
don't spot Brian and Madeline.

20   RESUME SCENE   20

Madeline grabs Brian's arm, pulls him toward the stairwell.

                         MADELINE
               The stairs...

Brian quickly opens the fire door. They hurry down the
stairs.

21   INT. STAIRWELL - DAY   21

They dash down the flight of stairs. Above them, they
hear the sounds of men's VOICES, SHOUTING. As they
pass a large metal trash dumpster, Madeline screeches
to a halt. Madeline reaches for the briefcase.

                         MADELINE
               Give me that.

                          BRIAN
               What are you doing?

                         MADELINE
               The police are outside!

She places the briefcase deep into the dumpster and
begins covering it with refuse. As she does, the
sounds of men's VOICES above grow louder.

                         MADELINE
                        (continuing)
               We'll come back tonight.

                          BRIAN
               Okay.
                        (very nervous)
               Let's get out of here.

We REMAIN on the dumpster as Madeline and Brian scurry
down the stairs. A beat, then the sound of slow, heavy
FOOTSTEPS making their way down from a flight above.

made to that particular page; however, first-draft scripts generally are typed on white paper. Subsequent revisions are typed on blue, then pink, then green, and, if necessary, yellow paper. The final production script usually is a "rainbow" of colors, each color indicating the number of revisions done to each page. Remember that, in this script format, as in most others, form follows content. Recognizing and using the scripting tools available in this and other formats require careful observation and sustained practice.

Following are the *specifications for the one-column three-camera script format.*

a. *Scene headings (descriptions).* Scene headings serve the same function for the one-column three-camera format as for the one-camera format. Because of the types of programs produced from the three-camera, "live-on-tape" script format, scene heading information is abbreviated to indicate only "INT." or "EXT." and a notion of place or location written in FULL CAPS, underlined, and placed between margin settings 15 and 35 using pica type. The hyphen is not used to separate each element in a scene heading. Although it is rare that more than one line is needed for a scene heading entry in the three-camera format, if necessary single-space between lines within each entry. Double-space down between transitions at the end of a scene and the beginning of the next scene heading. Also double-space between a scene heading and the first line of a stage directions entry.

b. *Stage directions.* Stage directions are also much more abbreviated in the three-camera script format. Write stage directions in FULL CAPS within parentheses between margin settings 15 and 46 using pica type. It is a common practice to single-space between lines in the same stage directions entry. Double-space to separate a stage directions entry and the next character designation or subsequent dialogue.

c. *Camera and sound directions.* In the three-camera script format, these directions are written as briefly as possible as separate entries and not included in stage directions notations, as in the other one-column script format. Camera and sound directions are written in FULL CAPS and are underlined. Both types of directions are placed between margin settings 15 and 35 using pica type. Only one line should be needed for each camera or sound cue. Such directions appear infrequently in this script format.

d. *Character designations.* Use regular upper- and lowercase letters when referring to a specific character in dialogue. Write character designations in FULL CAPS, beginning at tab setting 30, directly above the lines assigned to a particular character. Write character designations in FULL CAPS within stage directions to maintain style consistency. Double-space between scene headings or stage directions and a talent designation. Also double-space between the ends of lines assigned to one character and the next character designation.

e. *Character interpretation notes.* These brief interpretative notations are written in FULL CAPS and enclosed within parentheses between margin settings 15 and 36.

f. *Dialogue.* Words spoken by the talent are placed between margin settings 20 and 55 using pica type. Use regular upper- and lowercase letters to write dialogue. Double-space between the character designation and the lines assigned to that character. Double-space between lines of dialogue within one character's speech. If a character's lines continue to the next page, write "(MORE)" at tab setting 30, double-spaced down from the last line of dialogue for that character. Then, at the beginning of the next page, write "(CONT'D)" beside a repeat of the character designation on the same line to indicate that the character's speech continues from the preceding page.

g. *Scene transition notes.* Write scene transition notes in FULL CAPS, followed by a colon, underlined, and placed within margin settings 15 and 25 using pica type. Double- or triple-space between the end of dialogue, stage directions, or a scene heading and a scene transition notation.

h. *Beginnings and endings.* To begin the script, write "FADE IN:" (FULL CAPS, underlined and followed by a colon) at margin setting 15. After double-spacing down, write the first scene heading for the script as described earlier. The same scripting format is used at the beginning of each major program division if the script is divided into prologue, act, and tag or epilogue segments. To indicate the end of the script, write "FADE OUT:" (FULL CAPS, underlined and followed by a colon) at margin setting 15, triple-spacing down from the last line of stage directions or dialogue. Then write "THE END" (FULL CAPS and underlined) two spaces down at tab setting 15. In most cases, when this script format is used, "END OF ACT ONE" or "END OF ACT TWO" is written instead of "THE END."

Figure 3.8 illustrates many of the guidelines for the one-column three-camera script format. Figure 12.2 provides another illustration of this format.

(Bud)   JUNIOR/MINNIE/SCHOOLHOUSE #01

(ADD LOTS OF LAUGHS AT TOP)

(MUSIC: INTRO)

(DISSOLVE THRU ART CARD)

(KIDS LAUGH AND THROW PAPER)

                        MINNIE

        Children! Children! All right now,

        Junior, last week I asked you to start

        making a list of every single thing you

        eat. Has this changed your diet at all?

                        JUNIOR

        It sure has, teacher! Now I don't eat

        anything that's hard to spell.

(KIDS LAUGH)

(Bud)   ARCHIE/WILD LINE #11

(CIGAR PUFF)

                        ARCHIE

        Well, that means Junior won't eat anything

        with more than five letters or two

        syllables in it... and maybe not even

        alphabet soup!

Figure 3.8
Page from a one-column three-camera full-script for the syndicated television series "Hee-Haw."
Courtesy of Gaylord Program Services, Inc.

Scripting Approaches and Techniques

Each of the scripting forms described and illustrated in this chapter is shown in subsequent chapters to illustrate the application of specific formats to particular writing situations. Two approaches and techniques that have numerous scripting applications will be discussed in this section: computers can help make your work more efficient and flexible; storyboards can help you visualize and refine the visual elements in a presentation.

Using Computers

Each writer develops a preference for particular writing tools. Writers prefer the look, feel, and response of their chosen tools as they work. This is part of the pleasure of writing. Some writers work only with a pencil and notepad, others use only manual typewriters, and many others prefer electric typewriters. A growing number are turning to personal computers to generate the variety of script material needed in the scripting formats required. It makes no difference, however, how the creative process begins. Eventually script material must be typed and in proper form.

No matter which tools are used, writing for the electronic media requires interaction between the writer and others associated with a project. The final script is hammered out between people who express a variety of creative perspectives throughout the project's development. The writer's work is only the beginning of the writing/production process.

Computers can facilitate the necessary interaction between the writer and production personnel. Computers are used in print and electronic newsrooms, as well as in advertising agencies, continuity departments, and several kinds of business applications. Chapter 5 contains a full explanation and illustration of how computers are used in television newsrooms.

Capabilities and Advantages

Following are the capabilities of most computer systems. These items vary according to the system and software package used.

a. Basic scripting formats, described in this chapter, can be accommodated automatically using specialized and relatively inexpensive software programs.
b. Language usage, especially spelling, can be monitored.
c. Script changes can be made quickly, easily, efficiently, and electronically without disturbing essential script format requirements. Material can be added, deleted, moved, and saved as needed. For example, only a few keystrokes are required to change a character's name that appears numerous times in a script.
d. Automatic pagination and page headings generally are available.
e. Script material can be printed, stored, and delivered instantly.
f. Printers can produce a variety of typefaces and type styles.
g. Storage could be on floppy or hard disks, or to another kind of storage file for use later in another scriptwriting situation.
h. Modems can interconnect computer systems, using telephone lines. A modem allows you to contact others via electronic bulletin board systems and to share information and materials.

This is useful when you need to work with other writers not in your immediate geographical area. With a modem, your computer can tap vast data base files that provide resource and background information otherwise not readily available.

i. When combined with a FAX machine, the computer allows you to send material to another FAX machine virtually anywhere.

j. Computers can create a variety of graphics material—for instance, charts, graphs, and maps.

k. Lap-top computer notepads permit portability without restricting creativity. If you have an idea, capture it electronically on one of these small systems, which can be battery powered for a few hours and which have enough memory to tackle most short writing tasks—on location, in the field, or while traveling.

l. Computer software can accomplish tasks other than writing scripts—for example, preparing newscast lineups, capturing audio column material for on-camera teleprompter use or rehearsal by a narrator, handling production budgets and scheduling, and tracking equipment availability and usage.

Most writers who use computers agree that they maximize creativity and minimize concerns for the mechanics of scriptwriting. With most of today's computer software, you can concentrate on the creative aspects of writing and let the computer handle the necessary scripting format requirements. The result is greater production output in less time.

If you are going to use computers for scriptwriting, you will need to understand a few basic computer terms and processes. This is not meant to be a complete examination of all the considerations you will need to make before purchasing computer equipment for use in your writing. This brief discussion focuses only on microcomputers, or what are often called personal computers. This is the most common computer system used by scriptwriters—not the combined hardware/software systems, which are more complex and usually more expensive.

Terms and Processes

You will need to choose a "platform"—a combination of computer brand and operating system software. In selecting a system, such as the IBM PC family or the Macintosh, you then choose the software (computer programs) that will operate on that system. It is important to select a software package that offers flexible functions, ease of operation, and efficiency in time and energy spent.

Determine what you want a computer to do. *Word processing* software can handle scripts, but they are also useful for correspondence and other written presentations. *Data base* software is useful when you want to retrieve production information from your scripts, to locate information from centralized data bases, to prepare a budget or production breakdown by scenes, or to determine the number of locations needed or times a particular character is seen in a production. *Spreadsheets* can handle your financial and business needs, such as keeping track of your income or the taxes you have paid. Some writers purchase a software package that includes all three of these basic types of software. Generally these combination programs offer less sophisticated features and options than software programs limited to one function.

Full-time and professional scriptwriters generally use specialized word processing software packages. These handle the unique script formatting requirements of such productions as dramas, comedies, and instructional and corporate presentations.[3]

Developing Storyboards

A storyboard illustrates the camera's view of the essential shots in a sequence or segment of a production and shows the correlation between the sounds heard and the pictures seen. The frames in a storyboard show key shots, camera angles, and optical effects. The audio portion, which is written under each appropriate frame, indicates the music, sound effects, and voices to be heard.

Storyboards are useful in planning complex, highly visual presentations. Chapters 4 and 10 illustrate two applications of storyboards—television commercials produced by advertising agencies and animated adventure series produced for network television. A full-script usually accompanies a storyboard presentation.

A storyboard is not the same as a photoboard. A storyboard helps *plan* a production and refine a script. A photoboard shows key shots and accompanying audio from a *finished* production and a *completed* script. Chapter 4 shows examples of both a storyboard and a photoboard.

Advantages

Storyboards and similar visual presentations can help you and others involved in a project evaluate and adjust the visualization and sequencing of a production. Storyboards help you "see" the flow of sound and pictures and judge the structure, cohesiveness, and continuity of what is shown.

Storyboards are an invaluable planning tool when complex, lengthy productions involve expensive equipment or specialized personnel. Storyboards are often used by directors of high-budget motion pictures. A storyboard and a full-script may also be the basis for a client presentation at an advertising agency.

Storyboard material, once loaded into a computer, can be used as its own data base. This allows writers who also double as producer/director to manage a project efficiently. Computers can manipulate storyboard information and then plan frame-by-frame animation sequences or help build 3D models and move them through various positions to determine the best camera angles and movements to use. The integration of storyboard creation and computer manipulation can produce time-saving and money-saving options.

Storyboards help writers handle changes quickly and inexpensively. It is more efficient to make changes in a storyboard than to wait until a production is underway or nearly completed. Once production has begun, inefficiency causes production costs and time wasted to increase noticeably. This has made storyboards a cost-effective tool for corporate video work, as well as for feature films and commercial production.

Storyboards can be developed by one person or by a team of specialists. **Processes**
Some writers work as both artist and writer. Many writers use a scratch pad to draw a simple picture of a scene to help provide a visual reference as they write a script. Computer software systems are now available that allow a writer to create visual material that can be inserted into storyboard frames and woven into the video column of a script.

Complex productions may require a team approach. The writer can suggest visual treatments, an artist can suggest script changes, and a producer or graphics/computer specialist can indicate the availability of both visualization and scripting approaches.

As previously mentioned, specialized computer software programs are a **Methods**
quick, inexpensive, and easy way to create storyboard material; however, other techniques can also be used to produce a storyboard. Many times, you need only simple stick figures, hand-drawn on printed forms, to show what you envision. Perhaps you can create a few black-and-white sketches or use color photographs that show the scripted camera angles and talent positions.

No matter which method is used, remember to show *key* shots in the storyboard. A new "frame" or "cell" is needed for *each* important visual change—for instance, when a new camera angle is used; when a new character is shown; or when new graphics material, such as a client's logo, is inserted. A 10-second spot announcement may require only one or two frames. A 60-second spot announcement may require fifteen to twenty frames to show the essential shots.

This chapter presented the basic scriptwriting styles, formats, and tech- **Summary**
niques. The discussion of essential aural writing styles and techniques centered on how to select words, construct sentences, and integrate music and sound effects creatively into a finished script. The description of visual writing styles and techniques included suggestions for envisioning specific images (visualization) and combining images (sequencing) to visually convey a specific idea or perspective. There was an explanation of the mechanics of preparing script pages and the use of standard scripting styles. A wide range of scripting formats, approaches, and techniques was described and illustrated. A variety of full-script formats were examined in detail.

Preparing material in proper form is important for all writers, especially for those working in the electronic media. Careful attention to details is a hallmark of all professionals; however, writing a script in proper form is a mechanical process readily grasped by most writers. Even more important than proper script form, your scripts must display creativity, imagination, and innovation if they are to stand apart from many others.

Suggested Exercises and Projects

1. Prepare a cover page for one of the following, using the guidelines provided in this chapter: a television drama (teleplay), a screenplay, or an instructional television series.
2. Prepare script identification information, which would be found at the top left corner of a script page, for one of the following, using the guidelines provided in this chapter: a 30-second radio commercial for a local bank or automobile dealership, a 30-minute radio discussion program, or a 5-minute radio or television interview with the governor of your state.
3. Compile a list of five difficult-to-pronounce names or items from your area. These could be names of government officials, business leaders, athletes, coaches, street names, town names, and the like. For each name or item, provide both the regular spelling and your suggested pronunciation. Enclose each pronunciation notation in parentheses and use uppercase letters to emphasize stressed syllables.
4. Write each number in standard form:
    a. 1,218
    b. 215,750
    c. 618
    d. 1,800,000
    e. 2/3
    f. $20.50
    g. 16 ft.
    h. 33 St.
    i. 800-555-1212
    j. 1814 Briar Ave.
5. Use standard punctuation and editing marks to improve the effectiveness of each of the following sentences:
    a. Nate you says id comein over tonite
    b. Boy thats some tasty piz za
    c. Its goiing to be a good day break for the races
    d. Tigers elephants   and beers are featured in each performance
    e. He stopped turned to face her and suddenly began crying
    f. Is their a better reason to shop at Lakeside
    g. (Dialogue in a radio drama)

    | Boy | Struggling | I know what you mean |
    | Girl | Pensively | Please come in now |

6. Write five simple declarative sentences describing your hometown.

7. For twenty or thirty minutes, sit on a park bench, near a bus stop, or in any area where people gather to wait and converse. Report your observations about which topics or issues people discussed, the manner in which they selected and used words, how they constructed sentences, and how their conversations progressed. What are your conclusions about the current use of language, based on this experience?

8. Watch one of the following: a television drama, a television comedy program, or a current theatrical motion picture. Observe the use of language (words and sentences), music, sound effects, visualization, and sequencing. Report your observations and conclusions.

9. Monitor and, if possible, record several radio commercials. Report your observations about the use of words, voices, music, and sound effects in these commercials. If you recorded one of these radio commercials, try to write a full-script for the commercial to reflect what you heard on tape, using the scripting guidelines, forms, and techniques discussed and illustrated in this chapter.

10. Write a short segment for a radio commercial or radio drama in which you use sound effects to accomplish at least two of the following: establish a locale or setting, guide the listener's attention to a particular character or setting, establish or change the mood or tone, create a transition in time or setting, or indicate an entrance to or exit from a scene.

11. In one paragraph, written in the form of a mini-treatment, summarize one memorable scene from a movie you have seen recently.

12. Watch one of the following types of television programs: a documentary, a music/variety show, or a news magazine program. Prepare a television rundown sheet for thirty minutes of the program you watched. Prepare a semi-script for the same thirty minutes of the program viewed. Then try to write a script for a two-to-four minute sequence from the program you watched. Your full-script should mirror approximately what was seen and heard during this short sequence and should follow the scripting guidelines, forms, and techniques discussed and illustrated in this chapter. The capability to record the program on videotape will make it easier to prepare the full-script for the two-to-four minute sequence.

13. For the same thirty-minute program segment viewed in exercise 12, comment on the use and effectiveness of visualization and sequencing. In your judgment, which portions of the program were visually effective? Which portions were not effective? How would you have improved the scripting of these less-effective portions of the program?

Notes

1. The Annenberg Television Script Archive contains over 35,000 American television scripts, including most prime-time series, movies made for television, specials, and pilots aired on commercial television networks since 1976. The Archive continues to grow at a rate of approximately 1,500 titles per year. The Annenberg School is prepared to assist researchers in their use of the Archive. Access to the collection is by appointment only on application to this address: Television Script Archive, The Annenberg School for Communication, University of Pennsylvania, 3620 Walnut Street, Philadelphia, PA 19104.

2. The most complete treatment of screenplay and television dramatic script layout requirements and guidelines is contained in the *Professional Writer's Teleplay/Screenplay Format,* issued by the Writers Guild of America. See Appendix C for WGA addresses.

3. Computer software suppliers can provide current information about their widely accepted scripting systems. Comprehensive Video Supply Corporation (148 Veterans Drive, Northvale, NJ 07647) offers Script Master, a multicolumn script format system, and Movie Master, which is designed for writing one-column one-camera screenplays and providing an array of production breakdown information. (Script Master and Movie Master are registered trademarks of Comprehensive Video Supply Corporation, Northvale, NJ.) SnowBird Software (401 East College Avenue, Marquette, MI 49855) offers TVSCRIPT, a text formatter that puts a script typed on a conventional word processor system, such as WordStar or WordPerfect, into a two-column video format and prints it.

Commercials and Announcements

T he basic principles and techniques of persuasion apply equally to commercials, public service announcements (PSAs) and promotional announcements. The content of each type of message may vary, but writers tend to approach each in a similar manner. Solid, effective, persuasive writing and production techniques are needed in PSAs, promotional announcements, and commercials.

All commercials and announcements are intended to sell something. It could be a product, a service, an idea, a concept, or even an emotion or feeling. An automobile manufacturer wants to sell more cars. A bank wants to sell potential customers on the benefits of a new type of checking or savings account. A political candidate wants to create a favorable image or persuade voters to accept a controversial viewpoint on a key issue before election day. A social service agency tries to attract prospective volunteers by selling the concept of enhanced human values and life-styles. A television station wants viewers to trust the station's news department to deliver the news objectively and as comprehensively as possible, so a promotional announcement is designed, written, and produced to sell this concept.

This chapter will describe how the planning document, called a copy rationale, helps writers generate effective spot announcements, or "spots," by identifying the key elements to be used in the copy. Next will be suggestions about organizing an announcement—what to include and how to organize the material into an effective presentation. Several items relating to copy style and design will be discussed—how to use standard copy lengths to their fullest extent, how talent and production personnel styles of delivery influence the writer's work, and how to determine the most effective method of packaging or presenting the script material. Copywriting suggestions will be offered, along with examples of various kinds of commercial and public service spot announcements from different types of campaigns. Finally, techniques for writing effective on-air promotional announcements will be presented in an effort to show how the concepts, principles, and techniques described for commercials and public service announcements transfer to writing promotional spots. Examples from various promotional campaigns will illustrate these techniques.

Commercials, public service announcements, and promotional announcements generally are produced and recorded during reserved production times at local radio or television stations, at independent production facilities, or on location. Many stations have in-house production units that handle local station production, as well as outside production work, on a contractual basis. Independent production companies can develop jingles and musical logos needed by advertising clients handled by station sales staffs or by advertising agencies.

Developing a Copy Rationale

A full discussion of the development of multimedia campaigns is beyond the scope of this book. It is important to realize, however, that broadcast commercials and announcements usually are only part of a comprehensive multimedia effort. Commercials, public service announcements, and promotional announcements used on radio and television often use the same logos, music themes, and slogans to provide unity and to relate directly to efforts in other media by the same advertiser or client. To formulate and create multimedia messages for the same client, a campaign strategy and then a creative strategy are devised. Usually this is accomplished by advertising agency personnel in conjunction with the client or advertiser. The length of discussions and the volume of information collected generally are quite extensive.

A similar, although less extensive process should be followed when writing one or a limited number of electronic media advertising messages for a client or an advertiser. This planning document is called a copy rationale. Other labels attached to this process and the resultant document are copy platform, copy strategy, and copy policy.

The copy rationale allows the writer and the client or advertiser to determine the key elements to be used in the announcement(s) to accomplish certain stated objectives. It is a kind of map or blueprint that points the way toward the successful completion of a broadcast advertising goal. It is best to devise a copy rationale *before* writing advertising messages. Otherwise, commercials and announcements are written haphazardly, with no obvious unity within each message and between the messages of a consolidated campaign for the same client. It is best for a young writer to present a *written* copy rationale; experienced writers can usually quickly devise a mental copy rationale without committing such information to paper. Eventually the copy rationale should be presented in written form, albeit abbreviated, for approval by the client or advertiser and to serve as a guideline for future messages for the same client, product, or service.

Several elements should be included in a one-to-three-page copy rationale:

a. Client/product/service analysis
b. Audience analysis
c. Statement of objectives
d. Logical and emotional appeals
e. Copy style and design

    f. Competition and competitive claims
    g. Positioning statement
    h. Central selling point

The extent to which each element in a copy rationale is developed depends on time restrictions, as well as on the amount of detail needed by the client or by the individual writing the announcements.

Client/Product/ Service Analysis

Learn as much as possible about the client or advertiser, as well as the product or service to be advertised. The more you know, the easier it is to design effective spot announcements to meet realistic, identifiable goals.

Much of the needed information can come directly from the client. Information about specific types of businesses and services can be obtained from such organizations as the Radio Advertising Bureau, Inc., 304 Park Ave. S, New York, NY 10010 and the Television Bureau of Advertising, 477 Madison Avenue, New York, NY 10022-5892. Both the RAB and TvB provide information packets and booklets that contain useful national statistics and information on specific businesses. Industry periodicals and reference works directly related to a particular kind of business, client, product, or service also should be checked for additional background to assist in the writing process. Although such information usually provides a national perspective, the data will supply essential information and viable topic areas, which can be applied later to a specific local advertiser or client.

Client Analysis

The list of questions to ask a client can be endless. Some of the crucial questions to ask, before writing the copy, are the following:

a. *What has been done in the past?* What types of media have been used? What were the results? What kinds of campaigns and promotions have been used, with what results? What was the nature of the copy used? What has been the advertising or promotional budget in the past? What was the most successful campaign used? What was the least successful?

b. *What is now being done?* Type of media used? Kinds of campaigns and promotions? Nature of copy used? Current budget?

c. *What are the particulars about this business?* Hours of operation? When do most customers come in to the store or shop? When are most telephone calls received? What are the peak sales days and months? What are the seasonal business flows (winter, spring, summer, fall)? What types of products or services are offered? What brand names are carried? What co-op possibilities are there, so that advertising costs can be shared between the national manufacturer and the local retailer? Who are the owners and operators and what are their backgrounds in this business and in other businesses? What are the biggest sales events throughout the year? What are the special features of this particular business operation? What are the strengths and weaknesses of this business? How does the client or advertiser view business conditions, generally and specifically, in the areas of direct interest? What community projects does this advertiser participate in? What are the major community problems, from this advertiser's viewpoint? What are the client's short-term and long-term advertising goals and objectives? What are the *client's* opinions about the effectiveness of various media?

Product/Service Analysis

Some important questions to ask to analyze a product or service are the following:

a. *What exactly is the product or service to be advertised?* What are its strongest and weakest selling points?
b. *How is it used or made?*
c. *What are the special features or benefits of the product or service?* What are the color and size of the package?
d. *How has this basic product or service evolved over the years?* Or is this a new product or service?
e. *When is it bought or used?* Where? By whom? How often? What days of the week? Months of the year?
f. *How is the product or service distributed?* Where?
g. *How available is it?*
h. *Are there any restrictions on use?*
i. *What has been the pattern of development for this product or service?* Is it declining, growing, stabilizing?

Audience Analysis

You must identify specific audience characteristics in relation to the marketplace to create effective advertising messages. Basic audience composition and the characteristics of the target audience for the client's specific product or service are significant elements of a thorough audience analysis. Not only will you discover the makeup of the current market, but you will also learn something about the untapped potential market. To create specific types of messages, it is important to identify a target audience. Thus, the results of the commercials or announcements can be effectively measured.

Here are some of the questions that should be asked to formulate a thorough audience analysis:

a. *Who are the current customers?* What are their demographic characteristics, such as age, sex, income level, education, family size, life-style, and job status? Who are the prime customers? Where are they from? When do they shop or come into the place of business? What comments have they made to the client about the business? About the quality and frequency of past and present advertising? What keeps these prime customers coming back? What can be done to make them come back or to shop at this business more often? Does the client want to retain and strengthen this appeal to current customers?

b. *Who are viable potential customers for the product or service?* What are their characteristics? What are their shopping habits? What are their interests and priorities? What would attract them to the client's business or service? Should this be the target group for the commercials or announcements being written?
c. *How much do current and potential customers know about the client's product or service?*
d. *What are the attitudes of current and potential customers toward the client's product or service?* What client "personality" or "image" is conveyed? What misconceptions are there about the specific client or about the product/service category?
e. *Which attitudes should be reinforced? Which attitudes changed? Why? How?*
f. *What are the common, identifiable, consistent traits of current and potential customers?*

Much of the information needed to formulate both the client/product/service analysis and the audience analysis can be supplied through the collection of marketing data. Clients can supply the results of internal research projects. Independent research companies can provide general or specific information from store audits, consumer panels, and surveys.

The results of marketing research can provide insight into the attitudes and behavior of consumers—for instance, product consumption, brand and image preferences, and levels of product or service loyalty; determine product appeals and shortcomings—for instance, color, packaging, special features, and convenience; and help determine the client's position in the marketplace by examining such items as sales volume, distribution patterns, and industry trends. Marketing research techniques can be used to test advertising concepts and entire campaigns, both before and after the campaign is available in the market. Marketing research can be helpful when identifying problem areas, formulating objectives for future advertising, tracking current and future trends in the marketplace, and anticipating changes in the competition's strategies. It is an important tool in the decision-making process for the client and, ultimately, for the writer.

Find the common ground between the target audience and the advertised product or service. For example, it is not enough to show only Blacks in a commercial targeted to Black teenagers. It is also important to consider life-style, language, and cultural and attitudinal elements that may need to be incorporated into a script for a spot aimed at such a specific target group.

Statement of Objectives

The general purpose of any advertising message is persuasion. This broad objective must be more narrowly defined, however, to provide some means of measuring the results of the advertising and to save time and energy. The objectives of an advertising effort can be to create awareness or to inform consumers about a new product or service. For an established product or service, the objective might be to plant a name firmly in the consumer's mind and to motivate that person to buy the product or use the service. Perhaps the objective is to stress a new use or feature for the older, more established product or service. If the client is facing stiff competition in maintaining customers, the advertising objective can be to provide information about the client, to shape a positive attitude in the consumer's mind, or to provide additional motivation for selecting the client's product or service over the competition.

Be sure that the statement of objectives is *specific*. To whom is the advertising addressed? What specific action should be expected? Is the objective to convince nonusers to try your new or already established brand, to get former users to try your brand again, or to keep current users from switching from your brand to another brand, or to another product category altogether?

To be an effective tool for the writer, the copy rationale statement of objectives must be

- a. Expressed as a clear, positive statement of the communications job to be accomplished, aimed at a specific target audience or group, with a specific result over a specified period of time
- b. Realistic and capable of being measured
- c. Capable of being translated into a specific plan of action
- d. Based on a thorough analysis of the marketplace, the client, the product or service, and the consumer
- e. Agreed on by the client or advertiser before any advertising message is written or produced

The need to formulate a statement of objectives applies equally to commercials and to public service announcements for a noncommercial client and to promotional announcements written and produced by a station or network. Following are examples of statements of objectives for several kinds of clients and writing situations:

- a. To create awareness about a new detergent product among women aged eighteen to forty-five who will buy 100,000 units of this new product in the next thirty days
- b. To enhance the image of Bill's Clothing Store among men between the ages of twenty-five and forty-five who will spend a total of $75,000 on items offered by the client in the next ten days
- c. To motivate adults between eighteen and fifty-four in the community to contribute $50,000 to the local United Way campaign in the next thirty days
- d. To convince women between eighteen and thirty-four in the local television market to watch Channel 2's Late Afternoon Movie series, with the result that the size of this target audience for this program series will increase five rating points in the next ratings report for this market

Learn to identify and make effective use of the basic motivators of human behavior. These motivators often are referred to as the logical and emotional appeals used in advertising to persuade current and potential consumers to follow a particular course of action. *Logical,* or *rational,* appeals tap the intellectual and analytical processes of the consumer. *Emotional* appeals relate to the nonlogical, nonintellectual, humanistic, psychic, and personal aspects of the consumer. Logical appeals are effective when the product or service is being sold directly, without frills. Emotional appeals can be used to grab the audience's attention by presenting impelling motives and situations.

It is difficult to place a restrictive label on the wide variety of appeals that could be used in a commercial or an announcement. For the sake of identification and classification, however, the following are some of the major logical and emotional appeals available and often used in electronic media advertising.

Logical and Emotional Appeals

Self-preservation

Self-preservation is one of the strongest motivators of human behavior. Every individual is concerned about guaranteeing the continuation of life, personally and within a group or family. The listener or viewer wants to enhance the capability for self-preservation and to be alerted to situations that might threaten such enhancement. Public service announcements that appeal for funds to feed and clothe hungry and homeless refugees in a war-torn country use self-preservation as a primary appeal. Commercials for smoke detectors and air bags also emphasize appeals to self-preservation.

Security

Individuals want to be personally safe and comfortable, free from economic difficulties as well as psychological and social pressures. Security is a primary appeal in spot announcements for over-the-counter medicines, insurance company policies, and the use of automobile safety belts.

Reputation

Most people are concerned about the way others see them and how others feel and react toward what they own, as well as what they believe, say, and do. Most people seek recognition and approval from others. Reputation could be used as a primary appeal in announcements for a new automobile, furniture and interiors, appliances, and such personal items as bath soap, deodorant, and foot spray.

Self-respect

Most consumers set fairly high standards for themselves and their behavior and may be motivated to consider the purchase or use of a product or service because it would enhance this self-image. Hallmark's slogan "when you care enough to send the very best" tends to appeal to the self-image of the listener or viewer. A promotional announcement for a television opera series could use this appeal to entice viewers to watch the upcoming programs, since many viewers would want to consider themselves educated, refined, and naturally attracted to this type of high-quality television programming.

**Status/Power/
Prestige**

The need to feel reassured, confident, able to persuade others, and in direct control of their beliefs and actions may be overpowering in many consumers. Property, money, and power may be the overriding motivation in a person's life. Commercials for exclusive stores and shops, special clothing items, expensive cars, and exotic vacation spots may center on this need for status, power, and prestige.

Affection

Love, affection, loyalty, and sentimentality toward friends, family, church, school, country, or organizations are strong motivating forces for many people. When used expertly and creatively by the writer, this appeal can stir up strong, enduring feelings and emotions that are almost sure to inspire the listener or viewer. Commercials for Kodak and Hallmark are excellent examples of how this very strong emotional appeal can be used effectively.

Durability

Durability is one of the primary logical appeals you may decide to incorporate into a spot announcement. Every consumer wants to get the best value from each purchase—high performance, dependability, and low maintenance costs. Consumers may be willing to pay more at the time of purchase if they can be convinced that the item will last for a long time. Durability is a primary appeal used in commercials for Jeep, Duracell batteries, Maytag appliances, and Curtis Mathis television sets.

Economy

The initial or long-term low cost of a product or service may be especially attractive to a consumer. Saving money is a continuing, growing concern. Economy could be the basic appeal in commercials for gas-saving cars, energy-saving insulation, and low prices at supermarkets.

**Sense of
Adventure/Personal
Freedom**

Excitement, change, new experiences, adventure, and the personal freedom to act, speak, write, and think at will with no restraints may be the appropriate appeals to make. Most people are curious about the unknown. They want to feel or experience something that normally is not available to them. Relief from the monotony of the daily routine may be a constant motivating factor for a specific audience. Commercials for personal products, such as toothpastes, mouthwashes, after-shave lotions, and perfumes, could stress the unpredictable aftereffects of using them. The exhilarating experience of owning and driving a sophisticated foreign sports car could appeal in a special way to an individual's sense of personal freedom.

Although placed into an arbitrary classification system, logical and emotional appeals usually are not isolated for use in any one spot announcement. Rather, they are creatively fused to produce a specific, predictable effect on the listener or viewer and to identify a unique benefit to be derived from the purchase of a product or the use of a service. It is the conscious, calculated use of these logical and emotional appeals that often determines the overall success of a commercial, public service, or promotional announcement.

The implementation of the copy rationale or planning document is accomplished through the writing and eventual production of individual spot announcements. There are various presentational frameworks, approaches, or design schemes available to implement the copy rationale effectively. These are described later in this chapter.

Copy Style and Design

It is important that the copy style and design for each announcement match the product or service specifications identified earlier, implement the stated objectives, and incorporate specific logical and emotional appeals to make the message attractive and persuasive for the target audience. A decision may have been made to design announcements for use in several kinds of radio program formats or for specific types of television programs. The copy style and design statement should specify the adjustments needed to provide this customization.

The copy style and design statement should determine the selection and use of music, sound effects, and voices. If television announcements are to be written, there should be references to the kinds of shots, scene transitions, and special effects to be used. All the important aural or visual elements should be determined and identified and the use of each described and justified to create a particular mood or tone in each announcement. Clarity and precision in the copy style and design statement are necessary for implementing the copy rationale.

Competition and Competitive Claims

To place an advertiser or a client in perspective in the marketplace, compile information and form judgments about major competitors and competitive claims. It would be helpful to establish criteria for determining an advertiser's principal competitors. The criteria might include the amount of sales volume within the past year, visibility in the marketplace, and the amount of advertising purchased within a certain period.

Once major competitors have been identified, evaluate what each is doing. It is important to know the kind of advertising offered by each competitor—major brands sold, special sales, customer incentives, slogans used, claims made. Try to determine each competitor's identity in the minds of consumers. Determine each competitor's niche in the marketplace. It would be helpful to know what each has done in the past and is doing now. Track the development of each major competitor to better evaluate your advertiser or client. Information about competitors can be gathered by using market research techniques, through discussions with the advertiser or client or your local sales account executive, and by your own careful analysis and observations of the marketplace.

The notion of identifying and analyzing competitors applies most obviously to commercial clients and advertisers. The same kinds of considerations, however, can be applied to promotional announcements in which the competition is represented by the other stations and media outlets in the marketplace. Public service or nonprofit clients do not usually identify competing agencies but, rather, concentrate on other aspects of the copy rationale.

Positioning Statement

After analyzing the client, identifying the target audience, determining objectives and copy appeals, formulating an effective copy style and design, and evaluating major competitors, you can devise a positioning statement for the client. A positioning statement explains or anticipates the client's niche in the marketplace and describes how the consumer will regard the client, product, or service after exposure to the soon-to-be-created spot announcement(s).

Formulating a positioning statement forces you to identify a market vacuum and to determine how that vacuum can best be filled so that the client's products or services will be clearly set apart from the competition. Without a positioning statement, the client will blend into the competition and lose an effective means of marketplace identification.

Usually there is a noticeable overlap between competitors in the minds of consumers. The positioning statement could incorporate attributes shared by competitors but, in addition, should provide something unique to set the client apart from competitors. That feature might be a jeweler who offers custom ring designs or a pharmacy that provides free home delivery of prescriptions and an end-of-the-year statement of medical expenditures for tax purposes. Eliminate from the positioning statement the ineffective remnants of the client's past advertising efforts, as well as the insurmountable strengths of major competitors. From this process should emerge a clear, distinctive, consistent, and memorable personality or identity for the client. With enough probing and analysis, practically every client, product, or service can be positioned as offering something unique to its customers. All other things being equal, it is the *differences,* not the similarities, that make a person visit one store, buy one product, or use one service over another.

The positioning statement should be written as one sentence. If more is needed or if the sentence is loaded with dependent clauses, you have not focused your message. This could lead to weak creative work later. Following is a form that will help you construct a useful, effective positioning statement:

> For (target audience), (product or service name) is (single most important claim), because (single most important supporting evidence or fact).

Following is an example: ''For the frequent business flyer, United Airlines is the best airline, because United Airlines is the most attentive to the needs of business flyers.'' Here is another: ''For the investor with limited funds, XXX Mutual Fund offers the best value, because XXX Mutual Fund invests in highly rated municipal bonds and, therefore, produces tax-free income from secure accounts for the investor with limited funds.''

With a strong positioning statement, the client reaps the benefits: the client can match the competition now and anticipate future market developments from a position of strength and flexibility. A sound positioning statement should generate a main theme or stance from which subthemes with multiple possibilities can be developed.

Once the positioning statement has been formulated, you can determine the central selling point, or sales key. What is the central message, or sales pitch, to be delivered? How will the client's message be linked to the logical and emotional needs of the target audience? How can the statement of objectives and the client's position in the marketplace best be implemented? What will grab attention and sustain interest? How can the central sales message be expressed in a creative and interesting way? How can the listener or viewer best be persuaded to buy the product, use the service, or shop at this particular store? What should be stressed in each spot announcement? Would it be best to stress a particular event—for example, Christmas, Mother's Day, or back to school; a specific product feature, such as uses, size, and convenience; or special client services, such as free delivery, no service charges, convenient parking, or friendly sales personnel, or should these be combined for use in this set of announcements? Should emphasis be placed on the local client/advertiser or on the quality of nationally advertised and manufactured products available locally through the client?

These and many other questions must be answered before a strong, effective, and versatile central selling point, or sales key, can be formulated. All the other copy rationale considerations culminate in the central selling point, or sales key statement. In many instances, others will have determined the central selling point for you. You then take what is given and write the spot announcements. In other situations—for instance, small broadcast stations and some advertising agencies—you are expected to help generate the central selling point, or sales key, as well as the actual copy.

Central Selling Point

Despite the thorough analysis and careful documentation required to generate the copy rationale, you must still come to grips with the problem of what to include and how to organize each commercial, public service, or promotional announcement. The copy rationale should provide the answers. The primary function of such a planning document is to isolate and identify the information that *must* be included in each announcement and to suggest the most effective ways the information can be organized and presented.

Organizing the Announcement

Three suggestions should help you determine what to include in each announcement: (a) *use key attributes,* (b) *stress benefits,* and (c) *display both effectively.* Even a 10-second announcement should incorporate some of the key characteristics identified in the copy rationale. Although it is not possible to use all the key attributes, the one or two that must be used in every announcement should be obvious, even in a 10-second message. The key attributes of a client, product, or service should generate specific individual benefits, which must be stressed in each announcement if the consumer is to be reassured that something positive and beneficial will come from the purchase of this product or the use of this service. Both attributes and benefits must be linked in the consumer's mind by offering something tangible. What is included in each announcement must be organized and presented in an attractive, effective manner.

What to Include

How to Organize

It soon becomes obvious that there are many ways to organize an announcement. The writer's challenge is to devise the *best* organizational pattern, the one that will create a message that is attractive, interesting, persuasive, and memorable and that fulfills the essential objectives and conclusions of the copy rationale. Many writers recommend the use of a four-step persuasive process based on observations and conclusions about consumer behavior. This four-step process can be readily identified in what knowledgeable observers have determined are effective and successful commercials and announcements, no matter what presentational framework is eventually used. Although the four steps may not be presented in the same order as listed and a given step may be made subtly or combined with another step, all steps should be incorporated into each spot announcement. The four-step persuasive process includes the following:

1. Get and hold attention.
2. Build interest.
3. Create desire.
4. Get action.

The first few seconds of a commercial or announcement are crucial. You must have the attention of the listener or viewer before any other information can be presented. Use various devices both at the beginning and throughout the message to get and hold attention. These attention devices include the following:

a. An unexplained or unidentifiable sound or visual later clarified in the announcement
b. A startling or provocative statement or picture
c. An elaborate sound or visual effect
d. A rhetorical question that involves the audience
e. A well-known spokesperson respected by the audience
f. A sound effect or piece of music that evokes emotions, images, textures, colors, and shapes
g. A situation that immediately involves the audience because it relates to daily concerns

It is possible to build interest throughout the announcement by creatively using the elements of surprise, conflict, and suspense. Try to make the announcement somewhat unpredictable for the audience. Give them the unexpected. Create the impression that an important problem exists that must be resolved and hint that this problem could relate to the product, service, or client.

Using appropriate emotional and logical appeals, you must create a desire for the product or service in the minds of the listener or viewer. The listener or viewer must want to purchase the product, use the service, or shop at the client's store. However, this desire will be created in the audience's minds only if a tangible benefit is offered that impresses the individual consumer. You must plant in the audience's minds the idea that the problem presented earlier can indeed be resolved by the advertised product, service, or client. The individual listener or viewer must believe this connection can be made and that personal benefit will result from the purchase of a particular product or the use of a specific service.

The last crucial step in the persuasive process involves getting a response or an action from the audience. This response could be direct or implied. A commercial for a furniture store may conclude by urging the audience to buy specific items during a special sale. An institutional commercial for a major oil company may be written so that the audience understands and appreciates that company's efforts in finding new energy sources. The techniques used in a public service announcement may compel the listener or viewer to respond by being more sympathetic toward a certain cause, or the announcement may ask for a more direct response, such as contributions to a central fund. The announcement must be clearly and precisely organized so that the audience has no doubt about the needed action. The message must build to this final step and be based on the key elements identified in the copy rationale.

Methods of Presentation

An important part of the copy rationale, copy style and design, requires careful examination. Many creative alternatives must be considered before you can select the best possible method of communicating the client's ideas and objectives. Some of the most important creative variables include the following: standard lengths for announcements; styles of delivery, which will be determined by talent and production personnel; and the packaging of the finished announcement, in which the number of talent featured, the presentational frameworks used, and the copy makeup selected are important considerations.

The classifications and terminology used here are meant to place this information into some order for the purposes of understanding the creative writing process. Remember that many of these classifications overlap and that it is a common practice to combine several terms or classifications into one cohesive announcement that displays a sense of unity and direction for the audience. Understand the various classifications and terms. Become aware of the potential use for each item. Then select the combination that best fulfills the goals and objectives stated in the copy rationale.

Standard Lengths

Several standard lengths for announcements and commercials have evolved over the years to accommodate scheduling demands, convenience, and the purchase of advertising time by the client. The length of each announcement may be the result of placement (i.e., where the announcement will be used in the broadcast schedule); the conclusions drawn from the copy rationale; the type of client, product, or service featured; the nature of the program or the program format in which the announcement will be used; and a number of other considerations. On the average, spots are shorter than they were ten or fifteen years ago. The introduction of the 15-second commercial, which is discussed later in this section, helped encourage the use of short spots.

The use of standard lengths for commercials and announcements also provides a notion of the number of words needed. Nevertheless, only approximate word counts can be indicated for each standard copy length because words vary in length and in the amount of time needed to say them; some ideas are more complex and require a slower speaking rate for the audience to understand and to digest the ideas; some words or phrases require more emphasis through pauses and variations in rate of speaking; the talent may read faster or slower than you would like or had planned; and the kind, length, and number of music and sound effects inserted into the script usually decrease the number of words needed. The use of sustaining visual material, in which no audio element is included, must be calculated carefully when writing television spots.

To provide some assistance, each standard length is identified and an approximate word count and use for each length are suggested.

10-Second Announcement

Twenty-five words. The brevity of a 10-second announcement necessitates capturing immediate attention from the audience, since the announcement must focus on only one sales item or point from the copy rationale. The name of the client, product, or service and one consumer benefit are all that can be used. It is a length used infrequently in broadcast advertising.

15-Second Announcement

Thirty-five words. This is a useful length. It can incorporate one key sales point and one consumer benefit, mention the client's name at least twice, and still squeeze in a slogan or final client benefit.

20-Second Announcement

Forty-five words. This length is used infrequently. When it is used, however, it can incorporate one essential sales point, one or two benefits, and several mentions of the client's identity and it can embellish a slogan or add one final client reminder.

30-Second Announcement

Sixty-five words. The length of a 30-second announcement can accommodate specific details about a company, a product, a service, or an idea and expands the opportunity to present supporting claims and benefits. By a wide margin, this is the most common length used for both radio and television commercials and announcements on networks and local stations. "Split-30s" and "Interrupted-30s" are discussed later in this chapter.

60-Second Announcement

One hundred thirty words. The most elongated of the standard copy lengths, the 60-second announcement can be used to involve the audience longer and to disperse more information about the client/product/service. This length provides you with a broader canvas, allowing full development of the copy rationale, as well as more complete development of the characters, situations, mood, and atmosphere. It is a copy length used about as often as 10-second announcements.

Other commercial and announcement lengths are used for special reasons and under specific circumstances. For example, 5- and 45-second lengths have been created to accommodate special writing and broadcast sales needs, such as announcements used during program billboards or closing credits. Industrywide, however, these cannot be considered standard broadcast copy lengths. Advertising time is purchased in the standard lengths already described.

There is movement within the industry toward commercials and announcements longer than 60 seconds. Programs that have been underwritten by a single sponsor often feature announcements lasting as long as two or three minutes. The growth of cable systems' capacity to provide still more advertising opportunities and the use of commercial underwriting for the production of home video system videotape and videodisc programs should intensify the trend toward longer commercials and announcements. "Infomercials," or program-length commercials, have become a popular option on home shopping channels in cable-equipped areas. An extensive "sell" is given for advertised items.

The manner in which talent and production personnel deliver the commercial or announcement is another important consideration. Develop a versatility in writing that will allow you to prepare effective material for a specific kind of delivery style. This requires you to be flexible and to adapt such language usage components as word choice, sentence length, and syntax to different styles. Although you may indicate in the script the characterization, mood, pace, tempo, and atmosphere that are most appropriate for a particular message, talent and production personnel often exercise discretion when producing the commercial or announcement. Just as a composer's music is subject to varying interpretations when performed, the writer's script may be delivered in any number of styles in an effort to further enhance the message.

In the soft-sell presentation style, the message is delivered in a relaxed, informal manner. The talent's voice projects a soft, intimate relationship with the audience. A television announcement using this style would emphasize close-ups, dissolves, slow motion action, soft focus, more music, and less narration or dialogue. The soft-sell approach stresses personal, human, intimate, and emotional appeals.

The hard-sell style contrasts directly with the soft-sell approach in its strong, direct, no-nonsense, almost overpowering manner of delivering the message. Visually this style is characterized by quick cuts between shots, as well as fast zooms, pans, trucking shots, and attention-grabbing special effects. The pace and tempo are fast. A large amount of information is crammed into a short amount of time. The hard-sell approach invokes immediate action in the audience.

Other Lengths

Styles of Delivery

Soft Sell

Hard Sell

Straight Sell

The moderate pace and tempo of the straight-sell approach place it in the middle ground between soft sell and hard sell. The talent delivers the message in a conversational, yet persuasive style. In a television commercial, the full range of visual possibilities is used. This is the style used routinely in many commercials and announcements.

Avant-Garde/ Fantasy

Avant-garde/fantasy style is characterized by an emphasis on surrealism, sexual innuendo, nuance, and understatement. There is extensive use of sophisticated visual effects, bold colors, unusual camera angles, and often loud rock music. Characters appear emotionally cool, humorless, detached, and on the edge of decadence. The aim is to create an intense, memorable, and startling mood or feeling without a clear delineation of locale or description of circumstances. This delivery style has also been labeled experimental, new wave, high-tech, and new age.

An avant-garde delivery style has been used to enliven clients' stagnant consumer images or to add zest to a product or service category that needs a different look and approach. Commercial clients who have used the avant-garde delivery style on television include those that sell soft drinks, beer, cosmetics, clothing, and some foods. An avant-garde approach is especially effective for spot announcements used on networks or in programs that appeal to an audience with strong contemporary or progressive attitudes and preferences. Spots on Music Television (MTV) and music videos often use an avant-garde approach.

Be aware that using this delivery style presents a danger for the writer. This style often places the client's message behind the elegant, sophisticated, urbanized display of product user life-style. Technique tends to overshadow content and persuasive message. Stay in touch with the copy rationale.

Packaging

Consider carefully the many variables that influence how an announcement is formulated and finally written. These variables include the number of talent featured, the presentational framework or approach used, and the flexibility of the copy makeup selected. Each possibility must be explored completely and ultimately combined with other presentation factors to provide an effective, persuasive, memorable package.

Number of Talent

The three primary kinds of announcements based on the number of talent are single voice, dialogue or interview, and multivoice. Each can be an effective presentation tool. A *single-voice* announcement would be effective when using primarily logical appeals to convince the audience to buy a product or use a service; it allows an opportunity for strong one-to-one communication. *Dialogue* or *interview* announcements would be useful to create a realistic human situation or an imaginary, fantasy situation that highlights the attractiveness of the client's product or service; it permits the development of two distinctive characters who interact in a conversation.

Multivoice presentations can be beneficial if a wide variety of characters and situations are to be used; a clear differentiation between voices and characters is essential to the effectiveness of this presentational format.

Any of these three alternatives can be combined with music or sound effects. For the purposes of classification, however, think in terms of emphasizing the talent and not necessarily the music or sound effects. The same designations can be used to classify television presentational forms. Whether the talent performs live or is recorded on film or videotape, each of these alternatives can be used either on-camera or off-camera in a voice-over.

A *dramatization* can be devised to further refine a dialogue or multivoice presentation. In effect, you create a playlet, a happening or story that creates suspense, develops characters, and reaches a climax. Despite the limitations and restraints of advertising copy lengths, this presentational form can be effective if the standard dramatic structure conventions are used: exposition, conflict, rising action, climax, and resolution or denouement. Often the structure is provided through a narrative approach, using an announcer. Characters and plot must be developed quickly and well. It is one of the most difficult writing challenges because of the complexity of the dramatic structure needed. These spots often are called "slice of life," or vignette, announcements, since small pieces of real-life situations are created using bits of dialogue or action interspersed with direct or indirect information about the advertised product or service. Dramatizations have been used extensively by such commercial clients as Dean Witter, Glad, Hallmark, Kellogg's Cracklin' Oat Bran, and Campbell's.

Presentational Frameworks or Approach

Testimonials are another kind of presentational framework. Celebrities, ordinary consumers, or even the client could be featured. Testimonials must offer the audience someone they can trust, who can testify to the quality and effectiveness of the advertised product or service. Celebrities often are selected for such presentations in hopes of attracting those in the target group identified in the copy rationale. Ordinary consumers can provide testimonials through in-the-store interviews or similar devices. Clients often insist on presenting their own messages, usually with mixed results. The goal is to humanize what is often a cold, impersonal approach. Commercial advertisers who have used testimonials in broadcast advertising include Gatorade, with Michael Jordan; Wendy's, featuring founder Dave Thomas; 9-Lives, with Morris the spokescat; Chrysler, with Lee Iacocca; Remington, with company president Victor Kiam; Jell-O, with Bill Cosby; and Diet Pepsi, with Ray Charles.

Humor can be the basis for an effective advertising message. It can make a message stand out from many others. If the humor does not override the sales message, it can be a useful tool to get and hold attention and provide a memorable message for the audience. Humor tends to lower the audience's defenses, often makes the listener or viewer more tolerant of watching an advertising message, and can create a more positive attitude toward the product, service, or client. To be successful, the humor must reflect current life-styles and events, involve the audience in the characters and situations, and explore the full range of subtle satire, parody, and offbeat but believable humor. When selecting humor as the primary framework, you should determine whether humor is appropriate for this particular client, product, or service; whether humor helps ''sell'' effectively; whether the humor relates to human experiences and appeals to the target audience group; and whether the humor is indeed funny and attractive and enhances the message. Writing humor is very difficult. Writing sharp, incisive, memorable humor for broadcast advertising requires special talent developed only after many years of hard work, experimentation, and critique.

Jingles or *musical announcements* can add dimension and produce startling memorability and consistency in the minds of the audience. The use of music in announcements can evoke strong emotional responses. Even if potential customers do not hear the lyrics, the music can create a positive feeling that will usually transfer to the advertised product or service. Despite the high costs of creating original music, a theme or jingle can tie together a multimedia ad campaign and transfer easily from radio to television.

Although you are not responsible for composing the music, be aware of the various uses of music and how your work can be placed in a musical setting through the creative talents of professional musicians. You can suggest that music be used alone to present the message or with other presentational forms to heighten the central sales message. Musicians can customize their compositions through adjustments in instrumentation, vocal stylings, tempo, length, and lyrics to better match various radio programming formats and to target the message to specific audiences. A great deal of time and money is spent developing jingles or musical commercial announcements that sell an image. In most cases, the effort and expense produce worthwhile results. The commercial advertisers who have used this presentational framework include American Airlines (''We Love to Fly and It Shows''), McDonald's (''You Deserve a Break Today''), Oscar Meyer (''The Wiener Song''), and soft drink accounts, such as Pepsi-Cola and Coca-Cola.

A *demonstration* presentational framework allows the client to illustrate the uses or benefits of a particular product or service. Obviously a demonstration would be effective on television, where the audience can see what takes place. Nevertheless, a creative writer should not discard the use of a demonstration on radio, since the mind of the listener can be tapped by the innovative use of voices, music, and sound effects. The sound of a steak sizzling, a motorcycle roaring off into the distance, and the street noise of an exotic location, such as Hong Kong, all produce vivid, memorable images. If combined creatively with other elements, such sounds can produce an interesting demonstration. Among the commercial advertisers who have used a demonstration as the primary presentational framework are Lenscrafters, Black and Decker, Noxell (Clarion), Memorex, Duracell, Cheer, and Samsonite.

Animation is a presentational form used in several media applications. Whether alone or combined with live action, animation can simplify complex structures and processes, offer characters and situations more readily accepted by the audience, and provide an effective message that lasts over an extended period of time. Despite the high production costs involved, clients who have used animation generally agree that it offers unlimited freedom to communicate visually and that it is worth the cost, time, and patience necessary to produce an effective animated message. Commercial advertisers who have used animation or animation/live action campaigns include Green Giant, Star-Kist, the California Raisin Growers Association, and H. J. Heinz. The *process* used to write and produce animated material is described in chapter 10.

The creative copywriter recognizes the value of the *combination* presentational framework, in which no one method or form dominates; rather, several methods are blended to produce the commercial or announcement. As indicated earlier, the combination format is common. Examples of this combination form include Formby (demonstration, testimonial), Kmart (testimonial, dramatization), Oldsmobile (demonstration, dramatization), Keebler (animation, dramatization, humor), Pillsbury (dramatization, demonstration, animation), Luvs (demonstration, musical jingle), and 7UP (animation, musical jingle).

Clients and advertisers continue to seek ways to use your writing efforts in an efficient, flexible manner. The client usually is pleased when you find ways to devise an announcement or a commercial that offers the opportunity to present an attractive and persuasive message while providing flexibility, eliminating duplicate efforts, and saving money.

Copy Makeup

A *modulized* copy form has been found useful by many clients and advertisers. When a *set* of commercials or announcements is to be written, generate the longest copy length—for instance, 60 or 30 seconds. From that long-form copy, remove segments to produce the shorter lengths needed. This technique can be used in both radio and television applications.

In the *donut* copy form, a standard opening remains the same each time the announcement is used. The middle portion, or hole in the donut, is where the client inserts the special item for sale or a special service feature or bonus. A standard closing, like the opening, stays the same to remind the audience of the client or advertiser. Several variations of the donut copy form are possible: the length of each of the three segments can vary—for instance, :05, :15, :10 or :10, :10, :10; a jingle could be used for the opening or closing segment or both; one talent could be featured in the opening and closing segments while another voice or voices is heard in the hole segment. There are many other possibilities to explore. This is a very popular copy form for co-op messages, in which the national manufacturer provides the first and last segments and the local retail merchant inserts the middle segment to localize the client's message.

The *core* copy form also features three segments. The first and last segments may vary each time the announcement or commercial is constructed. The client can maintain various openings and closings in a library and select the particular segment necessary to give the message a flavor of difference while sustaining a strong identity with the audience. The middle segment forms the core and generally features an important sales point about the client, such as a unique service, an established reputation in the business community, or a special department. This middle segment remains the same when the core copy form is used. Using the core technique, you select from the available opening and closing segments or generate new ones and blend them with the central sales point in the middle segment to produce a smooth, even presentation.

Another possibility is the *open-faced* copy form, which features a standard opening, which is usually longer than the opening segment in the donut and core copy forms, and a variable ending. In this short closing segment, the client tops off the message by emphasizing a different copy point each time—for instance, a special sale, a key service, or a product feature.

A copy form used often in co-op advertising is the *tag,* in which the manufacturer's message is presented and then a short time is allowed for the listing of local dealers or distributors of the advertised products or services. In most cases, the national client or his or her representative insists on approving the local copy to ensure the proper emphasis of national and local advertisers and to provide access to valuable co-op dollars for local use.

Another popular copy form is the *lift,* or *simulcast,* in which the audio portion of a television message is lifted out and used in toto on radio. Many clients insist on this copy makeup to provide a readily available radio message and to enhance the uniformity of their multimedia campaign. Writers must be aware that a lift is anticipated and devise the television copy to permit effective use of this technique. The sound portion of the television message must be strong enough to sustain interest and to deliver a strong, persuasive message when used alone.

Since they were introduced in the mid-1980s, two forms of 30-second spots have posed special challenges for writers and advertising clients alike. *Split-30s* enable advertisers to buy 30 seconds of time and fill it with two spots, each 15 seconds long, for two different or two related products or services. A brief dip to black separates the two spots. There is disagreement about the impact and persuasiveness of such short spots, as well as about how the proliferation of such short messages might aggravate commercial "clutter" and possibly dilute the effectiveness of a series of messages delivered in tandem. *Interrupted-30s* are 30-second spots that are interrupted; a message for another client is heard or seen, and then the first spot concludes. You could write a commercial in which you present a problem—for example, a dirty kitchen floor—and then, after inviting the audience to stay tuned to see the results of using floor cleaner XYZ, wait for another client's short message before presenting the conclusion of your original spot. This copy form is not used often, since there is still some question about its effectiveness and its appropriateness for a variety of clients. Although both copy forms present 30-seconds of material, split-30s advertise multiple products, whereas interrupted-30s advertise the *same* product in *both* sections of the commercial.

An obvious writing hazard when using any of these copy makeup forms is the possibility that the various parts of the finished announcement or commercial will not blend to produce an effective, smooth, persuasive message. Careful planning, skillful writing, attention to detail, high production quality, and intense coordination among those directly involved in the creation and production of such hybrid copy forms will prevent many of the potential problems from developing into insurmountable obstacles. These copy makeup alternatives offer additional options for the client or advertiser, as well as for you as a creative writer.

A number of commercial script and copy strategy examples will help illustrate many of the concepts and techniques already discussed. A diverse selection of products, services, and clients is presented to show the wide range of copy design and form possibilities, as well as the creative strategies incorporated into various kinds of copywriting situations.

Examples of Commercials

Dyfonate

A Saatchi & Saatchi Wegener radio campaign for Dyfonate II 20-G insecticide from ICI Americas uses a combination of humor, storytelling, and side-by-side product comparison to reach corn growers who regularly treat their corn acres for soil insects. A tag provides a clear and specific reminder of the client and the thrust of the message. Figure 4.1 shows the copy rationale for the radio campaign. Figures 4.2 and 4.3 show two commercials from the same campaign.

Hallmark

Leo Burnett Company, Inc., developed a commercial for Hallmark shown during the award-winning dramatic series "Hallmark Hall of Fame." The copy strategy was to communicate that only Hallmark shows you care enough to send the very best. Other guidelines included the use of a simple, straightforward storyline, idealized people and situations, and the decision that the card must be the hero of the spot and pivotal to the situation.

This slice-of-life commercial creates an emotionally strong, deeply involving, and intensely personal situation. These kinds of dramatized situations allow the potential consumer to focus on benefits rather than product features, as emotional difficulties are resolved in a caring, personal manner. This two-minute commercial allows ample time to develop and enrich the characters and heighten the intensity and impact of the situation.

Figures 4.4 through 4.6 trace the evolution of this commercial—from preliminary ideas and concepts in the storyboard originally presented to Hallmark, to the final script of the commercial that aired, to the photoboard showing shots from the commercial seen during "Hallmark Hall of Fame" broadcasts.

ICI Americas Inc.

After two years of campaigns for Dyfonate II 20-G soil insecticide that were based primarily on print (4/color spreads and inserts) and 30 and 60-second television spots, Saatchi & Saatchi Wegener decided to switch emphasis to a media and in which they felt they could gain impact and memorability within certain budget constraints. Since the product category is not "top of mind" among corn farmers, S&SW decided to use humor, which can be attention-getting and memorable without being objectionable. A number of humorous executions were tested on farm audiences before a final decision was made.

1. Target

Growers with at least 100 acres of corn in the 12-state Corn Belt who regularly treat their corn acres for soil insects, mainly corn rootworm.

2. Strategy

Continue to position ICI's Dyfonate II 20-G soil insecticide in relation to the competitive Counter soil insecticide:

a. Control of corn rootworm is equal to Counter.

b. Has significantly less dust than Counter, i.e., less potential hazard to farmers when pouring granular material into their application equipment hoppers and when applying it in the field.

c. Costs less than Counter -- approximately $1.00 per acre less.

Executional format

A down-home, "storytelling" format in which the announcer relates humorous situations which put a unique twist in the thrust against Counter:

"Counter costs a dollar an acre more than Dyfonate II because Counter gives you three times more dust than Dyfonate II, whether you want it or not."

This tongue-in-cheek propositon presents the Dyfonate II positioning in a memorable fashion and permits a wide range of stories and situations.

MULTIMEDIA COPY - CREATIVE DIVISION SS—1056

| | PAGE 1 | OF |

| CLIENT | CLIENT'S APPROVAL | DATE |
| ICI AMERICAS | (AS RECORDED, 9/28/90) | 9/27/90 |

| PRODUCT | |
| Dyfonate II 20-G | YICA-0796 |

PRINT

| JOB NUMBER | SPACE | | SIZE |
| ICIDY-R1105A | | | |

| PUBLICATION | | | INSERTION DATE |
| Radio spot | :60 | "Parsley II" | |

RADIO TELEVISION

| TRAFFIC NUMBER | TYPE |
| | |

| SHOW | | DATE |
| | | |

| SUBJECT |
| |

VOICE: Yesterday morning I stopped at Willard's
          Cafe for breakfast. And when my order came out,
          everything had little sprigs of parsley on it. Willard
          explained that's what they did in high-class eating places.
          Then he gave me the check -- said the prices were up because
          of the parsley, whether I wanted it or not. "Willard,
          where'd you get this crazy idea?," I asked. He said he
          got it from a Counter salesman. "They charge a buck an acre
          extra for dust," he said, "even though no one wants it.
          Counter has <u>three</u> <u>times</u> more dust than Dyfonate II.
          Now, Dyfonate II gives the same rootworm control as
          Counter, same yield. Only difference is Counter has more
          dust." I said I'd skip the dust, save the buck an acre,
          and use Dyfonate II. "By the way," Willard said, "ice tea's
          gone up, too ...it comes with sugar now, whether you want it
          or not." Make the sensible choice -- Dyfonate II from ICI.
          It's a restricted use pesticide. So always follow label
          directions.

Tag: Dyfonate II, the sensible choice.

Figure 4.2

Script for a radio commercial based on the copy rationale shown in figure 4.1.
Courtesy of ICI Americas Inc. and Saatchi & Saatchi Wegener. (C) 1991,
ICI Americas Inc.

MULTIMEDIA COPY - CREATIVE DIVISION SS—1056

	PAGE 1	OF

CLIENT	CLIENT'S APPROVAL	DATE
ICI AMERICAS	(AS RECORDED, 11/16/90)	11/15/90

PRODUCT
Dyfonate II 20-G

JOB NUMBER	SPACE	SIZE
ICIDY-R1105A		

PUBLICATION | | INSERTION DATE
Radio spot | :60 | "Haircut"

TRAFFIC NUMBER	TYPE
	YICA-0876

SHOW		DATE

SUBJECT

VOICE: The world gets goofier by the minute. Just the other day I stopped in at Harley's barber shop, and I noticed he'd raised the price of haircuts a buck. When I asked him how come, Harley explained the extra buck was to cover the cost of a manicure from his wife, Hazel. "Harley," I said, "you're never going to see me with a manicure. What's gotten into you?" He said he got the idea from a Counter salesman. "They charge a buck an acre extra for dust," he said. "Counter has <u>three</u> <u>times</u> as much dust as Dyfonate II, and Dyfonate II gives the same rootworm control." "Harley," I said, "I'll just skip the dust and save the buck with Dyfonate II. And, I'll just skip the haircut, too, if you don't come to your senses." Make the sensible choice ... Dyfonate II from ICI. It's a restricted use pesticide. So always follow label directions.

Tag: Dyfonate II, the sensible choice.

Figure 4.3
Script for a radio commercial based on the copy rationale shown in figure 4.1.
Courtesy of ICI Americas Inc. and Saatchi & Saatchi Wegener. (C) 1991,
ICI Americas Inc.

Figure 4.4
Storyboard originally
presented to Hallmark
Cards, Inc., by Leo
Burnett representatives
when the commercial
entitled "Mrs. LaGow's
Gift" was being
developed.
*Used by permission of
Hallmark Cards, Inc. and
Leo Burnett Company,
Inc.*

Figure 4.4 (*continued*)

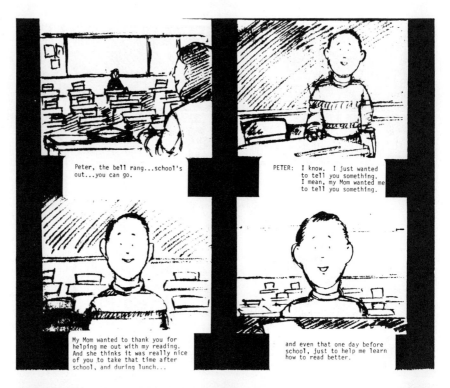

Figure 4.4 (*continued*)

 **LEO BURNETT U.S.A.**

35 WEST WACKER DRIVE, CHICAGO, ILLINOIS 60601
(312) 220-5959

HALLMARK CARDS INC.
2 Minute. Film
"MRS. LA GOW'S GIFT"
CHRISTMAS HALL OF FAME
HMHF1379

As Filmed and Recorded: 12/03/90 sjm

Job #: P15932

VIDEO	AUDIO
1 QUIET THIRD-GRADE CLASSROOM ON THE DAY BEFORE CHRISTMAS BREAK, SECONDS BEFORE THE BELL RINGS. SUPER: "MRS. LAGOW'S GIFT".	
2 KIDS RUN OUT OF ROOM AS BELL RINGS. TEACHER WAVES GOOD-BYE TO THEM.	TEACHER: Okay everyone. Now, I want you all to have a really good Christmas vacation. Have lots of fun. But don't forget everything we've learned so far this year because when we get back...
	SFX: (BELL RINGS)
	TEACHER: ...we're going to start on long division. Everybody have a good Christmas, I'll see you in a couple weeks.
3 CLOSER SHOT OF KIDS FILING OUT OF ROOM PAST THE TEACHER. TEACHER TALKS TO KIDS AS THEY LEAVE.	Merry Christmas. Do your homework.
	SFX: (KID LAUGHS)
	TEACHER: Merry Christmas. Bye-bye. Have a good break.
4 TEACHER GOES INTO HALL. WAVES GOODBYE TO KIDS.	See you in a couple weeks. Bye-bye. Merry Christmas.
5 TEACHER GOES TO HER DESK TO GATHER UP THINGS SO SHE CAN LEAVE.	MUSIC: (MUSIC)

Figure 4.5
Script for the finished television commercial "Mrs. LaGow's Gift," developed from the storyboard shown in figure 4.4.
Used by permission of Hallmark Cards, Inc. and Leo Burnett Company, Inc.

HALLMARK CARDS INC.
90-Second Film
"MRS. LA GOW'S GIFT"
CHRISTMAS HALL OF FAME
HMHF1379

As Filmed and Recorded: 12/03/90 sjm

Job #: P15932

VIDEO	AUDIO

6   SHE SUDDENLY LOOKS UP, AS IF SHE SENSES SOMEONE ELSE IS IN THE ROOM WITH HER.

TEACHER: Peter?

7   CUT TO A REVERSE ANGLE, WITH THE TEACHER LOOKING TO THE BACK OF THE ROOM, WHERE ONE LONE STUDENT IS SITTING AT HIS DESK.

Peter, the bell rang...

school's out... you can go.

8   STUDENT GETS UP SLOWLY AS HE BEGINS TALKING. HE APPEARS A BIT NERVOUS.

PETER: I know. I just wanted to tell you something. I mean, my Mom wanted me to tell you something. My Mom wanted to thank you for

9   MOVE IN A BIT CLOSER ON HIM AS HE BEGINS TO WALK TO THE FRONT OF THE ROOM.

helping me out with my reading. Because she thinks it was really nice of you to take all that time after school,

10   NOW HE HAS REACHED THE FRONT OF THE ROOM AND IS STANDING RIGHT IN FRONT OF HER.

and during lunch...and even that one day before school, just to help me learn how to read better.

11   CLOSE-UP OF TEACHER AS SHE TRIES TO INTERRUPT HIM, AS IF TO SAY IT'S NOT NECESSARY.

12   SHOT OF STUDENT AGAIN, AS HE CONTINUES.

Because if you hadn't spent all that extra time with me, I probably wouldn't be able to read much of anything. And...my Mom just wanted me to thank you.

Figure 4.5 (*continued*)

 **LEO BURNETT U.S.A.**

35 WEST WACKER DRIVE, CHICAGO, ILLINOIS 60601
(312) 220-5959

HALLMARK CARDS INC.
90-Second Film
"MRS. LA GOW'S GIFT"
CHRISTMAS HALL OF FAME
HMHF1379

As Filmed and Recorded: 12/03/90 sjm

Job #: P15932

<u>VIDEO</u>   <u>AUDIO</u>

13 CLOSE-UP OF TEACHER, AS SHE   TEACHER: Well, Peter...
    THANKS HIM.

14 BACK TO SHOT OF STUDENT.

15 HE PULLS OUT AN ENVELOPE WITH   PETER: and this is from me.
    HER NAME WRITTEN ON IT.

16 CLOSE-UP OF BACK OF ENVELOPE   Merry Christmas, Mrs. LaGow.
    WITH EMBOSSED HALLMARK LOGO.

17 TEACHER LOOKS AT THE CARD   TEACHER: Thank you.
    IN ENVELOPE AND IS GENUINELY
    TOUCHED THAT HE WENT TO SUCH
    TROUBLE.

18 HE SAYS ONE LAST THING TO HER   PETER: You're welcome.
    AND STARTS TO WALK AWAY.

19 SUDDENLY, HE STOPS IN HIS   Mrs. LaGow? Want me to read it
    TRACKS, LOOKS BACK AT HER AND
    FINALLY SAYS WHAT HE'S BEEN   for you?
    WANTING TO SAY ALL ALONG.

20 THE TEACHER WARMLY ACCEPTS HIS   TEACHER: I'd like that.
    OFFER.
                                                  I'd like that very much.

21 THE STUDENT COMES AROUND TO HER   PETER: (READING CARD) "There are some
    SIDE OF THE DESK AND BEGINS TO
    READ THE CARD TO HER.   special people, we meet along

                                             life's way, who make our

                                             journey..."

22 WIDE SHOT OF THE TWO OF THEM ALL   MUSIC: (MUSIC UP AND OUT)
    ALONE IN THE CLASSROOM, WITH HIM
    READING THE CARD TO HER.

Figure 4.5 (*continued*)

1. MRS. LAGOW: OK everyone, now I want you all to have a really good Christmas vacation.

2. Have lots of fun...

3. but...uh, don't forget everything we've learned so far this year...

4. 'cause when we get back... (SFX: BELL)

5. MRS. LAGOW: we're going to start on long division.

6. Everybody have a good Christmas. I'll see you in a couple of weeks.

7. (SFX: KIDS RUNNING AND TALKING)

8. MRS. LAGOW: Merry Christmas ...do your homework.

9. Merry Christmas...bye-bye.

10. Merry Christmas...bye-bye.

11. ...

12. ...

13. (MUSIC: UNDER THROUGHOUT) MRS. LAGOW: Peter, the bell rang...school's out...you can go.

14. PETER: I know. I just wanted to tell you something. I mean, my Mom...wanted me to tell you something.

15. My Mom wanted to thank you for helping me out with my reading, because she thinks...

Figure 4.6
Photoboard made from the finished television commercial entitled "Mrs. LaGow's Gift."

Used by permission of Hallmark Cards, Inc. and Leo Burnett Company, Inc.

Figure 4.6 (*continued*)

16. it was really nice of you to take all that time after school...

17. and during lunch...and even that one day before school, just to help me learn how to read better.

18. Because if you hadn't spent all that extra time with me...

19. I probably wouldn't be able to read much of anything. And my Mom just wanted me to thank you...

20. MRS. LAGOW: Peter...

21. PETER: and this is from me.

22. Merry Christmas, Mrs. Lagow.

23. ...

24. ...

25. MRS. LAGOW: Thank you. PETER: You're welcome.

26. Mrs. Lagow?

27. Want me to read it for you?

28. MRS. LAGOW: I'd like that. I'd like that very much.

29. ...

30. PETER: (READING CARD) "There are some special people, we meet along life's way..."

BACKGROUND

The United Airlines' commercial "Speech" was developed in 1989 and aired for the first time in September of that year. The commercial was part of the third pool of advertising developed since 1987 with a focus on business travel.

TARGET

The "Speech" commercial was developed to appeal to frequent business flyers (35-54, skewed male, HHI — $50M+, 6+ trips per year).

STRATEGY

The strategic direction behind the development of the "Speech" spot was to convince flyers that United understands the importance of personal service in maintaining customer loyalty while continuing to build on the friendly skies heritage. Thus, the strategy was:

> Convince frequent business flyers that United is the best airline because United is attentive to the needs of business flyers.

EXECUTIVE FORMAT

The execution is consistent with the current documentary style format used in the United business flyer campaign. It depicts United's understanding of the realities of the business world and is set to United's theme song, Gershwin's "Rhapsody In Blue."

The commercial has been praised by both business people and artisans for its creative insight. The relevance and impact of the message to the business community is evidenced by the hundreds of requests United has received for copies to be used as a motivating tool at sales force meetings and a general morale booster at corporate events.

Figure 4.7
Copy rationale and background information for the United Airlines commercial "Speech." *Reprinted with permission of United Airlines and Leo Burnett Company, Inc.*

Leo Burnett Company, Inc., developed a commercial for United Airlines entitled ''Speech.'' As the background information in figure 4.7 indicates, this commercial was part of the third pool, or group, of advertising messages developed since the late 1980s with a focus on business travel. Notice that the central selling point or strategy is succinct and well structured and that this strategy helps build on the friendly skies heritage of United Airlines.

United Airlines

Figure 4.8 shows the script generated from the strategy statement. Notice how the documentary-style dramatization copy framework helps reinforce the point that United Airlines understands the realities of the business world. The intended message of the commercial is clear: successful businesspeople need to travel to many locations, and United flies to many locations.

H&R Block

In a commercial, Bernstein Rein used two kinds of testimonial statements to reach consumers who prepare their own tax returns. To reassure those who may doubt H&R Block's ability to prepare all tax returns thoroughly and professionally, Bernstein Rein used actual H&R Block tax preparers to address possible concerns directly. The commercial concludes with Henry Block surrounded by the preparers, forming ''America's Tax Team'' (see figure 4.9). Notice how specific characteristics of the target audience are identified in the script shown in figure 4.10. This helps ensure that the specific segments of the target audience identify with those presenting the testimonials and that the sense of confidence about H&R Block's ability to handle any type of tax return is firmly established.

Examples of Public Service Announcements

Public service announcements are similar to commercials in approach and technique, but PSAs are produced and aired on behalf of nonprofit groups or activities and may advocate an idea, a viewpoint, or a policy endorsed by those groups or activities. Despite these essential differences, it is still important to approach the development of PSAs with the same vigor and creative spirit used for commercial clients. It is important to base *all* advertising campaigns, commercial and nonprofit, on a foundation of research and the identification of a target audience with a specific objective in mind.

Drunk Driving Campaigns

Many national and local public service campaigns have been mounted to try to curtail the death, injury, and destruction caused by drunk drivers. Two creative approaches are presented here.

WOW Radio in Omaha, Nebraska, produced a series of PSAs using performers who worked from a scenario or an outline, rather than a finished script. In effect, they created the spot on tape as music and sound effects were added, along with an announcer's voice, to conclude the spot with the key point. (see figure 4.11.) This approach illustrates the influence that a *blend* of creative writing and production techniques can have on the final version of the produced announcement.

A unique copy style was used by CKIQ, Kelowna, British Columbia, Canada, for a year-long safe-driving community involvement campaign. If one accepts the premise that the audience often becomes immune to scare tactics used in such announcements, then CKIQ's unique approach of a macabre parody of a game show is understandable. A strong, fast-paced delivery coupled with the grim realities reflected in the copy helped break

35 WEST WACKER DRIVE, CHICAGO, ILLINOIS 60601
(312) 220-5959

UNITED AIRLINES
60-Second Film
"SPEECH"
PASSENGER SERVICE
UAPF0606

As Recorded: 10/04/89 mct

Job #: P15777

VIDEO	AUDIO
1 OPEN ON EXTERIOR OF MANUFACTURING PLANT.	BEN: I got a phone call this morning.
2 MOVE IN AND BEGIN TO SEE CROWDED CONFERENCE ROOM IN PLANT.	From one of our oldest customers. He fired us.
3 CUT INSIDE FOR SALESMAN'S REACTION.	After twenty years. He fired us.
4 VIEW OF INSIDE BUSY PLANT WITH CONFERENCE ROOM IN BKGD.	Said he didn't know us anymore.
5 CUT TO CONFERENCE ROOM FILLED WITH NEARLY TWO HUNDRED PEOPLE. CHAIRMAN IS AT FRONT, BUT INFORMAL.	I think I know why. We used to do business with a handshake-- face to face.
6 CATCH ONE SALESMAN AS HE REACTS TIGHT SHOTS OF CHAIRMAN, STAFF, ROOM, ETC. WITH REACTIONS.	Now it's a phone call and a fax, and we'll get back to you later.
7 CHAIRMAN LOOKS OUT WINDOW AND REFLECTS.	With another fax, probably.
8 TIGHT SHOT OF CHAIRMAN.	Well, folks,
9 WE SEE SOME PEOPLE IN THE CROWD AND REACT TO WHAT THE CHAIRMAN IS SAYING. THEY'RE NOT INCREDULOUS BUT SOMEWHAT CURIOUS. ESPECIALLY, SINCE THE BOSSES' SECRETARY ENTERS A COVERED BOX AND WALKS THROUGH THE CROWD PLACES THE BOX NEXT TO HIM.	Somethings gotta change. That's why we're going to set out for a little face to face chat with every customer we have.
10 CUT TO SENIOR EXPERIENCED EXECUTIVE WITH A QUESTION.	SR. EXEC.: But Ben, that's gotta be over two hundred cities.

Figure 4.8
Script for the United Airlines commercial "Speech."
Reprinted with permission of United Airlines and Leo Burnett Company, Inc.

UNITED AIRLINES
60-Second Film
"SPEECH"
PASSENGER SERVICE
UAPF0606

As Recorded: 10/04/89 mct

Job #: P15777

VIDEO	AUDIO
11 LIFTS COVER OFF BOX TO REVEAL TWO HUNDRED AND TWENTY UNITED TICKETS.	BEN: I don't care.
12 AND HE BEGINS TO CALL EACH NAME OUT ONE BY ONE.	Edwards...Ryan...(UNDER) Nicholas...
13 WE SEE PEOPLE RECEIVING TICKETS, COMPARING, REACTING ETC.	ANNCR: If you're the kind of business that still believes personal service deserves a lot more than lip service...
14 BOSS HAS AN ASIDE TO ONE OF HIS SALESMEN.	BEN: (UNDER TO SALESMAN) Give Joe my best.
15 TWO GUYS GET TICKETS.	ANNCR: ...welcome to United. That's the way we've been doing business for over sixty years.
16 LAST TICKET IS TAKEN.	
17 BOSS LOOKS AT NAME...AND PUTS IT IN HIS OWN BACK POCKET AND SOMEONE FROM THE CROWD ASKS A QUESTION.	BEN: Willis. GUY: Ben, where you going? BEN: To visit that old friend who fired us this morning.
18 CUT TO AIR-TO-AIR.	ANNCR: United. Come fly the friendly skies.

Figure 4.8 (*continued*)

B E R N S T E I N   R E I N

Figure 4.9
Copy rationale for the
"Preparer Testimonial"
campaign.
*Courtesy of H&R Block
and Bernstein Rein.*

H&R BLOCK: **"AMERICA'S TAX TEAM"**

The "Preparer Testimonial" campaign was developed to address the concerns of the target customer.

Approximately 50% of all income tax returns prepared in the United States are self-prepared. When changes occur in the self-preparer's tax situation, they become the core target for H&R Block. Research with these potential customers indicated a skepticism about the "professionalism" and training of the average H&R Block tax preparer.

The H&R Block Income Tax School is possibly the most intense tax training course available. Each student is required to commit 70 plus hours of in-class and at-home study. The target customer was not aware of this level of training and qualifications.

Actual H&R Block tax preparers were selected throughout the country to be in the commercials. Each commercial was created to address specific target concerns of training, finding all deductions, getting the biggest refund, and standing behind their work.

1. <u>TARGET</u>

    A. Self-Preparer

        • Changes in tax situation
        • Skeptical of Block professionalism

2. <u>STRATEGY</u>

    Reassure the target of H&R Block's ability to thoroughly and professionally prepare a tax return, no matter how complicated or unique.

3. <u>EXECUTIONAL FORMAT</u>

    On-camera tax preparers discussing:

    - Training
    - Finding every deduction
    - Getting biggest refund
    - Stand behind our work

    Closed with Henry Block surrounded by actual preparers as "America's Tax Team."

4600 Madison / Kansas City, MO 64112 / (816) 756-0640 / Fax (816) 756-1753

MAN (WHITE HAIRED) SUPER: Robert Spradling Charleston, WV	MAN #1:	H&R BLOCK is prepared to take care of anyone's taxes.
MAN (MOUSTACHE,BEARD) SUPER: Vic Vandegriff Santa Fe, NM	MAN #2:	We have to know the changes. We have to know the forms. That's our business.
AMERICA'S TAX TEAM GRAPHIC	ANNCR: (VO)	America's Tax Team is ready for you right now.
HENRY BLOCK	HENRY: (OC)	We're prepared for all kinds of tax situations. From the simplest to the most complex.
BLACK WOMAN SUPER: Chris Jones Marietta, GA	WOMAN #1:	No matter how complex your tax return is, H&R BLOCK can handle your return.
WHITE WOMAN SUPER: Marjorie Hubny Millersville, PA	WOMAN #2:	It's satisfaction guaranteed.
SUPER: (H&R BLOCK LOGO)	ANNCR: (VO)	No wonder more people choose H&R BLOCK to get their tax return done right.
HENRY BLOCK WITH GROUP. AMERICA'S TAX TEAM GRAPHIC.	HENRY: (OC)	We're America's Tax Team. Put us to work for you.

4600 Madison / Kansas City, MO 64112 / (816) 756-0640 / Fax (816) 756-1753

Figure 4.10
Script for a television commercial in the "Preparer Testimonial" campaign based on the copy rationale shown in figure 4.9.
Courtesy of H&R Block and Bernstein Rein.

DRUNK DRIVERS KILL

30 seconds

WOW Radio   10/8

Figure 4.11
Transcript of a radio
public service
announcement on
traffic safety written
and produced by Shel
Fredericks, WOW
Radio, Omaha,
Nebraska.

(SFX:	CRACKLE OF VOICES ON POLICE RADIO)
(SFX:	TWO TELEPHONE RINGS BLENDED WITH POLICE RADIO SOUNDS...UP BRIEFLY AND THEN FADE UNDER)
MOTHER:	Hello...
MAN:	Mom?!
MOTHER:	Frank?! We've been worried sick! We expected you hours ago.
MAN:	Mom...Ther...there's been an accident.
MOTHER:	Are Shirley and the kids alright? (PAUSE FOR AT LEAST ONE FULL BEAT)
MAN:	Oh Mom!!!! (BEGINS SOBBING...KEEP UNDER)
MUSIC: GRINDING MUSICAL PHRASE, UP BRIEFLY AND THEN UNDER	
ANNCR.:	Drunk drivers kill!

[OPTIONAL TAG]

through audience apathy to produce a startling, memorable effect on listeners. The script, shown in figure 4.12, is an excellent example of humor used effectively to communicate a serious message. ''The Drinking Game'' announcement has received national and international awards from broadcast promotion organizations, the Canada Safety Council, the Hollywood Television and Radio Society, and the Radio Bureau of Canada. This PSA also received a CLIO award for public service.

American Physical Therapy Association

Over 80 percent of all individuals will suffer from back pain at some point in their lives. To emphasize the importance of a healthy life-style, the American Physical Therapy Association produced a 30- and a 10-second version of its public service announcement entitled ''Every Body That Moves.'' You should be able to visualize how the 10-second version of this PSA would be formed from the 30-second photoboard shown in figure 4.13. This is an example of the modulized copy makeup form described earlier in this chapter.

Notice the effective use of voice-over narration and close-up shots to convey the essential message. Notice, too, the use of a female artist as the principal on-camera talent to emphasize the importance of caring about every part of *every* body, male or female.

Broadcast Promotion

The promotion department at a station, network, or programming channel is involved in many kinds of activities, such as sales promotion, audience promotions and contests, the development of visual and aural logos, print ads and publicity, and special community projects. This section will examine on-air audience promotion and outdoor/transit advertising efforts, since they are the promotion activities that most directly involve creative writing.

The concepts, principles, and techniques already described for commercials and public service announcements apply equally to promotional efforts. There is a striking similarity between the creative process used to produce effective and memorable promotional messages and the process already outlined for producing commercials and PSAs.

Concepts of On-Air Promotion

On-air promotion is the broadcast station or network use of its own air time to create or enhance a specific image or profile for the broadcast facility among audience members, to inform and attract audiences for programming, and to develop audience awareness of the station or network's public service and community involvement.

The primary goal of on-air promotion efforts is to build audiences. This is best accomplished by formulating a strong individual image for the station or network, similar to the positioning statement recommended in copy rationale development for commercial clients, and then by projecting this image prominently and consistently in all on-air and related multimedia promotional efforts. This includes corporate identification items, stationery, order forms, billing forms, equipment, and vehicles. Often this image is capsulized in a graphic look, or logo. Once the station or network image or personality has become established in the minds of the audience, it is

JOHNNY:	It's time once again for..."The Drinking Game." Now, here's your toastmaster, Al Call!
AL:	Welcome to the Drinking Game. As you might remember, our contestant, Mr. Weaver, now has two impaired driving charges for a total of 20 big points! All he needs is another impairment, and he'll have another 10 points, a minimum three-month suspension and Johnny, tell him what else Mr. Weaver might get:
JOHNNY:	It's a jail sentence!
SFX:	CROWD CHEERS
AL:	Alright, get ready to spin your wheels Mr. Weaver, and good luck! Remember, you can stop drinking at any time. If you drink too much, you could hear one of these sounds:
SFX:	SIREN, CAR CRASH
AL:	And if you do, here's what you'll get:
JOHNNY:	It's a smashed up car!
SFX:	AUDIENCE CHEERS
JOHNNY:	But that's not all! You'll be driven in air conditioned comfort via ambulance for an extended stay in the Kelowna General Hospital!
SFX:	AUDIENCE CHEERS
JOHNNY:	Excellent accommodation and relaxation. Remember, KGH is hospitality at its best!
SFX:	AUDIENCE CHEERS ENDING WITH ECHO
STRAIGHT:	Every day, people play "The Drinking Game." They drink, and they drive...risking points, loss of driving privileges, fines, a jail sentence, or even injury or death. Don't play the Drinking Game, because when you do: You Bet Your Life.

Figure 4.12
Script for the radio public service announcement entitled "The Drinking Game."
Courtesy of Dale Baglo Broadcast Inc., Victoria, B.C., Canada.

American Physical Therapy Association

PSA :30 "EVERY BODY THAT MOVES"
(:10 ALSO AVAILABLE)

AUDIO: Even the most perfect bodies in the world don't just happen.

They're the result of hard work and careful planning.

Because even the most perfect bodies . . .

are subject to stress, fatigue, debilitation and over exertion.

So every body in the world . . .

needs a little help now and then. Even the healthy and the young.

A comprehensive approach to physical care is important.

For every body that moves.

A public service health message from the American Physical Therapy Association.

Figure 4.13
Photoboard for the finished television public service announcement entitled "Every Body That Moves."
Courtesy of the American Physical Therapy Association.

possible to accomplish other goals of on-air promotion—building audiences for programs and developing awareness and participation in a station's public service and community involvement projects.

Several companies provide customized versions of nationally distributed musical jingle and image packages. A station can create its own image package and have appropriate IDs and music beds and a logo designed to provide promotional consistency. A station or network image must be distinctive and indicative of a specific position in the market. This will help you focus each promotional announcement that you write. Often network-affiliated stations incorporate the network's image package into their own promotional efforts. This technique reinforces a strong network image and customizes the promotional message for local station use.

On-air promotion can be combined with other marketing strategies—for example, networks have found it valuable to team up with major retailers to promote new shows, especially in the fall. A network can provide on-air advertising space to link the network and the retail outlet in the audience's minds and promote the retailer's merchandise. The retail outlet can use contest entry blanks and in-store displays to promote the new network shows. Promotional tours of college campuses, malls, and comedy clubs have also been used to attract the elusive college audience, with in-person appearances by network stars from daytime game shows and dramas, primetime shows, and sports shows. Syndicators have also used this kind of retail/marketing tie-in to promote their line-ups of syndicated series.

Types and Techniques of On-Air Promotion

On-air promotion techniques are generally used for one of three types of messages: station identifications, program promos, and personality promos.

Station Identification, or ID

Station identifications are required of every radio and television station. Legally the ID must consist of the station's call letters and city of license or location; however, these mandatory IDs provide an excellent on-air promotion opportunity.

Station image or position can be reinforced by adding to the required station ID information a short promotional statement from a station personality or celebrity, a slogan, a short musical jingle, or a logo, for example:

```
ANNCR: This is Radio 90, W-A-A-H, Central City...
       your country music station since 1965!
```

or

```
VTR EXCERPT
W/LOGO/     NET.NEWSCASTER: Watch Channel 8 news
                              tonight at 11.

ID KEY-IN
```

Be sure to include the radio frequency or television channel number in the station ID. Broadcast audiences will remember "F-M 102," "Radio 14," or "Channel 2" more easily than station call letters.

**Program and
Personality
Promos**

Using the consistent image described earlier, promotion personnel can create promos for specific programs or program series, as well as personalities and celebrities featured in those programs. By using a station's umbrella image or by developing subthemes based on this image profile, on-air promos can be created to generate interest and to encourage audience acceptance of certain programs and personalities.

Promos could be developed for local programs produced by the station or for programs supplied by networks or syndicators. Any type of program can be featured: newscasts, news specials, talk shows, live sports broadcasts, special events, music programs, children's shows, movies, and network program series.

Program promos may be either generic or episodic. Generic promos are constructed for long-term use and to establish a program's image. Episodic promos tell the viewer or listener specific information about an upcoming episode or program in a series. Both types of program promos can be used effectively, although many prefer the episodic promo, since a clear benefit derived from the program can be emphasized. Just as in writing commercials, remember to analyze the program and target audience and then construct the message to provide an obvious benefit for the potential audience.

Personality promos can help establish station image and enhance the audience's attitude toward a specific on-air talent. This type of promo is used extensively to feature one or more members of a station's news staff and to highlight their strengths, summarize their achievements, and, generally, humanize their on-air presentation. Actors, performers, and celebrities also could be featured in personality or testimonial promos, which encourage the audience to watch for these individuals in an upcoming program or to recognize that a certain program or station effort has been endorsed by someone who is trusted and respected.

Choose from several *writing and production options* to construct effective promotional announcements. Practically all the commercial copy presentational formats described and illustrated earlier in this chapter can be used. In addition, audience and celebrity testimonials could be featured in promos. Voice-overs—in which promotional copy is read over program credits, film, or videotape—are used extensively in television on-air promotion. Program excerpts or segments can be edited together to help convey the excitement, action, and value of the program. Many of the writing and production techniques described earlier for commercials can be used to create a polished broadcast promotional announcement.

No matter what type of program or individual personality is featured in a broadcast promotional announcement, no matter which writing or production techniques are used, it is important that the information be presented clearly and directly, that the listener or viewer be given a good reason to tune in (benefit), and that where (channel or dial position) and when (day and hour) to tune in is stressed, especially at the end of the promo. As indicated earlier, the promotional copywriter's goal is basically the same as that of the commercial copywriter. In broadcast promotional copy, the writer can focus consistently on one client—the station or network. The conceptualization, development, writing and production techniques, and strategies follow similar paths for commercials, public service announcements, and promos.

WHYI FM's "Feel Like a Hundred" promotional campaign created a humorous framework in which to emphasize dial position (Y-100) and music format and to establish an identifiable, memorable campaign theme with multiple applications for the target audience. In the photoboard from one of the television spots in the campaign (figure 4.14), notice the continual emphasis on dial position in the words: in frame three, with the car radio set on 100; and in the final frame, in which Y-100's bold, distinctive, locally identifiable logo is displayed. Notice, too, the use of humorous situations punctuated by song lyrics heard on the station to highlight Y-100's program format. The repetitive copy line

```
...feel like a hundred -- Y-100
```

pounds home the theme and benefit for viewers and potential Y-100 listeners.

Although not electronic media writing, outdoor billboards and mass transit displays on cabs, trains, busses, and so on are used regularly in conjunction with on-air audience promotion efforts. When combined with other advertising media, outdoor and transit advertising can establish and reenforce the central theme of a multimedia promotional campaign.

KNX NEWSRADIO in Los Angeles, a CBS-owned and -operated station focusing on news/talk formats, produced a billboard to promote its coverage of University of Southern California (USC) football. Fred Bergendorff, Director of Advertising & Promotion at KNX, described how the billboard ad was developed:

> KNX carries USC football. We were looking for a special way of calling attention to that fact. In investigating possible paint bulletin [billboard] locations in this market, we decided, due to our limited budget, that we would order three boards during the Sept.–Nov. football season and place them near the L. A. Coliseum. Not only does USC play there but the NFL Raiders as well. We also discovered that between the two teams there were eighteen home games. The average home game attendance is over 50,000. So, over the course of the season our boards would be in a position to be seen by some 900,000 football fans, exactly our target audience.
>
> To get people to notice we decided to do something very different design-wise. We hired an expert paper sculptor who does work for many of the Fortune 500 companies. We took his beautiful eye-catching design and had it carefully photographed. Then we hired the best mural artists available to paint the board to look just like it was a three-dimensional paper sculpture. The results turned out to be striking and many people called us to say how much they liked the outdoor style we chose.[1]

Figure 4.14
Photoboard from one
of the television spots
in Y-100's "Feel
Like a Hundred"
promotional campaign.
*Courtesy of WHYI FM,
Y-100, Miami.*

Miami · Ft. Lauderdale

(Car tires screeching)

"It's not easy being a driving instructor."

"That's why I feel like a hundred – Y-100."

(Music: "Driving My Life Away")

"Things are tough all over."

"That's why more people all over..."

"...feel like a hundred - Y-100..."

"...Than any other station in Florida."

"It's not easy being a world famous brain
surgeon."

"Ooooooooops"

"That's why I feel like a hundred - Y-100."

"You feel like a million when you feel
like a hundred - Y-100." (Music: "Another
One Bites The Dust")

Figure 4.15
KNX NEWSRADIO billboard promoting USC football coverage.
Courtesy of KNX NEWSRADIO, Los Angeles.

Figure 4.15 shows the KNX billboard, which won a major design award from the Broadcast Promotion & Marketing Executives (BPME) organization.

The goal of an advertising copywriter is to create for a client, product, or service a positive, persuasive, and memorable commercial or announcement that effectively reaches a consumer target group with a central sales message. This is a challenging goal, but it is attainable. The following copywriting suggestions capsulize some of the concepts and techniques discussed in this chapter.

Copywriting Suggestions

a. *Keep the commercial or announcement in good taste.* Display your standards of creative professionalism and respect your audience. Let the goodwill of your client, product, or service come through in the copy you write. Avoid obvious exaggerations—unnecessary superlatives, false claims, and phone testimonials.

General Suggestions

b. *Know the facts.* Know your client. Get the background information necessary to write in a believable, accurate manner. Remember all the key elements from the copy rationale.

c. *Be as specific as possible when relaying information on prices, products, and services.* Your specificity should be tempered by the overriding need to be clear but also interesting, effective, and persuasive.

d. If known in advance, *adjust the style and content of the copy to the time of day and circumstances under which the announcement or commercial will be broadcast.* If appropriate, customize the copy to various program formats and uses.

e. *Stress benefits.* Tell listeners or viewers what is in it for them. Indicate why it is important to respond quickly to the commercial or announcement.

f. *Get and hold attention.* Know and use various writing techniques to get the message into the audience's consciousness. Build curiosity and suspense.

g. *Prepare a battle plan.* Know your objectives. Scrutinize the alternatives. Select the route carefully.

h. *Use slogans and catchwords effectively.* Often these capsulize the central sales message.

i. *Use the right appeal.* Understand the emotions and life-style of the target group. Understand buyer motivation and audience self-perception. Select and use the right blend of logical and emotional appeals.

j. *Use humor cautiously.* Make it work for the client, product, or service. Discard humor if it is inappropriate or less effective than other methods of presentation. Humor can noticeably improve the effectiveness of a spot announcement if the humor is consistent with and reinforces the central message. The humor must be an integral part of the announcement rather than an afterthought.

k. *Know the rules.* Know what is expected of you by the client, the audience, and the law. Be aware of the parameters. Recognize the circumstances in which creative experimentation will be stifled and those in which rules can be broken and creative energies released unimpeded.

l. *Work toward realistic creativity.* Expand your creative horizons. Become sensitive to as many creative options as possible, but know your limits. Know what is possible to accomplish and what will be acceptable to your employer, to the client, and to the audience. Temper your creative urges and talents with the realism of the competitive advertising environment.

m. *Make each message distinguishable.* Establish an identity with each commercial or announcement. Maintain a similar style, tone, theme, and personality among commercials or announcements for the same client. Use the same logo or identification symbol. Use easily recognizable production techniques, such as music, voices, sounds, camera shots.

n. *Polish until it shines.* Read your copy aloud. Check every nuance. Make every word, every image work for you. Rewind and play back your copy in your mind's eye until there is no room for improvement. Put yourself in the place of the listener or viewer. Calculate the effect of each part of each message. Make each commercial or announcement reflect your best personal and professional effort.

a. *Use only one principal selling idea in each spot announcement.* Make the point clear and unforgettable. Although the copy rationale statement may generate many viable selling points, focus the audience's attention on only one central idea in each message; otherwise, the audience's focus will be scattered, and this will produce mixed results.

Copy Design Suggestions

b. *Sell early and often.* Use every second to promote and enhance your client's central message. The first few seconds are especially crucial in gaining and holding the audience's attention. Make every part of the copy move the message statement forward. Do not bury essential information or lead off with trivia that stops the apparent forward motion of the copy.

c. *Emphasize the client, product, or service.* Make it the star of the message. Keep the spotlight where it belongs. Repeat the product, service, or client name often.

d. *Create an affordable, attractive need in the audience's mind.* Make the audience want to buy the product or use the service. Make the need urgent.

e. *Put the audience in the picture.* Make the product or service relate to the audience's life-style and current needs by carefully choosing settings, moods, atmospheres, words, music, and sound effects. Show tangible consumer benefits. Involve the listener or viewer.

f. *Use production elements creatively and effectively.* Be aware of the immense power and flexibility offered by music, sound effects, voices, pictures, movement, and color. Know the reason each production element is used and the effect each will have when combined with other script and production elements.

g. *Keep in touch with the copy rationale.* It is your blueprint. Design and construct your copy on the basis of the copy rationale.

h. *Monitor the structure of the spot announcement.* Like any narrative, your copy needs an obvious beginning, middle, and end. Your message should progress logically, clearly, and naturally from the opening sound or picture to the closing slogan or logo.

i. *Make your message attractive, clear, persuasive, and memorable.* Your copy must get and hold the attention of the target audience in the media environment in which it appears. The message must be clear and strong enough to become fastened in the target audience's memories until they perform the desired action or make the desired response.

j. *End the message with energy.* Build to a climax. Summarize the central sales point. Call for action or a change in attitude.

Language Use Suggestions

a. *Talk the audience's language.* Write for the ear, even when preparing television messages. Always write in a conversational manner. Use contractions and sentence fragments when appropriate. Choose words that express ideas clearly and directly.

b. *Use positive action words.* Stress urgency and immediacy. Use active verbs, adjectives, and adverbs. Paint pictures with words. Avoid hackneyed phrases that occupy space but do not enrich the message: "... an enjoyable dining experience ..." might be improved by writing "... secluded, candlelit tables overlooking the city skyline. ..."

c. *Do not overuse such verbal devices as alliteration, sibilants, fricatives, and plosives.* Consult your dictionary for definitions and examples of each of these.

d. *Make certain your grammar and spelling are correct.*

e. *Simplify your copy.* Make every idea as clear as you can. Nothing should be too wordy or too complicated to be easily understood.

f. *Remember the consumer's perspective.* Talk to the audience in terms they understand and in terms in which they think about the product or service.

g. *Avoid clichés, indefinite pronouns, and unnecessary numbers* unless they help the audience remember the central sales message.

h. *Construct sentences carefully and with purpose.* Make each sentence track smoothly and move logically, smoothly, and clearly from point to point. Be conscious of how the words flow together in each sentence.

i. *Use questions sparingly.* Questions can stimulate interest, increase audience involvement, and link the advertised product or service to the problem presented. However, too many questions can create a strong negative response.

Visualization Suggestions

a. *Storyboard your message.* Even rough preliminary sketches will help you visualize better and formulate more effective use of each visual and aural element.

b. *Scrutinize visual sequencing.* Make certain each shot and each scene builds logically, clearly, and effectively to a strong visual conclusion. Eliminate visual elements that do not enhance a strong progression of ideas. Make certain each shot creates, sustains, and builds audience interest in the client, product, or service.

   c. *Eliminate shots and scenes that do not relate to the central message of the commercial or announcement.*

   d. *Know the creative potential.* Be conscious of why each kind of shot is selected, how it is used, and what its effect will be. Anticipate the result when the various visual elements are blended into the final message. Fine tune each portion of the video in the script.

   e. *Remember the audio.* Make the sound portion of the message complement, reinforce, or counterpoint the video. Transfer from radio to television copywriting your concerns and skills for using music, sound effects, and voices.

A considerable amount of research has been conducted to identify techniques that can be used to increase the effectiveness of television commercials. Some of the principal conclusions from this research were reported in a study by David Ogilvy and Joel Raphaelson of Ogilvy and Mather.[2]

Ogilvy and Raphaelson based their conclusions on results from tests on more than 800 television commercials by the research firm of Mapes and Ross. These tests measured the ability of commercials to change an audience's brand preference, a characteristic Mapes and Ross found to be highly correlated with the ability of commercials to produce sales.

Commercials were classified according to the techniques used in their execution. The change in brand preference produced by commercials that used a particular technique was compared to the overall average for all commercials to determine whether the technique was above average or below average in effectiveness. The following types of television commercials were found to be above average in effectiveness:

   a. Commercials that provide the solution to a problem
   b. Commercials that start with the key idea or central sales point
   c. Commercials that use humor pertinent to the selling proposition
   d. Commercials that include a candid camera testimonial or slice-of-life enactment in which a doubter is convinced
   e. Commercials that provide news about new products, new uses, new ideas, or new information
   f. Commercials that include a demonstration
   g. Commercials that use supers, but the words on the screen must reinforce the main sales or copy point

The following kinds of television commercials were found to be below average:

   a. Commercials with extensive use of short scenes and several changes of situation or location
   b. Commercials that do not show the product's package

c. Commercials that end without the brand name

d. Commercials using cartoons and animation were found to be below average with adults but above average with children.

Ogilvy and Raphaelson do not suggest that these conclusions provide a magic formula for success, but they do believe that the judicious use of their findings will improve your chances of creating an effective television commercial.[3]

Suggested Exercises and Projects

1. Discuss the following topics:

   a. Evaluate the degree and quality of ethics and responsibility displayed in several local and area broadcast advertising campaigns.

   b. Discuss the use of deceptive and misleading advertising practices and techniques in several national and local broadcast advertising campaigns.

   c. Discuss the use of stereotypes in broadcast advertising. Cite specific commercials and announcements. How would you have changed the copy to eliminate the stereotyping but still convey the same information and persuasive value for a target audience?

   d. Discuss the use of logical and emotional appeals in broadcast advertising copy. When is the use of each type of appeal appropriate? Inappropriate? Determine the products, services, and clients that best use each type of logical and emotional appeal.

2. Monitoring projects:

   a. Watch and, if possible, record several television commercials by national advertisers. Formulate an abbreviated version of a copy rationale for each commercial. Comment on its effectiveness—central selling point, positioning, copy organization, style of delivery, and other criteria that you feel determine the effectiveness of a commercial announcement.

   b. Listen to and, if possible, record several radio commercials by national advertisers. Follow the process outlined in ''a'' and devise the copy rationale and provide comments on the effectiveness of each commercial.

   c. Follow the process outlined in ''a'' but for a number of television public service announcements.

   d. Follow the process outlined in ''b'' but for a number of radio public service announcements.

3. Examine carefully the style and content of a major metropolitan newspaper. Using standard reference material and your own observations of several issues of this newspaper, formulate a brief copy rationale for a set of commercials for this newspaper.

a. Write one 20-second generic radio commercial using a single voice/straight-sell presentational format. This would be a commercial that could be used throughout the broadcast day, with no seasonal restrictions.

b. Write one 30-second radio commercial for this same metropolitan newspaper, using the donut copy design format. The middle segment of the commercial should be approximately 15 seconds long.

c. Write one 60-second radio commercial for this same metropolitan newspaper, using one of the following presentational formats: dialogue, dramatization, humor, or testimonial.

4. Write two 30-second radio commercials for a local or area retail store that sells nationally advertised products and advertises regularly in your local or area newspaper. Clip sample newspaper advertisements and formulate an abbreviated copy rationale for the radio commercials. Construct the commercials so that they would be acceptable for co-op purposes; that is, your commercials should feature both a national manufacturer or advertiser as well as the local outlet or distributor for a particular brand of products. Use any of the following copy makeup formats: modulized, donut, core, open-faced, or tag. Types of clients that would best generate this type of broadcast copy include hardware stores, automobile dealers, clothing stores, appliance stores, furniture stores, department stores, agricultural products distributors, and franchised operations. Attach the newspaper ads used to generate the copy rationale and to write the commercials.

5. Write one 30-second television commercial for a local or area retail store, following the process and guidelines outlined in exercise 4.

6. Select a local advertiser whose business falls within one of the following client categories: furniture store, clothing store, shoe store, department store, pharmacy, carpet and floor covering, or jewelry store. Formulate a copy rationale for this client. Based on the copy rationale, write the following 30-second television commercials:

a. Voice-over copy for a single announcer. On-camera talent may be seen in the commercial but may not speak. Any video production elements may be used. Music and sound effects may be used with a single announcer.

b. A commercial written for a radio lift, or simulcast. That is, the copy must be designed so that the audio portion can stand alone and be appropriate for effective use as a self-contained, radio-only commercial. The visual material in this television commercial, however, needs to be sufficiently interesting and creative so that the information for television provides an impact specifically designed to interest a television viewer/consumer.

    c. Copy written in modulized form. The 30-second television commercial must be written so that one 10-second and one 20-second television commercial can be made from portions of the 30-second spot without substantial rewriting. Write the 10-second and 20-second versions as separate scripts.

    d. Copy written in a nonverbal manner. The video portion of this commercial must convey the appropriate persuasive message with only music or sound effects heard in the audio. Animation techniques and graphics may be used.

7. Select one of the following product or service categories: restaurants; appliance stores; real estate companies; banks or savings and loans; automobile dealers; sports, hobby, or toy stores; food stores and supermarkets. Compile as much information as possible about this product or service category and about a local commercial client whose business falls within that category. Prepare a one-page copy rationale for a set of commercials targeted to either Black or Hispanic young adults.

    a. Write three 30-second radio commercials using three of the following presentational formats: demonstration, dialogue, dramatization, testimonial, or humor.

    b. Write three 30-second television commercials using three of the following presentational formats: demonstration, dramatization, testimonial, or a combination of formats.

    c. Prepare a rough storyboard for one television commercial written in ''b.''

8. Pat Thompson and Chris Carothers are the only candidates in your state's next gubernatorial election. Prepare two 30-second radio or television spot announcements for either Thompson or Carothers. Provide a short narrative in which you show how your spots promote the candidacy of Thompson or Carothers and weaken the campaign of the opponent.

9. Select one local social service agency active in your area. Compile as much information as possible on the goals and projects of this group or organization. Prepare a one-page copy rationale for a set of public service announcements. Prepare appropriate copy material as described in exercise 7 ''a–c,'' but for a nonprofit, public service agency, group, or organization.

10. Follow the same procedures outlined in exercise 7 and/or 9, but work with others as a team to generate the specified copy rationale, spot announcements, and storyboard.

11. For a specified client, product, or service, prepare a 10-second, 20-second, 30-second, or 60-second radio commercial for use in one of the following radio programming formats: all-news or all-talk, easy listening, country music, rock music. The commercial should be written to match the radio station program format and to attract and persuade a target audience.

12. For a specific radio or television station in your area, prepare the following promotional copy:
    a. One 10-second legal station identification enhanced with a brief promotional message
    b. One 30-second news promo, which includes information about the news resources, facilities, personnel, or programming available at this station. This should be a generic news promo for use throughout the broadcast day, with no seasonal restrictions
    c. One 30-second program promo for a regular program series or a one-time-only special program
    d. One 30-second personality promo featuring one prominent on-air talent, who is heard or seen regularly on the station
    All of the information contained in each promotional announcement must be accurate. All of the promotional copy specified in this exercise would be for use *on* the selected station. Use standard broadcast industry reference material or contact appropriate station personnel as needed to compile the information necessary to write these promotional announcements.

13. You are the Promotion Director at WXXX Radio, an adult contemporary music station in your town. WXXX has faltered badly in the past three rating books, so management has decided to alter WXXX's format radically. In two weeks, WXXX Radio will become your town's first all-news/all-talk station. You have been told to devise a 10-second spot and a 30-second spot for use on local and area television stations during the first two weeks of this format change. The only information you have now is that half the programming will consist of news, sports, and feature material from the Mutual Broadcasting System (MBS) and the other half from local talk and call-in shows, plus live sports broadcasts. Write a brief memorandum to your station manager in which you analyze the radio formats and competition in your local market; identify the target audience to be reached; specify the objectives to be accomplished; indicate the copy appeals, styles, and designs to be used; and note the central selling point to be emphasized in the two promotional spots. Be sure to turn in both this narrative and the copy for the two spots.

Notes

1. Fred Bergendorff (personal communication, 6 March 1991).
2. See David Ogilvy and Joel Raphaelson, ''Research on Advertising Techniques That Work—and Don't Work,'' *Harvard Business Review,* July-August, 1982.
3. Results of the Ogilvy and Raphaelson study reported by the National Association of Broadcasters, ''Techniques That Increase the Effectiveness of Television Commercials'' (Washington, DC, 1982).

News and Sports

N ewscasts and sportscasts represent a station or network's largest daily commitment of time, effort, personnel, and facilities. They display the efforts of many individuals, working together as a team to gather, organize, write, produce, and report stories about the happenings of the day.

The competition to capture today's audiences is severe and is expected to intensify as the variety of choices and level of sophistication increase. National cable channels and systems, as well as local independent stations, now produce daily newscasts and sportscasts. The audience has developed personalized and often complex patterns of media use.

This offers a stimulating challenge: to provide brief stories about events that are interesting to and informative for a large, diverse group of people and to present this information under unforgiving deadlines in an accurate, clear, objective, and complete manner. Your writing talents must be combined with production skills so that, as a reporter working with others, worthwhile news and sports stories can be identified, covered, written, produced, and aired.

This chapter provides an overview of writing news and sports stories and examines the writing requirements associated with live sports broadcasts. Specifically this chapter considers the collection and processing of information; the factors that determine news value and establish news judgment; the sources of information used regularly; the techniques used in gathering, handling, and organizing information; the writing of stories; newscast and sportscast preparation; and the writing of specialized material, including scripts used for live sports broadcasts.

The principles and techniques of good writing described in this book apply to *all* writing for the electronic media, including the preparation of news and sports copy. The nature and complexity of news and sports reporting require the modification of some of these basic concepts, but essential principles of good writing remain intact. Also, it should be noted that only fundamental practices are presented in this chapter. Each news and sports operation imposes special writing and copy format requirements to meet its own writing and production standards. This chapter does not consider the important equipment and production skills needed for a full range of high-quality broadcast journalism work. See the suggested reading list in Appendix A for books that can provide this kind of information, and review the basic production principles and terminology described in chapter 2. Finally, it would be helpful to review "Regulations, Restraints, and Responsibilities" in chapter 1, since these laws also apply to news and sports coverage.

Process

News and sports stories begin and end in the newsroom, where it is decided which stories are to be covered and how they will be written and prepared. A newsroom is organized to provide the coordination and teamwork needed to get people and machines working together to produce effective news and sports reports.

Let's examine the organization and structure of a typical medium-size newsroom. The *news director* coordinates overall newsroom operations. There may also be assistant news directors, who handle the news director's primary responsibilities: personnel, operations, and finances. The *assignment manager* decides the stories to be covered and coordinates and monitors the work of the news staff, especially reporters and photojournalists if television news work is involved. *Producers* work with the assignment manager to determine the content and production requirements of each news or sports broadcast. *Technicians* handle most equipment requirements. Unless you work in a large newsroom, you will be expected not only to write stories but also to cover events and operate essential equipment, such as tape recorders, microphones, cameras, and lights. Large newsroom operations are intricate and encourage the specialization of personnel. Those who *only* write stories generally are found only in large newsroom operations.

Several steps are followed to develop each story. First, an idea for a story is suggested by a reporter, the assignment manager, the newscast producer, or someone else in the newsroom. Second, the idea is evaluated and a commitment is made to assign people to cover that story. Third, the logistics of covering the story are identified and finalized. Fourth, the story is covered. Fifth, the story is processed into finished form. Sixth, the story airs.

News Judgment

How do you determine what is newsworthy? Events and situations that are considered newsworthy have certain common characteristics. Not all news stories have all these characteristics, but a story's newsworthiness increases proportionately with the number of such characteristics it contains. These elements help newsroom personnel determine which events to cover, as well as which pieces of information to include in each story. The primary characteristics that determine newsworthiness are proximity, prominence, timeliness, impact, conflict, controversy, uniqueness, human interest, suspense, the need to update earlier stories, and available sound or pictures.

Audience members are more interested in what affects them personally, directly, and locally than in what happens in a distant location. Thus, *local* news tends to be considered more newsworthy than stories from other countries.

The more prominent or visible the person involved in an event, the more newsworthy that story is. Prominent locations or events also increase newsworthiness.

When an event occurs is sometimes just as important as what happens, who is involved, or where it takes place. Immediacy is a hallmark of electronic news coverage.

Consider the significance, impact, or consequence of a story on the lives, welfare, and future of your audience. Generally the more people affected dramatically and directly by a story, the more newsworthy it is.

Learn to recognize the ethical and emotional conflicts, as well as the physical confrontations, that heighten news interest. Assess their value and newsworthiness. Conflict often leads to controversy, which tends to fuel interest in a particular story. Ultimately that interest heightens news value.

Often an event or a situation is considered newsworthy simply because it is unique. Also, viewers and listeners are curious about other people, even those who are not well known. They like to empathize with the problems of others and share in their achievements.

Some events are newsworthy because their outcome is uncertain. Suspense heightens newsworthiness.

Stories are often written to update earlier reports. Natural disasters, rescue efforts, election returns, and legal actions in local fraud scandals are only a few examples of situations that require constant updating.

Available sound and picture also tend to increase the news value of a story. A story may have been newsworthy anyway, but the availability of vivid sound and picture can make the story especially newsworthy.

Sources

Where do you find the information you need to write what could be considered a newsworthy story? The reporter and the newsroom in which that reporter operates serve as a bridge between available sources of information and the audience for that information. You should know the basic sources reporters use regularly.

Public Sources

Several resources available to the general public can also be useful for news and sports coverage. These include standard reference works, government material, and public safety communications. Several kinds of standard reference works are available: dictionaries, thesauruses, encyclopedias, atlases, almanacs, telephone directories, and city directories.

The Freedom of Information Act described in chapter 1 provides an effective way to obtain information from government agencies. Government records, documents, and reports can supply essential statistics and data on almost any subject.

Most newsrooms routinely monitor the activities of police, fire, and ambulance agencies in their area. In a highly competitive market, this monitoring may also extend to the transmissions of competing news outlets; however, federal law restricts the direct use of this information. Most newsrooms use these transmissions as ''tips'' and then dispatch their own news personnel to cover the story. On the other hand, Citizens Band (CB) and amateur ham operator transmissions may be rebroadcast without special permission. It is always best to use these types of transmissions cautiously and only as news tips. It is also best to verify the information directly with key sources.

Private Sources   A reporter often relies on information from private sources: individuals, groups and associations, news releases, polls and surveys, newspapers and magazines, data bases, news wires, news services, and other news operations.

People are one of the best sources a reporter can use. They can make news reports come alive as they describe in vivid detail what they saw, heard, and experienced. Listeners and viewers can share experiences and determine points of view from the eyewitness accounts offered live or on tape.

Representatives of professional, civic, political, and special interest groups and associations have developed contacts and material that may be useful. Be aware, however, that most of these groups provide only information that presents their organizations in a favorable light.

Newsrooms receive news releases and handouts about upcoming events, generally in the mail or by FAX. Electronic news releases (ENRs), in audio or video form, are also provided by professional organizations and industries. Audio and video segments and complete stories can be supplied to newsrooms on tape or live via satellite. Newsrooms can often customize the material by having a local reporter ask questions of a guest via satellite during a national interactive session. This kind of hook-up provides access to an important news maker; prominently involves local on-air talent; and gives a company, an industry, or an organization air time it would not otherwise receive. The use of ENRs in corporate presentations is examined in chapter 11.

Stories occasionally cite the results of polls and surveys conducted by well-known national research companies, or even local research organizations. Be cautious and skeptical when reviewing and reporting such survey results.

Newspapers and magazines can help monitor the local and specialized interests of a newsroom. They can provide leads for stories to be developed by the newsroom staff. They offer depth and background about issues and situations that may be useful for the electronic news reporter and writer.

Data bases are computerized information retrieval systems accessed via telephone lines. Once a modem links a newsroom or laptop personal computer to a telephone connection, you have access to enormous electronic libraries. Both current and reference material are only a few key strokes away in an electronic newsroom.

A large share of the news and sports stories used on radio and television newscasts comes from domestic news wire services, such as the Associated Press. Regional and national bureaus offer a variety of services to the broadcasting and cable industries. Specialized wire services can provide weather information, sports scores and updates, agricultural reports, and local news coverage. Most newsrooms rewrite wire copy; some use wire stories only as tips.

Commercial news services, networks, and other newsrooms are additional sources of news material. Access to some of this information must be purchased, but newsrooms often forge a free information exchange agreement.

Internal Sources

Several sources of information can be tapped within the newsroom. These include future files, other newsroom files and records, and newsroom personnel.

Future files contain information about newsworthy events expected to occur in the future. Using ordinary file folders or sophisticated electronic data base systems, newsroom personnel catalogue such items as news releases, newspaper clippings, personal notes and reminders from reporters, and copies of previous stories used on the air. This material is reviewed on the date when the scheduled event occurs.

Newsrooms maintain other kinds of files and records that help generate story ideas and locate useful background information. Call sheets identify individuals contacted regularly for information and comments. Previous news or sports copy can be saved on computer disks or in files, boxes, or bundles. Audio and video material can be catalogued and retrieved from master reels.

Newsroom personnel are the eyes and ears of the operation. Full-time reporters cover breaking stories and often are assigned "beats," or subject areas, such as city government, education, entertainment, and sports, to generate stories with regularity. Correspondents and stringers may be hired to provide occasional coverage from outside the immediate area.

Gathering and Handling Information

The limited scope of this book prevents a thorough treatment of several topics associated with the work of a news or sports writer and reporter. Unfortunately, it is not possible to outline the equipment and techniques used to record and process audio and video material in newsgathering situations. Books listed as supplementary reading in Appendix A and trade publications listed in Appendix B can provide detailed information about these vital skills.

Following are suggestions for gathering and handling news and sports information efficiently and effectively as a reporter:

a. *When assigned to cover a story, verify the date, time, place, and person to contact.*
b. *Anticipate potential story coverage.* Be aware of current developments, personalities involved, and issues causing concern.
c. *Go prepared with the necessary reporting tools.* Determine what equipment will be needed to cover the story effectively. Remember your notepad and pencil, as well as recorder and microphone.

d. *Know your deadlines.* Know how much time you have to cover the story, write your copy, edit tape, and so on.

e. *Keep the newsroom informed.* Stay in touch by phone, two-way radio, or other means. The newsroom can relay information that may affect the story you are covering. You also may be reassigned if an important story develops unexpectedly.

f. *Be professional in your manner of dress, attitude, and conduct.* If you look and sound like a professional, you can expect to be treated like one.

g. *Maintain objectivity in your selection and treatment of story details.* Objectivity and accuracy are two prime ingredients of noteworthy news and sports reporting.

h. *Get the facts.* Good reporters are able to determine what details they need to gather as they cover a story. They make priorities. They develop the ability to assess the story quickly, to decide on the angle they want to develop, and to determine the sights and sounds they need to capture on tape before they are no longer available. *Before* leaving the scene of a news story, experienced reporters make certain they have all the necessary information, and they remember to check the quality of their tape recordings.

i. *Be sensitive to your sources.* Eyewitnesses to tragedies often have difficulty handling the demands of the news media. Compassion may prove to be more worthwhile than aggressiveness in sensitive newsgathering situations.

j. *Observe carefully.* Absorb as much information as possible. Be sensitive to the manner in which words are said, as well as the actions, posture, and attitude of news sources.

k. *Take notes.* If you are recording a personal interview or handling comments at a news conference or in a speech, make notes about excerpts that might be useful later. This can be done using the counter found on most tape recorders.

l. *Organize yourself and your story.* Know what you need and what you have. Determine why a story is newsworthy and how you can show this newsworthiness in selecting and treating the information. Place each story's ideas into a meaningful perspective. Understand the story yourself before trying to write it for others.

Organizing Information

Three steps are involved in organizing news sources: determine what you need to know, identify where to find what you need, and handle what you find.

Exactly what do you need to know? The more precise you can be, the more likely you will identify the source of the information you want.

Review the range of sources already described. What would be the *best* source for what you want? Would an eyewitness to a natural disaster be best? Maybe reference material would provide a better overview. Perhaps newsroom files can offer some insights.

After you obtain what you think you need, handle what you have found. Verify the information, and evaluate its merits. Put away your notes and organize the various pieces of the information puzzle. Plan how you will select key pieces of information to tell the basic facts of a story in clear and simple terms. Then, write the story.

Writing News and Sports Reports

There are various ways you can begin to tell a news or sports story. You need to understand how each type of lead sentence can be used effectively. You also need to learn how to organize the facts and comments you will present so that your story structure is sound. You also need to master the essential writing techniques and scripting formats that make news and sports writing an interesting challenge.

As indicated earlier, each newsroom imposes special writing and script format requirements to help standardize story development and presentation. The following practices should prove useful in most electronic news operations.

Leads

A lead is the beginning of a story. A good lead helps capture attention, prepares the audience for the story, and sets the tone or mood of the story that follows.

What information should you include in the lead sentence? The best guideline is to determine what makes the story especially newsworthy and include that information in the lead. Most experienced writers do not pause and then consciously identify or select a particular type of lead to use for each story. They simply write the best lead for the story that needs to be told. To help you get started writing effective leads for various kinds of stories, however, it may be useful to identify and describe some of the most common types of leads used to begin news and sports stories.

A *hard lead* presents the most important piece of information, conveys the essence of the story, and stresses the immediacy of the information:

```
Protesters continue to battle police this morning
at the Ord Nuclear Power Plant.

The Bears beat the Wolves last night to capture the
state basketball crown.
```

A *soft lead* indicates the general nature and impact of events and offers perspectives that might otherwise be overlooked:

```
The earth moved last night. An earthquake
measuring four-point-four on the Richter
Scale shook Southern California in the
early morning hours.
```

What began as a good day for the quarterback
ended as a disaster for the team. Although Eric
Johnson broke a school record for the most passes
completed in a single game, his team lost the game.

An *umbrella lead* combines two or more related stories into one lead:

Three murders have been reported in the city
overnight.

The selection of expansion teams in the league has
had a significant financial impact on the three
cities chosen.

A *question lead* can help reflect questions that may be on the minds of listeners and viewers. If used sparingly, question leads can increase interest and focus attention by clearly announcing the nature of the story.

How would you like to be the only person in town
without a name? That's what happened to Pat Jones
today when she discovered...

What's it like to be the owner of a national
championship team that has never defeated
its crosstown rival? We'll find out tonight
when...

Several factors influence the type of lead you eventually use: the nature of the story, the manner in which you plan to reveal details, the length of the story to be told, how a story is packaged or presented, and directives from newsroom supervisory personnel. Some of these factors relate to story structure and scripting formats.

Story Structure

Leads provide only the essential "foundation," or beginning, for a news or sports story. The "girders" of the story are supplied by its structure—that is, the manner in which the story is organized and presented.

Like any story, a news or sports story must be complete. The beginning must draw you into the story, transitions should help bridge key ideas, and the ending should finish the informational process.

When you write a story, you are creating the pieces of an informational puzzle. You shape, connect, and hone bits of information, trying to find the *best* way to arrange the facts and comments you have gathered. Some writers find that they can achieve an effective *progression* of information in each story by responding to key questions the audience may formulate as the story unfolds. For example, after indicating that a major traffic accident has occurred overnight, the natural questions would be the following: What happened? Who was injured? How? When? Where did the accident occur? Any charges filed against any of the drivers? Answering these questions can help you write a well-organized, informative story.

Although each story deserves its own unique treatment, various organizational patterns can help form this basic story structure. Perhaps a chronological arrangement would work best, as in the story about the fatal car crash. A topical organizational pattern would be useful to summarize the important decisions made at a local governmental meeting. Opposing points of view could be presented in a report on a heated labor dispute. Select the story structure that best matches the nature and importance of the story and that presents the information in a clear, straightforward manner.

Following is a suggested process for developing, writing, and structuring the first version of a story. The same steps could be used to revise or rewrite the same story to provide a fresh perspective for later newscasts or to rewrite stories written by other reporters or news sources.

1. *Read the original source material carefully and thoughtfully.* Understand the essence of the story, why it is newsworthy, and what impact it might have on the potential audience.
2. *Underline or highlight the main points* in the original source material.
3. *Put away the source material.*
4. *Tell the story informally* to a friend, fellow newsroom reporter, or your keyboard.
5. *Determine how the story can best be told.* Think of the *structure* that might work best—chronological, topical, or opposing viewpoints. How will you begin *and* end the story?
6. *Write the first draft.*
7. *Reassess your plan of attack:* lead sentence, organizational pattern, and ending.
8. *Check your copy against the original source material* to ensure accuracy, balance, and objectivity.
9. *Revise your copy.*
10. *Read your story aloud, not* in your mind. Improve your word choices, sentence structure, story organization, flow, rhythm, and pace. "Tighten" your copy: limit the amount of information you include.

Good story structure results from digesting facts and comments, assessing their value, and then devising the best possible way to organize and present that information in an interesting and compelling manner. Good newswriters are also good storytellers.

Scripting Formats

It is important to standardize the written presentation of news and sports stories within each newsroom. The following basic copy format guidelines are based on practices in a majority of the electronic media newsrooms across the country.

Figure 5.1
Radio copy format for
a reader or copy story.

APEX FIRE
9/20....9am
J. Jones

10 lines

     Arsonists may have caused last night's big fire....Fire
Chief Bill Atkins today blamed arsonists for last night's
fire, which destroyed the Apex Paint Company Warehouse on
South Third Avenue.
     Chief Atkins reports that ten empty gasoline cans were
found near the incinerator in the building. So far there
are no clues to the identities of the suspected arsonists.
     City police are fingerprinting an abandoned car found
near the warehouse. There were no injuries. No damage
estimate is available at this time.
     Fire and police officials continue their investigation.

-0-

Radio

In this section, an imaginary fire story will be used to illustrate both story structure and acceptable radio script formats. The facts presented in each report remain the same, but the formats vary.

Figure 5.1 shows how the fire story could be written if reported only by a radio newscaster or anchor. This is usually called a *reader* or *copy story,* since the newscaster simply reads the news copy.

Figure 5.2 illustrates how the same fire story might be written if a comment from the Fire Chief were to be inserted. This recorded excerpt generally is called an *actuality* or *soundbite.*

Figure 5.3 on page 160 illustrates a third scripting possibility. Have the newscaster read an introduction to a report about the fire and then play a *voicer,* or summary of the story read on tape by a reporter. Figure 5.4 on page 161 shows a different scripting format some newsrooms use for a voicer report. Radio network newsrooms often provide additional precision and copy flexibility by attaching to the copy what are often called *verbatim sheets* (the verbatim transcript of an actuality or a voicer report). Figure 5.5 on page 162 shows the verbatim sheet used by ABC Radio News for the news copy shown in figure 5.4. If the voicer scripted in figure 5.3 had included an actuality from the Fire Chief, this would be called a *voicer wraparound* or simply a *wrap.* The voice of the reporter would wrap around, or surround, the Fire Chief's brief comments. Wraps and voicers are scripted in a similar manner.

A few copy format comments are needed for the scripts that appear as figures 5.1 through 5.3. Notice how each story is identified by a *copy slug* at the top left-hand side of each script page. The number of lines of copy, or

```
 _____
/ APEX FIRE     \
| 9/20.....9am  |
| J. Jones      |
_____/
```

```
 _____
/ 8 lines                    \
| PLUS :12 ACTUALITY         |
_____/
```

Figure 5.2
Same news story as
shown in figure 5.1
but written to include
an actuality.

Arsonists may have caused last night's big fire....Fire
Chief Bill Atkins today blamed arsonists for last night's
fire, which destroyed the Apex Paint Company Warehouse on
South Third Avenue.

CART:	In Cue:	"From the evidence..."
	Out Cue:	...was set on purpose."
	Length:	12 seconds
	SUMMARY:	Chief Atkins reports that
		ten empty gasoline cans
		were found in the
		building. Chief Atkins
		believes the fire was set
		on purpose.

So far there are no clues to the identities of the
suspected arsonists. City police are fingerprinting an
abandoned car found near the warehouse. There were no
injuries. No damage estimate is available at this time.
Fire and police officials continue their investigation.

the line-count, and the recorded length of the actuality or voicer appear at
the top right-hand side of each piece of copy. This notation helps anticipate
the length of each story in the newscast or sportscast. *Line-counts* can provide a reasonably accurate estimate of reading speed. Newscasters can determine their personal reading speed by counting the number of lines read in
one minute; if a newscaster reads sixteen lines in 60 seconds, for example,
an eight-line story would be read in approximately 30 seconds, a four-line
story in 15 seconds, and so forth. Newsroom computer systems have timing
capabilities and can eliminate some of these arithmetic gymnastics. Material
not meant to be read aloud is boxed or circled. For each cart, or recorded
report, the first few words, the last few words, the length, and a summary
are written on the copy page. The summary of the recorded material may be
provided to ensure a smooth transition by the newscaster or sportscaster,
who would have to recover and read something if there were technical problems. Summaries are also useful as ready-made rewrites of stories to be used

Figure 5.3
Same news story as shown in figures 5.1 and 5.2 but written as a voicer or voicer wrap.

APEX FIRE
9/20.....9am
J. Jones

2 lines
WITH #:32 VOICER

Arsonists may have caused last night's big fire. Radio 90's Jeff Smith has details.....

<table>
<tr><td>CART:</td><td>In Cue:</td><td>"Fire Chief Bill Atkins..."</td></tr>
<tr><td></td><td>Out Cue:</td><td>"...their investigation. Jeff Smith, Radio 90 News."</td></tr>
<tr><td></td><td>Length:</td><td>32 Seconds</td></tr>
<tr><td></td><td>SUMMARY:</td><td>Radio 90's Jeff Smith reports that Fire Chief Bill Atkins blames arsonists for the Apex Paint Company fire last night. Gasoline cans were found in the building. An abandoned car is being fingerprinted. There were no injuries. The investigation is continuing.</td></tr>
</table>

-0-

in later newscasts or sportscasts. Since summaries are meant to be read on the air, always use complete sentences. Notice that regular paragraphing and capitalization are used. Some newsrooms insist on no paragraph indentations and the use of FULL CAPS, as well as the use of an *end mark* to indicate that the story is finished. Following are a few end marks you could use: "–O–" or "end" or the date you wrote the story or perhaps your initials to indicate that *you* wrote the story.

The content and story structure of the copy in figures 5.1 through 5.3 should not be neglected. Notice how a hard lead is used to provide a quick update on an important, ongoing story. The copy is relatively short, even when an actuality or a voicer report is used. All the essential information is attributed to a recognizable source. Notice how the details are unveiled—briefly, directly, one key piece of information at a time, all relating to the lead sentence that begins the storytelling process. A topical story structure is used—each key item in the story is included. The Fire Chief's comments provide the specifics about the new developments in the story that make it newsworthy. The last few sentences in each report take care of the related information about injuries and damage estimates and indicate that the story continues to develop, thus creating the expectation of a future rewrite or update of the story in a later newscast.

```
        hardt      Tue Oct 20 17:48  page   2

                              -0-


    SEEMS THE PENTAGON WAS MAKING HOME-MOVIES OF YESTERDAY'S U-S NAVY ATTACK

    ON 2-OF IRAN'S OIL PLATFORMS IN THE GULF! ABC'S BOB ZELNICK GOT A LOOK

    AT THE MOVIES TODAY:


                      CAT# 127
                  O; THE FOOTAGE
           (5)    T; 23
                  C; ABOARD THE SHIPS


    IRAN IS STILL THREATENING TO GET-BACK AT THE U-S FOR THE ATTACK ON ITS

    OIL PLATFORMS.
```

Figure 5.4

Example of another radio copy format for a voicer news report.

Courtesy of ABC Radio News. From Peter E. Mayeux, Broadcast News Writing and
Reporting. *Copyright © 1991 Wm. C. Brown Publishers, Dubuque, Iowa. All Rights
Reserved. Reprinted by permission.*

161

```
CAT#  WHO           NC  CODE      SLUG            ? RUNS PROCESSED

127  BOB ZELNICK     ABCrruuu   WHAT FOOTAGE SHOWS  Q  :23 Oct 20 16:45
     WHAT:

WHERE:PENTAGON              EVENT TIME:   445P   FACILITIES/QUAL:DOD AUTO

TAKEN BY:silverst   CREDIT/RESTRICTION:ASK/ZELNICK

OPENS:THE FOOTAGE..            RUNS:23  CLOSE:....THE SHIPS.

NEWSCALL DESCRIPTION:
=================================================================================

THE DEFENSE DEPARTMENT HAS RELEASED FOOTAGE OF YESTERDAY'S DESTRUCTION OF AN

IRANIAN OIL INSTALLATION - AND MILITARY OUTPOST - IN THE PERSIAN GULF. FROM THE

PENTAGON, ABC'S BOB ZELNICK TELLS US WHAT THE FOOTAGE SHOWS....




VERBATIM: THE FOOTAGE SHOWS THE OVERWHELMING MIGHT OF FOUR DESTROYERS UNLEASHED

AGAINST A VIRTUALLY UNDEFENDED STATIONARY TARGET, BANGING AWAY AT THE ROSTOM

PLATFORM AT WHAT AT TIMES APPEARS LITTLE MORE THAN TARGET PRACTICE. AFTER MORE

THAN A THOUSAND FIVE-INCH SHELLS AND SOME 45 MINUTES OF FIRING, A NAVY

DEMOLITION TEAM MOVES ON TO THE WRECKAGE. THE EXPLOSION FROM ITS CHARGE BRINGS

CHEERS FROM THE MAN ABOARD THE SHIPS.
```

Figure 5.5
Verbatim sheet for the radio copy shown in figure 5.4.
Courtesy of ABC Radio News. From Peter E. Mayeux, Broadcast News Writing and
Reporting. *Copyright © 1991 Wm. C. Brown Publishers, Dubuque, Iowa. All Rights
Reserved. Reprinted by permission.*

Several presentation formats are used routinely for television news or sports stories. An on-camera anchor could simply read the story with no additional video used; as previously mentioned, this is called a reader or copy story. Graphics could be included in readers by using a character generator (CG) to electronically produce letters and numbers seen directly on the screen or by using an electronic still storer (ESS) to store and retrieve graphics and photographs and place them in the picture with the anchor. Another presentational format possibility is to have an anchor read over edited video material shown full-screen; this is called a *voice-over* or *VO* story. You could also combine VO copy and soundbites so that the viewer sees and hears a short comment made by a person associated directly with a particular story; this is generally labeled a *VO/SOC* story. *Remote* stories include both an anchor who introduces the story and a reporter who files an update from the site of the event. A *reporter package* or *wrap* in television is similar to a wrap in radio news; the anchor leads in to the reporter's story, which includes voice-over narration, soundbites, and *stand-ups,* in which the reporter appears on-camera. Material included in the wrap is edited to specifications noted on production worksheets.

Television scripting formats are more intricate than radio scripting formats. You must indicate both sound and picture components for each television news or sports story.

Most television newsrooms use computers to prepare news and sports stories, as well as newscast line-ups, which are described later in this chapter. The scripting formats used at KIRO TV in Seattle are typical of those used in computerized television newsrooms across the country. The following is how KIRO TV introduces its copy format requirements to its writers:

> As is usual with news scripts, the video instructions appear on the left side of the script, the anchor copy on the right side, lined up for the teleprompter. Unlike a typewriter, the NewStar computer doesn't let you type on the left side and the right side. Your entire script, video directions and anchor copy, is written in one big block. All video instructions, though, are written in what the computer manual refers to as "reverse video". You can tell the reverse video because it has a green field behind the letters.

> On the sample scripts [shown as figures 5.6 through 5.10], the video instructions are indicated by boldface type; on the NewStar computer, the video instructions would be over a green field.

> At the very top of the script, above the story slug, is the story's "status line". The first set of six numbers refers to the date, the second set of four numbers refers to the time of day the script was printed. The two initials that follow are those of the script's author. The numbers after that are the estimated time for the story (if you see ???? instead of numbers, it means the author did not file the estimated air time). The final series of numbers and letters is the printer code for each story.[1]

Several production terms, used routinely in presenting KIRO TV news stories, can be retrieved and inserted into scripts by pressing a rapid access key and then a letter or number to type out the full production command.

COPY STORY

05/14/87 15:18 ml 0:27 #1+11YuppieC

YuppieCoke
5
O/S BOX (OS) One of the four
men accused in Seattle yuppie
coke ring is on trial this week
--and the case is expected to
go to the jury by tomorrow.
 40-year old Thomas Everts
today testified that he did
give accused ringleader
Michael Sofie 34-thousand
dollars, but he claims it was
part of a real estate deal--
not a drug deal.
TOTAL=

VOICE-OVER ("VO")

05/14/87 15:24 hh 0:28 #1+11CopMemo

CopMemorial
5
LIVE (L) Amid all the downtown
construction noise, came the
plaintive sounds of "taps" today.
CAS_____/NS VO (VO) It was
played at an annual ceremony
remembering police officers
who've died in the line of duty.
(AT+   )CG=P*Seattle Mayor
Charles Royer was among those who
praised the 53-killed on the job since 1881.
 For several years, a large
wreath has been sent--
anonymously---for the ceremony
outside the Public Safety Building.
 It was there, once again, today.

VO/SOC

Figure 5.8
Computer-generated
television news
VO/SOC script format.
*Courtesy of KIRO TV,
Seattle.*

05/14/87 15:24 h4 0:45 #1+11Securit

SecurityClearance
5
LIVE (L) The U-S Defense Department
has set new rules involving the three   .
million people who carry security
clearances.
CAS_____/NS VO (VO) The rules aim
to tighten security in light of
recent spy cases..but gay activists
charge the motive is to black list
homosexuals.
 For the first time sodomy has been
listed as one of many forms of
sexual misconduct..grounds for
denying a person access to
classified information.
AT :16 SOC (SOC AT :16)
RUNS= :08 ENDS: "...NEVER PROVE."
TCT= :24
LIVE (L) The Pentagon says it is
just as concerned about a married
person having an affair as it is
about a homosexual...because the
threat of blackmail makes a person
a security risk.
 Pentagon officials say an avowed
homosexual should not have a
problem getting a security clearance.
TOTAL=00:51

Figure 5.9
Computer-generated
television news live
remote script format.
*Courtesy of KIRO TV,
Seattle.*

05/14/87 15:13 dh ?:?? #1=11R!Sonic

R!Sonic
5
LIVE-OS BOX (OS) It's never
happened before in the Northwest:
it's mid-May and the Seattle
SuperSonics are still alive in
the NBA playoffs AND the Mariners
are in first-place!
 But it's happening tonight, in
what may be the story of the
month.
 The Sonics tonight try to do
what the oddsmakers said wouldn't
happen-advance to the semi-
finals in the NBA playoffs.
 It'll happen with a win tonight
in the Coliseum.
REMOTE FULL 2 HOLER ( ) That's
where Ron Callan is right now
with the answer to the big
question: Will the game be on
TV?
REMOTE FULL (REMOTE)
(AT=   )CG=S*Callan LIVE
(AT=   )CG=L*Seattle Coliseum
(AT=   )CG=L*

2-HOLER ( ) TOSS BACK

WRAP

Figure 5.10
Computer-generated
television news wrap
script format.
*Courtesy of KIRO TV,
Seattle.*

05/14/87 15:13 nw 1:57 #1+ArsonEd

ArsonEdmonds
5
LIVE (L) A rash of arson fires is
making news once again.
 This time, the target was an
apartment complex in the
Edmonds area--not far from where
five fires were set last week.
 Nick Walker reports.

CAS_____/SOC   (SOC AT :00)

(AT=   )CG=P*Edmonds
(AT=   )CG=N*Mike Noriega/Asst. Manager
(AT=   )CG=S*Walker
(AT=   )CG=P*Edmonds/May 5
(AT=   )CG=N*Jack Weinz/Edmonds Fire Chief

RUNS=1:355app   ENDS: "KIRO NEWS."

TOTAL=01:57

Following is a directory of some of these rapid access keys, the words that will appear in the scripts when these keys are pressed, and the meaning of the terms used frequently in KIRO scripts and shown in figures 5.6 through 5.10:

L	O/S BOX	Live read by anchor, with an over-shoulder graphic
l	LIVE (L)	Live read by anchor
c	CAS____ /NS VO	Natural sound video from a 3/4″ videocassette, with an anchor reading copy over the natural sound
C	CAS___ /SOC	A videocassette with sound on; used for reporter wraps or for soundbites. "(SOC AT :00)" would indicate that sound can be heard at the beginning of the videocassette playback.

N	(AT =) CG = N*	The place in the videocassette where the person shown is identified. Name and/or title are to be written exactly as they will appear on screen.
P	(AT =) CG = P*	The place in the videocassette where the location of the video is identified. Words must be written exactly as they are to be shown on the screen.
S	(AT =) CG = S*	The place in the videocassette where the KIRO reporter is identified. The name is provided just after the asterisk.
7	(AT =) CG = L*	Where a live report originates. The location is identified just after the asterisk.
q	RUNS=0:00 ENDS: ". . . KIRO NEWS."	The end of a KIRO reporter's package, with the standard KIRO Eyewitness News tag. Fill in the running time of the package after "RUNS."
2	2-SHOT	A 2-shot, used mostly for on-set reports that include both an anchor and a reporter in the studio
3	3-SHOT	A 3-shot, used mostly for getting into sports and weather segments

The following terms also appear in figure 5.6 through 5.10 scripts but are not retrieved by rapid access keys:

AT :00 SOC	The place in the videocassette at which the viewer begins to hear the sound of someone associated with this story. This is the soundbite of the newsmaker.
TCT	The total length of material on a videocassette recording
2 HOLER	Two elements on screen at the same time—for example, the anchor and a reporter at a remote location
REMOTE FULL	The remote location shot is seen full-screen.
TOSS BACK	The reporter at the remote location returns, or "tosses back," control to the anchor for the next story.[2]

The following suggestions should help you write effective radio and television news and sports copy: **Suggestions**

a. *Provide concise, accurate reports in an understandable form.*
b. *Work for clarity.* The essentials of a story must be clear and memorable when heard or seen only once. Limit the information. Use only one central idea in each sentence.
c. *Choose words that enhance the smoothness and readability of your copy.*
d. *Simplify sentence structure.* Use short declarative sentences with an easy-to-follow subject/verb/object sentence arrangement.
e. *Use present tense and active voice.* Present tense verbs stress the immediacy and continuing action of a story. Active voice lets the subject of the sentence perform the action.
f. *Use punctuation marks that make the copy easy to read and understand when read aloud.*
g. *Use numbers sparingly.* When you do use them, try to indicate the significance of the numbers.
h. *Remember attribution.* Be sure to indicate who is being quoted. Identify, by name, title, or position, who is heard or seen during a story. Attribution adds credibility and clarity to stories and often avoids potential legal problems.
i. *Write for the ear and not the eye.* This is true even for television reports, since audio often carries the essential information for the story. In television, remember that pictures tend to predominate and that sound should support the pictures and often can provide additional information or material not necessarily shown on the screen in a television news story.
j. *Read the copy aloud.* This is the best way to check its effectiveness, clarity, and length.
k. *Write within time limits.* Know the length of the story needed. Most radio stories are 10 to 30 seconds long, whereas television reports average one to two and one-half minutes.
l. *Check legal points.* Read each story carefully, with an eye toward avoiding problems involving libel and slander, objectivity, fairness, balance, and completeness within the limits of time constraints.

Newscasts

The newscast pulls together the resources of the newsroom to present one installment, one report highlighting the day's news or sports events. The newscast is the culmination of the day's work by the newsroom team: individual stories have been assigned and covered; copy has been written, rewritten, and timed; tape has been edited and matched to the copy; and production details and contingency plans have been devised.

Selecting Stories

The criteria described earlier in this chapter (see "News Judgment") are used by the newscast producer to select and place stories in the newscast or sportscast. In addition, the length, placement, and "packaging," or presentational format, of each story may be influenced by such variables as the news philosophy and policy established by the newsroom, the amount and quality of information available in a given day or other time period, the on-air newscast and sportscast format already established, the coverage area and target audience of the station, and the time of day the newscast is presented.

The newscast producer follows several steps to coordinate the building of the newscast: first, identify what is available; second, determine how much time you have in the newscast after deducting time for commercials, transitions, and so on; third, construct the newscast segments.

Line-Ups

As the day progresses, the newscast producer prepares a tentative line-up for the newscast or sportscast. A line-up is also called a *rundown* or *budget.* It is the written plan that guides those involved in getting and keeping the newscast on track. It provides an overview of the various copy, talent, and production elements necessary to produce each story. The line-up is continuously revised and updated, up to the last possible moment, to accommodate late-breaking stories, new facts about stories already included, live remote reports, and emergency situations.

Line-ups are used primarily for preparing television newscasts. Some computerized radio newsrooms also prepare line-ups. Many regularly scheduled radio newscasts are produced using routine sheet formats, such as the one that was shown in figure 3.3.

Figure 5.11 shows a line-up for a radio newscast. In some line-ups, each newscast item, or *event,* is numbered consecutively. In others, a three-digit number or a letter-number combination indicates the position of each item in a specific segment. Thus, the first three items in segment 1 could be numbered 101, 102, 103 or A1, A2, A3. Other notations are generally included for each item in a newscast line-up: the story slug or event designation (e.g., *open, commercials, overnight report);* the initials or abbreviated name of the on-air talent expected to read or handle each item; the initials of the reporter, writer, and/or editor responsible for preparing each item; the source(s) of the video or audio to be used (some line-ups indicate specific playback machines to be used); the length of each news or sports item; the cumulative, or "running," time for the newscast; and the production or presentation format to be used—for instance, VO/ENG, PKG WRAP, SOT.

The content, pace, and flow of the newscast is controlled by adjusting the length, placement, and presentation of each story; by clustering related stories, and by using obvious transitions between story or topic clusters. The refinements of preparing a line-up and producing newscasts and sportscasts are beyond the scope of this book.

SLUG	ANCHOR	WRITER	CART NO.	COPY	TAPE	TOTAL	CUME
OPEN				0:13			0:13
NEIGHBORHOOD MGT#2	DILLON	wright	A/ 24	0:36	00:21	0:57	1:10
POLICE AND GANGS 4	DILLON	roy	38	0:49	00:15	1:04	2:14
RADAR LOCATIONS				0:10			2:24
COMMERCIAL				0:60			3:24
ABC NEWS	DILLON	abc	ABC 3	0:00	00:58	0:58	4:22
2ND SPONSOR CREDIT				0:07			4:29
RIGGS ON PROTESTERS	DILLON	ap	WIRE	0:47	00:00	0:47	5:16
MISSING RUSSELL FOLKS	DILLON	dan/ap	READER	0:39	00:00	0:39	5:55
2ND COMMERCIAL				0:60			6:55
OVERNIGHT REPORT	DILLON	white	PD1	0:00	02:27	2:27	9:22
3RD SPONSOR CREDIT				0:07			9:29
NEA-W RECALL 2	DILLON	zoglman	34	0:34	00:29	1:03	10:32
FINNEY MONEY 2	DILLON	zoglman	6	0:35	00:20	0:55	11:27
UNION VOTE#2	DILLON	wright	8	0:26	0:17	0:43	12:10
HAYSVILLE NEEDS 1	DILLON	roy	READER	0:28	00:00	0:28	12:38
DIAMOND LIL' #2	DILLON	vandruff	H - 5	0:48	00:16	1:04	13:42
3RD COMMERCIAL				0:60			14:42
SPORTS				0:30			15:12
WEATHER				0:30			15:42
CLOSE				0:06			15:48

Figure 5.11
Computer-generated line-up for a radio newscast.
Courtesy of Dan Dillon, KFDI Radio, Wichita, Kansas.

Specialized Reporting

Specialized opportunities often evolve after reporters have gained extensive professional experience, additional education or training, and refinement of their basic writing and reporting skills. The results of these specialized activities often become regular newscast segments. The principles of solid news judgment, objectivity, fairness, accuracy, completeness, and clarity of expression, as well as the process of gathering and handling information, preparing stories, and structuring newscasts, apply to general news writing and reporting as well as to these specialized areas.

Specialized reporting involves the use of specialized sources of information and the exploration of particular topics. The specialty reporting areas examined in this section are sports stories and live sports broadcasts, agriculture and business, consumer affairs, science and health, education, and features that conclude newscasts.

Other segments often included in newscasts are examined in other chapters. These include editorials and commentaries in chapter 6, documentaries and investigative reports in chapter 7, and interviews in chapter 8. Weather reporting is not covered in this book because information sources and coverage techniques are essentially the same as those already outlined for general news writing and reporting. Also, a large portion of weathercasts, especially in television, is not scripted.

Sports

The comments made thus far in this chapter apply to sports reporting as well as to news reporting. Writing a sports story and preparing material for live sports broadcasts require special consideration.

People and paper are the sports reporter's best sources. Coaches, players, and school and team officials can be interviewed personally, at regularly scheduled news conferences, or even at arranged times before or after games and matches. Paper sources include newspapers, sports magazines, media guides and brochures, sports almanacs, written and electronic news releases, and wire services, including special sports wires.

Sports reporting can involve several kinds of presentations. A few include round table discussions of sports issues, investigative and documentary reports, live reports from the scene of a sports event, special programs and features, in-depth analyses of people and issues, and magazine program series. Individual sports news stories are used routinely.

Various types of sports news stories can be done: previews of upcoming matches—player profiles, coaches' projections, league standings, and medical updates; scores and highlights from completed games and contests; sports business items, such as signings and deals, trades, and coaching changes; awards and recognitions; legal investigations and rules infractions; records that are broken; and even sports trivia questions and answers. *Local* sports coverage affects and interests local sports fans most directly. It is a key ingredient for effective local sportscasts.

Live play-by-play sports broadcasts require specific kinds of script material and writing skills. Generally a routine sheet is used. In addition, stand-by material is outlined to provide information that will heighten audience interest and clarify the sports action described in ad-lib fashion. The stand-by material generally is prepared by the color commentator, who tries to provide perspective about the progression of the contest within the description of the action by the play-by-play announcer. The stand-by material might note individual or team statistics, the significance of the specific contest, human interest stories, or observations about the crowd, playing field, or arena.

Figure 5.12 shows a routine sheet for a live broadcast of a football game. Notice that the announcements to be inserted in the live broadcast are numbered consecutively under the column "Position Number." Also notice that the length and source of each commercial break are specified in the columns on the right. Sometimes the Mutual Broadcasting System (MBS) uses the break time, and sometimes the station uses it. The last page of figure 5.12 shows additional production notes used by stations carrying this broadcast. Cueaways by the live announcers are provided for each break. Notice,

1990 COLLEGE FOOTBALL BOWL GAMES

Figure 5.12
Routine sheet used
for a live sports
broadcast.
*Courtesy of the Mutual
Radio Network.*

POSITION NUMBER	CUTAWAY CUE	MBS	STATION

Broadcast start is 20 minutes before scheduled kickoff.

A	Broadcast opens with theme, intro, and network billboard. The network billboard ends "THAT'S THE LINEUP OF NETWORK SPONSORS FOR (the name of the bowl game) ON MUTUAL." After a one-second pause, talent will fill for 15 seconds, and pause again for one	:15	
B	second. Stations may roll over the fill with a 15-second local billboard.	+	:15 (opt.)

PREGAME COACH'S SHOW

1	Coming up, the Pre-Game Show, after this for _____.	:90	
2	More of the pre-game show after this time-out for _____.	:90	
3	Back to the pre-game show and (the name of the bowl game) in just a moment.		:90
4	More in a moment. This is (the name of the bowl game) on Mutual.		:90

PRE-KICKOFF WARMUP SEGMENT

5	The kickoff's coming up after this time-out for _____.	:90	

FIRST QUARTER

6	Time out on the field. Now this for _____.	:30	
7	This is (the name of the bowl game) on Mutual.		:30
8	With the score _____, there's a time-out. Now this for _____.	:60	
9	Time out on the field. Now this for _____.	:60	

END FIRST QUARTER

10	That's the end of the first quarter with the score _____. Now this for _____.	:60	

Figure 5.12 (*continued*)

POSITION NUMBER	CUTAWAY CUE	MBS	STATION
SECOND QUARTER			
11	This is (the name of the bowl game) on Mutual.		:30
12	Time out on the field. Now this for _____.	:30	
13	Time out with the score _____. This is (the name of the bowl game) on Mutual.		:60
14	With the score _____, there's a time out. Now this for _____.	:60	
END OF FIRST HALF			
15 and 16	That's the end of the first half, with the score _____. Now this for _____. (Station :60 follows Network :60 with no cue)	:60 +	:60
HALFTIME			
17	We'll be back after this for _____.	:90	
18	More of halftime after this for _____.	2:00	
19	Our halftime feature continues in just a moment. This is (the name of the bowl game) on Mutual.		:60
20	Back to halftime after this for _____.	2:00	
21	The score at halftime: _____. This is (the name of the bowl game) on Mutual.		:60
PRE-KICKOFF			
22	Coming up, the second half kickoff. But first, this time-out for _____.	:90	

Figure 5.12 (*continued*)

POSITION NUMBER	CUTAWAY CUE	MBS	STATION
THIRD QUARTER			
23	This is (the name of the bowl game) on Mutual.		:30
24	Time out on the field. Now this for _____.	:30	
25	This is (the name of the bowl game) on Mutual.		:30
26	Time out with the score _____. Now this for _____.	:60	
END THIRD QUARTER			
27	That's the end of the third quarter with the score _____. Now this for _____.	:60	
FOURTH QUARTER			
28	Time out on the field. Now this for _____.	:30	
29	This is (the name of the bowl game) on Mutual.		:30
30	Time out with the score _____. This is (the name of the bowl game) on Mutual.		:60
31	With the score _____, there's a time out. Now this for _____.	:60	
END OF GAME			
32	The final score _____. Now this for _____.	:90	
WRAPUP			
33 and 34	Our wrapup will continue after this for _____. (Station :60 follows Network :60 with no cue)	:60 +	:60
35	A final word after this message.		:60
END OF BROADCAST			
C	At the end of the broadcast, talent will read the network billboard and then the final cue: "A SUBSIDIARY OF WESTWOOD ONE, THIS IS THE MUTUAL BROADCASTING SYSTEM."	:15	

Figure 5.12 (*continued*)

ADDITIONAL PRODUCTION NOTES

All Station positions will be filled by the Network with promotional
or public service announcements. Stations rejoin on a time basis at
the end of all Station positions. For greater ease in rejoining, 30-
second Station positions will run 31 seconds, 60-second Station positions will run 62 seconds, and the 90-second Station position will
run 93 seconds. If all Station positions are not accomodated during
game play, makegoods will be inserted during the WRAPUP after position
#34 and before position #35, on this cue: "WE'LL BE BACK FOLLOWING
THIS (60-) (30-) SECOND MESSAGE FROM YOUR LOCAL STATION."

"FLOATERS": As game action permits, Network and Station "floater" pos-
            itions will be aired, following this rotation: Network,
            Station, Network, Station, Network, Station, and all
            thereafter Network. All of the "floaters" will be 30
            seconds in length, and will be inserted in each quarter
            (where possible) after all regularly scheduled positions
            have aired, IF additional time-outs or touchdowns occur.

NETWORK Floater Cue: "More after this time-out for _____.

STATION Floater Cue: "More after this special 30-second message."

STATION I.D. Cue: "We pause briefly for station identification. This
(on the hour)   is Mutual, your network leader in radio sports."

too, that each segment of the broadcast is clearly identified. This makes it
easier for the live talent to handle ad-libbing responsibilities and still provide the necessary cues for breaks.

Sometimes script material is prepared in advance to accommodate the
unpredictable nature of live sports broadcasts. Producers of live broadcasts
try to conclude such presentations as close as possible to the next regularly
scheduled program. Figure 5.13 shows a routine sheet for a *long* closing to a
live basketball telecast. Figure 5.14 shows the *short* version of the routine
sheet in figure 5.13.

Raycom Sports televises more college basketball games than all of the
major networks. Six regional broadcasts showcase college basketball's top
conferences.

Agriculture and Business

There are several similarities between agriculture and business news: a noticeable intertwining with general news developments; the use of specialized
sources; the influence of time of year and geographical area; and reports that
must inform those directly involved in either industry while also appealing
to those without such direct interests. The popular term *agribusiness* under-
scores this deepening correlation of agriculture and business.

Although business and agricultural information can be presented in
various forms—for example, features, announcements, interviews, magazine
programs, and documentaries—the most common form is individual news
stories. To write such stories well, you need to include specific kinds of information and to use special sources and writing techniques.

Long Closing Copy with Chyron and Music
(Copy 1:45)

Figure 5.13
Routine sheet used
for the closing to a
live sports broadcast.
*Courtesy of Raycom
Sports.*

"The final score is _____.

(Pause for Re-Cue)

"Today's game has been brought to you by...

_____

and by _____

and by _____

and by _____

(Pause for Re-Cue)

The Executive Producer of Raycom Sports is..............................Peter Rolfe

Raycom Senior Coordinating Producer...................................Johnny Tyous

The telecast of today's game has been produced by.....................Jim Zrake

... directed by..Doug Freeman

Technical Director..._____

and our Associate Director.._____

(Pause for Re-Cue)

Ad-lib upcoming game(s) - off chyron

(Pause for Re-Cue)

This has been a copyrighted presentation of the University of Washington.

Figure 5.14
Alternative routine
sheet used for a
shorter closing to a
live sports broadcast
than shown in figure
5.13.
*Courtesy of Raycom
Sports.*

<u>Short Closing Copy wth Chyron and Music</u>
(Copy :30)

The final score is _____

(Pause for Re-Cue)

Today's game has been brought to you by...

_____

and by_____

and by_____

and by_____

and by_____

(Pause for Re-Cue)

Ad-lib promo for upcoming game(s)

(Pause for Re-Cue)

This has been a copyrighted presentation of the University of
Washington.

Some of the sources of agricultural information include wire services
that provide daily summaries of items relating to agriculture; state and federal departments of agriculture, which provide written and electronic news
stories about the results of tests, surveys, and technological developments;
extension services at nearby agriculture-oriented colleges and universities;
specialized journals and publications; local and area agriculture organizations and representatives; and *local* commodity market exchanges and reporting services. Additional sources of information will emerge as you begin
working regularly with this kind of specialized information.

Following are some items often included in a regularly scheduled
Midwest agricultural report: weather forecast and current conditions;
world/national/state news items that relate directly to agriculture—for instance, governmental regulations, international trade agreements, and new
uses for standard agricultural products; local and area grain and livestock
market reports; a calendar of future events and issues; and features about
people and events associated with agriculture, especially local and area
agricultural interests.

A variety of sources can be used to gather business and financial news: business publications, such as *The Wall Street Journal, Business Week,* and *Money;* the wire services, which provide various kinds and levels of business and financial information, as well as reports on world and national events that affect business developments; local business organizations; local public interest and consumer groups; local economists, analysts, consultants, and brokers; major employers in the area; and governmental publications.

The following items have general appeal for the business community: stock market quotations and trends; statistics that measure business activity and financial vitality, such as unemployment, inflation, and interest rates; local investment strategies and trends; personnel changes in local and area businesses and industries; and corporate mergers and acquisitions. The emphasis should be on stories that have a grass roots impact, stories that directly affect local businesses and workers.

As was true with agricultural reports, it is best to include world, national, state, and local news stories that could directly influence business developments. Both agricultural and business audiences need this broad base of information to make knowledgeable decisions about future investments and activities. Both business and agricultural reports require clear and precise use of technical terms so that the impact of the reported information is evident.

Consumer Affairs

People want the best value for the money they spend. They want to know that someone cares about their interests and concerns. That is the principal responsibility of the consumer affairs reporter—to examine the effects of business and industry policies and products on the consumer. Sometimes the business reporter also handles consumer information.

A variety of sources are used for such reports: consumer groups, product testing labs, specialized and general distribution publications, local consumer consultants and home/family specialists, regulatory agencies at all levels, and court cases and laws related to consumer concerns.

Here is a sample of the possible range of consumer stories: scams and frauds, false advertising, product recalls, money management, consumer services, and the impact of technological developments on the general public.

Science and Health

Science and health considerations have become crucial for many of our daily decisions about food, shelter, and work and leisure activities. This is a reporting and writing specialization that occupies a regular time slot on many newscasts, especially on stations with medical and scientific research facilities nearby.

People are the best sources. Patients, physicians, scientists, and researchers offer a human and practical application of scientific and health developments.[3] Another excellent source is the meetings and publications of professional scientific and health organizations.

Story ideas for this specialty are extensive. Here are a few possibilities: nutrition and fitness, environmental issues, life sciences, high technology, and energy issues and developments.

In writing for this specialty, monitor your clarity and precision. Explain terminology in clear and simple language, but maintain accuracy and reasonable completeness.

Education

Educational concerns are shared by practically everyone. Parents, students, teachers, and administrators are interested in the quality of education. Local property owners and taxpayers, who provide a large share of the money used to support education, want to know that public funds are being spent wisely.

Again, people are the best sources—those already mentioned, as well as public officials and parent-teacher, home-school, and local citizens' groups. Printed material is also helpful—meeting agendas, public documents and records, and national and local publications.

Good education reporters go beyond the obvious stories—school board meetings and personality features. They also tackle specific issues and concerns—for instance, disputes and controversies about how the school system is operated, hiring and firing practices, curriculum changes, the impact of long-range planning and budgeting goals, the training and education of teachers, union activities, laws and regulations affecting education, and evaluations of the work done by students, teachers, and administrators.

Features

The specialists previously described regularly produce breaking news stories that require immediate coverage. However, sometimes they develop a feature story that relates to a specialized area but also provides insights into the people, places, things, or events that surround us each day but to which we pay little or no attention. Some reporters develop a knack for finding and developing interesting stories, and features become *their* specialty.

Features (sometimes called *kickers*) are written and produced using the same principles of newswriting and reporting described earlier in this chapter. However, story structure, point of view, and treatment tend to be more personal and flexible when preparing features than hard or breaking news stories.

Since features are developed for many kinds of programs besides newscasts and sportscasts, let's examine the principal types and sources of feature stories, as well as the approaches and techniques used to identify, organize, write, and produce effective feature stories for the electronic media.

Types

The categories identified in this section are not rigid and are presented only to help you better identify and develop effective features.

General news features are stories that are newsworthy but do not require the immediate attention and treatment that crucial breaking stories do.

Special events features cover in-depth one aspect of a larger breaking story. For example, feature stories could be developed about various activities surrounding the local visit of a foreign dignitary or the effects of a nearby oil spill.

News backgrounders trace the development and progression of a significant news story currently receiving attention, such as long-standing hostilities between neighboring countries or extended hostage situations.

Historical features examine the importance and relevance of past events—for instance, the anniversary of a major local crime or the series of events that evolved into a tense international situation.

Personality sketches or profiles can provide a better sense about the character, motivation, goals, ambitions, activities, and concerns of an individual—for example, a newly elected public official, a former astronaut or sports star, or the controversial spokesperson for an antienvironmental organization.

Descriptive features focus on places to visit and events to watch or participate in—for instance, recreational areas, fairs, festivals, pageants, or a behind-the-scenes look at a circus, carnival, or rock concert.

Seasonal features spotlight annual events or observances. Examples include religious or patriotic holidays, local fairs, and harvests or community activities.

Human interest features are the most common type of feature story. They offer the odd, unusual, humorous, and offbeat incidents and personalities that help keep life in perspective.

Sources

Where do ideas for feature stories originate? Some come from viewers or listeners who contact the newsroom suggesting a particular story idea or from friends or newsroom associates who talk about an interesting incident or person they have encountered. Others evolve from breaking news stories covered by you or other media, such as newspapers or magazines.

The best source is you and your sensitivity to the world that surrounds you. Cultivate an interest in a variety of subjects and activities by exploring new hobbies and enlarging your circle of friends. Look and listen carefully and thoughtfully to each part of your day. Always be alert to potential story ideas, breaking news as well as feature stories. Sensitivity will alert you to potential stories. Creativity will help you shape the stories you decide to develop.

Approaches and Techniques

Anything that arouses your curiosity could be developed into an intriguing feature story. The most memorable features center on people—who they are, what they do, why they act a certain way, and so forth. Listeners and viewers never seem to tire of learning about the activities of others. Place the audience in the position of an individual so that they understand and appreciate that person's concerns and interests. Let the individual tell the story from a personal perspective and in his or her own words, if possible. Even complex issues and situations can best be understood if presented from the point of view of a single individual.

The development of features requires flexibility. Approach feature stories with a tentative plan of development or structure in mind but without firm, preconceived notions or viewpoints. Try to offer a fresh, creative treatment for each feature story you develop.

The following is a process to follow to nurture and develop a feature story idea:

1. *Create a tentative story outline or structure.* This will help you identify the "spine" of the story—that is, the essential structure of what you expect to report—and help you determine whom to contact, what to gather, and so forth.
2. *Continue to shape and adjust the outline as you gather facts and comments.*
3. *Log the contents of the recorded material and highlight your written material* to better assess the quality of what you have gathered.
4. *Arrange recorded comments and notes into a rough sequence and revise the outline.*
5. *Write the first draft of the feature story,* molding words, sounds, and images into the finished piece.
6. *Refine and polish the script.*
7. *Refine and edit the tape.*

Writer John Holden's features have been used for many years by networks and nationally syndicated news services. Figure 5.15 shows the rough draft of his script for the opening segment of a human interest feature about inhabitants of a town that carries their namesake. Notice how pace and rhythm are affected as he begins a sentence and finishes it with a short recorded comment or inserts one- or two-word exclamations or comments to punctuate or accent a specific point ("Peeples" names). The use of several short, taped comments creates a distinctive rhythm and pace and is an interesting way to begin a feature story to point out quickly to the audience the unusual nature of the story.

Perhaps a few scripting observations would help you appreciate the process used to assemble this type of feature story. In the video column, notice how all name supers are clearly identified and how a combination of videotape footage and timing notations help locate specific pieces of videotape from the three worktapes used to gather video material for this feature story. In the audio column, notice how the three voice-over tracks by John Holden are identified and how the incues for each videotape excerpt are also provided, even when the excerpt is only one or two seconds long; this information will help the videotape editor when searching the three worktapes to be certain that the correct videotape excerpt or soundbite has been located, edited, and placed into the story as scripted.

Peeple town		LENGTH: 2:09
~~CITRUS CENTRE~~	6 PM	
Slug		**NEWS4**
HOLDEN CARLOS 8-25-87		57A
Writer Photo Editor Date		Page

VIDEO, SUPERS		AUDIO, SOUNDBITES
		(UP MUSIC...:05)
		VO1
S/ HOLDEN REPORTING	08-12	YOU'D NEVER KNOW IT NOW BY LOOKING AT IT...BUT
S/ LA BELLE 12-15		ONCE UPON A TIME, THIS STRETCH OF GRAZING LAND
		ON THE NORTHERN EDGE OF THE EVERGLADES WAS A
		1920'S BOOM TOWN! YEP...BACK THEN, CITRUS
		CENTRE WAS FILLED WITH LOTS of PEOPLE!
S/ DON PEEPLES	#1 1142	IN: ''PROBABLY ABOUT FOUR OR FIVE HUNDRED PEOPLE!
FORMER XXXXXXXX		AND NOW? IT'S JUST ME, DONALD PEEPLES, :05
TOWNSPERSON		**VO2**
:18-:23		WELL, THAT'S NOT QUITE TRUE: THERE'S STILL A FEW
		PEOPLE LEFT IN TOWN...
	#3 1:39	IN: ''WHAT'S YOUR NAME? DONNY PEEPLES . . :02
	#1 :54	IN: ''THIS IS BILLY PEEPLES. YOU'RE BILLY PEEPLES?
		:02
	#2 1128	IN: ''I'M DOROTHY PEEPLES..:01
	#2 1145	IN: ''I'M JIM PEEPLES :01
		XBEDEKBNIXKKNNBRBRSIMMXXX
	#2 115-8	IN: ''I'M KEVIN HOWARD. :01
		VO3
		AND KEVIN COULD JUST AS WELL BE A PEEPLES: YOU
		SEE, HE'S THE HIRED HAND FOR THE PEEPLES FAMILY,
		AND THEIR TOWN IS NOW THE PEEPLES RANCH. RXMEMER
		SO, DO THE-LAST REMAINING PEOPLE OF CITRUS
		CENTRE INEXXASTXREMRONONCXPEOPLEXBRXIIXBOXSSSXXXXX
		INEXXASTXREMX EVER GET LONELY BEING THE ONLY
		PEOPLE LEFT IN TOWN? NO...
		XX: ''
	#3 1:27	IN: ''JUST NICE, QUIET AND, PEACEFUL. :02
	#3 3:06	IN: ''NOT MANY PEOPLE, DON'T LIKE A LOT OF PEOPLE :02
	#3 3:46	IN: ''. . AND IF YOU WANT TO GO TO TOWN, YOU JUST GO
s/ JIMMY PEEPLES		TO LABELLE OR SOMETHING, AND YOU SEE ALL THE R
''REERKES RANCH''		
''PEEPLES		PEOPLE . . AND YOUR'E READY TO COME BACK. :05

Figure 5.15

Rough draft of the script used to produce the opening segment of a feature story by John Holden.

Courtesy of WTVJ-TV, Miami, Florida. From Peter E. Mayeux, Broadcast News Writing and Reporting.
Copyright © 1991 Wm. C. Brown Publishers, Dubuque, Iowa. All Rights Reserved. Reprinted by permission.

Summary

This chapter presented an overview of the principles and practices needed to write effective news and sports copy. Special consideration was given to the writing approaches used for live play-by-play sports broadcasts, specialized reporting areas, and feature stories. Specifically this chapter considered newsroom organization and structure; the process used to select and develop individual news and sports stories; the factors that determine news value and establish news judgment; the sources of information used regularly by reporters; the steps involved in gathering, handling, and organizing information; the copy formats and techniques used to write individual news and sports stories; and the preparation of newscasts and sportscasts.

Several points should be remembered when writing this kind of material; the importance of such information cannot be overemphasized. Literally the livelihood of viewers and listeners may be affected by the accuracy, completeness, clarity, objectivity, and balance provided in the stories you write. Fulfilling this responsibility is made even more difficult by the large volume of information that must be handled and the deadline pressure under which you must work. Format and copy style must become second nature. There is no time to second guess or mull over scripting formats and production practices.

Despite the difficulty, many writers find that this is the only kind of writing they want to do regularly. There is a unique personal and professional satisfaction for the writer who completes a solid news or sports story, develops a feature item that touches a strong human chord in a viewer, or produces a report in a specialized area, such as health or consumer affairs, that helps explain the personal impact of a complex process in clear, simple terms. Without the writer's skill and care, this kind of information would not touch so many lives so directly and with so much impact.

Suggested Exercises and Projects

1. Get permission to accompany a radio or television news or sports reporter into the field for coverage of a local story. Be sure to allow several hours for this. Note the process used to assign, cover, assess, report, write, produce, and present the story. As time permits, ask the reporter for comments about working as a news or sports reporter. Gather comments about the reporting methods used, the job satisfactions and frustrations, the writer's reporting accomplishments, and memorable stories the reporter has covered. Report your impressions and observations.

2. From a local governmental agency, obtain a recent news release about a significant issue or project and the agenda for an upcoming meeting or seminar associated with this agency. Write a 20-to-30-second radio or television reader story by doing *one* of the following:
   a. Rewrite the news release.
   b. Develop a follow-up report on an important issue described in the news release or discussed at the meeting.

    c. Preview the upcoming meeting, using the agenda as a reference.

    d. Attend the meeting and use the agenda to write a story about the important items discussed.

3. Write a short (:10–:20) anchor reader story for either radio or television based on *one* of the following abbreviated fact sheets:

    a. Shooting

- Andrew Williams was arrested early this morning at his family home in the southeast part of your town.
- District Attorney Sue Roy filed murder charges against Williams at noon.
- He is accused of killing his wife, Sarah, with gunshot wounds to her head.
- Sarah was dead on arrival at a local hospital.
- No weapon has been found yet.
- Neighbors report they heard no shots overnight.
- Williams' arraignment will be tomorrow morning.

    b. Robbery

- The Texaco gas station at 17th and A was robbed last night.
- Station attendant Phil Rodriguez described the supposed robber as about twenty, with dark hair, wearing sandals and a beret, and carrying a brown bag. Rodriguez says this jerk bought chewing gum and then demanded money without flashing a weapon.
- Phil claims the thief took the attendant's envelope containing cash and then fled around the corner.
- Local police have no suspects, but they are still looking for a blue scooter with a noisy muffler that was heard just after the robber ran around the corner.

4. Monitor a local or national radio or television newscast. Provide the lineup sheet for the monitored newscast.

5. Arrange to record two radio or television network newscasts that are broadcast simultaneously. Compare and contrast the newscasts in terms of the selection, length, treatment, and placement of each story; the writing style; and the use of sound or picture.

6. Use a recent edition of a metropolitan daily newspaper to do the following:

    a. Write the individual stories needed for a three-to-four-minute newscast or sportscast. The items can be local or national.

    b. Prepare the lineup for the newscast.

7. For an upcoming local sports event, prepare a preview story based on published reports, such as newspaper accounts or news releases. When the event concludes, prepare another story that includes highlights from the event. Provide *all* the written

material used to prepare *both* stories. The stories could be written for radio or television and in the presentational format that you think is the best for the story.

8. Prepare a routine sheet for a local athletic event that could be broadcast live on radio or television. Include the full-script material needed for the opening and closing of the broadcast, as well as all cue-aways for announcements during the broadcast.

9. Select one of the following reporting specialties: agriculture, business, consumer affairs, science, health, or education. Develop a newsworthy radio or television story related to this specialty. Select the length and presentational format you think will best present the information you have compiled, edited, and written. Turn in your news copy and your original source material.

10. Prepare the full-script for a one-to-three-minute radio or television feature to be used in a local station's newscast. The feature may relate to news, sports, business, or other specialized reporting areas described in this chapter.

Notes

1. *KIRO TV News Stylebook* (Seattle, WA: KIRO TV, revised March 1990), 18.
2. Condensed from *KIRO TV News Stylebook* (Seattle, WA: KIRO TV, revised March 1990), 15, 16, 28, 29.
3. Journalists can call the SIPI (Scientists' Institute for Public Information) Media Resource Service at 800–223–1730 toll-free (in New York State, 212–661–9110) for the names and telephone numbers of experts who have agreed to speak with media representatives directly or via recorded comments on scientific, medical, technological, environmental, and energy-related issues and topics. The mailing address for SIPI is 355 Lexington Avenue, New York, NY 10017.

Editorials and Commentaries

A t one time, the electronic media hesitated to express opinions on controversial issues, problems, and personalities. There were fears of government-imposed restraints, as well as criticism that such comments would unduly prejudice listeners and viewers. Today editorializing is not only allowed by the Federal Communications Commission, but it is encouraged. Editorializing is one way to demonstrate a station's level of community involvement and commitment.

There is an apparent decline in the use of editorials and commentaries. Some claim that there is insufficient time, facilities, and qualified personnel to research and prepare editorial comment of consistently high quality on a regular basis. Others fear that a delicate situation may develop when tough editorial stands on crucial local issues place the station management and sales staff at odds with the viewpoints and positions of current or prospective advertising clients. They also fear that some community leaders may disagree with a station's strong editorial stance. As noted in chapter 1, the FCC's elimination of the fairness doctrine in 1987 caused profitability concerns to overshadow public service commitments in facilities that used to air editorials and commentaries regularly. Others do not editorialize because they contend that it would be wrong to impose on viewers and listeners only a single viewpoint on controversial issues.[1]

Editorials and commentaries are supported by many for several reasons. They help highlight key issues and provide viewpoints that often lead to further thought and discussion. They help place news events in perspective, giving the audience a way to stand back and examine the meaning of events and developments and how they might affect their lives. They help audience members form and articulate their own opinions. Thoughtful, reasoned, and well-researched analyses and opinions help a station or network sustain an image of community involvement and enhance news credibility; image and credibility are vital to the success of local and network news broadcasts. Editorial leadership is an excellent way to demonstrate an attitude of responsibility toward an audience, its needs, and its concerns. Often emerging issues are identified as editorials and commentaries are developed; this can provide clues to meaningful news coverage. Editorials represent a level of recognition and community participation that distinguishes one station or network from another, both in community attitudes and often in financial success.[2]

This chapter will examine the writing process and techniques used to generate editorials and commentaries. The difference between an editorial and a commentary will be explained so that you understand the kinds of messages to be written and the perspective from which each type of comment originates. News-related and special-purpose commentaries will be described and illustrated. The principal types of editorials will be examined to help you determine their specific purposes and assess their impact. The selection and development of editorial subjects will be traced to identify more closely the writer's participation in this process. The logistics associated with the presentation of editorials will be reviewed. Several editorial examples will illustrate the writing suggestions offered.

Although there are similarities between radio and television editorials and commentaries and their newspaper counterparts, there are also differences that should be noted. The editorial writer for the electronic media must adhere to strict federal regulations, whereas the newspaper editorialist does not. Although both the print and electronic media must handle regulations governing libel and invasion of privacy, broadcasters must observe additional regulations, enforced by the FCC. Because legal regulations, restraints, and responsibilities bear directly on the preparation and use of editorials and commentaries, you should review chapter 1. Specifically review the rules and regulations governing defamation (libel and slander), invasion of privacy, and political broadcasts by candidates and those supporting candidates in editorials.

Editorial writers and commentators must not only understand the process involved in generating such material, but they must also remember ethical and moral obligations and responsibilities that should be an integral part of such writing. You cannot always measure the power and impact of editorials and commentaries by identifiable audience responses. There is an intangible influence that is not easily measured.

Definitions

"Editorial" has been defined in various ways. It has been called an expression of a licensee's opinion, which usually consists of comments on current issues and events. An editorial has also been labeled as a statement that may criticize, praise, or simply discuss the actions and policies of a public official or group. An editorial is much like an essay in that it often reflects the personality of the author.

The FCC describes a station editorial as "a statement representing the view of the licensee of the station, such as its owner, a principal officer or the manager or another employee if he is permitted by the licensee to speak for the station."[3] As noted in chapter 1, the term *licensee* can be described essentially as the owner(s) of a broadcasting station.

A concise, workable definition of the term *editorial* is supplied by the National Association of Broadcasters. The NAB identifies an editorial as "an on-the-air expression of the opinion of the station licensee, clearly identified as such, on a subject of public importance."[4]

Commentaries are viewed as being distinct from editorial statements. Generally commentaries reflect *individual* opinion rather than the official opinion of the station licensee. Many commentators are hired by individual stations, but more likely by group-owned stations, networks, and syndicated production companies, based on their background and reputation and their ability to write well, hold attention, and have something significant to say. Although editorials may accomplish some of the same objectives, commentaries generally analyze an issue or event and provide historical and contemporary perspectives on concerns of the day. Commentaries often focus on dominant national and international issues and events. Commentaries feature the nuances, implications, and effects of people, places, and events in the news on the minds of listeners and viewers. Commentaries provide a reflective perspective from an individual who has examined the intricacies and implications of events.

Commentaries

A large share of commentaries are news-related and appear within or adjacent to news broadcasts. Many special-purpose commentaries are also used as segments in entertainment, music, and magazine programs seen on stations, networks, and cable channels. John Chancellor tends to emphasize politics in his commentaries for the "NBC Nightly News." Other special-purpose commentary subject areas include sports issues and personalities, the economy or business, health, religion, international affairs, and consumerism.

In figure 6.1, notice how quickly John Chancellor focuses the audience's attention on the issue at hand. He links addiction to drugs with addiction to foreign oil. His opinions are sprinkled with pertinent background information to make his arguments clear and persuasive. Short, repetitive phrases throughout the commentary create a staccato effect and a steady pace to emphasize key points and sustain an effective conversational style. This commentary is especially noteworthy because of its logical organization, simple but effective word choices, smooth-flowing sentence structure, and thoughtful observations by an experienced journalist who has reported world events for several decades.

Entertainment commentaries are also prevalent. With sufficient background, training, preparation, and experience, an individual could be employed to provide regular reviews of and observations on the entertainment industry. At the network level, Gene Shalit's "Critic's Corner" on NBC's *Today* has become a staple for early morning viewers. His crisp, biting, satirical writing style reflects his varied experience as a reviewer and an observer of the entertainment scene.

Figure 6.1
John Chancellor's
commentary for "NBC
Nightly News,"
December 6, 1990.
*Courtesy of John
Chancellor.*

You hear a lot about drug addiction these days, but how about oil addiction? The United States is hooked on oil, addicted to foreign oil, hopelessly dependent on oil from the Persian Gulf. We import more foreign oil today than ever before. America's thirst for oil from the Persian Gulf has tripled in the last five years.

We're addicts, so we keep two sets of ethical books. We didn't try to rescue Tibet when China took it over. No Oil. We looked the other way when Morocco annexed Spanish Sahara. No Oil. But as many as 400,000 Americans could be ordered to fight in the Gulf next month because oil-rich Iraq grabbed oil-rich Kuwait. If Kuwait were only Kitty Litter we wouldn't care. But if Saddam Hussein gets to keep Kuwait, he'll own one-fourth of all the world's petroleum reserves. Therefore, hundreds of thousands of young Americans may be ordered to face death to stop him.

Protestors say, "Hell no, we won't go, we won't fight for Amoco" or other big oil companies. But Americans will have to risk fighting for oil as long as their country won't conserve it. Remember the price hikes and the gas lines of the 1970s? Your government has forgotten. Conservation is a joke. Gas prices are lower than in any big country because it pleases the voters. There is no national energy strategy.

Let the good times roll. And the next time some tinhorn oil dictator like Saddam Hussein throws his weight around, we'll have to go through all this again. It's a classic case of substance abuse.

Notice in figure 6.2 how Shalit begins an entertainment commentary by clearly identifying the movie to be reviewed. It is important to be this specific early in such commentaries so that the audience is set up for the opinions that follow. Shalit then offers an overview of the movie and launches into his personal retelling of the story without revealing the ending so that viewers who want to see the movie will not have their experience spoiled. Shalit mentions noteworthy individual performances before concluding the review with his personal assessment of the movie and his recommendations for the audience. Notice the clever word choices. The structural pattern for this type of commentary generally follows that shown in figure 6.2. Still photographs and film clips from the movie can offer visual enhancement. This kind of special-purpose commentary is particularly suitable for reviews of radio and television programs, stage plays, musical performances, and even contemporary novels.

"The Godfather--Part 3" opens on Christmas Day, which is the equivalent of finding coal in your stocking. After the critical and popular success of the first two Godfather films, Director Francis Coppola decided to cap it off with a Part 3. He should have quit while he was ahead. Mr. Coppola has cast his daughter Sofia in a pivotal role...and unfortunately she can't pivot. This movie may give nepotism a bad name. Apart from Al Pacino, who dominates the movie, there is little to commend it. As the murderous Godfather, Don Corleone, who has risen to defame and misfortune, Pacino delivers a vivid and steely performance. Where the first two Godfather pictures were devoted to family relationships and mafia matters, this one takes us into the sly finance of high finance. Don Corleone is determined to take over an international conglomerate that's tied into the Vatican. He offers to pay $600 million to a church emmisary, evidently hoping to become a holy owned subsidiary. He soon discovers that the difference between his pals in New York and the European businessmen he's dealing with, is that his New York pals *admit* that they're gangsters. So many people are killed in this movie that it would be appropriate to list the cast in order of their *dis*appearance. The principal characters are Joe Montagna as a rival boss who can pull some triggers of his own; Eli Wallach, impressive as an old, grovel-voiced dissembler; Talia Shire, a combination of Morticia and the Wicked Witch of the West; and Pacino's principal henchman, the fast-rising Andy Garcia. Diane Keaton's talents are totally wasted. Too bad she has only a few scenes. Whenever she's on, she adds class to the proceedings. Although there are several sequences of explosive violence, most of the story slogs along, braked by its rudimentary script. Some of the dialogue is incomprehensible. I know gangsters like to whisper, but from time to time they ought to let the audience in on it. What's good about "The Godfather Part 3" is Al Pacino's indespensible performance, the vigor and vitality of Andy Garcia, and Eli Wallach's old reprobate. What's not good is almost everything else. After all the hype and hope, this movie ends up on the heap. [COPYRIGHT 1990 BY GENE SHALIT]

Figure 6.2
Review by Gene Shalit first broadcast on NBC-TV's "Today" in December 1990.

Editorials

It is important to know the principal types of editorials, the process used to select and develop subjects, and the details involved in presenting editorials on-the-air.

Types

It is sometimes easier to talk about types of editorials in the abstract without examining realistic problems and situations. Once you have selected a particular type of editorial writing approach, your opinions can be formulated to match the nature of the topic. This will help you achieve an identifiable audience response. Knowing when to use a particular type of editorial approach often becomes a decision as crucial as selecting the topic and expressing the opinions.

Although a given editorial may fulfill more than one purpose, most can be categorized on the basis of their predominant purpose. There are basically five types of editorials.

The *informative editorial* restates the principal facts of a news story and tells of, or explains, a particular occurrence or series of related happenings. This type is used to lay the groundwork for future editorials on a subject or to give you time to research the topic in depth and to determine the station's stand on an issue or event.

The *interpretative editorial* presents the facts of a particular event briefly and then tells what the licensee feels is the real, vital, and hidden significance of the event. This type of editorial may also present a conclusion for the audience to consider and may advocate a line of thinking for them to adopt.

The *argumentative editorial* takes a present condition or event and argues logically what will happen from cause to effect. This type of editorial requires clear organization, sufficient documentation, and convincing reasoning to be effective and to have impact on the audience. It is one of the most difficult types of editorials to write.

The *call-for-action editorial* states a problem or situation, details a solution, then finally calls for specific action by the audience or by a particular group, agency, organization, or individual. This is one of the easiest types of editorials to research and to write because the issue involved generally is well known. Its effectiveness, however, is diminished by constant ''calls to action'' on almost all issues considered.

The *entertaining editorial* uses satire, humor, and comedy in an effort to entertain but also to gently persuade. This type of editorial strives to provide a light approach to the day's important and seemingly unimportant events and newsmakers.

Subject Selection

If editorials are done regularly, it is best to select a person or to establish an editorial board to supervise editorial policy. This will provide guidance for the selection and development of editorial opinions. At some stations, the licensee retains this editorial responsibility. Most stations, however, form an editorial board composed of a few or all of the following: the licensee or the licensee's representative, the station manager if not also the licensee, the program director, the public affairs director, an editorial writer/researcher/director, and another member from the station's management team or an individual from outside the station who is involved in community and philanthropic activities. A common practice is to separate editorial efforts from news department concerns to avoid potential conflicts.

Topics for editorials, however, may be suggested by news department personnel, as well as other station employees. The editorial writer often works through the ranks of the news department and, thus, continues to monitor local and state news events, which provide the majority of editorial topics. The important thing is to have someone or a group in place to decide what subjects to discuss in editorials, who will write them, whether the final version of each editorial is accurate and meets with station policy on each issue, when to broadcast the editorial, who voices the editorials, and who handles reaction and rebuttal to the editorial.

The process established by WCVB-TV in Boston is typical of how most stations that editorialize regularly coordinate editorial efforts. Marjorie M. Arons-Barron, Editorial Director of WCVB-TV, works with a researcher/writer. This editorial staff meets once each week with a ten-member editorial board. The staff makes presentations on about four issues they have selected. Recommendations are made regarding the position the station should take on each issue. Vigorous discussion among the board and staff usually follows and results in an editorial position. The editorial mandate is limited to a ''sense of the board.'' This becomes two or three principal points that are to be incorporated into each editorial. That is the end of the board's involvement; there is no board review of scripts.

Here are suggestions to help you select and research potential editorial topics:

    a. *Select a topic or subject that has impact for your immediate audience.* Since your audience is more concerned about issues and problems that affect them directly, you should stress local, state, and area issues rather than national and international problems. Management should be committed to a strong editorial policy. It is a necessary ingredient for successful editorializing. Realistically, only local, state and regional issues can be properly researched by the station's staff. It is only these kinds of issues on which the station can realistically have some impact within the community it serves. How the strike at a local steel factory affects the ten thousand employees and their families is more important than a transit strike in a distant city that may affect more workers but has little or no impact on the local audience.

b. *Select a subject that is current, timely, and most directly related to your audience's life-style.* Unless your audience can relate to the issue or problem discussed, your success as an editorial writer and the impact of the station on community concerns will be less than desirable.

c. *Select a subject that is important enough to discuss.* The audience must understand that the subject you are presenting is urgent and requires immediate attention. Although occasional editorials on patriotic and safety topics may be regarded by some as part of the editorial service of the station, it is the hard-hitting, vibrant, sensitive, and tough subjects that command respect and attention from your audience and from the community at large.

d. *Select and develop an editorial subject that will gain and hold attention.* This may be accomplished by focusing on controversial subjects or perhaps by using striking graphics and visuals during a television editorial. Your audience deserves and expects only the best in topic selection, development, and presentation.

e. *Focus on a problem or situation not yet resolved.* Although many excellent editorials have been written as reactions to events or situations, effective editorializing can also *lead* events rather than only follow them. Editorials can look to the future as well as assess events from the past.

f. *Limit the scope of the editorial subject.* The station's editorial staff must be capable of handling the topic. Station managers must recognize and accept the fact that sufficient staff and time must be provided if worthwhile editorial comments are to be offered regularly. If the subject is so broad that regular editorial staffers cannot handle it, more personnel should be assigned to help in the project. Perhaps the subject should be limited in scope or dropped in favor of another topic that is more readily researched, written, and presented.

g. *Identify a subject in which the public interest conflicts with the interests of an individual or a special group.* Theoretically, when the station expresses an editorial opinion, it is seeking what is best for the public as a whole rather than for one individual or group. Editorials that express this attitude are usually the most effective.

You can tap various sources to select and research excellent editorial subjects. Here are a few to use: the previous newscasts of your station; other station staff members; the station's last ascertainment survey of community needs; files on previous meetings and decisions of local public bodies; library resources and references; personal contacts and informed sources; unsolicited audience comments and opinions; and simply your solid editorial judgment acquired after many years of experience. Sometimes editorial subjects are assigned by the station licensee or by the editorial board. As an editorial writer, you may be in a position to suggest and help develop appropriate editorial subjects. Topics for station editorials may come to mind as you read an impressive magazine article or hear a startling local news story on the afternoon newscast. Always be aware of what is happening around you and be sensitive to potential editorial subjects as you progress through your routine assignments.

Once the editorial subject has been selected and the station's basic position on an issue confirmed, you can then research the subject in some depth and begin writing. When assembling information to be used in the editorial, you can tap basically the same sources used to select the subject. Although the research for any given subject never will be complete, enough information must be compiled to formulate the first draft of the editorial. This will allow the licensee or editorial board an opportunity to review the information and to confirm final approval of the station's opinion before any editorial stance is broadcast.

Subject Development

Once your essential research is completed, sift out the information to be used and organize the material clearly and concisely. Often it is helpful to outline the information available and the tentative order in which the information will be presented. At times, this outlining process may indicate that a particular subject is not worthy of an editorial. The licensee or the editorial board should then be consulted and an adjustment made in the selection or development of the topic, or, at this juncture, the topic may be discarded and another subject selected for development.

If the subject does seem to lend itself to a worthwhile editorial, write the first draft. Read it aloud and listen to how it sounds. Edit it for grammar, spelling, word choice, sentence structure and length, tone and treatment, persuasiveness, and, of course, content and accuracy. Does the editorial gain and hold attention? Is it written in a conversational style? Is it written in a clear, concise, logical, and unified manner? Are the language mechanics of grammar and spelling used correctly and effectively? Do all your word choices express precisely what you wish to communicate? Is the station's position on the issue or problem clear, especially after only the first reading? Does the editorial display a strong, persuasive, and constructive tone by offering thoughtful analysis and treatment of an issue, along with practical ideas and solutions to the problems? Above all, does the editorial clearly express an opinion or a stand on an issue of vital importance? If these and other concerns have been satisfied, then you can begin to prepare a subsequent or final draft of the editorial.

If the editorial is to be broadcast on television, consider the use of various types of visual material to accompany the written editorial comment. Nothing is as dull as a television editorial showing only the presenter's face and a cold table top. Consider using charts, graphs, maps, videotapes, and photographs to add visual reinforcement and information to the editorial statement. Stations often broadcast television editorials from a studio using ESS graphics as the minimum visual support. B-roll from the station's news film/videotape library can be used. Shooting editorials on location can add impact and a sense of immediacy to the presentation. Remember, the viewer has become accustomed to rather sophisticated television presentations. Any legitimate television production tool that will enhance the viewers' attention, produce a greater impact, and supply supplementary information should be considered when designing, writing, and producing television editorials.

Most often, radio editorials feature a single voice delivering the station licensee's opinion. On occasion, it may be appropriate to consider the use of other radio production tools to better communicate and reinforce the opinion expressed. Careful use of other voices, music, sound effects, or "location sound" could create in the listeners' minds a sharper, more graphic, and more memorable impression than is possible with only a single voice. Only occasional use of these additional production tools is recommended and only when appropriate for the circumstances.

Some components can be used in either radio or television editorials—natural sound, interviews, news coverage excerpts (or soundbites), perhaps even music segments and excerpts from commercials and entertainment programming. Unless you consciously enliven an editorial's content, chances are good that the expressed opinion will be ignored, misunderstood, or quickly forgotten.

Another factor to consider at this stage of the writing process is whether the station licensee wants a single editorial or a multipart editorial series prepared. Besides presenting individual editorials on a variety of subjects, stations on occasion prepare a series of editorials on a major topic. These multipart editorials may be presented on consecutive days or offered as events and issues develop over a period of weeks or even months. Some editorial writers question the advisability of consecutive-day presentation, since it presumes that the listener or viewer has been exposed to all portions of previous editorials in the multipart series. On the other hand, consecutive-day presentation allows the station to keep the issue before the audience, to follow through on developments, and to make it known that the station is committed to its stance and will continue to report and editorialize on an issue of community importance. Careful planning and coordination are required to develop an effective multipart editorial series.

Logistics and Presentation

Several details are involved in presenting editorials in the electronic media. Awareness of these details will help you thoroughly complete the editorial writing process.

Although an editorial is technically the opinion of the station licensee, the licensee does not necessarily have to present the editorial. Most stations use the same presenter or announcer for all station editorials. Others prefer to use various station representatives; each presenter or announcer is used only for specific editorial subject areas. Whoever delivers the editorial on-the-air must have an acceptable delivery style; otherwise the editorial's full effectiveness may be lost. Make certain the audience knows that the expressed opinions represent those of the station licensee, even if the licensee does not present the editorial personally.

Editorials tend to be brief. Many are only 30 to 40 seconds long. A few last about 60 seconds.

Although editorials generally are scheduled near the times of newscasts, editorials should be separated from the newscasts as much as possible so that the audience does not confuse opinion with straight news items. Irrespective of whether editorials are broadcast on a daily, weekly, or occasional basis, the important rule to follow is to air an editorial several times, in carefully selected time slots, on the day it is scheduled to be used. This maximizes the number of people who will hear or see the editorial and respond to it. If a multipart editorial series is presented, it is even more crucial to broadcast each editorial in the series at the same time each day.

Although no longer required to do so, most stations that editorialize provide rebuttal time to responsible citizens and groups who disagree with editorial viewpoints and wish to express dissenting opinions. Generally editorials conclude with a standard statement offering such an opportunity. The station licensee decides whether time should be given to each party that applies for response time.

One practice is highly recommended to avoid potential problems and to promote healthy dialogue within the community. Before each editorial is aired, send copies to community leaders as well as individuals and groups directly involved in the subject of the editorial. Although a station is not likely to reverse its opinion because of negative feedback from such mailings, this kind of response from important community members provides additional perspectives for the station to consider and displays the station's attitude of cooperation and goodwill within the community.

Each editorial must be read on-the-air exactly as it is written. For each editorial, use a standard opening and closing statement. Ad-libbing an editorial can prove to be a costly shortcut. Announce that the editorial is the opinion of the licensee and offer to provide response time for responsible groups and individuals. Keep copies of each editorial script for future reference in case of disagreements or lawsuits. It is also a good idea to record the editorial on tape.

Editorial Examples

The technique of writing editorials for the electronic media is best illustrated by examining editorials from stations that have received awards from professional organizations and associations. The editorials in figures 6.3 through 6.5 are only a sample of each station's editorial efforts throughout the years.

Figure 6.3 shows one of the editorials that helped WTMJ win national honors from the National Broadcast Editorial Association (NBEA). Notice the use of recorded material in this editorial aired on both radio and television. Although only a transcript of the spoken words is shown in the script, pictures of the two officials in this heated exchange added intensity to their

Figure 6.3
Interpretative editorial
that concludes with a
pointed call-for-action.
*Copyright WTMJ, Inc.
1990.*

WTMJ, Inc.

EDITORIAL

27-183

WTMJ-TV at 10:00 p.m., Saturday, Apr. 22, 1989.

*WTMJ Radio at 6:15 p.m., Saturday, Apr. 22, and 8:35 a.m.,
Monday, Apr. 24, 1989.*

WKTI-FM at 12 midnight and 5:00 a.m., Monday, Apr. 24, 1989.

One of the sidebar factors in the resignation of Police Chief
Robert Ziarnik may have been the verbal abuse he took the
other day from Alderman Robert Anderson.

(Anderson: "...put those others on, out on the street." Ziarnik"
"You run it then." A: "I will run it." Z: "Go ahead." A: "When
do you want me to come over?" Z: "Any time." A: "I'll be over
tomorrow. Have the coffee ready. I want them taken out. You
don't know what you're talking about. Why don't you resign?"
Z: "You'll get that soon enough." A" "Good. Good.")

As City Hall people know well, that was a modest version of an
Anderson outburst. Throughout his career as an Alderman, he
has delivered even more severe tirades to a lot of other
people. There are even indications that the Common Council
has modified its procedures in efforts to avoid Anderson's
verbal explosions.

So, Alderman Anderson, if you can't behave as a responsible
elected official and as a gentleman, let us ask a question with
which you're familiar. Why don't you resign?

Broadcast by Ed Hinshaw

Editorial

WCVBTV **BOSTON, CHANNEL 5**
Editorial Department
5 TV Place, Needham Heights, MA 02194-2303
(617) 449-0400

Title: Rejecting School Committee Negativism

Presented By: Marjorie Arons-Barron, Editorial Director

Broadcast: July 21: 6:57 AM; 12:28 PM; 6:55 PM; 3:40 AM

Reference No.

100-89

Figure 6.4
Argumentative
editorial from
WCVB-TV Boston.
*Copyright WCVB-TV
Boston.*

The Boston School Committee has hit a new low in cowardice. The problem: the Committee's afraid to close under-utilized schools. Sure, that's always a tough vote, certain to anger some neighborhood people. But we elect Committee members to make those hard decisions.

The case for closing schools is clear. Four thousand excess high school seats with a budget $4 million over the limit set by the Mayor. And it's not just the money. Some schools don't have enough students to support complete academic programs, so the kids can't take the courses they want. So excess seats are bad educationally as well as financially.

Nine members of the School Committee were so afraid of taking the heat on school closings that they voted for an independent commission to make the hard choices. But four of those who had voted for the commission then voted against its recommendations. Those four were Gerald Anderson, Robert Cappucci, John O'Bryant and Jean McGuire. Remember their names.

They turned their backs on the children of Boston, who can't learn at half-empty schools with barebones programs. We expect more than this from our School Committee members. And if current members can't live up to those expectations, voters this fall should find replacements who will.

EDITORIAL

No. 4338
Aired: November 27 & 28, 1989

TACOMA DRUGS

I'm Ken Hatch for the Editorial Board of KIRO.

The Tacoma police department is now distributing fliers with the names and pictures of people they've convicted for drug selling.

That's a good approach, but we think it's also time the Tacoma police go farther. If they're distributing fliers with drug sellers on them, Tacoma police should also distribute fliers with the names and pictures of those convicted for drug *buying*. We think the threat of popping up on a drug poster would be a significant deterrent to casual drug use.

Police have long insisted they need to go after both sides of the drug demand cycle, the seller and the buyer. Tacoma should go all the way and add convicted users to their drug posters.

Reprints only with credit to KIRO, Inc.
Excerpts only with permission of KIRO, Inc.

comments when shown on television. Although the Ed Hinshaw editorial concludes with a rhetorical call-for-action question, the primary purpose of the editorial is to interpret a local situation.

WCVB-TV in Boston has received numerous awards for its editorial efforts, including national Editorial Excellence Awards from the NBEA. Figure 6.4 shows a WCVB-TV editorial that considers the consequences of not closing underutilized schools. It is an excellent example of an argumentative editorial. It logically argues for closing some schools, and it chastises specific elected officials who failed to take action on a crucial local issue. The editorial displays excellent structure, documentation, logic, syntax, and persuasiveness.

Figure 6.5 shows a call-for-action editorial in which the Editorial Board of KIRO-TV applauds the action already taken by Tacoma police but calls for more action to attack both sides of the drug demand cycle. The editorial is brief and focuses directly on an important local concern.

Summary

This chapter examined editorials and commentaries. Network and station examples illustrated the two forms. The process of selecting, developing, and presenting editorials was also discussed.

With strong managerial support and encouragement plus sufficient time, personnel, and research facilities, broadcast editorials can be an effective tool to enhance station image and to provide a catalytic spark for community improvement. A station's strong editorial policy indicates its strength within and commitment to the community.

1. Critique several commentaries broadcast on national radio or television networks. Comment on the selection and development of subjects, writing and presentation style, tone and treatment of the subject, documentation presented, persuasiveness, impact, and compliance with broadcast editorial guidelines.
2. Write a short 30-to-40-second radio or television commentary on a current national or international topic of importance.
3. Write a short 30-to-40-second radio or television entertainment commentary on a current motion picture, stage play, or musical performance in your area.
4. Outline and then write a short 30-to-60-second radio or television editorial on a current local or state topic of importance.
5. Write a series of three radio or television editorials on the same topic. Prepare the editorials to be used in sequence, on consecutive days, on a local broadcast station.
6. List five topics or issues suitable for local station editorial comment. Indicate why you selected each topic or issue for potential development and use as a broadcast editorial.
7. List ten key community leaders in your area who you feel should receive advance copies of editorials broadcast by local and area broadcast stations. Indicate why you would recommend each person on your list.

1. A thoughtful discussion of this viewpoint is presented by Doug Halonen in "The Vanishing Editorialist," *Electronic Media* (24 September 1990): 1, 16.
2. G. Donald Gale provided a thoughtful analysis of "The Need for Broadcast Editorials" in *RTNDA Communicator* (May 1987): 10–11. The article was reprinted in *The Masthead* (Spring 1988): 37–38.
3. From *The Law of Political Broadcasting and Cablecasting*. Federal Communications Commission, Federal Register, Vol. 43, No. 159, 16 August 1978, 36387.
4. National Association of Broadcasters, *Radio and Television Editorializing* (Washington, DC: National Association of Broadcasters, 1967), 2.

Documentaries and Investigative Reports

7

Networks, local stations, and production companies continue to invest large sums of money and a substantial amount of time, energy, and talent to develop documentaries and investigative reports. These types of presentations have an inherent value for the public and the telecommunications industry.

Competing media have intensified their efforts to capture large shares of the audience by offering provocative and entertaining programming. Radio and television stations and networks continue to search for cost-effective ways to offer documentaries and investigative reports that address pressing personal and public concerns, as well as attract large audiences.

Topics for such programs address contemporary and powerful human concerns. They are often developed as segments in news magazine programs.

Those who write and produce documentaries and investigative reports acknowledge the power of the electronic media to effect change. However, they must also determine how their work can be used at a time when profitability and entertainment, rather than news value, are growing priorities.

This chapter will examine documentaries and investigative reports, focusing on the writer's participation in the creative process. There will be a description of the basic types of documentaries, as well as the criteria used to evaluate such creative efforts. The chapter will outline the progressive steps used by the writer to generate a documentary and investigative report: selecting and developing meaningful subjects, gathering information, preparing script material, developing a program structure and organizational pattern, handling the production process, and working with narration. Script examples will be presented at the end of the chapter to illustrate the writing principles described.

Definitions

It will help to differentiate between the terms *documentary* and *investigative report*. This will be useful when you begin developing subjects in-depth.

Documentaries

Documentaries present facts about a relevant subject from real events, persons, or places to reflect, interrelate, creatively interpret, or comment on current concerns and realities. Documentaries should be designed to create a cohesive, dramatic presentation with intellectual and emotional impact. Reality is the basic criterion for a documentary.

Documentaries may be classified according to their ultimate objective—information, interpretation, or persuasion. Certainly such classifications can be combined and altered to provide an even more effective documentary presentation. If the intent is information, a documentary may simply explore a subject in an organized manner; facts are carefully selected and organized to provide as complete and objective a report as possible. Interpretation may evolve from this informational base; the documentary presentation could be designed to provide insight and perspective into a sensitive or controversial subject. A documentary could arouse concern and present solutions to specific problems that have been factually and objectively identified, outlined, and creatively interpreted. In effect, the persuasive documentary incorporates information and interpretation to present persuasive arguments.

Two developments have provided additional dimensions for these primary documentary classifications. In *cinéma vérité,* the audience is allowed to witness an event for themselves and, thus, to form their own inferences, perspectives, and interpretations of what the camera simply records. The documentarian controls, to an extent, the view of the event by selecting camera angles, editing long sequences, and omitting some material, but it is the viewer who ultimately determines the impact of what is seen and heard. Such program series as CBS's "48 Hours" use cinéma vérité techniques effectively. *Docudramas* are essentially fictional accounts based on actual events, persons, and situations. They are a hybrid program form that usually emphasizes fictional dramatic entertainment and plot structure. Docudramas are discussed fully in chapter 12, "Dramas and Comedies."

Investigative Reports

Investigative reporting is a form of documentary. It requires the acquisition and presentation of carefully documented facts to substantiate specific charges, to explain changes in society, and to serve as a guidepost for societal ethics and standards. It should lead to a direct knowledge of events, actions, and facts that have been concealed. Revelation is the essential characteristic of investigative reports.

Good investigative reporting requires an emphasis on accuracy, objectivity, and documentation. These are acquired only through hard work that is painstaking, careful, logical, thoughtful, and as complete as possible. A good investigative reporter gathers pertinent facts from various kinds of sources and presents these facts in a logical, understandable, and interesting manner.

The selection and development of a topic often determine the success of an investigative report. Engaging and effective investigative reports tend to focus on corruption, fraud, hypocrisy, and illegality by public officials and agencies, private corporations, political organizations, charities, and foreign governments. Other viable topics may evolve from personal injustices, scandals, intimate details about notorious celebrities, and societal inequities. Later in this chapter, specific suggestions will be presented to help you select and develop effective topics for investigative reports.

Ethical and legal concerns often impinge on the use of certain investigative reporting techniques and practices. These concerns include the methods of gathering information; how human sources of information are treated and rewarded; the personal integrity, objectivity, and perception of the investigative reporter; how information is prepared for presentation; the individual's right to privacy versus the public's right to know and react to certain kinds of information; and the formulation of composite persons who typify real characters. The investigative reporter faces the difficult challenge of deciding what actions and practices are illegal or unethical and then following a carefully documented path that leads to the objective presentation of previously concealed facts. The investigative reporter continually walks a tightrope, balancing delicate moral and ethical standards and the documentation and interpretation of complex issues, events, and actions.

Developing the Documentary or Investigative Report

Several considerations are involved when selecting and developing subjects for a documentary or an investigative report. These two steps come early in the developmental process and help determine the success of the rest of the documentary or investigative report project.

Selecting Subjects

The topic of a documentary or an investigative report must capture and sustain the attention and interest of the audience. The most effective topics usually relate directly to contemporary life-styles and affect the heart, health, and pocketbook of the audience. Topic selection is the crucial first step in generating an effective, engaging documentary or investigative report.

The initial idea for such presentations may come from any number of sources. Make a conscious effort to become aware of current developments and concerns. This usually yields many worthwhile subjects. Excellent sources for ideas include regular reading of pertinent magazines, newspapers, and books; audience research information compiled for program ratings or community ascertainment purposes; unsolicited audience comments and reactions; routine review of available public records; newscast stories, which often indicate the spark of an idea that could be more fully developed; and suggestions and comments by fellow staff members or from a formally established advisory board.

Developing Subjects

The idea for the documentary or investigative report must be developed. How the idea is developed usually depends on such variables as the established developmental procedures you are expected to use, the nature of the topic, available personnel and production resources, and the writing and production timetable. In large production operations, a special unit is assigned the task of producing documentaries and investigative reports. Limited staff and budget generally require that routine news coverage responsibilities be combined with such production tasks.

No matter what process is used to develop a subject, generally this scheme is followed:

$$\text{information} \longrightarrow \text{knowledge} \longrightarrow \text{understanding} \longrightarrow \text{exposition}$$

Each essential step leads to the next. Information provides knowledge, which leads to understanding and, ultimately, to an exposition of the material in a clear, logical, poignant manner. Although an experienced documentarian or investigative reporter may combine or even bypass some of the specific steps outlined, the recommended procedures are isolated for the purposes of discussion and evaluation by the novice writer. These procedures are only recommendations based on general practices within the industry. Usually several steps are under development simultaneously.

Gather Preliminary Information

Many of the same sources used to select a topic can be tapped to gather preliminary information to formulate a tentative plan of action for further development. At this point, complete enough research to know something about the topic, but not so much that you form a prejudicial perspective and, thus, preclude alternate methods of presentation and development. In effect, this phase should be a *preliminary* examination of the topic. Remain objective and alert to identify the parameters of the topic and the sources of information that will be pursued at a later time. Continue your research as the documentary or investigative report is developed and finally produced.

Besides the sources already listed for selecting a subject, it might be helpful to seek out experts, technical advisers, or people who have lived through a particular experience; to visit certain locales that might be used in the final presentation; to complete a preliminary examination of relevant written material and documents; and to determine the availability and usefulness of archival material—films, slides, pictures, newspaper accounts, historical objects, and so on.

Prepare a Treatment

The treatment is an explanation of the essential idea or storyline around which a presentation revolves. The treatment for a documentary or an investigative report contains the same kind of descriptive information all treatment statements provide—the purpose of the program; the intended audience; the content and length of each major sequence; and the style, mood, emphasis, and shape of the presentation. In addition, a treatment for a documentary or an investigative report should reflect the quality and nature of the preliminary information gathered and indicate a tentative point of view, tact, or "feel" that will be explored, developed, and adjusted later by the writer and production staff.

Some production facilities require the approval of each idea after preliminary information has been assembled and a treatment statement has been prepared. This may be one of the first of many checkpoints you will encounter; other reviews may occur at other crucial points in the writing and production process. These checks are done generally by upper management personnel for budgetary as well as other financial concerns.

At this point, return to those fertile research sources identified earlier. Now each source should be explored fully to refine and focus the topic. Specific material should be gathered, recorded, filed, and organized. There should be a continual review of the accumulated material and the treatment to determine what is known and what needs to be known to provide a complete report. Every reasonable effort should be made to examine and probe all available resources that relate to the subject.

Complete Research

At this point, as the writer/researcher, you should begin to place each piece of information into perspective, to determine its place and function. The outline could be written as research progresses. Often it is written after most of the research has been completed.

Formulate an Outline

It must be a dynamic outline, one that progresses dramatically and remains reasonably flexible. The outline serves as a guidepost for writing the documentary or investigative report. It must be a "living" document, adjusting to new information and new perspectives. The outline must be clear, concise, and cohesive and must logically display the relationship between main points and supporting ideas. As a developmental step, the outline may substitute for a treatment statement.

A thoughtful, carefully written outline normally suggests the most effective structure for a particular documentary or investigative report. The program structure must be "dramatic"; that is, it should have an identifiable beginning, middle, and ending, progressing to a climax or conclusion. The beginning must capture audience attention and clearly indicate the nature of the program. The middle must examine the topic, issue, or event in practical human terms. It should explore the subject in a compelling manner. The ending must provide the essence of the program, as well as focus and interpretation that adds meaning to what has been presented. It should make the audience think about the significance and impact of the subject. It may be appropriate to suggest a course of action to resolve a problem or issue.

Determine Program Structure

Various organizational patterns can provide a clear and logical program structure and allow a progressive exposition of the topic. Some of the more common patterns are problem-solution, cause-effect, chronological, geographical or spatial, topical, and various classifications—for instance, age groups and political subdivisions. Select the appropriate organizational pattern that reflects the nature and anticipated development of the topic.

Several kinds of formats can be used to structure the program. Short-form formats include news magazine and mini-documentary reports. Long-form formats include news specials and full-length programs. The use of each kind of program format will influence the shape and style of the final presentation.

Short-form formats are used frequently. *News magazines*—which display diversity, flexibility, and a fast pace—tend to attract large, loyal audiences. When structuring a news magazine presentation, the intent is to provide short but complete reports on a variety of topics of direct interest to the audience. The reports or segments are positioned during the presentation to attract and sustain audience interest. On-air anchors introduce each program segment and often interact with correspondents as preproduced reports conclude. Each of the three or four segments in a *single-theme* news magazine program should be a story, complete with a beginning, a middle, an end, and a payoff that precedes a break for spot announcements. *Mini-documentaries* are a series of brief, interrelated presentations on a subject of prime importance to the audience. Mini-docs can provide coverage of immediate, emerging topics not requiring full-length program treatment. They create interest and suspense as the various parts or episodes are presented, usually on successive newscast programs, building to the final, climactic episode. Each episode is usually two to five minutes long. Three to twelve episodes may be presented within regularly scheduled newscasts or public affairs program series over a period of one week or even several weeks. Each episode must be able to stand alone and yet still interrelate with all other episodes in the series to provide a complete and unified perspective of the topic. Since it is unrealistic to expect that the audience will see or hear all parts of a mini-doc series, each episode, except for the first, begins by briefly recapping previous episodes and placing the upcoming episode into perspective. Each episode, except the last, usually ends with a preview of the next installment to help arouse audience interest. The final episode could review the entire series and offer additional insights.

Long-form formats are useful for a full exposition of a topic within a single program. *News specials,* which usually are broadcast in primetime or just after the late-night newscast, are programs that explain or interpret the significance and impact of a particular contemporary news event or development. Such specials concern an event, a person, or an action that significantly dominated the news events of the day. It could be the death of a nation's leader or a popular entertainer, military or political changes in a developing story, a natural disaster, or a human tragedy. Archival material as well as recorded reports often are used during such broadcasts. *Full-length programs* are the more traditional thirty- and sixty-minute documentary or investigative reports centering on one topic for the entire broadcast. The dramatic program structure outlined earlier would be used to develop such programs.

A popular option is the single-theme full-length news magazine documentary, such as CBS's *48 Hours*. The interrelated segments in such a program format attract large audiences and respond well to budget constraints often imposed on documentary and investigative reporting productions. A combination of presentational formats can be used in these full-length or full-form presentations. For example, there could be a central, on-air anchor introducing the topic and serving as the transitional device or "glue" for the program that integrates recorded segments from several correspondents. Another possibility is to intersperse live, interactive, satellite-generated interviews or discussions with periodic, recorded segments introduced by one or more reporters. Still another format is a combination of studio- and field-produced segments with live and recorded interviews introduced by several principal anchors, who conclude the program with an assessment of what has been presented. Select the presentational format or style that best suits the topic. The format should be a means to a predetermined end, not an end in itself.

It is possible to combine short- and long-form program formats into an effective program structure. For example, it is possible to develop a five- to ten-part mini-doc series on a particular topic. These episodes could be written and produced to be used as "interlocking modules." That is, the individual mini-doc episodes could be consolidated into a unified, long-form, full-length thirty-minute documentary. The opening and closing sequences of each installment would have to be deleted, but there should be no need to change the crucial middle portion of each episode. When combined, the episodes would present the full exposition of the subject, just as though they were originally designed for broadcast in this way. Thus, a station or network could present the mini-doc series in its entirety and also offer the opportunity to see or hear all the parts in one program. Careful writing and production planning are necessary to make this multiple use feasible.

Select the Production Process

Before you write the script, determine how the documentary or investigative report will be produced. As indicated earlier, you may be in a position to work as the producer or director of the production as well as the writer and researcher. Select the production process carefully and early.

Many documentaries are *field-produced programs*. After the outline for the program has been completed, interviews are conducted in the field with the principals involved. These remarks are transcribed and reviewed. Useful recorded comments are underlined and numbered to permit retrieval from the production work tapes. Then, narration can be written and additional visual and aural material recorded to further illustrate what is said in the field recordings and to bridge gaps between program segments. These elements are then assembled in the editing room into the final program. Field-produced programs generally rely on a carefully devised outline to begin the production process. Since the final assembly of the program is done in the editing room, a full-script may or may not be developed. After the program has been assembled, a transcript may be prepared for recordkeeping purposes and as a final check on program content.

Studio-produced programs can make use of a full-script, since they normally include preproduced reports, archival material, and a primary anchor. This is a more carefully controlled production environment, which allows the scripted use of already available, timed material.

Write the Script

A full documentary script cannot always be written in advance because usually it is not possible to anticipate every content and production possibility. Enough preparation and scripting must be done in advance, however, to keep the documentary on track and still provide an opportunity to react flexibly to evolving situations and to adjust the content and structure of the documentary. A producer who goes into the field to gather material for a documentary unprepared, expecting that such material will add up to a cohesive presentation, is likely to run aground. Although a script might not be written on paper before production begins, it has to be all but written in the mind of the person who will be gathering material in the field and providing even a tentative structure for the final presentation.

Whatever form of scripting used, whether it is an outline, a semi-script, or a full-script, the script must at least indicate the parameters of the subject and the particular program elements to be emphasized. However, the script still must permit future creative involvement to mold and shape the final documentary presentation. Most documentaries use the standard scripting formats already described and illustrated; however, these standard formats often are modified to accommodate specific writing and production situations.

Here are suggestions you may find helpful for preparing scripts for field-produced programs and segments:

a. *Prepare as detailed an advance script as possible.* It may be only an outline, but make the outline as comprehensive as possible.
b. *Divide program elements into those that are under your control and those that are not.* Prepare script material for what can be controlled or anticipated.
c. *Make the controllable elements serve as pegs or building blocks for the rest of the program or segment structure.* A usable, "dynamic" program outline is essential.
d. *If possible, provide a full-script for the opening and closing sequences.* Scripting these two crucial parts will help determine the shape and tone of at least some of the presentation.
e. *Transcribe interviews and log the content of the material recorded in the field.* This might include shots of buildings and photographs and ambient or location sound.

When reviewing field-produced material, mentally inventory the essential production elements already gathered: recorded comments, or sound bites taken from interviews; scripted or ad-libbed narration and stand-up and voice-over segments; ambient or natural sound; and stock shots or sounds for sustaining or uninterrupted segments. The initial structure for the documentary can be built around these recorded elements. *Scripted* transitions using voice-over narration generally are added last in field-produced documentaries.

Narration is used often in both field- and studio-produced programs and segments. Narration can be used effectively in many kinds of presentations, including news and sports stories, compilations, special events segments, corporate and instructional presentations, and even dramas and comedies. You should understand why narration is used and how to write effective narration.

Write the Narration

The basic functions of narration are to clarify, interpret, enhance, and reinforce what is presented. In general, narration should be expository, explaining what is seen or heard. It can help control the flow of information, forming bits and pieces of information and comments into unified segments and, ultimately, into a recognizable whole. To be effective, narration must be an obvious, integral, justifiable part of the structure of the documentary or investigative report.

Narration has several specific applications: to establish a scene or situation, to make effective transitions between ideas and program segments, to keep the audience on track, to provide additional information, to call attention to something easily overlooked or misunderstood, and to preview or review what is presented.

Here are some techniques that will help you write effective narration:

a. *Write narration for either on- or off-camera use.* A mix of the two can also be effective.

b. *Involve the audience.* Present the subject matter in meaningful, human terms. Use second person and active voice.

c. *Provide narration that sounds natural and conversational.* When using material taken from the printed media such as excerpts from books, magazines, newspapers, or poems, it may be necessary to adapt or "translate" such material or to use only short excerpts.

d. *Avoid unnecessary statistics, long lists, complex terms, jargon, and trite hackneyed expressions.* These distract the audience easily and usually add nothing significant to the narration or the overall exposition of the subject.

e. *Make the narration clear, precise, and easy to understand.*

f. *Stick to the subject.* Each piece of narration must relate directly to the structured development and exposition of the subject.

g. *Use controlled experimentation.* This might include the use of contrasting narrators, the voices of people directly involved in the subject, or human voices for inanimate or even animalistic situations and characters.
h. *Narration should work in tandem with other production elements.* When a new idea begins to unfold in sound or picture, a new sentence should also begin in the narration.
i. Although narration usually matches what is seen or heard, *consider using narration as a contrasting element, counterpointing aural or visual material.* For example, stark pictures of a war-torn city could be juxtaposed with a soft, melodic, poetic narration about what the city used to resemble.
j. *Do not inundate the program with too much narration.* This usually causes the audience to become confused, bored, distracted, and irritated.
k. *Make the narration sparse.* Let the real or imagined pictures, sounds, actions, and situations create the mood, convey the meanings, shape perspective and interpretation, and move the program along. Narration should supplement and complement the main body of information. It should not dominate the program.
l. *Leave some breathing room.* Allow time for the audience to think about what is said, especially after a provocative or startling statement. Use short, musical segments or let natural sound carry some of the burden of telling a story or enhancing a mood.
m. *Do not use narration when a picture or sound will communicate the information or mood more meaningfully.*

The procedures used for writing narration are as varied as those used to formulate an effective outline for a program. Each project involving narration necessitates a slightly different process. Some of the factors that interact to determine the narration writing process include the nature of the subject, the production and research timetable, the division of production and writing team responsibilities, and the preferences of writers and directors.

Bits and pieces of narration may be written as material is collected. The narration can then be rewritten to fuse with other elements to produce a solid, unified structure. The narration style and approach may change as new material is gathered and as the script moves through the various developmental stages. A certain degree of flexibility is necessary. The intended function of the narration must be determined early, as the treatment and outline are developed. It is not uncommon, however, for the material or content of the program, whether pictures or sound, to mold and shape the length, style, and mood of the narration.

The narration should not dominate and determine program content. On the other hand, neither should the content unilaterally dictate the nature of the narration. Both must work together to produce an effective presentation.

Timing is an important consideration when writing narration. In some situations, the narration is written first and then the visual or aural material is edited to fit that predetermined length. In other cases, the narration is written after this editing step has been completed. In most situations, the narration is written or rewritten as other program material is assembled, usually in the editing room. An important variable is the reading speed and other vocal characteristics of the narrator. A rapid, light, almost flippant narration style will necessitate a different kind of writing style and approach than if the narrator bellows the words in a slow, deliberate, dramatic style.

Unfortunately, you will not always know who will read the narration. The writer does not select the narrator unless the writer also serves as the producer for the program. Narration may be written and then the narrator is selected. If the narrator is already determined, try to write the narration to match the narrator's voice characteristics. The best test for the effectiveness of narration is to evaluate how well the edited program material and the narration come together in the final assembly of the program and then to adjust each program element as necessary.

Finish the Project

Several steps should be completed before the documentary or investigative report is considered finished and ready for use. The structure, style, and "look" of the presentation should be finalized and refined. First and subsequent drafts of the script must be written and evaluated. Management officials and legal consultants should review the product after all writing and production details are completed, especially if there are concerns about individual or corporate rights violations or potential losses in advertising revenue caused by the final presentation.

Profiles

Two local station programs will be examined in this section to illustrate the application of many of the principles and techniques already outlined. Each illustrates a different writing, research, production, and program format approach.

"Newsfile: A Bankrupt Court"

WJR-AM, Detroit, produced a series of investigative reports on that city's Federal Bankruptcy Court. Rod Hansen, acting news director of WJR, and Gene Fogel, federal beat reporter, were tipped by interested parties of some "problems" in the conduct and relationships of certain officers of U.S. District Bankruptcy Court and certain attorneys practicing in the court. After cross-checking verified these irregularities, Fogel broadcast hard news stories. After these stores aired, allegations from within and without the Bankruptcy Court surfaced—establishment of cronyism, irregularities in procedure and judgments, sexual favoritism, and apparent judicial incompetence.

Hansen and Fogel investigated these charges, checked casefiles, and interviewed judges, lawyers, and court clerical employees for more than two months before writing rough drafts of the first series of special reports. The script drafts were submitted to another WJR newswriter, who then wrote the programs as they were heard on the air. Each subsequent series of reports was handled essentially the same way. After each series was written in final form, it was submitted to an attorney retained by WJR for comments and suggestions to protect the station from any potential defamation or invasion of privacy judgments. Due to the care and thoroughness with which the scripts were written, the attorney had few suggestions for rechecking information or revising the scripts.

In a departure from standard scripting and production practices, the three-minute reports were written in ALL CAPS and in "newspaper form"— all narration, with no actualities. The decision to use straight narration in these reports was made early and for a variety of reasons: most of the sources could not be quoted by name and would not be interviewed on tape; the story was complex and difficult to explain, and it would have required extra verbiage to introduce actualities and sound bites; a single voice would help keep the story concise and clear; extra time and attention would be needed to integrate the actualities, time better spent gathering more material to enrich the information. WJR officials felt that, if the writing did its job and the reporters did theirs on the air, the programs would be interesting and understandable without using taped comments. The complete script for one report in WJR's third series of reports on the Federal Bankruptcy Court is shown in figure 7.1.

The WJR investigation led to the removal or resignation of two federal judges, the removal and conviction of the chief federal court clerk, the removal of all Detroit bankruptcy trustees and the disbanding of their panel, an FBI investigation of the way certain bankruptcy cases had been conducted, several significant changes in the "blind draw" assignment of judges, and a tightening of codes of conduct and lines of authority for those working in the bankruptcy court system. This WJR investigative report series received not only George F. Peabody and Society of Professional Journalists national awards, but also the National Headliners Public Service award, the grand award of the Investigative Reporters and Editors, the Radio-Television News Directors Association International Award for investigative journalism, and the American Bar Association Silver Gavel award.

"Did They Die in Vain?"

It is difficult to offer a new perspective for such an often-discussed and sensitive topic as racial desegregation in the Deep South. However, that was the topic handled by Bob Noonan, news projects director for WLOX-TV in Biloxi, Mississippi.

Noonan outlined how the idea for the documentary evolved and the difficulties he encountered while writing, producing, and narrating this award-winning television program:

> I first came up with the idea of writing "Did They Die in Vain?" after reading about the controversy surrounding the movie *Mississippi Burning.* "Did They Die in Vain?" is a one-hour documentary detailing the true story behind the 1964 murders of three civil rights workers in Mississippi. While critics raved about the film, historians cringed—it was factually inaccurate. "Did They Die in Vain?" sets the record straight. We interviewed the key

NEWSFILE: A BANKRUPT COURT. I'M GENE FOGEL WITH A SERIES OF REPORTS ON THE UNUSUAL WAYS THE SCALES OF JUSTICE ARE BALANCED IN DETROIT'S FEDERAL BANKRUPTCY COURT.

IN OUR INITIAL SERIES, CONSIDERABLE TIME WAS SPENT EXAMINING THE BLIND DRAW SYSTEM IN THE COURT. SOME DESCRIBE THE BLIND DRAW AS THE CORNERSTONE OF THE COURT'S INTEGRITY. BUT THERE ARE SERIOUS QUESTIONS IN FEDERAL BANKRUPTCY COURT IN DETROIT AS TO JUST HOW BLIND THE DRAW HAS BEEN.

YOU MAY RECALL THAT IN THE FIRST SERIES IT WAS DISCLOSED THAT THE PROMINENT BANKRUPTCY LAW FIRM HEADED BY IRVING AUGUST HAD UNCANNY SUCCESS IN KEEPING ITS SIGNIFICANT CASES OUT OF THE REPUTEDLY TIGHT FISTS OF JUDGE GEORGE BRODY. WJR NEWS DISCOVERED THAT IN THE MORE THAN ELEVEN MONTHS THAT HIS GIRLFRIEND WAS HANDLING THE BLIND DRAW AS INTAKE CLERK, ONLY ONE OF AUGUST'S 44 CHAPTER ELEVEN CASES FOUND ITS WAY TO BRODY. A UNIVERSITY OF MICHIGAN STATISTICS PROFESSOR CALCULATED THE ODDS OF THAT HAPPENING IN A TRULY BLIND DRAW AT ONE IN 100-THOUSAND.

SUBSEQUENT TO THAT FINDING, WJR NEWS ANALYZED THE ASSIGNMENTS OF ANOTHER LARGE BANKRUPTCY FIRM, GOLDSTEIN, GOLDSTEIN AND BERSHAD, AND FOUND THAT IT TOO WAS EMINENTLY SUCCESSFUL IN AVOIDING JUDGE BRODY. COURT FILES INDICATE THAT DURING THE SAME TIME SPAN, NOVEMBER FIRST, 1979 TO MID-OCTOBER, 1980, THE FIRM FILED 19 CHAPTER ELEVEN REORGANIZATION PETITIONS. TWO WERE CONSOLIDATED INTO ONE -- AND THAT LEFT EIGHTEEN. ONLY ONE WENT TO BRODY, WHILE FOUR WENT TO JUDGE DAVID PATTON AND THIRTEEN WENT TO SENIOR JUDGE HARRY HACKETT.

COURT RECEIPTS INDICATE THAT IRVING AUGUST'S GIRLFRIEND DREW THE VAST MAJORITY OF THE ASSIGNMENTS FOR THE GOLDSTEIN, GOLDSTEIN AND BERSHAD FIRM. IN FACT, AVAILABLE RECORDS SHOW THE FIRM NEVER FILED A CHAPTER ELEVEN CASE WHEN SHE WAS NOT ON THE JOB.

Figure 7.1
One of a series of investigative reports on the Federal Bankruptcy Court in Detroit.
Courtesy of WJR, Capital Cities Communications, © 1981 by Capital Cities Communications.

Figure 7.1 (*continued*)

BASED ON THE BLIND DRAW ASSIGNMENT FORMULA GIVEN HIM PREVIOUSLY, U of M STATISTICS PROFESSOR MICHAEL WOODRUFF PLACED THE ODDS AT ONE IN 300 THAT THE GOLDSTEIN FIRM'S CASES WOULD HAVE BEEN DISTRIBUTED AS THEY WERE IF THE DRAW HAD BEEN BLIND.

SEVERAL PERSONS WORKING CLOSE TO FEDERAL BANKRUPTCY COURT HAVE TOLD WJR NEWS THAT WITH CO-OPERATION IN THE RIGHT QUARTERS IT WOULD BE RELATIVELY EASY TO SUBVERT THE BLIND DRAW. AS DESCRIBED TO WJR, A PETITIONING FIRM WOULD ARRIVE AT THE INTAKE WINDOW WITH SEVERAL CASES, ONE OR MORE COULD BE CHAPTER 11 BUSINESS REORGANIZATIONS AND SOME OF THEM RELATIVELY SIMPLE CHAPTER SEVEN BANKRUPTCIES. IN CASUAL CONVERSATION, THE PERSON FILING MIGHT SAY SOMETHING LIKE..."I NEED A JUDGE." THE NEXT BLIND ASSIGNMENT CARD IS DRAWN. IF IT'S NOT THE JUDGE THE LAWYER WANTS, FOR THE IMPORTANT CHAPTER 11 RE-ORGANIZATION CASE, HE HANDS THE CLERK A MINOR CASE TO WHICH TO ATTACH THE CARD. THE PROCESS IS REPEATED UNTIL THE RIGHT JUDGE COMES UP...AT WHICH TIME THE CHAPTER 11 CASE IS HANDED THROUGH THE WINDOW TO THE CLERK, WHO ATTACHES THE ASSIGNMENT CARD.

CONTACTED BY WJR NEWS...STANLY BERSHAD OF THE GOLDSTEIN FIRM SAYS HE WAS NOT EVEN AWARE THAT THE ASSIGNMENTS MIGHT BE OUT OF BALANCE ADDING HE DOESN'T CARE WHAT JUDGE HE GETS. BERSHAD SAYS, "IF YOU DO A GOOD JOB YOU DON'T HAVE TO WORRY ABOUT WHAT JUDGE IS HEARING IT." ASKED IF HE THOUGHT IT WAS UNUSUAL THAT THE SAME CLERK ALWAYS SEEMED TO DRAW HIS FIRM'S CHAPTER 11 CASES, BERSHAD SAID HE WASN'T AWARE OF IT, THAT SEVERAL OF HIS FIRM'S EMPLOYEES FILE CASES AND IT WOULD BE IMPOSSIBLE TO KNOW WHO DREW THEM ALL.

TOMORROW AN UNUSUAL CHAPTER 12 RE-ORGANIZATION CASE WHEN OUR NEWSFILE SERIES CONTINUES...I'M GENE FOGEL, FOR NEWSFILE.

players in the 1964 investigation—FBI agents; the sheriff of Neshoba County, where the murders took place; relatives of the victims; and residents who witnessed the circus-like atmosphere surrounding the search for Andrew Goodman, Mickey Schwerner, and James Chaney.

We did not run into any major obstacles during our work on this documentary, though at one point tapes with interviews of former civil rights workers and FBI agents were stolen from our car as we sat in a movie theater watching *Mississippi Burning*. We had conducted the interviews earlier in the day. Fortunately, we had taken our camera equipment back to the hotel prior to going to the theater.

We worked approximately four weeks on "Did They Die in Vain?" In that period we traveled the state, conducting interviews, shooting video, writing the script, and going into production. It took me two full days, locked in an editing bay, to write the script for the sixty-minute program.

"Did They Die in Vain?" opens with interviews with the director and actors featured in *Mississippi Burning*. We gave our viewers a look at the events as seen through Hollywood's eyes and then presented the facts through firsthand accounts.

The documentary was broadcast throughout the state. It was well received, though some criticized our program as well as the movie for "opening old wounds." For many, this program was the first time they had heard the entire story about the murders and the resulting investigation.[1]

The documentary was divided into three segments: an assessment of the movie *Mississippi Burning,* a retelling of the facts surrounding the slayings, and an examination of the progress Mississippi has made in its racial relations in the past few decades.

Figure 7.2 shows the actual production script for the closing minutes of the documentary. Refinements of spelling, grammar, syntax, copy form, neatness, and so on usually are not evident in such working scripts. A clean final production script in standard form is always useful. Notice how sound-on-tape (SOT) excerpts are noted: the time into the field tape where the sound bite is to be found, the incue and outcue of the sound bite to indicate the words heard as the excerpt begins and ends, and the length of the excerpt. Also notice how Bob Noonan's narration serves as a transitional device and helps pull together related comments as the program concludes.

"Did They Die in Vain?" received a national award for television enterprise from the Associated Press, as well as a George Foster Peabody Award for distinguished broadcasting. Judges said the program demonstrated what a small-market television station with a capable and dedicated staff can contribute to the understanding of issues that are both complex and important.

STORY: ___PT 3 P 2___   DATE_____   PAGE_____

WRITER:_____ SOURCE_____ SHOW_____   TIME_____

VIDEO	AUDIO

THE CITY OF PHILADELPHIA WILL FOREVER BE MARKED BECAUSE OF WHAT

HA-PEDN IN THAT SUMMER OF 1964...SEGREGATION IS A THING OF THE PAST
                    AS
THOUGH IN MANY CITIES, THERE IS A BLACK SECTION OF TOWN AND A WHITE

SECTION OF TOWN,...THERE ARE SOME HERE WHO BELIEV FATHER TIME MOVES

FASTER THAN CHANGE IN THIS EAST MISSISSIPPI TOWN...

SOTIN AT: 8:27 MONUMENT TAPE IN: THERE'S STILL
                          OUT: TO DO, YOU KNOW, 5 SECS.
                                   THE MT. NEBO
A MONUMENT XXXXXSXXXXXXXXXXXXXX ON THE LAWN OF A BAPTIST CHURCH BEARS THE

NAMES AND PICTURES OF THE SLAIN CIVIL RIGHTS WORKERS,...IT IS THE

ONLY RECOGNITION GIVEN THE THREE INSIDE XXXXXXXXXXX THE CITY LIMITS,...

SOTIN AT: 13:24 IN: IF IT WEREN'T FOR
                   OUT: CHANGED A LITTLE, RUNS: 26 SECS.

DISSLOVE: CART-------

THERE WAS SOME QUESTION AS TO WHETHER MISSISSIPPI BURNING WILL BE

SHOWN IN PHILADELPHIA,...WELL, THE THEATORS OWNERS NOW SAY YES,...

SOTIN AT: 16:21 IN: THAT'S THE TRUTH
     MONUMENT   OUT: CAN'T HIDE, RUNS: 17 SECS.

DISSOLVE: SOT IN AT: 3:53 DEWEESE IN: IF YOU WANT
                           OUT: MOST EVERYBODY, RUNS: 30 SECS.

BUTT--SOT IN AT: 7:54 IN: I THINK PHILADELPHIA
                 OUT: COME A LONG WAY, RUNS: 12 SECS.

DISSOLVE TO TALLEY(NAACP) IN AT: 5:15 IN: THIS AREA HAS
                           OUT: NO COMPARISON, RUNS: 35 SECS.

   FORMER SHERIFF RAINEY HAS MOVED AWAY FROM NESHOBA COUNTY...HE NOW

LIVES IN MERIDIAN...ITONICALLY HE IS EMPLOYED BY A BLACK MAN...HE×NB
HE IS A SECURITY GAURAD IN A LOCAL MALL,...HE NO
LONGER WEARS THE STETSON HAT, THE COWBOY BOOTS OR THE SIX SHOOTER...

SOTIN AT: 20:43 RAINETY IN : THE NEWS MEDIA
                    OUT: HIS COMPANY, RMMS(LAUGH) RUNS: 30 SECS.

E.E. MCDONALD OWNS THE SECURITY SERVICE...HE SAYS HE AND RAINEY ARE LIKE

BROTHERS,...BUT THAT RELATIONSHIP APPARANTLY HAS COST HIM BUSINESS AND EVEN

abc NEWSWATCH 13 /WLOX-TV BILOXI, GULFPORT, PASCAGOULA

Figure 7.2
Last two pages of the production script for the documentary entitled
"Did They Die in Vain?"
Courtesy of WLOX-TV and Bob Noonan.

Figure 7.2 (continued)

STORY: PT 3 P. 3 _____ DATE_____ PAGE

WRITER:_____ SOURCE_____ SHOW_____ TIME

VIDEO | AUDIO

SUPPORTERS WITHIN ██ THE CHURCH IN WHICH HE SERVES AS PASTOR...

SOTIN AT: 3:26 MCDONALD   IN: THERE ARE PEOPLE
                          OUT: ANY OTHER INDIVIDUAL. RUNS: 25 SECS....

DISSOLVE: CART------
    AS FOR CECIL PRICE, HE STILL LIVES IN PHILADELPHIA,...EMPLOYED BY THE

MAN WHO OWNS THE PROPERTY WHERE THE BODIES OF SCHWERNER, GOODMAN AND CHANE

WERE BURIED,...

DISSOLVE: CART-----
    ████████ MEANWHILE ██████████████████ 25 YEARS AFTER HIS SONS

MURDER, BEN CHANEY ████████ REMINISES...HE DOES SO WITH PRIDE,...█████

███████████████████████████████████...

                         ████ ALONG WITH GOODMAN AND SCHWERNER
QUIETLY ANNOUNCING THAT JAMES ████████████████ DID NOT DIE IN VAIN,...

SOTIN AT:18:30 ████ DAD IN: ITS OK NOW
                          OVER AGAIN. (NOD HEAD) █ 50 SECS.

DISSOLVE TO CLOSE,...RUNS: 1:10

Summary

An effort was made in this chapter to describe and illustrate the basic writing and organizational process for documentaries and investigative reports. Each step in the process leads logically, progressively, and dynamically to the next step, until an engaging and cohesive presentation is achieved. Topics for such programs must be selected carefully and developed in a manner that clearly indicates their contemporary significance for the audience. Sufficient information must be gathered and then organized to provide convincing documentation and to devise a flexible treatment or an outline of the subject and eventually a finished script. A clear, logical, and flexible program structure and format must be developed to allow a progressive exposition of the topic. The production process to be followed must be determined before the appropriate kind of script can be written. The effective use of narration provides still another tool for the writer of documentaries and investigative reports.

Suggested Exercises and Projects

1. List five topics that could be developed into effective documentaries and investigative reports for use on a local radio or television station. Explain why you selected each topic.
2. Prepare a schedule of interviews and tentative research sources you would suggest to help develop further one of the topics listed in exercise 1.
3. Gather preliminary information, prepare a treatment, and complete research for one of the topics listed in exercise 1. Then prepare an outline for a five-part (two to four minutes per part) mini-documentary or a full, thirty-minute documentary on the same topic.
4. Write the full-script for the documentary or investigative report outlined in exercise 3. The script must be written in one of the following ways:
   a. Entirely in a voice-over, narration form
   b. For effective use on *both* radio and television
5. Write the full-script for a five-part radio or television mini-documentary using one of the topics generated in exercise 1. Then indicate how this script could be modified for use as a full-length, thirty-minute documentary or investigative presentation using the interlocking module scripting format technique described in this chapter.
6. Complete the research and write the script for a prospective radio or television documentary news special on a current prominent world leader.
7. Complete the research, formulate the outline, and write the full-script for a four-to-six-minute report that could be used in a local or national news magazine program series.
8. Monitor a network documentary or an investigative report. Prepare a report in which you critique the selection and development of the subject or topic, the effectiveness of the program structure and the organizational pattern or scheme, the accuracy and completeness of the information presented, and the overall writing and production style.

Notes

1. Bob Noonan, personal communication, March 1991.

Interviews and Talk Programs

When regular radio broadcasting began in the 1920s, among the first types of programs to appear on local station and network program schedules were those that featured interviews with prominent celebrities and discussions of contemporary ideas and issues. These talk programs (interviews, news panel programs, and discussions) have remained on the program schedule. Usually they are placed under the general program category of "public affairs" or "community affairs."

The interview and talk show genre has expanded over the years. Traditionally structured programs remain on-the-air, but this category has been expanded to include shows that incorporate live call-in comments from viewers and listeners who want advice about a variety of subjects. Some audience-participation talk shows are limited to a narrow set of topics, such as financial planning and investments, automotive repairs, or personal relationships. A mixture of formats can be used to present facts and opinions about current topics and issues. This might include recorded information packages, commentaries, and discussion segments.

An interesting hybrid talk program format, "This Week with David Brinkley," was developed in 1981 by ABC. This hour-long Sunday morning broadcast features a brief newscast of events "since the Sunday morning newspaper," as well as news panel interview segments, usually on related topics, and a discussion or round table segment led by David Brinkley, in which news reporters and correspondents freely express their views on events and issues of importance. Although the program segments appear in a regular pattern in each program, there is flexibility to expand or contract portions of the show to maintain viewer interest. Thus, in one program, several types of talk program segments are featured—interviews, a news panel interview or discussion, and a round table or panel discussion. Other hybrid program formats will be described later.

The sources of such programs have also expanded. Some series appear only on cable channels, whereas others are on local stations or national networks. Others are provided by syndicators who produce and distribute the shows via satellite. Program producers try to identify and target demographic groups for each interview and talk program series they develop.

Most talk programs are presented as a regularly scheduled series. Talk shows can be produced as television programs, with the audio portion then "lifted" and used for radio purposes. Talk shows often generate comments from newsmakers, which can be used on regularly scheduled newscasts. Notice that many of the news panel programs are presented on Sundays, when very few of the regular news sources are active and readily available. The skillful editing of comments from these programs usually produces several newsworthy excerpts for use in Sunday evening newscasts.

In most facilities, the news or community affairs director coordinates efforts with production personnel to produce regularly scheduled interview and talk programs. Often a producer or producer-director is assigned to work on such programs. Except for commercials, news and public affairs program production occupies the majority of a station's local production time and effort.

In many talk program situations, the writer's work is combined with other on-air production responsibilities. In very large production facilities and situations, the writer may simply be expected to provide only the necessary abbreviated prescripted material and leave the on-air duties to appropriate production personnel. At smaller broadcast stations and facilities, and even in a few network, cable, and syndicated program production situations, however, the writer carries a hybrid title. Examples are writer-interviewer, writer-producer, or even writer-producer-program host or moderator. Thus, as a writer, you should be prepared to participate fully as needed in the preparation of material for talk programs—helping to select guests, researching a guest or topic, or devising an outline of topics to be discussed or a preliminary list of questions to be asked during a program. This combined set of responsibilities provides the full creative vehicle for you to accomplish the tasks necessary for the successful production of various types of talk programs. Specific suggestions for handling these on-air responsibilities will be offered later in this chapter.

As noted in other chapters, the writer's work still must precede the production of such programs. Some degree of preparation, even if minimal, is needed to ensure the success of each program. The nature of talk programs usually requires that writers who work with the script on-the-air perform the largest share of their task orally and spontaneously as the program progresses, rather than in a formal, fully-scripted manner. Although the amount of writing required is minimal, it is important for you to understand and master the written and oral presentation techniques needed to produce effective interviews and talk programs.

This chapter will consider the major types of talk programs—interviews, news panel programs, discussions, and interactive talk shows. For each type, there will be a description of the nature of such programs and the kinds of preparations involving the writer, plus suggestions that may be useful when approaching such assignments, as a writer and as on-air talent. It should be noted that the interviews described in this chapter are not the same as interviews completed for news and sports stories.

Each of us does several interviews every day. We ask questions to find out **Interviews** information, to determine feelings, to get reactions, to solicit comments. It is a basic part of our everyday communication pattern and routine.

In a similar way, interviews constitute a basic part of many types of programs—feature programs, music and variety shows, live sports broadcasts, game shows (when contestants are interviewed on-the-air by the host), magazine programs, documentaries, and investigative reports. Although an interview may constitute the entire program, often it is used as part of a larger program format or concept—for instance, in some types of instructional and corporate presentations. The importance of this basic programming form cannot be overemphasized. As a writer, you should have a firm grasp of the principles and techniques used to prepare effective interviews. This will pay dividends when you develop other types of programs.

Electronic media interviews are done under a variety of circumstances—live or recorded and edited for later use, in the studio, on the telephone, or on a remote location in the field.

This is a brief discussion of the essential steps needed to prepare and conduct full interviews for electronic media use. Several books listed in Appendix A illustrate more fully the various aspects of the interview process. This includes selecting topics and guests, compiling and organizing research information, preparing questions, developing interviewing strategies, conducting interviews, and editing and processing interview comments.

There are three primary types of interviews. The precise delineation of each **Types** type is difficult, since there are obvious similarities among the three. Nevertheless, knowing the primary types of interviews will help you determine the principal purpose or function of each interview situation and, thus, the approach needed to prepare and conduct each interview on-the-air. The three types of interviews are the information interview, the opinion interview, and the personality interview.

The *information interview* focuses on factual material. No opinions are expressed overtly, and no attempt is made to delve into the personality of the person being interviewed. News reporters, as well as public service, civic, and institutional organizations, use the information interview extensively.

The *opinion interview* centers on the ideas and beliefs of an individual. Although information or background on a topic is provided during the interviews, the primary purpose of such interviews is to obtain specific viewpoints, beliefs, and opinions. Such interviews may consist of on-the-street comments on a contemporary issue or topic, audience phone-in or write-in responses to editorials or programs, or simply interviews with individuals in which they express opinions on controversial issues.

The *personality interview* features a public figure or a celebrity in a human interest situation. The interview subject often is selected because of past events or activities, recent developments involving this individual, or simply the position this guest currently holds in the public eye. Motion picture stars, television personalities, sports figures, artists, and comedians are some of the people who fit this category. The interviewer in this situation must be flexible and sensitive in approaching the guest and in discussing topics. Also the interviewer must carefully adjust his or her language and delivery style to complement the background and temperament of the guest.

Approaches

Whether you are preparing an information interview, an opinion interview, a personality interview, or a combination of the three, there are essentially five methods of approaching the task. Each approach is isolated in this section for the purpose of description; however, they can be combined to prepare for a particular interview.

Several factors determine the approach you would use to prepare an interview:

a. The style of the interviewer
b. The comfort and wishes of the guest(s)
c. The time available for preparation of the interview
d. The nature of the topic or guest(s)
e. (At times) the interview policies of the station or network. Some prefer spontaneous, unrehearsed interviews. Others prefer a more structured, predictable interview situation.

If at all possible, for each interview, prepare at least a show format (rundown sheet or routine sheet), if not a semi-script, which includes an introduction and closing to the interview, specific questions, and approximate timing for each interview segment. The factors just listed influence the amount of preparation needed or desired and the result of such preparation efforts. There are five basic approaches used for on-the-air interviews.

The *ad-lib method* involves virtually no preparation by either the interviewer or the guest. This can be a deadly approach, especially for an inexperienced interviewer. More than one interviewer has made a serious mistake in an interview because there was no time to meet with a guest and to discuss in advance the topics and issues featured in the interview.

A more desirable approach involves the *preparation of an outline of the topics or points* to be covered during the interview. The interviewer ad-libs or formulates questions from the outline as the interview progresses, while the guest ad-libs the responses.

A highly recommended approach entails the *preparation of specific questions* as the interviewer expects them to be used in the interview. When combined with other elements of a show format or semi-script, this approach allows the interviewer to prepare material more precisely but still incorporate the elements of informality and spontaneity, which are necessary for an effective interview.

Another approach is the *preparation of specific questions and then briefing of the guest(s)* about the topics to be discussed. Some interviewers show the questions to the guests in advance, whereas others prefer to indicate only the general line of questioning prior to the interview. At such a briefing, the guest may prefer only to preview the topics; others prefer to make brief notes to use in answering some or all of the questions, especially those that require a precise response. Once briefed, some guests may inform the interviewer of the general line or tone of responses. The danger of such a practice is that the guest will over-rehearse and not provide a spontaneous, informal response to the question when asked on-the-air. Such preinterview comments by a guest, however, may help the interviewer correlate prepared questions and discover other pertinent topics that could be included in the interview.

The *full-script approach* usually results in what is often referred to as a "canned" interview. That is, the interview, when heard or seen, usually sounds or looks artificial and rehearsed. When using this approach, the writer prepares a complete script that includes the introduction to the interview topic and guest(s), specific questions, word-for-word responses for each guest, transitions between topic areas or guests, and a formal conclusion to the interview. The full-script approach is *not* recommended for effective on-the-air interviews.

First, *obtain as much information as possible* about the topics to be discussed and the guest(s) to be interviewed. This may require detailed and exhaustive research in the local library, an examination of old newspapers or newscasts, or conversations with the guest's friends and acquaintances.

Preparations

Next, *sift the accumulated information* so that only the most important topics or issues remain. Keep in mind the approximate length of the interview so that a sufficient amount of interesting information is available. As you sift through the information, keep two important questions in mind:

a. *What questions would the audience want to ask or be most apt to ask if given the opportunity to talk to this guest?*
b. *How can I create a desire for information on the part of the audience?* How can I motivate them to want to know more? Select only the most important, potentially interesting, and significant information that will have a direct impact on the audience's emotions, beliefs, life-style, and pocketbook.

Prepare for the interview using one or a combination of the approaches already described. Organize the interview using one of several schemes: by geographical location (north, south, east, and west; uptown, downtown; national, regional, statewide, and local; or any other similar pattern); by chronology of events (before, during, and after or past, present, and future); by divisions of the subject matter (problem, solutions, results or background of the issue, personalities involved, issues, prospects for the future); or by divisions of the audience (men, women, and children or elementary, junior high, and high school students).

Present each interview in an easy-to-follow, recognizable pattern. An organized interview will still permit enough flexibility to keep it conversational and interesting but also allow you to use the thorough research and precise interview strategies you might have developed. A systematic approach to the preparation of on-the-air interviews will ensure that your work as a writer is efficient and that the interview will look and sound professional to the audience, as well as to the interviewer and guest. *Sometimes* interview guests are available for preinterview briefings, at which you can confirm facts and preview the topics to be examined. However, either the guest or the interviewer may choose not to participate in such a briefing. Compare the approaches and techniques used by Bob Costas and Jim Bohannon described later in this chapter.

Determine the structure of the interview program. Unless you are helping to design the format of a new interview series, generally you will work within an established program structure devised by the series producer or community affairs director. If you do help develop a format for an interview program series, there are several factors to consider. Many interview programs begin and end with standard voice-over copy identifying the program and inserting the names of the guests and participants for each program; questions are then provided for participants. Some programs begin with a short teaser about the topics or guest to be featured, or perhaps the guest gives a startling response to whet the audience's interest in listening for more. Prepared video or audio packages may be inserted to illustrate specific comments made during the interview. The tact or purpose of the interview series, whether to probe, attack, persuade, or inform, often influences the program's structure. It is best to prepare a short and a long ending for interview and talk programs; the long ending can be abbreviated into a shorter closing to provide only essential information about the guest, the topics, the program name, and the name of the host or announcer. The material would be prepared similar to the closing copy that was shown in figures 5.13 and 5.14 for live sports broadcasts.

Profiles

Remember that no one system or approach always works best or is used by every interviewer in all situations. As noted earlier, several factors determine the approach used to prepare an interview. It would be useful to profile various preparation techniques used by notable interviewers.

Jim Bohannon

When preparing for his Mutual Broadcasting System talk programs, Jim Bohannon tries to gather material that will relate to the guest and the topics selected by the production staff. Wire service news reports might provide background information for a political candidate. Skimming, if not reading, a book by an author scheduled to be interviewed might suggest pertinent questions to ask.

Bohannon confides that he has rarely prepared specific questions to ask interview guests, but he does write down notes about areas he wants to explore and then tries to put them into a logical sequence before each interview.

Bohannon generally meets his interview guest only a few moments before airtime. As Bohannon explains,

> I never talk to a guest before the program. [Interview] guests have a tendency to want to talk shop, and I don't want them giving their first, which is usually their best, spontaneous answer to me. I want them to give it to the audience.[1]

Several factors determine the strategy Bohannon uses to conduct an interview: the interview time available, the topics to be discussed, the nature and quality of the interview guest, the amount of experience a guest has had dealing with the media, and a guest's predisposition toward a specific topic.

Telephone callers are not screened before they are heard on Mutual Broadcasting System talk shows that Bohannon hosts. Callers are asked only where they are calling from and to turn down their radios. Bohannon thinks this keeps his call-in program segments interesting and stimulating.

Here is how CBS news reporter Mike Wallace responded when asked, "What's the secret of an interview? How do you prepare?":

Mike Wallace

> What I try to do is write out in categories maybe 50 questions. Questions on money, power, relationships, inconsistencies. Then the producer comes in with his own questions. It's in the research. You read transcripts of other interviews that have been done. You sit there quietly by yourself and think—what in the world would *I* really like to know about this individual? By the time I'm through with the questions—maybe in the final analysis I won't use more than a half dozen of them. But I'll know from having written them down, from my reading. I'll be so well grounded by the time I sit down across from him or her that I will be a good interviewer. Then I'll listen, listen, listen. Throw away the questions and let the interviewee carry me. If you listen carefully, and then let something drop, all of a sudden you're off on another tack. It's a combination of exploration, skepticism, psychoanalysis, even simple conversation.[2]

To prepare interviews in the NBC series "Later . . . with Bob Costas," extensive profiles are written after a preinterview session with the program guest, and after research is read and analyzed by the show's producers.[3] These profiles provide perspective on and key events in a guest's life and career. The producers also prepare "agenda cards"—key items from the profiles that Bob Costas can use during the interview. Figure 8.1 shows a portion of these notes.

Bob Costas

A day or two before taping an interview, the executive producers and producers meet with Bob Costas and show him what has been gathered and how the staff suggest certain items be handled or presented. When Costas reads the research and looks at the video that the staff has collected, he makes notes onto the "agenda cards." These 5 × 8-inch orange cards remind Costas of the points he wants to make or the topics he wants to emphasize as he interviews each guest. Figure 8.2 shows a set of agenda cards.

Figure 8.1
Excerpt from research
notes used to prepare
one of two thirty-
minute interviews
with Carl Reiner.
*Courtesy of NBC
Productions, "Later . . .
with Bob Costas."*

inspired with the alien concept, he created an alien and built a sitcom
around it -- It was Mork & Mindy.

6 - Here is Reiner's assessment of The Van Dyke Show: "It was the best.
I swear to God it's not because I had anything to do with it. Sometimes I
see a show and it's like, it's the first time. I was really laughing. I didn't
care who wrote it. I was just having a good time."

The New Dick Van Dyke Show

In 1971, Reiner went back to t.v. and created The New Dick Van Dyke
Show. In this one, Dick was a Phoenix talk show host -- with wife Hope
Lange -- and zany friends Marty Brill and Fanny Flagg. The show started
slowly and by it's third year it was doing very well. They changed the
setting so Dick was now on a soap opera. That year, the program was
consistently in the top 15.

The show one week was to be about a little kid walking by and seeing his
mother and father making love. The CBS executives said no, it "wasn't
Dick Van Dyke's image." Reiner said, "Wait a minute. I am Dick Van
Dyke. I know his image better than you." They told Carl that you
couldn't show couples having sex just for fun -- they had to be trying to
conceive a baby. With that, Reiner & Van Dyke quit. Now it was written
in Carl's contract that the shows he wrote had to be produced -- they did
not have to air. So this show was produced and shown later in Canada to
great acclaim. It has never been seen in the United States. Reiner has a
copy and told me he would send it to us. That's a helluva hook for us.
Never seen before. The show that drove Carl Reiner out of network t.v.
for good. He says, "I wouldn't do another series unless my last pair of
socks had a hole in them. What happens is that in t.v., you have people
making decisions on your work that you don't have as much respect for as
you might have." All this is because of that incident and if we get the tape,
it's a great thing to discuss.

CARL REINER - SHOW #1   10-29-90

ACT ONE

I. THE DICK VAN DYKE SHOW
- A. What makes it special/groundbreaking
   1. Scene at an office
   2. Father doesn't know best
   3. Laura in pants - no pearls
- B. Wouldn't date shows for re-runs - No slang
- C. Birth of Show
   1. "Head of Family" - Reiner stars
   2. Get Van Dyke - Johnny Carson
   3. Mary Tyler Moore - Danny Thomas remembers her
- D. The Show & Episodes
   1. Reiner as Alan Brady - Not seen in first 2 years
   2. "Coast To Coast Big Mouth" - Brady is bald
   3. Autobiographical - Reiner & Dick shake at proposal
   4. JFK and Pony
   5. Carl's favorite episode

ACT TWO
II. "SHOW OF SHOWS" AND MEL BROOKS
- A. First as performer - Then invited to writers' room
   1. Suggestion French movie satire - 3rd rehearsal
- B. Favorite Caesar sketch
- C. Creative Process - The writers' room
   1. Woody Allen
   2. Neil Simon
   3. Larry Gelbart
   4. Mel Brooks
- D. "2000 Year Old Man"
   1. Born with Louis Nye at "Inside USA"
   2. Start at parties - Brooks & tape recorders

ACT THREE -- NEW DICK VAN DYKE SHOW
- A. The Show that made Carl quit
   1. Kid watches parents making love
   2. "Not Dicks image"
- B. Ever do series again?

Figure 8.2
Typed copy of agenda cards prepared by Bob Costas for the first of two thirty-minute interviews with Carl Reiner.
Courtesy of NBC Productions, "Later . . . with Bob Costas."

Figure 8.3

Rundown sheet prepared after taping and editing one of two Carl Reiner interviews. Segments 17 through 22 were assembled based on information shown in figures 8.1 and 8.2 ("Act Three").

Courtesy of NBC Productions, "Later . . . with Bob Costas."

	SEGMENT	SEG TIME	CUM
1.	CLIP - "Titles" (The Dick Van Dyke Show)	:09	1:30:50
2.	INTERVIEW	3:02	1:30:59
3.	CLIP - "In Office" (The Dick Van Dyke Show)	:41	1:34:01
4.	INTERVIEW	1:00	1:34:42
5.	CLIP - "Dick Van Dyke" (The Dick Van Dyke Show)	:42	1:35:42
6.	INTERVIEW	3:19	1:36:24
7.	CLIP - "MTM - Dick Van Dyke" (The D.V.D. Show)	:28	1:39:43
8.	INTERVIEW	:29	1:40:11
9.	FEATURE - "If My Friends Could See Me Now" by Sammy Davis, Jr.	:57	1:40:40
10.	SHORT TITLES w/Feature Music	:06	1:41:37
11.	**COMMERCIAL #1**	2:04	1:41:43
12.	INTERVIEW	2:54	1:43:47
13.	CLIP - "Tub" (The Dick Van Dyke Show)	:57	1:46:41
14.	INTERVIEW	1:40	1:47:38
15.	CLIP - "Alan Brady" (The Dick Van Dyke Show) w/HICON	:29	1:49:18
16.	**COMMERCIAL #2**	2:04	1:49:47
17.	INTERVIEW	1:00	1:51:51
18.	CLIP - "Titles" (The New Dick Van Dyke Show)	:11	1:52:51 - **VIDEO FLAGGING AS PER ORIGINAL TAPE**
19.	INTERVIEW - Insert "New D.V.D." @ 01:53:43 - Insert "New D.V.D." @ 01:54:10	1:20	1:53:02
20.	CLIP - "Cavalry" (The New Dick Van Dyke Show)	:12	1:54:22 - **VIDEO FLAGGING AS PER ORIGINAL TAPE**
21.	INTERVIEW	:53	1:54:34
22.	CLIP - "The New Dick Van Dyke Show" w/HICON	:42	1:55:27 - **VIDEO FLAGGING AS PER ORIGINAL TAPE**

Video segments are inserted in editing after an interview is recorded and timed. The research sometimes indicates to Costas the video material available to the production staff and appropriate for the interview topics noted earlier. If he chooses to do so, Costas can ask a question that will solicit an answer that could lead smoothly into a particular video clip. Once the interview is taped, the producers must work quickly to identify the needed clip, locate the material, and secure the permissions and fees needed to use specific pieces of video on the air. Figure 8.3 shows the rundown prepared after the first of two Carl Reiner interviews had been taped.

Figure 8.4 shows pages of a semi-script prepared for an interview segment on the "Home" television series. This is a daytime magazine program that includes several interview segments. One of the guests, Cathy, had appeared on the program several times to discuss various aspects of her breast cancer diagnosis. In figure 8.4, notice the precision with which questions are worded and answers are outlined. This helps ensure that the information is organized and specific to best use the limited interview time available. This semi-script illustrates the result of thorough research and careful planning by the series writers and producers.

"Home"

Virtually an unlimited list of recommendations can be made to prepare for and to interact in an on-the-air interview. Following are some essential recommendations for both writers and interviewers:

Guidelines and Suggestions

a. *Select the topic carefully.* If you are responsible for selecting the interview topic, be certain the subject is important enough to interest the audience. You should feel comfortable about the selection and potential development of the topic. You should not feel embarrassed to discuss a sensitive or potentially controversial topic.

b. *Know as much as possible about the topic.* Become an informed surrogate member of the audience. The more background and information you have available, the better the interview questions that can be formulated.

c. *Limit the topic.* It is better to cover a few items well than many items poorly. Expand or contract the subject to match the time available for the interview. Focus only on key areas to guide the audience in connecting ideas and absorbing information or opinions.

d. *Establish and reinforce the importance of the topic.* This must be done early in the interview and at appropriate junctures throughout the dialogue. Give the audience reasons for listening or viewing.

e. *Formulate developmental questions.* Devise questions that bring out the crux of the situation or issue and that point up the guest's information or opinions about the history of the problem, the people involved, current procedures, and proposed solutions.

f. *Develop a sequence of questions that will explore, in an interesting and organized manner, the topics planned and the guest's viewpoints you want to hear.*

g. *Pace the exposition of the topic.* Prepare background questions to familiarize the audience with the scope, nature, importance, and direction of the topic. Formulate a "break" question, which will be the high point of the interview, the culmination of responses to that point. This should be planned in advance, even if a better break question turns up in the course of the interview. Then the

INTERVIEWS AND TALK PROGRAMS   231

SHOW #537
AIRS: APRIL 4, 1990
ACT #5
"SECOND OPINION CANCER"

23

SEG. TIME:
(6:00)

Figure 8.4
Script pages prepared
for a "Home"
interview segment.
*Courtesy of Woody
Fraser, Cece Caldwell,
Marty Tenney, Richard
Camp, and James E.
Witte.*

NO BUMPER IN

TALENT:
GARY, DAPHNE, CATHY, DR. KIVITZ

SEG. PROD:
(LISA MORIN)

HOMBASE

GARY

We're back with Cathy. Joining us now is Dr.
Philip Kivitz, Director of the Regional
Cancer Foundation in San Francisco.

APPLAUSE

(AD LIB GREETINGS)

Dr. Kivitz, you are the director of a unique
program that offers a free second opinion to
anyone with cancer. Tell us about it.

CHYRON:
PHILIP KIVITZ, MD

(DR.:
BOARD FORMED AS ANSWER TO RISING COST OF
CANCER...BECAUSE COST IS SO HIGH, MANY PEOPLE
CAN'T AFFORD SECOND OPINION.
* BOARD CONSISTS OF PANEL OF 9 "JURY" EXPERTS
  WHO EVALUATE A PATIENTS MEDICAL HISTORY.
* THE ONLY REQUIREMENT IS THAT THE PATIENT
  MUST BRING A REFERRAL FROM HIS/HER DOCTOR.
* MOST CASES ARE CONSIDERED WITHIN 2 WEEKS,
  AND GIVEN A SECOND OPINION A FEW DAYS
  AFTER THE PATIENT IS SEEN BY THE PANEL.)

DAPHNE

Dr. Kivitz, why a panel of doctors?

(DR.:
WITH A PANEL, THE PATIENT GETS 9 EXPERT
OPINIONS REGARDING THE BEST POSSIBLE CANCER
TREATMENT FOR THEM, AT ONE TIME.
* OFFER A RANGE OF EXPERTISE.
* THE PANEL CONSIST OF 2 SURGEONS, 2 RADIA-
  TION THERAPISTS, 2 MEDICAL ONCOLOGIST,
  1 DIAGNOSTIC RADIOLOGIST, 1 PATHOLOGIST,
  1 NUCLEAR MEDICINE SPECIALIST.)

DAPHNE

Cathy, did you consult a second opinion
panel?

(MORE)

SHOW #536
AIRS: APRIL 3, 1990
ACT #5
"SECOND OPINION CANCER"

(CATHY:
* HAD OPPORTUNITY TO VISIT TUMOR BOARD,
  EXPLAINS....
* SECOND OPINION ONLY CONFIRMED WHAT FIRST
  DOCTOR DIAGNOSED.
* THE CANCER CONSULTATIVE SERVICE IS A GREAT
  IDEA BECAUSE ALL SPECIALISTS CAN DISCUSS A
  CASE AT ONCE...TOGETHER.)

GARY

How often does the panel disagree with the
first doctor's diagnosis?

(DR.:
*IT HAPPENS....DR. KIVITZ WILL GIVE EXAMPLE:
A MAN HAS A TUMOR IN HIS BLADDER; DOCTOR
ADVISED REMOVING THE ENTIRE BLADDER; PANEL
SUGGESTED REMOVING ONLY TUMOR, LEAVE
BLADDER AND TREAT IT WITH A NEW FORM OF
TREATMENT; 8 YEARS LATER, MAN IS FINE
WITH BLADDER INTACT.)

DAPHNE

What's so wonderful about this program is
that it is completely free!˜ How can you
afford to do this?

(DR.:
*THE FOUNDATION IS NON-PROFIT.
*OPERATES ON DONATIONS & GRANTS
*ALL 100 PHYSICIANS ARE VOLUNTEERS.
*BECAUSE THEY FEEL IT'S SO IMPORTANT TO GET
THAT 2ND OPINION.)

GARY

For anyone seeking a second opinion and who
might not have access to this service, what
are the best questions to ask?

(MORE)

233

Figure 8.4 (*continued*)

SHOW #536
AIRS: APRIL 3, 1990
ACT #5
"SECOND OPINION CANCER"

CHYRON: (W/BANNER)
QUESTIONS TO ASK
2ND OPINION DOCTOR:
1. DO YOU HAVE
THE NECESSARY
INFORMATION?
2. ARE THERE ALT-
ERNATIVE TREATMENTS?
3. WHAT SHOULD I
BE DOING RIGHT NOW?

(DR.:
QUESTIONS TO ASK 2ND OPINION DOCTOR:
1. DO YOU HAVE ENOUGH INFORMATION TO FORM
   A SECOND OPINION? DO YOU HAVE ENOUGH
   TESTS, X-RAYS, UP TO DATE INFO, ETC.?
2. ARE THERE OTHER KINDS OF TREATMENT BEING
   DONE FOR THIS WHICH ARE ACCEPTABLE? ANY
   CLINICAL TRIALS BEING DONE?

3. WHAT SHOULD I BE DOING NOW TO HELP
   OVERCOME THIS DISEASE...I.E. REDUCING
   STRESS, CHANGING DIET, EXERCISE, ETC.)

DAPHNE

Cathy, anything you'd like to add?

(CATHY:
*DON'T BE AFRAID TO LET YOUR DR. KNOW THAT
 YOU WANT TO SEEK OUT SECOND OPINIONS.
*DON'T GO HOPING PHYSICIAN WILL TELL YOU
 DON'T NEED TREATMENT.
*HAVING A SECOND OPINION MAKES YOU FEEL LESS
 LIKE A VICTIM, AND HELPS TO MAKE YOU DECIDE
 THAT THE FORM OF TREATMENT SUGGESTED IS THE
 BEST TREATMENT TO SAVE YOUR LIFE.)

GARY

Dr. Kivitz, how can people get a free second
opinion cancer service in their town?

(DR.:
*FIRST, GET A FEW (CAN BE AS FEW AS 2 OR 3)
PHYSICIANS WHO SPECIALIZE IN CANCER TREATMENT
INTERESTED IN THE SERVICE....AND WHO WILL
VOLUNTEER THEIR TIME.
*GET FUNDING: DONATIONS   FROM   LARGE
COMPANIES, THROW FUND RAISERS, ETC.
*WHEN YOU GET THIS FAR, YOU CAN COME VISIT
US IN SAN FRANCISCO, AND WE'LL WORK WITH YOU
TO HELP START ONE UP ON YOUR OWN.)

GARY/DAPHNE

(AD LIB THANKS)   (INTO BUMPER #5/CMX 5)

interviewer has the choice of using either break question. If a break question is planned, it is best to *build* up to the explosive and controversial question than to ask this important question at the beginning of the interview and then have nothing worthwhile or interesting for the audience for the rest of the dialogue. On occasion, the break question may be asked at the beginning of the interview for dramatic effect or shock value.

Writer/ Interviewer

As indicated earlier, not only must writers prepare for interviews by researching the guest and topics and perhaps preparing the questions to be used, but they may also be expected to produce the interview program, determine the series format, and *conduct* the interview on-the-air.

The following are additional suggestions that will be useful if you need to handle the responsibilities of an on-the-air interviewer:

a. *Select interview guests carefully.* If you are responsible for this step, be sure guests are willing to participate. The length and quality of their answers will determine the success of your interviews.

b. *Determine the ultimate goal of each interview.* This should be linked to one of the three primary types of interviews already described—information, opinion, or personality. Each interview should provide a thought or viewpoint that is interesting and generally not commonly known or heard.

c. *Determine the interview approach you will use.* This is generally determined by the nature and quality of the information you have, the guest to be interviewed, the topics planned, the interview setting, and the interview time available.

d. *Conduct the interview.* Guide the interview so that you accomplish what you want and obtain the comments you need. Interview questions should progress logically from one another, growing out of comments made during the interview and anticipating what your audience needs to know and wants to hear.

e. *Pace the interview.* Ask general questions that encourage the guest to talk. If the interview timetable permits, save tough, sensitive questions for later. Controversial and sensitive material is best addressed after a few easy-to-answer questions.

f. *Try to have a conversation instead of an "interview."* Interact with the interview guest. Show interest in the guest's responses.

g. *Listen to the answers.* Listen to what is said, but also to what is left *unsaid.* This will help you formulate follow-up questions.

h. *Look around.* Carefully observe and objectively note how the guest is dressed, the quality of eye contact, and the guest's body positions, word choices, and reliance on notes and prepared remarks. If the interview is done out of the studio, notice the features of the room or setting, as well as the items prominently displayed.

i. *Watch your physical attitudes.* Your attitudes and expectations can be revealed by your body language, facial expressions, and vocal inflections, as well as the words you choose for your questions. Remain neutral in your attitudes during interviews.

j. *Reassure the interview guest* about his or her understandable nervousness, the production equipment to be used, the importance of the information and comments the guest will give, and your competence as an interviewer.

k. *Do not answer your own questions.* Avoid loaded questions that presuppose the answer.

l. *Ask questions simply and directly.* Ask one question at a time.

m. *Ask questions that require specific, short answers.*

n. *Ask for clear explanations of technical terms and jargon.*

o. *Conclude effectively.* If time permits, it is best to identify the guest fully, using his or her name and title or position related to the interview topics; summarize the information or comments presented; provide final reminders, such as an agency to contact or the time or place to be to participate in a particular activity; your name; and the name of the interview program.

In addition to the general suggestions already offered for handling on-the-air interviews, you can use the following techniques to make *live* interviews easier to do and to elicit more worthwhile information:

a. *Place yourself next to the interview guest* to establish an open, interested attitude and to give the guest the necessary quality of attention.

b. *Make microphone or camera placement as unobtrusive as possible.*

c. *Tell your interview guest in advance how long the live interview is expected to last.*

d. *Since interview time is limited, ask only one or two key questions of immediate interest.*

e. *Predetermine how the interview will end.* Prepare a short and a long version of your interview closing to accommodate technical and timing changes that are likely to occur.

f. After your last question has been answered and before you conclude your live interview, if you are standing, take a short step away from your interview guest as a *signal that the interview is over and that the next part of the report needs to begin.*

The results of any interview depend on the quality and completeness of an interviewer's preparation, organization, poise, composure, curiosity, on-the-spot wit, and flexibility. To be successful, an interviewer must simultaneously listen, observe, inquire, respond, and record information and impressions.

News Panel Programs

News panel programs are a special type of interview situation. The producers of such programs invite a current prominent newsmaker to be questioned by a panel of newspeople drawn from print and electronic newsrooms. The panelists conduct what is generally regarded as a news conference with the guest. Questions focus on current topics, issues, concerns, and problems of direct interest to and under the jurisdiction of the guest. The newsmaker questioned may be from the government, labor, business, the arts, the sciences, international organizations, or many other fields.

The objective of a news panel program is to offer a thoughtful, fair, and informed view of news events and issues. This kind of exchange between newsmaker and news gatherer should provide a spirited discussion of the relationship between news events and broader issues and trends.

The format for news panel programs usually is simple and direct. Generally the format consists of an opening question; the introduction of the guest and panelists by the moderator, who may or may not participate in the questioning; a continuation of the questioning; intermittent commercials or public service announcements; and a brief summary by the moderator or a final comment by the guest.

The general approach used to prepare most news panel programs is rather conservative. A subdued setting and straightforward format allow the audience to concentrate on the guest's comments and the issues raised by the panelists' questions.

It is not uncommon for a writer to serve also as the producer or moderator of a news panel program. Producing such a program involves selecting panelists and arranging for interesting guests. A writer/producer also gathers and organizes research material related to the guest—for example, information on the guest's activities, interests, previous comments and positions, and current concerns or causes. Moderating a news panel program requires the use of techniques similar to those already outlined for interviews.

Discussion Programs

Discussion programs allow for the purposeful, systematic, and oral exchange of ideas, facts, and opinions by a group of individuals. Such programs follow a variety of patterns in their structure and presentation to fulfill the overall objective of interchange among individuals.

Types/Formats

Each type of discussion program sustains the overall objective just described but also permits the ideas, information, and opinions to be expressed in a slightly different way. Each type is a legitimate talk program format.

Panel Discussion   In a panel, or round-table, discussion, a small group of participants analyzes a problem or an issue for the benefit of the audience. The participants, who should represent various backgrounds and perspectives appropriate to the topic(s) under discussion, should engage in open, informal interplay. A specific solution to the problem or issue does not necessarily have to be devised. The moderator may summarize the position(s) taken by each participant at the end of the discussion.

Group Discussion   In a group discussion, participants attempt to solve a problem or reach a conclusion about an issue by objectively and cooperatively examining all facets of the situation and then forming a consensus. This type of discussion program shares some of the characteristics of the panel discussion format. It is important that each participant share available information and opinion and that the discussion be approached without preconceived notions. The group must reach a collective decision by defining and limiting the problem or issue to be discussed, determining the causes of the situation, reviewing available solutions, and then selecting a solution or course of action to follow.

Symposium   Just as in the panel discussion, a small group of participants in a symposium analyzes a policy, a process, a problem, or an issue. The presentational framework differs from a panel discussion, however. In a symposium, each participant delivers a reasonably short prepared speech without interruption. Each speech explains a particular viewpoint, explores one aspect of the problem or issue, or offers an individual approach or solution to a complex problem. Speakers follow each other in turn until all participants have been heard. Usually the same amount of time is provided to each speaker. The moderator simply introduces the topic of discussion, introduces each participant, and then closes the symposium at the conclusion of the last speech.

Debate   Two distinctly opposite points of view should be obvious in a debate. The debate could be between candidates for public office or proponents and opponents of a particular policy, process, problem, or issue. Usually the moderator briefly introduces the topic(s) for debate and the participants and may summarize the principal points made by each side at the conclusion of the debate. Each side presents an initial prepared argument or point of view. Then each side gets an opportunity to rebut the opponent. Finally each side is provided an opportunity to make a final statement, in which the main arguments are highlighted for the audience.

Forum   A forum consists of general audience participation, usually after a presentation has been made, such as a panel or group discussion, symposium, or debate. During a forum, the audience may participate in the discussion from the beginning. Thus, a forum can be attached to other discussion program designations to indicate that the audience participates in some way. The choice of when and how the forum portion of the program will be integrated into the discussion rests with the program producer and the moderator.

Participants may also exchange comments during a forum if the program format allows it. A popular type of forum, interactive talk shows, will be examined more closely later in this chapter.

It is often appropriate to combine the different types of discussion programs to produce a more lively and flexible program format. A forum, perhaps the easiest format to integrate with others, can enliven the discussion by including input from the audience. The audience may contribute to the discussion directly in the studio, through the moderator, or perhaps via telephone lines from a remote location. Another combination format is a symposium-group discussion, in which the standard symposium portion of the program is followed by interaction between the symposium participants in an effort to arrive at a solution collectively. Other combinations are also possible. The topic(s), the type of participants, the setting for the discussion, the length of the program, and the kind of interaction desired should govern the design of a combination discussion format.

Another type of combination is achieved when a discussion program format is combined with recorded segments or reports. A typical pattern or format for such a program series is to begin with a teaser, a short taped segment or live comment meant to entice a listener or viewer to stay tuned. After the program is introduced, guests and topics can be identified. Short recorded segments can highlight a particular aspect of the topic or issue examined. This will help guide the discussion among guests or the audience, who are often available in the studio or by phone.

At KUSA-TV in Denver, Barb Simon produces a weekly half-hour public affairs program series entitled "Making a Difference Today." Each program includes recorded news stories and features, as well as interview and discussion segments. The combination of presentation formats allows some flexibility to present issues and topics in a unified manner.

In a program segment on interracial marriages, Simon included a short, recorded profile of the concerns and life-styles of an interracial couple who had been married for nine years. This was followed by an in-studio interview with a different biracial couple, who expressed concern about raising their children and handling contacts with their family and friends. The combination used in this KUSA-TV presentation is guided by the charter or mission statement for the series:

> It [the series] should provide an opportunity for members of the Black, Hispanic, Asian, Native American, and other minorities to present information of interest to the larger general audience. It is a community interest program.
>
> It should be 2/3 minority, 1/3 community- or nonprofit organization–oriented. The community bulletin board type [of] information should be included in each program. While it is 2/3 minority interest information, it can also include some religious and political information.
>
> It should not be a talking head show. . . . It should be a show which is timely and utilizes the strong video resources of the station. . . . It should be one of the best efforts of the station.[4]

Simon described how the program content is assembled and the show is produced:

> The biggest consideration is in following the charter for the show. . . . We try to hit minority issues hard, community issues almost as hard. From there, we look at what we've done in the previous week [in the newsroom], and what we missed (often the minority issue is set aside for something more visual, exciting, dramatic, etc.). Therefore, we have to make do with existing resources. That means recycling preproduced packages, vo's or vosot's [see chapter 5 for a description of these terms]. We try to have on-set interviews, but not so much that we have an entire twenty-five minutes of talking heads. As you can imagine, trying to do so much (in meeting the standards of the mission statement) with so little (it's basically me, the host, and the director giving input to the show, and carrying out most of the work) is a unique challenge.[5]

Approaches

In most cases, for the types of discussion programs already described, you would be wise to prepare at least an outline of the topic areas. It would be best to prepare a written rundown, routine sheet, or semi-script. Such programs could be produced live or recorded for later use.

The writing and production approach should reflect the kind and quality of interaction, informality, and spontaneity desired in the program. Generally the more spontaneity desired, the less structured and formal the script and program should be.

Preparation

Discussion program participants and moderators, as well as writers also serving as participants or moderators, should complete the same kinds of preparations and use the same on-the-air presentation techniques already outlined for interviews and news panel programs. The preparation and presentation techniques are similar.

Other preparations are also needed for discussion programs. Background information on the topic must be compiled and organized. An outline of the information gathered should be prepared. Then, depending on the discussion program format, each participant must prepare to contribute to the program based on the parameters established by that format. For example, participation in a debate will require a different kind and level of preparation than that used in a group discussion or symposium-forum.

Even minimal preproduction planning will help ensure that a discussion show adheres to the structure, content, and pace envisioned and avoids unnecessary duplication of effort or information. A full-script should *not* be used; if the script is too detailed, valuable spontaneity will be lost.

Following is the "ideal" set of scripting material to provide for most discussion programs: a routine sheet that indicates the approximate length of key program segments; a fully-scripted opening that includes the program title, its identification, the participants' credentials, and a brief overview of the nature and importance of the topics and issues to be examined; an outline of the topics or a list of the specific questions to be asked; transitions to be used between program segments and to cue-away for spot announcement breaks; and a fully-scripted closing that summarizes the discussion, offers conclusions, identifies the participants, and names the program.

Interactive Talk Shows

Live, call-in talk shows are enlarged forums in which individual audience members provide information, make comments, express opinions, or ask questions on various topics of current interest. Essentially such programs are large group conversations or discussions moderated or coordinated by a program host. Sometimes an interview guest or expert is added to the mix of program elements.

Two points made earlier in this chapter apply to this type of talk program: minimal scripting is needed, and the writer is often required to produce and host this program on-the-air, especially at local stations. The popularity of audience participation talk shows is expected to continue to increase. A writer would do well to know the variety of formats used to produce this kind of program, as well as the techniques that work best when handling on-air responsibilities.

Formats

Some interactive talk programs focus on specific topics or issues—for instance, medical or legal advice, personal or life-style information, consumer issues, automotive repair, or financial counseling. Other programs center on specific controversies or issues of the day. Many programs focus on one topic or issue and allow a discussion of any topic of immediate concern to the audience.

Several factors determine the format, approach, and procedures used: the time of day, the style and preference of the program host, management policies and philosophies, and commercial commitments. Consumer issues might receive more attention in morning programs, whereas investment or legal advice is more welcomed at night or on weekends. Some program hosts have educational and professional backgrounds that determine the focus of their discussions and the selection of their guests, such as an attorney, a psychiatrist, or a certified public accountant. Program time, topic selection, and topic development may be limited.

Preparation

The nature of interactive talk programs generally precludes the use of formal, standardized scripts. The majority of such shows are ad-libbed and informal. The personality, attitudes, education, background, and life experiences of the host come together to shape the program's style, pace, and approach. *Some* scripting is usually done.

Although such shows need to sound spontaneous, most program hosts follow various regimens to prepare their programs and to generate ideas for the various topics, issues, and guests to be featured. Most successful program hosts are voracious readers of several daily newspapers, weekly news magazines, and books. They often use extensive personal filing systems to organize and retrieve the clippings and notes they have accumulated. Portable personal computers are especially useful. Personal research efforts can supplement the material program guests have supplied. Marketing information may also be useful. Any and every information source may eventually be used by an active talk program host.

Procedures

Since interactive talk programs often are regarded as modified interview situations, the procedures and preparation techniques described earlier for interviews should also apply to this type of talk program. It would be useful to review a few procedures that generally are used to handle incoming telephone calls from audience members.

The call-in portion of such programs can be handled in various ways. Most calls are intercepted by someone other than the program host. The caller may be asked only to indicate where the call originates and to turn down the radio or television set to avoid feedback when the caller is heard on the air; this is the procedure followed by the producers of the Mutual Broadcasting System's interactive talk programs (review Jim Bohannon's comments earlier in this chapter). For other shows, callers are also asked their name, telephone number, and address and the nature or topic of their question and comment. The caller is then placed on hold.

After the call has been intercepted, the program host is alerted that a caller is ready on a particular phone line. This can be accomplished electronically, using a computer screen or lights for each phone line, or by simple mechanical means, such as holding up cards or fingers, indicating the phone line, topic, and so on.

Whatever cueing system is used, eventually the caller is placed on-the-air. Some telephone conversations are used in "real time," as they happen. Those involving controversial issues or guests generally require a five-to-seven second delay in the conversation to help the program host eliminate inappropriate or obscene comments. The effective use of such a time-delay system hinges on the skill, talent, and experience of the program host.

Guidelines and Suggestions

The following guidelines may be useful as you tackle on-air responsibilities for interactive talk shows:

a. *Do your homework.* Know the scheduled issues and guests.
b. As needed during the program, *provide background information or insights drawn from your preparation.*
c. *Prepare some script material.* Until you acquire enough experience handling on-air duties, prepare at least an introduction and a closing for the program. Write short "fillers" to be used during the program when the conversation becomes slow and repetitive. These could be 10-to-20-second items that include statistics, quotations, and personal anecdotes related to the program topic or guest.
d. *Stay on course.* Maintain control. Know where the discussion is going.

e. *Make notes.* Keep track of the points made, the identity of callers, and the phone numbers the audience should use.
f. *Be prepared for the unexpected.* Through practice, learn to handle the frequent crackpot as well as the welcome local expert.
g. *Question the validity or completeness of unsubstantiated comments.* You can do this effectively only if you have prepared well and possess strong interviewing skills.
h. *Be sensitive to the attitude and mood of each caller, as well as the listening audience.* Through experience, develop the skill to know when to pursue an idea or to move to another topic.
i. *Learn when and how to terminate a call.* Experience is the best teacher.
j. *Pace yourself and the program.* Make the last part, as well as the first part, of each program interesting, informative, stimulating, and entertaining.
k. *Remind the audience who you are and what you are doing.* Give the name of the program, your name, the featured topic or guest, and especially the telephone number to call to participate. Do this often throughout the program, especially when making a transition to a commercial break or to a new topic area.
l. *Develop strong interviewing skills.* They are especially essential for this type of situation.

Larry King

Larry King's informative and entertaining radio talk show is heard each weekday throughout North America on the Mutual Broadcasting System. King does not prepare his comments or guests in advance. His natural curiosity generally makes his interviews a success. He prefers not to screen callers but adds that a call-in audience can be trained to know that they had better stay on the topic and contribute interesting comments or their call-in conversation will soon be terminated. King regards himself as an editor, deciding when to continue or conclude a call based on his feel for what his loyal audience would prefer.

King brings the same curiosity and versatility to Cable News Network's (CNN) primetime viewers. The one-hour "Larry King Live" features a diverse line-up of guests and topics—from top celebrities to powerful decision makers to detailed discussions of timely topics. During the program, King shares the interviewing duties with viewers, who frequently call in with very candid questions.

Figure 8.5 shows a portion of a rundown sheet prepared for a "Larry King Live" ("LKL") telecast on CNN. Notice that program guests and their locations are listed. Telephone numbers are also listed for both domestic and international callers to use to talk to King and his guests. Program segment times are listed on the far right side of the rundown. Cumulative program times are also noted on the right, within the block identifying the content of each segment. Segment 5 contains a short, recorded piece introducing Willard Scott, who is identified by VF (video font); the outcue for this

```
SLUG                    WRITER    DAY/DATE/TIME    REV  BY  ON              STATUS TIME
LKL RUNDOWN             falco     Sat Jan 19 14:03 mcrae,c  Jun 10 10:40 HOLD    1:18
=============================================================================
MUSIC CATALOG #:  CAV98-11-37
THURSDAY, JUNE 5, 1991                          billboard:NONE

GUESTS: LINDA WOJAS - DC (INSIDE)
        AL JOHNSON - DC
=============================
        WILLARD SCOTT - DC              back half

+++++++++++++++++++++++++++++++++++++++++++++++++++++++++++++++++++++++++++++
segment 1: LINDA WOJAS - DC (INSIDE)
           AL JOHNSON - DC
              TEASE: 202-408-1666
              BILLBOARD: NONE                             9:08:00
=============================================================================
LK 1      VF: Los Angeles
              September 20, 1990
-----------------------------------------------------------------------------
1ST COMMERCIAL BREAK                                      2:00
=============================================================================
segment 2: PHONES
                   INTL #:202-408-4821
                                                          9:15:00
=============================================================================
LK2   ???????????????????????????????no font info yet

=============================================================================
2ND COMMERCIAL BREAK                                      2:00
=============================================================================
segment 3: PHONES
LK-3            from Columbia
                                                          9:26:30
-----------------------------------------------------------------------------
3RD COMMERCIAL BREAK                                      1:45
=============================================================================
LK-4:            CUE TONE TEASE                            :20
            PREPRODUCED!!!!!! OC "no way jose"

-----------------------------------------------------------------------------
-----------------------------cuetone break----------------------1:15
=============================================================================
segment 5: WILLARD SCOTT - DC
LK-5:      sot/vo :10/:55   oc "to die for"/pads to  :55
           VF: Washington                                 9:36:00
               Yesterday
-----------------------------------------------------------------------------
5TH COMMERCIAL BREAK                                      1:45
=============================================================================
segment 6: PHONES
LK-6:    Courtesy NBC News
                                                          9:45:00
-----------------------------------------------------------------------------
6TH COMMERCIAL BREAK                                      2:00
=============================================================================
segment 7: PHONES
LK-7:    VF: Saudi Arabia
             August 15, 1990
-----------------------------------------------------------------------------
7TH COMMERCIAL BREAK                                      1:45
=============================================================================
```

Figure 8.5
Rundown sheet for a "Larry King Live" show.

```
TRANSCRIPTS TAPE (ROLLS FROM PLAYBACK / MUSIC ON TAPE & CART!!)
segment 8:PHONES

close tape & copyright
9:57.50==================================================================
+++++++ FULLSCREENS!! +++++++++++

10:101 FROZEN COPYRIGHT WITH LOGO & MICROPHONE
10:103 NY PHONE NUMBER:   212-643-0077
10:104 OLD TRANSCRIPT - EMPTY SET
10:105 BLANK SPLIT
10:106 INTERNATIONAL CALL-IN #:    202-408-4821
10:107 DC PHONE NUMBER: 202-408-1666
10:108 LOGO WITH MICROPHONE
10:109 MICROPHONE
10:110 1991 copyright
10:111 old BLANK background
10:112 dc/ny split
10:113 NEW PROMO BACKGROUND (same as moving background!)
10:114 LA / WASH SPLIT
10:115 6TH ANNIVERSARY LOGO
10:116 LOS ANGELES TRANSCRIPT BACKGROUND
10:117 6TH ANNIVERSARY TRIANGLE              DISK 88
10:118 LA PHONE NUMBER: 213-469-5533         HDO 7
10:119 LKL SIGNATURE
10:120 6TH ANNIVERSARY SMALL LOGO
60:431 small logo
60:432 BIG logo
60:433 Larry King signature
60:434 5th anniversary logo
60:440 triangle (live only!)
dc IFB #:    202-842-2987
10:271 old split
26:30
GOOD FONT STYLE: HUMANIST 521
```

Figure 8.5 (*continued*)

introduction is "to die for." Graphic material is loaded and retrieved from computer-type disks, using specific numbers shown on the *second* page of this "LKL" rundown sheet.

Computers make it relatively easy to generate the rundown sheet for each "LKL" program. The basic outline for all shows is readily available through a "boiler-plate," or "masking," technique that allows program producers to insert specific information for each show into the established rundown for the series. Such techniques ensure consistency among shows in the series, yet they allow specific guests and topics to be featured in individual programs.

Summary

Although a limited amount of formal scripting is required to produce interviews and talk programs, a writer must understand the formats and approaches commonly used, practice specific techniques needed to generate the necessary script material, and be prepared to handle on-air talent duties for such programs. Appropriate script material helps production and on-air personnel present a smooth, organized, and interesting program. You need to know the requirements of such programs before you can write effective script material.

Suggested Exercises and Projects

1. List five topics appropriate for a five-minute interview segment on a local radio or television magazine or news program. For one of the topics, explain in a few sentences why you think this would be an effective topic and how you would design the interview to stress information or the opinion or personality of a guest. Finally list three local guests who could comment on that topic. Write a short, fully-scripted introduction for one of the guests.

2. Prepare a semi-script for the topic and guest selected in exercise 1. Write a full-script for the opening and closing of the interview. These two fully-scripted segments should include your name, the guest's name and credentials related to the topic, and a brief overview of the topic, in which you indicate its importance and impact. In addition, list five to eight questions in full and on a separate sheet. These questions should anticipate the development and progression of the interview.

3. If time and facilities permit, produce and then critique the interview program segment you designed and scripted in exercises 1 and 2.

4. Select one person to interview. Prepare a show format (rundown or routine sheet) for a five-minute information interview with this individual. The interview could be for either radio or television. Then, using the same guest, prepare separate show formats for an opinion interview and a personality interview. If possible, record and then critique one of the interviews.

5. Monitor and, if possible, record a network radio or television interview. Comment on its effectiveness: the selection and development of the topics; the completeness and accuracy of the information presented; the interviewer's opening, closing, transitions, and comments; the effectiveness of the questions; the organization of the interview; other favorable and unfavorable comments about the interview; and suggestions for improvement.

6. Monitor and, if possible, record a radio or television news panel program. Comment on the effectiveness of the program: the selection of the guest and the panelists; the format of the program; the selection and development of the topics; the effectiveness of the questions; other favorable and unfavorable comments about the program; and suggestions for improvement.

7. Prepare a semi-script for a local thirty-minute television news panel program. The guest is the mayor of your city. Identify four local and area news reporters who, realistically, could be the panelists. Create a name for the program. Provide a full-script for the introduction to the program, in which you preview the guest, panelists, and topics to be discussed; the closing to the program; and the transitions to and from two one-minute commercial

breaks inside the program. Provide approximate timing cues for each significant program segment. If time and facilities permit, record the program for use on a local cable access channel.

8. Select one of the following types of discussion programs: panel discussion, group discussion, symposium or debate between candidates for a local or state political office. Select a topic suggested in exercise 1. Prepare a show format (rundown or routine sheet) for a local thirty-minute radio or television discussion program of the type selected.

9. Follow the directions in exercise 8. Divide into groups of three to five persons each. Select one individual's show format; that person serves as moderator for the discussion show as it is recorded. Other members of the group serve as panelists. *Each* member must turn in his or her proposed show format. Critique the writing and production skills of each group's presentation.

10. Provide a rundown sheet and a one-page description of the contents and structure of a thirty-minute, locally produced public affairs program you have designed. In this program, there should be three to five segments and two or three breaks for spot announcements. Each segment should focus on issues and concerns developed around and prompted by classic or current movies or television programs. Segments might cover such topics as child abuse, homosexuality, violence and drugs, or family traditions. A variety of presentation formats must be used during the program. This might include the use of news or sports features and stories, spot announcements, editorials or commentaries, short investigative reports, interviews, discussions, musical profiles or performances, and animated segments.

11. From a local newspaper, select an article that focuses on an important, controversial issue. Write a short introduction to the topic and list three or four key aspects of the issue you think would make an interesting discussion for an interactive radio or television program. Simulate or actually record a five-to-ten-minute segment of this program in which you serve as host. Critique the quality of your preparation and performance as a writer/host.

Notes

1. Jim Bohannon, personal communication, 24 September 1991.
2. Tom Bier, "What Makes '60 Minutes' Tick?" in *Communicator* 45, no. 9 (September 1991): 13. Courtesy of RTNDA *Communicator*.
3. Fred Rothenberg, personal communication, 24 September 1991.
4. Barb Simon, personal communication, 23 July 1991.
5. Simon.

Music and Variety Programs

9

M usic and variety programs require similar preparations and considerations and use approximately the same type of script material. Often, various elements of both these types of programs are integrated into composite programs or series. Variety programs often include musical segments, as well as interviews, news and feature stories, and other writing and production options, described and illustrated elsewhere in this book. Music programs need to display the same qualities of pacing, unity, variety, and entertainment necessary for a successful variety program.

A hybrid variety program form, the talk-variety show, has become pervasive. Programs of this type use many of the elements associated with a traditional variety program but offer a blend of various program elements, such as comedy routines, interviews, news stories, spot announcements, and music videos.

Chapter 10 includes illustrations of other types of programs that are similar to talk-variety shows in their scripting requirements and program structure. Magazine programs and musical year-in-review presentations are two such programs. (See figures 10.1 through 10.5.)

In this chapter, for the purposes of discussion and illustration, we will consider music and variety programs separately. That is, we will identify and describe the elements that make each type of program distinctive, even though a *combination* of elements probably will be used in the final version of each program.

This chapter will present the following information for both music and variety programs: an overview and a survey of current perspectives, the role and function of the writer, the process followed and techniques used to prepare music and variety program material, and examples of written material. From this discussion, you should obtain enough insight and information to begin writing the material needed to produce music and variety programs for the electronic media.

Music Programs

Music is the basis for much of the programming on radio and television. For example, music can be the primary program element that identifies a radio station's format in a competitive market. Music can also be used by the audience as a backdrop for activities, such as working, relaxing, and exercising. It can also be combined with other program elements in variety shows. Music can convey specific moods and meanings in commercials and announcements, as well as in documentaries, dramas, and game shows.

There has been a noticeable increase in the number and quality of music program series and specials produced for syndication to local television stations and for distribution on cable systems. Producers continue to offer attractive, creative, and versatile music programs that meet and often anticipate the needs of specific audiences.

Contemporary music anticipates and reflects trends and priorities in today's society. Music has become an important part of most people's lives. It often identifies who they are, as well as who they hope to become. Your ability to work effectively with music is almost as important as your ability to communicate meanings, ideas, information, and feelings through words.

Music on Radio

We will examine three elements associated with using music on radio: formats, the role of the writer, and producing radio music programs, especially those that require extensive scripting.

Formats

Format is an important concept in radio station music programming. *Format* is the preplanned control of all elements in a radio station's presentation, which creates the consistency needed for that station to be successful in a competitive climate. Essentially a station's format identifies the kind of programming it offers, such as news, talk, country, classical, adult contemporary, contemporary hit radio (CHR), or urban music.

Labeling a radio station's music format helps its management team identify the station's image, shape that image, and project it into the minds of the listeners. The format designation helps the station develop a distinctive "sound," or niche in the competitive marketplace. Unless this distinction is carefully developed and clearly projected to listeners, a station's format will blend with others in the same market, producing a blandness often criticized by the audience.

Generally listeners attach their own labels to radio stations' programming efforts. Ideally a station's designation of its format should match the listeners' format label, but often it does not. It is important for everyone involved with a station, including writers, to know the intended, as well as the perceived, format of the station.

Role of the Writer

Most local radio stations allow air personalities to ad-lib comments between music selections. The announcer becomes an "oral writer," creating material spontaneously. Although an effective on-air radio personality makes the presentation appear effortless and carefully prepared, such a quality performance requires extensive experience and the creative use of promotional material and entertainment news gleaned from a variety of sources. The success of such presentations relies more on the announcer's extemporaneous ability than on carefully written formal script material. It is beyond the scope of this book to consider the various elements involved in such extemporaneous presentations. See Appendix A for suggested readings that can supply this kind of information.

So, what is done to prepare most local radio station music programs? The on-air personality selects or is given the music to be played, based on the station's format. This announcer then comments, as appropriate, on the recording artist, the music, upcoming station programs, and activities and contests and very frequently simply provides the current time and temperature. A format clock or wheel is devised to help guide music selection and use, as well as other programming elements, such as community activity announcements, station promotions, and contests. The clock or wheel divides the contents of an hour of radio programming into wedges. Each wedge helps visualize the major elements of a format. Colors are often used for similar elements, such as announcements, music categories, and promos. The placement and length of each element are visible on the format clock or wheel.

Some preparation is necessary to ensure the success of any program; however, most local radio station music formats require minimal written preparation. A full-script is rarely prepared; it can disturb the effectiveness of a key ingredient of such programs—the spontaneity of the air personality, who provides the flexibility and energy that is essential for the programs' success.

Even nationally syndicated program music services usually do not prepare fully-scripted material for the many formats distributed via satellite or on tape to radio stations around the country. Knowledgeable announcers are employed to provide appropriate extemporaneous comments about the music and performers as the program is assembled. Stations receive only a rundown or cue sheet for the music, sent via FAX or simply enclosed with the recorded tape reels or CDs. Figure 9.1 illustrates a typical rundown sheet sent to stations using a syndicated oldies rock music program format.

Generally a writer concentrates on the *structure* of a music program, particularly of a contemporary music program. You might help select the music to be used and determine its placement in the program. You would probably write only essential continuity for the music program: opens, closes, transitions, and announcements.

Producing Radio Music Programs

It should not be inferred that formal and extensive script preparation is never used to prepare radio music programs. Every music program requires at least a firm mental rundown sheet. A semi-script or even a full-script may be appropriate for such programs as a musical year-in-review or a program highlighting the musical progression of a particular era, recording artist, or composer. Formal script preparation is essential when special effects, gimmicks, recorded dialogue, or humor is used or when an engineer operates the equipment for the announcer and script material is needed to ensure consistency

Length of Selection	Selection Title	Artist	Record Label	Music Licensee[1]
3:16	1. Sister Golden Hair	America	W.B.	A
3:46	2. For the Good Times	Ray Price	Columbia	B
2:50	3. This Will Be	Natalie Cole	Capitol	A
4:47	4. Wildfire	Michael Murphey	Epic	B
2:35	5. I'd Really Like to See You Tonight	England Dan/ John Ford Coley	Casablanca	B
2:41	6. It Don't Matter to Me	Bread	Elektra	B
2:54	7. My Cherie Amour	Stevie Wonder	Tamla	B/A
3:00	8. Best of Both Worlds	Lulu	Epic	
4:43	9. Slip Slidin' Away	Paul Simon	Columbia	A
3:27	10. Autobahn	Kraftwerk	Vertigo	A
3:10	11. Daytime Friends	Kenny Rogers	U.A.	B
3:33	12. Eres Tu (Touch the Wind)	Mocedades	Tara	A
4:41	13. Hello It's Me	Todd Rundgren	Bearsville	B
3:38	14. We're All Alone	Rita Coolidge	A&M	A
3:10	15. Daybreak	Barry Manilow	Arista	B
3:40	16. The Long and Winding Road	Beatles	Apple	B
3:15	17. Changes in Lattitudes, Changes in Attitudes	Jimmy Buffett	ABC	B
2:37	18. House at Pooh Corner	Nitty Gritty Dirt Band	U.A.	B
4:45	19. Me and Mrs. Jones	Billy Paul	Phil Intl.	B
3:28	20. Have You Never Been Mellow	Olivia Newton John	MCA	B
3:45	21. Garden Party	Rick Nelson	Decca	B
3:54	22. The Way I Feel Tonight	Bay City Rollers	Arista	B
2:20	23. Mr. Tambourine Man	Byrds	Columbia	A
3:30	24. Don't Give Up on Us	David Soul	Private St.	A
3:28	25. Once a Fool	Kiki Dee	Rocket	B
2:51	26. Sentimental Lady	Bob Welch	Capitol	A
2:58	27. To Love Somebody	Bee Gees	RSO	B

[1]A = ASCAP; B = BMI. Individual subscribing stations pay these music licensing fees.

Figure 9.1
Rundown or cue sheet for a syndicated music tape service.
Courtesy of Broadcast Programming, Inc.

and to avoid confusion. In these circumstances, precise information and timing are important. This precision can best be achieved through formal script preparation.

Two radio music program series profiled later in this chapter will illustrate this point. In addition, figures 10.1 through 10.3 will trace the preparation of a country music special featuring recording artists from a previous decade. Compilation techniques described in chapter 10 are often used to prepare such musical specials.

For *any* radio music program, you should

a. Plan the musical selections.
b. Check the music clearances. ASCAP and BMI require music licensing fee payments.
c. Note the timing of each selection.
d. Prepare for emergencies.
e. Follow the designated music format consistently.

When *preparing contemporary music programs,* consider these recommendations:

a. Select music that is appropriate for the designated format and that consistently reinforces a predetermined image.
b. Know the music by keeping abreast of current developments through the music trade press, local music stores, and television and radio entertainment news.
c. Know the available music library, its contents and cataloguing system.
d. Be aware of scheduled breaks for announcements, station IDs, and other programs.
e. Pace the program by controlling the general intensity of the music—tempo, lyrics, featured groups—and by providing a smooth continuity of sound.
f. Analyze the potential target audience. Take them seriously. They take you and the music seriously. Music is an important part of their life-style.
g. Match the language used to the type of program prepared.
h. Keep it simple. Provide only the essential facts. Make ''information with a purpose'' your watchword.

All these suggestions for preparing contemporary music programs also apply to several of the other standard radio music formats—for example, country, oldies, big band, and easy listening.

Additional suggestions should be considered when *preparing jazz and classical music programs,* since often these types of music shows require more extensive scripting preparations:

a. Know the music thoroughly. Regular listeners for these kinds of programs expect intelligent and informed commentary and musical interpretation, since often they are already very familiar with the music. This audience is unforgiving when, for example, in an introduction to a musical selection, an important fact is omitted or a prominent composer's name is mispronounced.
b. Use standard music reference works. Assemble your own personal music literature library.
c. Read the backs of album jackets and material placed in CD cases. Often, valuable and interesting information is provided.

d. Provide comments and biographical information about composers. Also be sure to include a pronunciation guide for difficult-to-pronounce names.

e. Provide information about each musical composition. This might include anecdotes, the historical circumstances surrounding the music, other musical developments during the same period, or an analysis of the construction of the composition.

f. Provide comments about the performer(s), such as background, previous recordings, and repertoire.

g. Prepare brief "filler" material to accommodate time requirements and equipment difficulties if the program is broadcast "live."

To better illustrate the process and many of the principles and techniques used to prepare jazz and classical music programs for radio, let us trace the development of two program series. One is a limited jazz series and the other is an ongoing classical music series heard on National Public Radio (NPR) stations throughout the United States.

"Jazz Birthday Celebrations" Beth Schenker produced and distributed a radio series celebrating the birthdays of six jazz trumpet players. Over sixty-five public radio stations used the five-minute programs funded by a grant from the Gilbey's National Jazz Service Organization Community Jazz Program. Some stations used each program as a "hook" to lead into a longer presentation featuring music by the same artist. Others used the short programs as modules in a magazine program, such as NPR's "All Things Considered" or "Morning Edition," and replaced a magazine segment or module with the programs in this limited jazz music series.

In assembling the material needed to produce the programs in the series, biographical information was gathered on the entire group of trumpeters (Charlie Shavers, Bill Coleman, Benny Carter, Michael Mantler, Art Farmer, and Kenny Dorham). Figure 9.2 shows the notes assembled for one of the trumpeters.

Next, for each trumpeter, Schenker says she

> tried to get a sense of what important times in their life were, in terms of recording, and started to make some long lists of what albums I thought would be important. That might mean particular people that they played with, or that played with them . . . a particular era during the time of their career. . . .
>
> Some [of the artists] were fairly obscure, in terms of availability of music, so I got all of my records through a record store in New York. . . . I tried to get about six albums for each artist because I knew I needed to have a good variety, and there might be specific parts of music that I needed to find. Because I couldn't just go to the store down the street two days later and find what I needed, I had to really plan. And I wound up using usually at least one cut from each of those albums.

Bill Coleman: August 4, 1904   Died August 24, 1981

Bill Coleman began his musical career with the clarinet
converting to trumpet after hearing a recording of Louis
Armstrong. In the early 1930's he played in Benny
Carter's and Charlie Johnson's band. Although he played
trumpet as early as 1916 audiences really didn't get
acquainted with him until his 1935 recordings with the
Teddy Hill band and Fats Waller.

Later that year he moved to Paris to work with Freddie
Taylor and the Great Willie Lewis Orchestra. For the next
five years Paris became his home base. He enjoyed the
lack of discrimination found in the US and was pleased
with his acceptance by the Europeans. While in Europe he
recorded solos with Dickie Wells and the Willie Lewis
Orchestra and guested and recorded with the Hot Club of
France Quintet, becoming a celebrity in the process.

In 1940 he came back to the US to work in New York with
Jazz artists Teddy Wilson, Benny Carter, Lester Young,
Coleman Hawkins, Mary Lou Williams and Sy Oliver. At the
same time there was a rise of popularity in Bebop and
trumpeters such as Dizzy Gillespie might have made life a
little less comfortable for Coleman so in 1948 he
responded favorably to a telegram to return to work
opportunities in France.

He commuted regularly to other European countries and in
the 1950's his recordings showed a new confidence and
maturity. Coleman's playing was noted for the elegance
and fluidity of his phrasing and his highly musical
melodic ideas.

He continued to play and record until his death in Paris.

Figure 9.2
Research notes
compiled for one
program in the
"Jazz Birthday
Celebrations" series.
*Courtesy of Beth
Schenker, Jazz Radio
Producer.*

I had to think about who my audience was . . . who did I expect to be
listening to this so that I would know the kinds of facts [to gather] and how to
present that information.[1]

The target audience for the series was identified as

the people who are already jazz enthusiasts who might know a lot about these
people, but would enjoy hearing about them. And then, the person who hasn't
heard much jazz, but this might catch their ear and might result in them going
out and finding out more about this particular artist and buying an album. . . .
I felt like I needed to be fairly broad in what I was trying to do. . . . [Each
program] needed to be . . . [produced] with a professional approach.[2]

Once the target audience was identified, Schenker worked on each program.

> So, I had my music and my bio information. I sat down at the computer and started a very rough draft . . . setting out main points in that person's career that I felt were really important for the listener to know about.
>
> I'd listen to the music one time, and then I made some notes of interesting things in some pieces that might work well for the show for various reasons. Maybe there was a portion of a solo that seemed especially nice, or maybe there was interaction with another instrument, with another musician, that was an important relationship that needed to be talked about.[3]

Even with only six programs in the series, it was important to maintain continuity and establish a common thread among the shows. To accomplish this, the programs were designed to be used in chronological order. Each program began with the musician's date of birth, place of birth, and distinctive contribution—for instance, performing, performing and composing, or conducting. Each program featured six or seven musical excerpts from each artist's career, as well as biographical information presented by the host, who was the same for each program in the series: internationally acclaimed trumpeter Jon Faddis.

Beth Schenker explained what she tried to accomplish with each program:

> Overall, I tried to give people a clear idea of who this artist was, and what he accomplished within his career, or at least up to that date. Three of the artists were dead, and three were not. . . . Plus, I wanted to be able to give as many musical examples as I could.[4]

Figure 9.3 shows the final production script for the program on Bill Coleman that was developed from the notes assembled in figure 9.2. Notice the excellent blend of narration and music throughout the program, as well as the compactness of the information and musical excerpts.

Schenker has been producing radio programs since 1983. Her work has been heard on stations in San Francisco, Tucson, and Newark, as well as across the country on National Public Radio programs, such as "Morning Edition," "Let's Hear It," and "Performance Today." What is her advice for those who research, write, and produce jazz music programs?

> The main thing that I keep in mind, above all else, is to be true to the music, and that the music ultimately is what's telling the story.[5]

She says that, if the music "works"—if it has a nice flow and pace—and if the script interacts with the music, enhancing its value or quality, then the combination of words and music has added enrichment for listeners.

"Performance Today" This timely classical music program series is heard Mondays through Fridays on over 100 radio stations in the United States. The series emphasizes performances taped live on the scene and broadcast soon after the performance.

```
                    BILL COLEMAN
                    PROGRAM #2
```

(Open with Joe Lewis Stomp or Ol'Man River)

Trumpeter Bill Coleman was born on August 4, 1904 in
Paris, Kentucky. Jazz audiences discovered Coleman during
the mid-thirties while he was playing and recording with
the Teddy Hill Band and Fats Waller.

(Opening cut out by 'Orchestra in Paris)

In 1927 Bill Coleman moved to New York and then on to
France in 1935. Here he is with the Willie Lewis
Orchestra in Paris.

(Bill Street Blues, start in the clear)

That's Bill Coleman with his own composition, "Bill
Street Blues." Can Bill Coleman swing? Or can he swing!

(Begin classic tenor collage under host)

(Fade out under by 'Europe his home)

In 1940 Bill Coleman returned to the U.S. and played with
many Jazz greats including Benny Carter, Teddy Wilson,
Coleman Hawkins, Lester Young, and Mary Lou Williams.

He returned to Paris in 1948 and said, "it was a mellow,
cultural city where you were accepted for what you were!"
As with many American Jazz musicians, Bill Coleman made
Europe his home.

                    ---MORE---

                         1

Figure 9.3
Final production script
based on material
shown in figure 9.2
for one program in
the "Jazz Birthday
Celebrations" series.
*Courtesy of Beth
Schenker, Jazz Radio
Producer.*

Figure 9.3 (*continued*)

FINAL DRAFT
Bill Coleman
PG. 2

(Begin Back Home Again in Indiana in the clear)

Here is Bill Coleman in Switzerland from a 1957 live
recording of "Back Home Again in Indiana." That's him on
trumpet (PAUSE HERE) AND singing!

He has a never-ending flow of ideas no matter what the
instrument.

(Indiana emerges here and take it out)
(Begin L & L Blues at top of host)

July 4th 1973 finds Bill Coleman at the Montreux Jazz
Festival playing an original composition entitled L and L
Blues. In this performance you can hear a maturity to his
trumpet voice; he's clearly found a way to focus all that
energy, AND get it to swing...ALL at the SAME time!

Bill Coleman died in 1981 in Toulouse, France.

Jazz Birthday Celebrations is made possible by a grant
from the Gilbey's/National Jazz Service Organization
Community Jazz Program; and is produced by Beth Schenker
for KZUM FM in Lincoln, Nebraska. I'm Jon Faddis.

(Fade out on L & L)

---END---

2

Don Lee, senior producer of the series, outlined the process used to design, plan, script, and produce each program:

> We sit down at 11:15 each morning and review the show we just did for a few minutes, its strengths and weaknesses. Then, we move on to the next day's show, which will have been planned already. . . . At the end of each morning's meeting, we make writing assignments, and talk about any overarching [or dominating] shape to hours that isn't obvious [with the commentary and music already planned]. And then everybody goes off to his or her own corner and writes scripts.[6]

By the end of each day, scripts have been reviewed and the next day's program produced and ready for broadcast.

The structure of each program is monitored closely. Each hour-long show consists of three segments.

> The A [first] segment of each hour has several smaller subcomponents. We begin the hour with a 60-second billboard that highlights what will be coming up during the hour. That's followed by a five-minute cut-away. . . . It's an opportunity for stations that want to carry NPR newscasts to drop them in there. . . . We typically put a short CD into that slot. It presents a challenge because for many listeners it's the beginning of the show and it should be "catchy," but for stations who cover it with news, it's a "throw-away." . . . Then, at six minutes past the hour, we come out of that cut-away and reestablish the show. . . . It's tricky, for at this point, for many listeners, it's the beginning of the show, really. So, we have a little [musical] "button" suggesting our theme once again. The host, Martin [Goldsmith], reintroduces himself, and then he'll read a short bit of music news, if there happens to be any that day. . . . We move at that point into a piece of music, and we try to make that just about the freshest piece of music we have on the shelf.[7]

The rest of each program is built around regular guests, as well as special observances that have been planned for weeks, often months, in advance.

> Feature material [presented in the last third of each hour's program] often will "drive" the focus of each hour. Not always, but if there is thematic unity to an hour, it usually comes from that [regular features on such topics as musical jargon and new classical music CDs, as well as special features based on such events as anniversaries and birthdays].

> We try to fill in the week's features the Thursday previous to the week [of production], but . . . we know about anniversaries and other events months in advance, so we're thinking about them. We have a weekly futures meeting on Friday where we discuss ideas months down the pike. . . . Some things don't get filled in until a couple of days in advance because they don't have a "peg" . . . as the saying goes.[8]

An excerpt from the *Performance Today Stylebook* provides insights into writing and producing material for this continuing series:

> Because our overriding goal is to point out the vitality and contemporaneity of classical music in our culture, we should emphasize the here and now in introducing the music we play. That means we should always try to say interesting things about the performance or the players rather than recite a lesson in music history or theory. . . .
>
> Avoid any usage or construction that explicitly or implicitly presumes the listener is very familiar with classical music or with *Performance Today*. Examples:—Use of the phrase ''of course'' in any but the most obvious cases;—Use of the definite article so as to imply that anyone listening should be familiar with what is in reality a pretty obscure bit of information . . . (''Robert Simpson, *the* English composer and Nielsen biographer . . .'') . . .
>
> [The tone and style of the writing should be] informal, approachable, inclusive, occasionally humorous and irreverent, aware that classical music and its listeners are part of a wider world. We can achieve that tone by using everyday language and simply-structured sentences. Write for a friend rather than ·a member of some classical music elite.[9]

Music on Television

Music programming has been an integral part of public television programming since its inception. Local public television stations and the PBS (Public Broadcasting Service) network have provided a wide range of dazzling music programs over the years for their diverse viewing audience.

Commercial television networks and program syndicators offer music series and specials, most featuring contemporary music. Some of these programs showcase a number of stars. Others feature the talents of a single entertainer. These programs are often combination music-and-variety programs. Many are offered during holidays and ratings sweeps periods, when television outlets try to hype the programs to improve their ratings.

The amount and diversity of music available on cable systems and in the home video market continue to grow. Pay-television systems produce several music specials and limited series, most featuring rock and country music performers, as well as a combination of music and comedy performers.

Music Videos

Music videos are part of today's music industry lexicon. Recording artists incorporate video as well as audio conceptualizations into their plans for new recordings. Music videos often serve as the basis for the design of contemporary commercials, instructional and corporate presentations, and other specialized presentation situations.

Originally music videos appeared only on cable channels, such as MTV and VH-1. Video jockeys (VJs) occasionally offered comments about the music, interviews with contemporary music celebrities, music news items, and gossip about entertainers and recording stars. Today a growing number of cable channels, as well as local stations, present a regular program series of music videos. Some programs are thirty or sixty minutes long; others are short, tightly structured programs that feature one or two music videos sandwiched between commercials, transitions, news items, and comments by an on-camera host. This attractive, creative type of visual presentation can be used for many kinds of music, including rock, country music, and jazz. Marketing survey results can help sales and programming personnel match the style, mood, theme, pace, and tempo of a specific music video to a specific target audience.

Music videos can be used to sell products and services, as well as motivate children to learn certain skills in school. A versatile tool for both writers and production personnel, a music video generally can be identified as one of three types: performance video, concept video, or compilation video.

A *performance video* is simply a live, or live-looking, stage performance of the musicians presenting the music.

In a *concept video,* the performers set a mood for their viewers by adding settings or actions to their lyrics. Concept videos have been called "video mini-movies" or "three-minute visual fantasies." In a concept video, sometimes a visual narrative or story line is tied to the lyrics of the song. Generally musicians are shown in one of two ways, simply as a musician or as a character in the story line of the musician's song. In videos that feature a narrative, the soundtrack can operate like a narrator's omnipotent voiceover, guiding the visual action.

A *compilation video* is less common than performance and concept videos. Compilation videos are more of a subtype. They consist of preexisting material adapted for and edited to a song, such as videos of early rock groups performing on stage or rehearsing in a recording studio. Another possibility is to create a video of a song from a motion picture soundtrack by intercutting shots from the movie and shots of the group performing.

Many music videos combine category designations. For example, there might be a dramatic narrative in progress, then a few shots of a live performance, before returning to the original story line. Special effects might be combined with any of the three types of music videos. Categorizing the music video to be produced will help you write material that will meet or exceed the objectives that are determined *before* production begins.

Many music videos, especially concept and compilation videos, are labeled "controversial" because of their depiction of sex and violence, their negative portrayals of women and minority groups, and their rough and sometimes prejudicial language, as well as the strong perceptions such videos create for young, vulnerable viewers. As discussed in chapter 1, those who write and produce material for the electronic media need to exercise restraint and display a responsible attitude toward the quality and value of their work. This sense of responsibility produces material that is not indecent, obscene, or blatantly offensive to the audience.

Role of the Writer

Generally the writer's contribution to the preparation of music material for television is limited. You might be involved in the preparation of short musical introductions or transitions, a rundown sheet for the music featured in a broadcast, or a semi-script for an interview with a music performer. In many situations, the actual full musical score becomes the script used by production personnel, with only minimal scripting added to provide continuity.

The principles and techniques presented earlier for radio music programs transfer with little modification to similar programs for television. You still must emphasize pacing, continuity, unity, and diversification in the selection, placement, and use of the music. The tastes and expectations of the audience remain a primary concern. The obvious difference between radio and television music programs is the visual presentation of the music.

Producing Television Music Programs

If you do become directly involved in the production of music presentations for television, then you can make a different kind of contribution. The intensity and fullness of the music can be visualized, and the visuals can display new dimensions because of the music. The music can be interpreted visually based on the lyrics, a suggested locale or theme, or even the personality of the performer. The variety of interpretations is limited only by your imagination. The full range of visual alternatives can be tapped and new dimensions offered by the use of such art forms as dance, pantomime, slides, films, videotapes, drawings, sketches, paintings, buildings, abstract representations, colors, and shapes. The shooting, assembling, and editing of musical productions is beyond the scope of this book. See Appendix A for a list of works that describe and illustrate specific types of production techniques.

Minimal scripting is needed for musical productions on television. Later in this chapter, there is an illustration of the scripting used for a musical segment in a variety program special.

Music videos can be "scripted" as a treatment accompanied by a storyboard. The treatment for a music video could describe, in narrative form, key shots and sequences, as well as the anticipated visual progression, theme, tone, pace, and mood. Before writing such a treatment, however, you need to understand thoroughly the music and lyrics (if any) of the musical piece. This understanding includes both intellectual and emotional elements. Before you write such a treatment, determine the purpose or objective of the music video. Will it simply enhance intellectual or emotional points already established or understood? Will it attempt to persuade the viewer to adopt a less-than-popular viewpoint? Will it simply illustrate lyrics, with scenes called to mind as the words and music blend to create an effect or a feeling?

Variety Programs

At one point in the development of radio and television programming, regular variety series were an industry staple. These shows featured music, dancing, and drama/comedy sketches, often with well-known vaudeville and stage stars, who brought their entertainment magic to the airwaves to delight millions across the country. Such programs as "The Ed Sullivan Show," "Show of Shows," "The Carol Burnett Show," "The Jack Benny Show," and "The Hollywood Palace," to mention only a few, for many years consistently filled the audience's need for entertainment. These kinds of shows were just plain fun to watch and often were used by young entertainers to sharpen their performing skills.

Today variety program *series* are rare. Because of high production costs and a lack of general audience appeal, only networks, syndicators, and packagers (individuals or companies that assemble the creative talent necessary for a production) now produce such programs. Variety shows tend to be produced as specials rather than as a series and generally feature a theme or celebrity. Hybrid variety program forms have evolved, in which diverse elements are presented to attract and hold audience interest. The talk/variety program and magazine programs now fulfill many of the same audience needs once served by the more traditional variety program forms.

Categories

Besides the fact that a variety program can be produced either as a special or as part of a regular series, such shows can also be identified by the emphasis placed on certain elements in the program. There are three common categories of variety programs: performer-oriented, theme-oriented, and talk-variety.

Performer-Oriented Programs

In a performer-oriented program, the performance of one or more entertainers is emphasized. For example, this emphasis could be displayed as a vaudeville or music hall show, in which individual acts lack any obvious connection or relationship. Another possibility is a solo performance by such talents as Garth Brooks, Bill Cosby, and Guns n' Roses. This type of variety program might feature one main performer or a regular cast of performers, along with special guests; examples include "The Tonight Show with Jay Leno" and "The Arsenio Hall Show," as well as the ensemble performances on "Saturday Night Live" and "Hee Haw."

Theme-Oriented Programs

In theme-oriented programs, the topic dominates, rather than individual performers. Such variety program specials have emphasized such themes as patriotism, holidays, and even television. Perhaps the theme could be the songs of a particular composer or the anniversary of a significant historical event. A locale or setting could also be used as a variety program theme. For example, perhaps the plain, homespun people of a certain mountainous area could be the backdrop and connecting link between musical and comedy segments for a country music variety special featuring several entertainers who return home for the holidays. The continuity, or "glue," of the program is its theme, which must be evident in each segment.

Talk-Variety Programs

Networks, syndicators, and cable programmers have found the talk-variety program structure an attractive alternative to the traditional variety show format emphasizing performers or themes. Talk-variety programs offer viewers entertaining, often informative conversation, as well as guest appearances by singers, dancers, musicians, actors, athletes, authors, and specialty performers. Often comedy sketches are featured. On some programs, co-hosts share the spotlight with the featured talent and provide a sense of continuity for a limited set of programs. Talk-variety is a hybrid form, offering elements of comedy, music, and entertainment, as well as conversations with interesting guests.

One of the dangers of placing all variety programs into a limited number of classifications is the implication that each type of program must be developed in isolation, with no attempt to blend creative elements. Obviously a variety show emphasizes several elements. For example, a Christmas special could feature a Christmas theme reinforced with guest interviews, music performances, and explorations of wintry locales. In this situation, performers, themes, music, conversation, and perhaps even a comedy sketch could be blended into the fabric of the program.

Role of the Writer

Practically all variety programs are staff written. Established writers who have worked on similar programs contract to write material with other writers sharing similar backgrounds. For a variety program series, a staff of six to ten writers generates the majority of the material for the entire series. Usually the writers of a variety program special have worked with the program producer or packager on previous programs or series.

Generally the writers inherit the variety program idea or concept formulated by the packager or producer. They also inherit the general content and approximate length of each major program segment. Rarely does a staff writer help formulate and develop the original program idea or even the general nature of most of the program segments, unless the writer also serves as the program producer or packager.

The writers *can* help *enhance* variety programs, however. Research may be needed for a particular segment only outlined in the original treatment for the program. Perhaps a writer can help determine a specific song to be sung to present the best that a particular performer can offer or can determine how long a dance routine should be to blend well with the words and movements to be scripted into a comedy sketch or monologue. Maybe a guest needs a special introduction or a sensitive approach for questions to be asked during an interview. Precise script material must be prepared for music and drama or comedy segments. Writers also may suggest alternative segment ideas, which might or might not be accepted by the producer or packager.

Variety program development produces a unique writing environment. In most cases, the individual writer must interact with other writers and production personnel, respond to their suggestions, offer creative ideas and insights, and still conform to a program structure that has been determined by someone who may not necessarily help write the required script material. This kind of intense program development situation requires a strong, seasoned writer who has faced the turmoil and inevitable compromises inherit in such circumstances.

The steps in packaging, producing, and directing a music or variety program live or on tape are beyond the scope of this book. See Appendix A for works that provide this type of information.

Producing Variety Program Material

Despite what may appear to be limitations placed on you when a variety program idea or concept is developed, as a writer, you place the flesh on the bones of a variety program outline or rundown sheet. Working with others, you can contribute significantly to the success of the program by providing specific script material and ideas to enhance the quality of each program segment. Following are techniques and suggestions that can help you accomplish this writing task.

Know the audience. Identify the target audience for the program. This should be done not only for variety programs but also for any other form of communications, especially in the mass media. Once the audience is identified, the purpose or intent of the program should also become clear. The cultural diversification of audiences and the proliferation of program sources, especially on cable systems, require the careful targeting and preparation of material to reach a specific audience with a particular program. In the first few decades of television programming, music and variety shows were structured to reach a wide, diverse family audience. Music and variety programs no longer have that kind of mass appeal. A variety program format could be used effectively to reach elementary school students, for example, with specific kinds of information from any number of subject areas.

Know the available resources. Aside from your own personal writing resources, you must know about the creative and production talent. As you write specific script material for the program, you should be aware of the performers' range of talents and skills, as well as the preferences they have expressed or implied. On the production side, you ought to discover what is possible to produce and what is not. You might find that the personal preferences of key production personnel or the availability of the production facility or equipment will impose certain limitations or offer additional creative opportunities.

Work with the schedule. Variety programs are produced under severe time constraints. Although some of your work can be completed before production begins, it is during the grueling six to ten days of production that a writer's metal is tested. It is important to know the complete development and production schedule, but especially your participation in that schedule. This will help you avoid unnecessary conflicts and a reduction in expectations. The more you work on this kind of program, the better you can evaluate the progress that is being made and the level and quality of your contributions.

Stress teamwork. Writing a variety program normally is not a solo effort. It is done within the pressure cooker environment of human interaction. There are disagreements, conflicts, and sometimes constant bickering; however, there is also a sense of accomplishment as several individuals pull together to create something that, by themselves, they could not have achieved. Variety program development, as well as most of television production, requires a concerted group effort to produce consistent, high-quality work.

Build program unity. Even if the variety program is destined to be performer oriented, a clear, attractive central theme must exist to connect and unify the various program segments. The unity expected in a variety program is like that of a drama or comedy show. Each program segment must exhibit unity and excellence within itself. Each segment hinges on the effectiveness of the segments that precede and follow it. Together all of the segments provide a sense of unity for the audience and often build to a final climactic segment, which features the principal performers in a dazzling display of technical quality and high entertainment value.

Maintain program diversity. Allow each segment to shine with its own special qualities and contribute to the general effect of the program. If the show is to be considered variety, it must exhibit some contrast and diversification, but with the ultimate goal of effectively joining all of the program segments. The variety provided by each segment should fall into place under the unifying umbrella of the program idea or concept.

Monitor continuity and pacing. A key to the success of any program is conscious control over its continuity and pace. The various program elements must flow and blend. Initially, continuity and pacing are established by the order, length, and content of each segment. For example, two comedy segments normally do not run back to back. The same would be true of musical or dance segments. Instead, these segments are mixed together to provide a smooth, easy movement throughout the program. You can enhance the flow of a program by providing carefully written transitions between segments and appropriate introductions to guests and by working with others on the creative staff to drain as much as possible out of each performer and program segment. Without continuity and pacing, the program will appear disjointed, but when these two characteristics are displayed in the program, the creative staff and, more important, the audience will attain a firm sense of organization and unity among program elements.

"Texaco Star Theatre . . . Opening Night"   Today's television variety programs use scripting formats that are not noticeably different from those used in earlier decades, when music and variety shows dominated television screens. To better illustrate many of the principles and techniques used to prepare an effective variety program, let us examine the NBC-TV music/variety program special entitled "Texaco Star Theatre . . . Opening Night." This one and one-half hour salute to the American musical featured top celebrities from the stage, movies, and television. Figure 9.4 shows one page from the revised rundown sheet for this program. Program segments often are recorded out of sequence. The page numbers indicated in such rundown sheets are not always consecutive. The columns in the rundown sheet indicate, from left to right, the consecutive numbering of each segment as broadcast; the content of each segment, along with the names of the performers; the original script page (in parentheses) on which each segment begins; the length of each segment; and the cumulative or program running time.

22. ANN JILLIAN PERF. "Diamonds are a Girls Best Friend" (SC-45)	(71)	2:25	36:37		
23. PARTY INTRO #4 (Into My Fair Lady) (Steve Allen,Charles Nelson Reilly) (SC-49)	(76)	1:00	37:37		
24. ROBERT GUILLUAME PERF. "Ordinary Man"/"Accustomed To Her Face" (SC-50-51)	(78)	2:20	39:57		
25. PARTY INTRO #5 (Into Trouble) (Charles Nelson Reilly,Steve Allen,Donald O'Connor") (SC-52-53)	(83)	:14	40:11		
26. DONALD O'CONNOR PERF. "Trouble" (SC-54-55)	(84)	3:42	43:53		
26A ANIMATED BUMPER	(93)	:03	43:56		
27. COMMERCIAL POSITION #4	(94)	1:32	45:28		
28. NBC PROMO	(95)	:31	45:59		
29. PARTY INTRO #10 (Into Enchanted Evening) Carol Burnett,Placido Domingo, (Zsa Zsa Gabor,ANNIE kids) SC61,66	(96)	1:01	47:00		
30. PLACIDO DOMINGO PERF. "Enchanted Evening" (SC-67)	(98)	3:01	50:01		
31. PARTY INTRO #14 (Into Chorus Line) (Annie Kids)	(101)	:14	50:15		
32. A CHORUS LINE SEGMENT Intro :05 a. "What I Did for Love" (Cast) (SC-78) (2:32)	(102)	4:24	54:39		
b. "One" (Cast) (1:35) (SC-79)	(106)				
33. COMMERCIAL POSITION #5	(109)	1:02	55:41		
33A ANIMATED BUMPER	(110)	:03	55:44		

Figure 9.4
Rundown sheet from the NBC-TV special "Texaco Star Theatre . . . Opening Night."
Courtesy of Passetta Productions, Inc.

This theme-oriented variety special appeals to a wide cross section of the audience because of the way the music and performers are featured. The wide range of available talent is used well. Notice also how the musical party theme is reinforced throughout the show and is used as a transition into individual and group performances of music and comedy. The quality of each segment shines through and contributes to the overall effectiveness of the entire program.

The program structure displays good contrast, diversity, continuity, and pacing. Notice how the emphasis shifts from group performances, such as segment 32, to individual performances, such as segments 22, 24, 26, and 30. Continuity between segments is provided by the party settings, such as in segments 23, 25, 29, and 31. Continuity is also maintained with animated ''bumpers,'' or transitions, that lead viewers into and out of commercials and promotional announcements. The various program segments flow and blend well to present a strong, diverse, yet unified presentation.

Figure 9.5 shows the scripting format and writing techniques used for one of the segments featured in this, as well as most, variety programs. Segment 32 (A CHORUS LINE SEGMENT) contains two musical numbers. The segment begins fifty-four minutes and thirty-nine seconds into the program. Segment 32 was originally labeled segment 39A on page 102 of the final script. A short monologue blends into a musical number by a single performer. The full cast participates throughout this first song. A visual and musical transition is made on the bottom of script page 105 to the second and probably most identifiable song from this long-running musical.

In figure 9.5, notice the use of a slightly modified three-camera scripting format. This modification was done to help create a feeling of rehearsed spontaneity. Dialogue in a variety program tends to be light and paced quickly, in an effort to bridge easily and naturally into the music. Script pages 102 through 108 illustrate how musical numbers are written. Notice how song lyrics use triple spacing and FULL CAPS. Talent directions are in FULL CAPS and enclosed in parentheses. Sufficient space is provided for the director to note camera shots, singer and dancer movements, and technical changes, such as scene changes and background adjustments.

"The Tonight Show with Jay Leno" This is one of the most popular late-night performer-oriented television variety programs on-the-air. Writers, performers, and producers have tried to enhance the long-standing ratings success of this program series hosted for many years by Johnny Carson. Figure 9.6 on page 276 is a preliminary rundown sheet used to produce one program in this weeknight network series. Production personnel associated with this NBC-TV series admit that extensive script material is not usually prepared. Except for a few fully-scripted segments, most of the program is ad-libbed by host Jay Leno, using a rundown sheet similar to the one shown in figure 9.6.

"CHORUS LINE" SEGMENT   "CHORUS LINE" SEGMENT
"WHAT I DID FOR LOVE"   "WHAT I DID FOR LOVE"
(Cast)   (Cast)

DISSOLVE TO BARE STAGE WITH ENTIRE
CAST IN REHEARSAL CLOTHES SITTING AROUND.   SC. 78

PIANO INTRO SLOW - 4 -

          ZACK (SPOKEN OVER MUSIC)

But if today were the day you had

to stop dancing, how would you feel?

        GAYE MARSHALL

KISS TODAY GOODBYE

THE SWEETNESS AND THE SORROW

WISH ME LUCK

THE SAME

TO YOU ----

BUT I CAN'T REGRET

WHAT I DID FOR LOVE

WHAT I DID FOR LOVE -----

(FULL ORCHESTRA COMES IN)

LOOK MY EYES ARE DRY

THE GIFT WAS OURS TO BORROW

        (MORE)

Figure 9.5
Script pages from the NBC-TV special "Texaco Star Theater . . . Opening Night."
Courtesy of Pasetta Productions, Inc.

                        GIRL LEAD (CONT'D)

    IT'S AS IF WE

    ALWAYS

    KNEW ----

    AND I WON'T FORGET

    WHAT I DID FOR LOVE

    WHAT I DID FOR LOVE ------

    GONE

    LOVE IS

    NEVER GONE

    AS WE

    TRAVEL ON

    LOVE'S WHAT WE'LL REMEMBER

(MODULATION)

                    FULL CAST

    KISS TODAY GOODBYE

Figure 9.5 (*continued*)

GIRL LEAD

AND POINT ME TOWARD TOMORROW

                                    CHORUS

                    POINT ME TOWARD TOMORROW

          FULL CAST

WE DID WHAT WE

HAD

TO

DO ------

WON'T FORGET

CAN'T REGRET

WHAT I DID

FOR

LOVE ------

WHAT I DID FOR LOVE ------

          GIRL LEAD

WHAT I DID FOR

               (MORE)

_____

Figure 9.5 (*continued*)

FULL CAST

LOVE ------

(APPLAUSE)

_____

(AS THE NUMBER ENDS...THE ORCHESTRA BUILDING
WE SEGUE TO A FULL PRODUCTION SET...AS THE   SC. 79
MUSIC VAMPS, WE SEE A MONTAGE OF "CHORUS
LINE" POSTERS FROM ALL OVER THE WORLD. AT
THE CONCLUSION OF THE MONTAGE, THE LAST POSTER
FLIES OUT, AND WE REVEAL THE MIRRORED SET FROM
THE FINALE. AND COMPANY ENTERS AND SINGS....)

_____

Figure 9.5 (*continued*)

(39B)

"CHORUS LINE" SEGMENT
"ONE"
(Cast)

"CHORUS LINE" SEGMENT
"ONE"
(Cast)

ORCHESTRA "ONE" VAMP TRANSITION (:15)

SC. 79

                    CAST

        ONE

        SINGULAR SENSATION

        EVERY LITTLE STEP SHE TAKES

        ONE

        THRILLING COMBINATION

        EVERY MOVE THAT SHE MAKES

        ONE SMILE AND SUDDENLY

        NOBODY ELSE

        WILL

        DO-----

        YOU KNOW YOU'LL NEVER BE LONELY WITH

        YOU

        KNOW

        WHO ------

        ONE -----

                    (MORE)

Figure 9.5 (*continued*)

(39B)

FULL CAST (CONT'D)

MOMENT IN HER PRESENCE

AND YOU CAN FORGET THE REST

FOR THE GIRL IS SECOND BEST

TO

NONE ----

SON ----

OOH! SIGH!

GIVE HER YOUR ATTENTION

DO I

REALLY HAVE TO MENTION

SHE'S------

THE -----

SHE'S -----

THE -----

SHE'S -----

THE ----

(MORE)

Figure 9.5 (*continued*)

(39B)

FULL CAST (CONT'D)

ONE ------

(ORCHESTRA VAMPS TO FADE OUT) _

(APPLAUSE)

(INTO: COMMERCIAL POSITICN #5)

_____

Figure 9.5 *(continued)*

GUESTS: PETER ONORATI (DAVE)   HOST: JAY LENO
          THE CHIEFTAINS W/ (MIKE)   ANNCR: EDD HALL
          ROGER DALTREY & NANCI GRIFFITH   COND: BRANFORD MARSALIS
          JEFF STILSON (MIKE)

          5:30:00 (11:35:00)   6:00:00 (12:05:00)

1. THEME/OPENING VT/ANNOUNCE/CHYRON   9. TITLE BUMPER (MUSIC)

2. JAY - MONOLOGUE   10. ROGER DALTREY & NANCI GRIFFITH
   CHILDREN'S LETTERS   (PANEL)

3. BUMPER (EDD v/o) COMML (VT):   11. BUMPER (EDD (v/o) COMML (VT):
   NABISCO/LENS/GALLO (t/f/f)   FORD/DOW/WRIGLEY (t/t/t)
   LCI/BUMPER   LCI/BUMPER

4. PETER ONORATI   12. ROGER DALTRY & THE CHIEFTAINS
                                           (SONG)

5. BUMPER (EDD v/o) COMML (VT):
   MAZDA/NUTRASWT/VALVOLINE (t/t/t)   13. BUMPER (EDD v/o) COMML (VT):
   LCI/BUMPER   W. UNION/MAZDA/NUTRSWT/ARM-DIAL/
                                           NBC PROMO (:30)/BUMPER VALVOL
6. PETER ONORATI   (t/t/t/f/f)

7. BUMPER (EDD (v/o) COMML (VT):   14. JEFF STILSON (STAND UP TO PANEL)
   MARS/PONTIAC/WENDY'S (t/t/t)
   LCI/TITLE BUMPER   15. VT BUMPER (EDD v/o) COMML:
                                           LOCAL (SLIDE) (PROMO) VT BUMPER
8. NI VI
   STATION BREAK (1:25)   16. NANCI GRIFFITH & THE CHIEFTAINS
                                           (SONG)/GOODNIGHTS

                                       17. CRAWL (VT-1)/TAG (VT)

                                       18. NI VT
                                           BLACK (28:55)

Figure 9.6
A rundown sheet used to produce a network music/variety program series.
Courtesy of The Tonight Show with Jay Leno.

Figure 3.8 illustrated script material from another type of performer-oriented variety program series. "Hee Haw" features a regular group of performers along with special guests who appear in musical and comedy segments. This popular syndicated variety program series is seen in over 170 television markets covering approximately 90 percent of the United States.

Summary

This chapter examined music and variety programs and the writer's work associated with each type of presentation. Although the preparation of each kind of program calls for distinctive writing techniques, you can approach each of these writing opportunities with a similar set of concerns and interests: creatively selecting elements that enhance to the fullest each program segment yet provide a unified presentation that blends creatively and coincides with audience expectations; providing the variety, contrast, and diversification necessary to sustain audience interest and involvement and to control the pace and intensity of the presentation; making full use of available resources (talent, music, settings, etc.); and using simple, direct language and syntax to guide and hold audience attention throughout the program.

Music and variety programs offer still another opportunity for you to work cooperatively to prepare entertaining and often informative material. Because of the different elements involved, writing for such programs makes you stretch, creatively and professionally. It is a challenging writing opportunity.

Suggested Exercises and Projects

1. Select a popular music recording group. Write a full-script for a thirty-minute radio or television program that features several of the group's recordings and traces its musical style and development.
2. Follow the steps outlined in exercise 1 but for a prominent composer or composer/performer.
3. Select a theme, motif, or special event for a thirty-minute radio music program. Select the music and write a full-script that will develop the theme, motif, or special event.
4. Write a full-script for a two-hour radio music program to be distributed nationally to local stations. The script must include specific information about the recorded music used (title and length of each selection, composer, performer, and record label). The program must feature one of the following types of music: rock, country, jazz, or classical.
5. Record one of the "Performance Today" programs or a similar classical music program heard on National Public Radio. Prepare a rundown sheet for that program. Critique the selection and use of music, as well as the written continuity. Review the guidelines and writing processes described earlier in this chapter for the preparation of programs in the "Performance Today" series.

6. Read one of the major articles or special feature stories in a current issue of one of the following publications: *Billboard, Cash Box, Radio & Records, Variety.* Write a brief summary of the article.

7. Prepare a rundown or routine sheet for a one-hour radio or television music or variety program. Use a special holiday or event as the theme for this special program. Following are a few possible themes: Valentine's Day, spring break, spring, summer vacation, Fourth of July, Labor Day, Christmas. Write a full-script for one short segment of the program.

8. Assume that you have access to your choice of leading show business performers. Design a one-hour television variety program. Write a show format (rundown or routine sheet). Provide a brief justification for your program design. The justification statement should include the rationale for the selection and placement of each act or performer into the structure of the program, the tone and pace of the program that you envision as illustrated by the segments planned, and the target audience for the program.

9. Follow the directions given in exercise 8, but work with other members of a group. Each member of the team concentrates on developing and writing the material for one segment of the program, but all participate in the overall planning. Each member could be assigned a specific job associated with the show, such as producer, director, talent coordinator, writing supervisor, music coordinator, comedy coordinator, or technical adviser, but each must participate in some way in the writing of the program. An oral or a written group presentation should be made and evaluated.

10. Monitor and, if possible, record a one-hour television network or syndicated variety program. Prepare a rundown sheet for the show. Then critique the program, using the writing techniques and suggestions contained in this chapter.

11. Monitor and, if possible, record one music video shown recently on television. Write a one-page treatment that describes its theme, tone, pace, and visualization. Critique the quality of the music video.

12. Individually or as a member of a creative writing and production team, write a treatment for a four-to-five-minute music video. Consider providing a storyboard for one sequence in the music video. If time and facilities are available, work with production personnel to produce the sequence described in the treatment and shown in the storyboard.

Notes

1. Beth Schenker, telephone interview, 1 November 1991.
2. Schenker.
3. Schenker.
4. Schenker.
5. Schenker.
6. Don Lee, telephone interview, 4 November 1991.
7. Lee.
8. Lee.
9. *The PT Stylebook* (Washington, DC: NPR, n.d.), 2, 3. Used with permission.

Special Writing Situations

10

I n *every* writing situation, it is important to identify and analyze the creative *process* that will efficiently produce the most effective presentation for a target audience. Once this has been done, you can use the appropriate writing techniques and principles to provide the type of script material needed for that particular situation.

Although each type of writing situation included in this chapter could be expanded into a separate chapter, such depth is outside the scope and objectives of this book, which is only an introduction to the principal forms of writing for the electronic media. The special skills necessary to write material for many types of programs will be acquired at a later stage in your professional writing development. The information in this chapter provides insight into potential writing career specializations, which are discussed in chapter 13.

The types of programs examined in this chapter often interrelate and use similar preparation and scripting techniques and processes. For illustrative purposes, however, each type of writing situation has been isolated. A diverse group of script examples illustrates essential writing principles.

The special forms of writing examined in this chapter include compilations, magazine programs, special events, programs for special audiences, religious programs, children's programs, animation projects, and game shows. The content and purpose of each type of program or writing situation will be examined, and specific writing techniques and suggestions will be offered.

Compilations

Compilation is the creative process of combining appropriate program elements to construct an effective, synergistic composite presentation. The writer functions as a creative compiler, pulling together various bits and pieces of material from numerous sources to write the finished script. Each part of the scripting puzzle is examined critically to determine what is known and what is still to be learned. Sometimes the pieces fall easily into place. Often, composite pieces must be forged and blended into the fabric of the script. This synergistic process should yield an enhanced combination of program elements. The result should be a cohesive, balanced presentation, offering a new perspective for the audience.

Compilation is a necessary organizational technique for all writers. As you learned in chapter 1, it is used in research, to gather material to write a script. Compilation is also useful for other kinds of writing projects in which divergent material must be collected and arranged into a cohesive, attractive pattern. Most of the types of programs discussed in this chapter make use of compilation techniques. In addition, compilation techniques are useful for preparing commercials, interviews, music programs, documentaries and investigative reports, features, instructional and corporate presentations, year-in-review music or news specials, and "instant" specials, which provide same-day coverage of significant news or sports events.

Chapter 9 included a description and illustration of the compilation process used to write and produce a series of radio programs featuring jazz trumpeters ("Jazz Birthday Celebrations"). Other kinds of compilation projects were illustrated in chapters 5, 7, and 8. The public affairs series "Making a Difference Today," described in chapter 8, also uses compilation techniques.

Approaches

Your approach to the compilation process is determined by the interaction of many variables:

a. *The nature of the writing project.* Each writing assignment requires a different kind and level of compilation activity. Documentaries, for example, necessitate extensive research. Variety programs, on the other hand, entail minimal compilation of information.

b. *Your depth and diversity of experience.* Steps that both save time and energy and produce more effective results become part of the work habits of a person who writes more and more scripts for different kinds of programs.

c. *The number of writers/compilers involved.* A different level and type of compilation activity are required when a writer works alone on a script than when writers work together as a team.

d. *The writing and production timetable.* The time available for compilation may be unlimited or restrictive. The time factor often determines the depth and extensiveness of compilation activity. Usually writers complain that they never have enough time to gather material or to think through a complex or emotionally charged sequence. A professional writer's continuous quest for excellence produces the unsettling concern that detailed knowledge about the subject of a script is incomplete.

e. *Budget constraints.* Meaningful compilation activity requires adequate time, money, and personnel. Sufficient funding should be provided to complete the compilation process. Despite budgetary limitations, use ingenuity and innovation to complete the necessary compilation work.

f. *The nature and extent of available resources.* Determine the quantity and quality of the available material and ferret out less obvious but valuable sources of information and comment.

g. *Quality requirements.* Although most writers contend that they strive for quality at all times, the exigencies of deadlines and budgets often force compromise. Ideally both deadline and script quality demands always will be satisfied. Realistically quality often is a secondary concern—a worthwhile bonus but not the primary focus.

There are several *approaches to the compilation process:*

a. If the premise of a program script is already established, this will determine the contents and depth needed in preliminary research, in the tentative outline, in the initial treatment statement, and in subsequent drafts of the script. This is a very common sequence for the writer who develops the finished script from an already accepted idea. Industrial, educational, and instructional scripts follow this pattern of development. The editorial writer often works from ideas initially generated by the station manager. General ideas, concepts, and issues often form the basis for dramas.

b. If only a large volume of material on a topic is available, and if no specific program concept or premise has been established, then it is the writer's responsibility to determine the nature, quality, organization, and depth of the compiled material. From this determination, the program script idea can be formulated. This leads to a distillation of resource material so that only appropriate items are included. At the same time, a tentative, flexible script outline should be devised. A treatment statement may be prepared before initial and subsequent drafts of the script are written. This compilation approach is useful for year-in-review programs, in which significant events and personalities are featured. The year-in-review could highlight music, entertainment, news, sports, medicine, finance, laws, or any number of other subjects. "Instant" news specials also use this approach when it is necessary to produce quickly a program that places a complex issue or series of events into proper perspective. The general idea or objective of the program may have been determined before compilation began, but the results of the compilation process will provide the means to identify and crystallize the unique aspects of the topic that should be included in the final script.

c. The material to be written may be compiled all at once, in the aggregate, or cumulatively over time. For example, a year-in-review music program, featuring the top artists and recordings in a particular music format, can be prepared at the end of the year, when final record sales and recording awards have been determined. Within a short period, you can assemble the necessary material, determine the appropriate music selections, and write the necessary script fragments. Another approach is to formulate preliminary comments for each top-selling recording and artist throughout the year. At the end of the year, these preliminary script fragments can be reviewed. The language and length of each fragment can be adjusted to fit timing constraints and to accommodate industry developments, as well as new material written for additional top artists and recordings. All the fragments are then pulled together into a smooth, cohesive script. A similar process could be followed for year-in-review programs featuring news, sports, or entertainment items. At the end of each week, a short summary can be written of the top events, issues, and personalities featured in daily reports. At the end of the year, these preliminary weekly summaries are reviewed, rewritten, and forged with other events, personalities, and topics from other weeks. An alternative method is to wait until the end of the year and then review all the stories. This delay sometimes provides a better perspective of the year but is more time consuming and allows for a less critical analysis of the material.

d. You may complete the compilation process alone or in a group. Working alone provides the freedom to explore new concepts and techniques without constraints and to avoid some of the confusion and duplication of effort that often occur when others are involved. Nevertheless the volume of work may be overwhelming. You run the risk of losing perspective, and you do not derive the usual benefits resulting from interaction with others. The success of joint writing ventures often hinges on an individual's willingness to cooperate, share, coordinate information, and contribute a strong personal sense of organization and dedication to quality.

These approaches to the compilation process are most effective when combined creatively to meet the requirements of each writing situation. For example, you may come up with an idea for a short feature on a community project. The specific premise, tack, or angle for the feature may be determined after conversations with people involved in the community or the specific project, a short visit with the news director, or informal talks over coffee. Several individuals may conduct the research. Whether working alone or with another writer or the program producer, you would distill this information and prepare a tentative outline or treatment for the feature. Short segments could be written as the information falls into logical sequence. The initial scripted segments could be edited and rewritten to meet time, budget, production, and quality requirements. Other writing situations necessitate a similar combination of compilation approaches to produce the best possible script.

a. *Remember the purpose of the script to be written.* Then compile only essential and pertinent information to reinforce the key ideas associated with this objective.

b. *Explore viable leads.* Gather as much pertinent material from as many sources as possible.

c. *Work from a flexible, evolving outline,* which allows meaningful accumulated material to shape the final, effective treatment of the topic.

d. *Continually analyze and evaluate material,* allowing each piece of information to find its niche and to help shape the flexible, evolving outline.

e. *Remember the value of script, audio, and video archival material.* Know what is available and how to obtain such material for use in current script projects.

f. *Rewrite continuously.* A new fact, a startling archival voice or picture remnant, a fleeting image or impression, a significant new development—all should cause you to reexamine the collected material, the manner in which it is organized, the style of presentation, and the length of the segments. The compilation process is a continual, progressive effort to provide the most complete and effective presentation possible.

Writing Techniques and Suggestions

Let's examine a year-in-review country music special featuring performers from a previous decade. Tracing the compilation process used for this project will illustrate many of the principles and techniques described in the previous section. The steps examined in this section comprise the process currently used for compilation programs involving the presentation of music.

The country music special we will examine is distributed by TM Century, Inc., based in Dallas. As noted in chapter 9, compilation techniques are often used to prepare script material for year-in-review music specials. Several production companies, such as TM Century, produce a variety of specials and then syndicate them to stations around the country. Often these companies also produce weekly music countdown programs for several standard program formats, such as rock and country music, using the same compilation process described in the following paragraph. Year-in-review specials are often included as part of the package of programs these companies produce and distribute.

First, "unpositioned" script fragments are written for each music selection. When the program is finally produced, these fragments will have to be rewritten for content and length and then fused with other program elements. However, by writing these script fragments early, you have time to assess what you have written and then weave into the final script your own musical insights, as well as such trade publication information as record sales and updates about the featured recording artists. It is not recommended that you wait until the crunch of final production to write your initial script material.

Country Music Special

Figure 10.1
Unpositioned script
fragment for a
year-in-review country
music special.
*Courtesy of TM Century,
Inc., Dallas, Texas,
distributor,* Country '82.

HAGGARD, MERLE & G. JONES "YESTERDAY'S WINE"

COUNTRY '82 SCRIPT   CUT #_____

NOW, HERE'S A DUET BY TWO PERFORMERS WHO AS SOLOISTS HAVE
CAPTURED JUST ABOUT EVERY MAJOR AWARD THAT THE COUNTRY
MUSIC INDUSTRY HAS TO OFFER. ONE HALF OF THIS SINGING TEAM
WAS THE COUNTRY MUSIC ASSOCIATION'S MALE VOCALIST OF THE
YEAR, AS WELL AS ENTERTAINER OF THE YEAR IN 19-70, WHILE
THE OTHER HALF HAS NAILED DOWN THE MALE VOCALIST AWARD
TWICE...IN 19-80 AND 19-81. THE DUO IS, OF COURSE, MERLE
HAGGARD AND GEORGE JONES. THIS YEAR, THEY COMBINED THEIR
TALENTS FOR SONG NUMBER ____ IN OUR SHOW...HERE'S "YESTER-
DAY'S WINE."

Figure 10.1 is an example of an unpositioned script fragment written
soon after the music was selected for this program. Notice that the recording
artist's name and the title of the music selection is provided only after the
background information is given. This technique encourages listeners to participate in the program by trying to determine who is being introduced before the name is supplied.

When it comes time to assemble the final year-in-review program,
all of the unpositioned script fragments are reviewed and adjusted in content and length. To make these adjustments, however, it is necessary to
determine the placement and length of all the music to be used, the
amount of commercial matter to be inserted, the length of the opening
and closing to the program, and the length and placement of musical jingles, introductions, interviews, and program segment transitions.

Figure 10.2 is the rewritten version of the unpositioned script fragment
shown in figure 10.1. Notice how the previous program selection is identified before the next selection is introduced. This provides a smooth flow and
continuity. The handwritten notation "→ 1 :38" indicates that the first recording of this copy by the narrator lasted 38 seconds and is the recording to be used in the final program. Actual "tape recording" is now done
on digital hard drive work stations for distribution on digital compact
disk rather than on analog tape or vinyl records, as was done a decade or
two ago. Years of experience producing such year-in-review programs
show through when one notices that very few changes were needed in the
final version of this script fragment. It is obvious the writer knows the music
well. Sentence length and vocabulary help establish the pace and create the
intensity needed for the selection. The copy is crisp, succinct, and in tune
with the musical life-style of the potential target audience.

"WHEN YOU FALL IN LOVE" BY JOHNNY LEE, NUMBER 80 ON
COUNTRY 82. NEXT IS A DUET BY TWO PERFORMERS WHO AS
SOLOISTS HAVE CAPTURED JUST ABOUT EVERY MAJOR AWARD THAT
THE COUNTRY MUSIC INDUSTRY HAS TO OFFER. ONE HALF OF THIS
SINGING TEAM WAS THE COUNTRY MUSIC ASSOCIATION'S MALE
VOCALIST OF THE YEAR, AS WELL AS ENTERTAINER OF THE YEAR
IN 19-70, WHILE THE OTHER HALF HAS NAILED DOWN THE MALE
VOCALIST AWARD TWICE...IN 19-80 and 19-81. THE DUO IS, OF
COURSE, MERLE HAGGARD AND GEORGE JONES. THIS YEAR, THEY
PUT THEIR TALENTS TOGETHER FOR THE NUMBER 79 SONG OF THE
YEAR...HERE'S "YESTERDAY'S WINE."

⟶ 1:38

Figure 10.2
Rewritten version of
the unpositioned
script fragment shown
in figure 10.1.
*Courtesy of TM Century,
Inc., Dallas, Texas,
distributor,* Country '82.

Figure 10.3 is the final rundown sheet for the first three segments in
the program. Segment, or "element," times are noted in the far right column. The running time for the program tape appears in the far left column.
The script fragment examined earlier is used in segment 1/B, eight minutes
and 22 seconds after the first hour of the program begins. Notice how a
musical jingle is used on each side of each commercial insert to reestablish
the name and theme of the program.

Magazine Programs

In a magazine program, several topics are featured in segments combined
into the framework of a single program or series. A radio or television
magazine resembles the conventional print media magazine format in that
separate stories or features are fully developed but always placed within the
context of the entire magazine's goals or objectives. Although the overall
objective of an electronic media magazine program series may be to entertain, particular programs in the series or segments within a single program
may also inform, persuade, or provoke action on a specific issue. Magazine
programs provide writers and producers a unique opportunity to identify target audience groups and then to fashion program content to meet specific
tastes and interests.

Magazine presentations have proliferated in the television industry, on
both cable and conventional channels. The instructional and corporate sectors have also begun using magazine programs to meet their unique communications objectives. Chapters 3, 8, and 11 contain various types of magazine
program script material.

Some magazine program series that begin as local productions eventually are distributed regionally or nationally. Script and program ideas, as
well as production and distribution costs, can be shared by the stations and
channels carrying such series.

Figure 10.3

Final rundown sheet for the first three segments in the "Country '82" year-in-review country music special.

Courtesy of TM Century, Inc., Dallas, Texas, distributor, Country '82.

SCHEDULED START TIME	ACTUAL START TIME	ELEMENT	ELEMENT TIME
00:00		1/A COUNTRY '82 THEME AND OPENING OF HOUR 1 #82 WHATEVER/Statler Brothers INTERVIEW/Larry Gatlin #81 IN LIKE WITH EACH OTHER/ Larry Gatlin & The Gatlin Brothers Band COUNTRY '82 JINGLE	6:52
6:52		COMMERCIAL INSERT	1:30
8:22		1/B COUNTRY '82 JINGLE #80 WHEN YOU FALL IN LOVE/Johnny Lee #79 YESTERDAY'S WINE/Merle Haggard & George Jones EXTRA: ALMOST PERSUADED/David Houston (#1 of 1966) COUNTRY '82 JINGLE	9:43
18:05		COMMERCIAL INSERT & COUNTRY '82 CUSTOM LOCAL ID	2:10
20:15		1/C COUNTRY '82 JINGLE INTERVIEW/Ed Bruce #78 LOVE'S FOUND YOU AND ME/Ed Bruce #77 HEY! BABY!/Anne Murray COUNTRY '82 JINGLE	7:03
27:18		COMMERCIAL INSERT	1:30

Group-owned stations have also found that high-quality programming can be produced and shared within the group when writing and production capabilities are pooled. "Videomax" is a monthly magazine program series produced by six Pulitzer Broadcasting stations. Each station in this group contributes at least one feature for each program and provides a host to give the show a local identity. The programs, aimed at nine-to-fourteen-year-olds, are carried on all of the Pulitzer stations from Lancaster, Pennsylvania, to Albuquerque, New Mexico.

Various kinds of magazine programs, both regular series and specials, at all levels of production and distribution, offer audiences a wide selection of program content. Such programs are produced by print magazine companies, cable systems, local stations, networks, and syndicators. Segments may focus on such diverse topics as news, sports, entertainment, exercise, food and nutrition, gardening, fashion, personal enhancement, life-styles, travel, medicine, health, science, finances, consumerism, and celebrity and human interest profiles. The length and objectives of each magazine program, as well as the number and placement of program segments, determine the kind of development needed for each topic within individual segments.

Various scripting and production formats and techniques are used for magazine programs. Segments may be designed as interviews, discussions, call-ins, or regular newscast-type reports. Segments, and even entire programs, may be produced live, recorded on tape, or by a combination of production methods. Most magazine programs are produced as a regular series for use five days a week, generally in late afternoon or early evening time slots. Regular series hosts provide visible continuity for the programs, whereas special contributors may be featured in individual segments.

Approaches

Effective magazine programs are carefully planned, designed, and structured. They display cohesiveness, as well as flexibility. Segment themes can be designed in advance and can be used either "vertically" (in each program) or "horizontally" (inserted periodically and regularly but not in each program). For example, regular vertical segments might be those featuring news headlines, an interview, local entertainment notes, or a health tip. Horizontal segments, included regularly on specific days of the week, might include personal finances on Mondays, exercise on Tuesdays, travel on Wednesdays, and so on. Thus, the magazine program could be designed to use the skeletal structure provided by the vertical theme segments to establish stability and continuity for the series, and then each program could be "fleshed in" with horizontal theme segments. This approach is an excellent way to maintain the pace and flow of the program series but still permit the use of immediate and contemporary issues, topics, concerns, and personalities.

Regular magazine program series generally are prepared from a standard rundown sheet, which is used to map out the various segments for each program. The length of each segment is determined in advance and ranges from one to five or six minutes. Other script forms, described in chapter 3, are used to write and produce each segment. The choice of script form depends on the nature, topic, or subject of the segment, as well as the availability and requirements of production and talent personnel, budget, timetable, and facilities. For example, an interview segment could use a routine sheet. A cooking segment might be produced from a semi-script. Full-scripts would be useful for entertainment or life-style commentaries, news, or sports features recorded in advance. The standard opening and closing to the program could be fully-scripted and often is produced on tape to begin and end the program in an effective manner.

Writing Techniques and Suggestions

a. *Keep program objectives in mind at all times.* Information program series and segments should stress information. Entertainment programs and segments should spotlight entertainment news and features.

b. *Remember the audience.* Give them what is interesting, important, innovative, and expected from the type of magazine program produced.

c. *Offer the innovative, with reference to the familiar.* Unusual, startling, or controversial material can be presented, but always should be clearly linked to more familiar, easily accepted information and concepts. A thorough, practical knowledge and acceptance of your audience's characteristics will help you present the unfamiliar in terms of the familiar.

d. *Make abstract information concrete* by presenting specific, real-life material that can be easily identified and understood by the audience.

e. Prepare program segments that *provide a flexible, contemporary approach to modern living.*

f. *Organize each program segment.* Get and hold audience attention and interest. Present supporting material that logically and effectively moves the listener or viewer from point to point, idea to idea. End each segment smoothly and climactically, with an eye to how the ending of each program segment will make an effective transition to the next portion of the magazine program.

"Pulse"

As indicated earlier, it is not uncommon for locally produced program series eventually to be offered in syndication to stations and outlets in other markets. Bob Montgomery is the producer of "Pulse," a weekly medical magazine show, produced at KXTV in Sacramento. The twenty-six shows produced each season are also shown on The Discovery Channel. Talks are underway to expand the series distribution into overseas markets. Figures 10.4 and 10.5 provide information used to plan, write, and produce programs in the "Pulse" series.

Special Events

A special event is the broadcast of a particular actual happening whose outcome is undetermined. Many special events are witnessed by all media rather than just the electronic media. The event must be unusual and of direct interest to a substantial number of listeners or viewers. It is heard or

PULSE - SHOW STRUCTURE

Segment One

```
Billboard.................................... :50
Talent Intros First Story.................. :15
Story One..................................5:00
Talent Outro/Tease.......................... :15
Bump Out.................................... :10

BREAK......................................2:00
```

Segment Two

```
Bump In..................................... :05
Talent Intros Tip........................... :10
HealthTip..................................4:00
Talent Outro/Tease.......................... :15
Bump Out.................................... :10

BREAK......................................2:00
```

Segment Three

```
Bump In..................................... :05
Talent Intros Second Story................. :15
Story Two..................................5:00
Talent Outro/Tease.......................... :15
Bump Out.................................... :10

BREAK......................................2:00
```

Segment Four

```
Bump In..................................... :05
Talent Intros Quiz.......................... :10
Quiz.......................................3:00
Talent Reads Letter......................... :25
Reply to Letter............................. :45
Talent Goodbyes............................. :10
Credits....................................1:00
```

Figure 10.4
Program format used to produce "Pulse," a weekly medical
magazine program series.
Courtesy of KXTV/A.H. Belo Corp.

Figure 10.5

Guidelines used to produce material for "Pulse," a weekly medical magazine program series.

Courtesy of KXTV/A.H. Belo Corp.

Story ideas for Pulse come from a variety of sources. We read the wire services daily, follow other health broadcasts (such as the nationally syndicated radio show hosted by Dr. Dean Edell), and scan most of the available general circulation health publications. We also stay in close touch with the public information office at UCDMC, since they're often able to provide information upcoming new or unique medical procedures.

The story process usually begins with a brief telephone interview with the primary physician or other caregiver in a particular case. The involvement of hospital professionals is extremely important to the outcome of the story, since the caregiver is often the conduit to the patient. Because of California's patient confidentiality laws it is extremely difficult to get access to patients without physician approval.

Field producers are entirely responsible for the shooting, writing and production of stories. Producers are expected to do all interviews. Stories scripts are reviewed for writing style, narrative qualities, and medical accuracy prior to editing.

The stories we produce tend to fall into one of three categories. The first we like to call "medical miracles". It's really a variation of the old boy-meets-girl story, except that in our case it's boy gets sick / boy goes to the hospital / boy gets well. The second category is what we refer to as "gee whiz" stories. These present the latest and greatest in medical technology, with special emphasis on original research being conducted in the University of California system. The third category is personality profiles. These generally occur when we find a particularly engaging individual who's performing some sort of valuable function. In the past we've profiled a pediatric anesthesiologist who uses humor to put his young patients at ease, a cancer nurse who helps children through the throes of chemotherapy, and a female oncologist whose twin passions in life are saving patients and collecting African art. In all cases we place a great deal of emphasis on telling interesting and emotionally affecting stories about <u>people</u>.

seen ''live,'' in ''real time,'' as the event unfolds. The broadcast may be a recording, but the sequence of events follows the pattern of the actual occurrence. The outcome often is unknown to the audience until the final, climactic moments—for instance, the winners declared in a sporting event, an election, or a beauty pageant or the safe return of astronauts, which is not assured until the final camera shot at the landing site.

There are many events that might be labeled as special. Some of the types of occurrences that could be classified as special events, worthy of electronic media coverage consideration, are special news coverage (late breaking news stories reported ''live'' from the scene of the event, election-night reports, funerals of public figures, and political conventions), news conferences, speeches, political candidates' debates, sports and auto shows, parades, dedications (of such things as buildings, shopping centers, transit system facilities improvements, or a special wing in a library), banquets, awards presentations, beauty pageants, fairs, expositions, telethons, and auctions or fundraisers. Script material used in live sports events coverage was shown in figures 5.12, 5.13, and 5.14.

Under the proper circumstances, these and many other occurrences could be considered special. This designation hinges on a determination of the nature of the event, the degree and quality of interest in the unfolding of the event, the importance of the result, and its impact on the audience. The decision to cover an event as a special is made by programming or sales personnel, who have considered the situation carefully and determined that such coverage would be beneficial to the audience, the station, the network, or the company. The writer then helps prepare material that makes the special event interesting to and worthwhile for the audience.

The immediate, spontaneous, and developing nature of most special events generally prevents thorough planning and complete scripting. Nevertheless, a minimal level of preparation is necessary to anticipate the exigencies of the event and the special circumstances involved. Ad-libbed rather than full-scripted comments are used to communicate information in these situations. Thus, most special events presentations are produced using a show format (rundown or routine sheet) or a semi-script. Like many other types of programs already discussed, the approach used to prepare script material for a special event often is contingent on several interrelated factors:

Approaches

a. *The nature of the event.* For example, experienced sports play-by-play announcers require a minimum of prepared script material to provide interesting sports coverage. On the other hand, the live telecast of a parade or an awards presentation requires more precise anticipation of events and, thus, more complete scripting.

b. *The availability of information.* Although some information can be accumulated for each special event, there may not be enough information available in advance for you to prepare detailed script material. As always, you should use whatever pertinent information is available and prepare the type of script needed for an interesting and effective presentation.

c. *The timetable.* Working under a deadline, there may not be sufficient time to prepare extensive script material, even if this would be desirable. For example, a late breaking local news story that occurs during the early evening newscast permits the preparation of only a very brief introduction to the reporter ''live'' at the scene, who then ad-libs the information about the incident.

d. *The preferences of talent and production personnel.* Extensive script material may be unnecessary and perhaps confusing to those responsible for producing the program. They may be accustomed to and expect to encounter less formal, more spontaneous script and production formats.

Writing Techniques and Suggestions

a. *Adhere to the predetermined concept.* If the special event is a local community awards presentation, prepare script material to provide essential background information on the recipients. If special election night coverage is prepared, gather background information for preproduced segments on major candidates, campaign issues, and political party policies.

b. *Make the special event the focal point.* Write material that enhances the immediacy, reinforces the structure or organization, and anticipates the conclusion of the special event.

c. *Collect as much information as possible about the event*—what is planned, who is involved, and when and where specific parts of the event are scheduled to occur.

d. *Abstract pertinent and interesting information* for use in preparing script material.

e. *Prepare "digests," or summaries,* of the abstracted information in the form and length to be used by the on-air talent. This could be done on either standard-size paper or on index cards. Using index cards provides the talent with immediate access to essential script material and makes it easier for the producer to accomplish last-minute program line-up adjustments by simply shuffling the index cards into the revised order.

f. *Anticipate as much as possible.* Prepare script material for openings, closings, and transitions, as well as for possible emergency situations. Thoughtful, well-written, brief filler material, prepared in advance and not during the heat of the emergency situation, has rescued many special events programs.

g. *Prepare script material for short, prerecorded program segments* that can be used to overcome inevitable delays and production problems and to control the pace and tempo of the program. For example, for a live parade telecast, prerecord features that focus on the history or traditions surrounding this annual event, the preparation of floats, techniques used to apply clown makeup, or comments by participants, especially visiting band members or celebrities.

h. *Keep the script material and coverage interesting, timely, and informative* so that the audience does not become bored or distracted.

i. *Work with the special events program producer and director* to adjust the coverage if necessary if the event develops in a direction not already anticipated. Be prepared with alternative methods of adjusting to the changing events. If necessary, prepare script material to accommodate these alternatives.

Barry Downes has written scripts for many special events telecasts. He traced the process and principle steps he followed when preparing script material for a Macy's Thanksgiving Day parade. Telecasts of parades are becoming more common on local channels, as well as national television outlets.

Thanksgiving Day Parade

a) First, you look over the general layout of the show. How many commercials? How much time is available to include special entertainment segments? Who is the [on-air] talent going to be? . . . What do they do best? Have they done the show before? What can we do with them to establish a relationship and show what each will be doing? . . .

b) The writer meets with the producer/director (in this instance, Dick Schneider). We've worked together many times before and in the weeks to follow we start to bounce around a number of ideas for talent, possible Broadway shows that might provide some special segments, what problems Dick feels may arise and what ones I can anticipate. Perhaps most important at this point is trying to be as loose as possible. We're both looking for ideas that may be different, [to] solve problems that we've had in previous years, [to] help to capture the television audience.

c) Dick and I review the tentative rundown of parade elements and talent that Macy's has been developing over the year. Dick has also been at earlier meetings with Macy's discussing the parade and its elements, sometime before I have been officially hired.

d) Macy's will be revising and updating their rundown and talent lineups right up to the last week of the parade. They also send over to me a good deal of background material, information and renderings on new floats and the entertainment that will be on them. I also have an early meeting with Jean McFaddin of Macy's (who is the lady in charge of really putting this event together). She fills me in on her thoughts and ideas. . . .

e) Fact sheets are now starting to come in on the bands who will be appearing in the parade, bio material on celebrities, press kits on Broadway shows, films, opera companies, dance companies, cartoon characters—all kinds of elements scheduled to be in the parade. I also start trying to see any Broadway shows and other productions that might have entertainment elements which could be included in the parade. Some are suggested to me; others I may suggest to Dick and Jean.

f) I start writing first draft material on the script. At this point, I also look back at previous parade scripts. The only purpose for this is to make sure I'm not repeating copy or ideas. The event is fun and the material should be fresh. My job is to have fun writing it. The amount of words is not nearly so lengthy as an event such as the Rose Parade, so I enjoy the luxury of doing a good deal of rewrite and polishing.

g) As the script starts to take form, I submit a first draft to Dick Schneider for his comments and then (with corrections included) that draft is sent to Macy's per their contract with NBC.

h) Notes of possible errors or changes in the parade lineup come back from Macy's and I review them and incorporate what changes seem appropriate. There is no pressure here since we've all worked together before.

i) Final scripting is being completed. Special pieces are being written. Special dialogue for animated characters, a song lyric, various comedy pieces—whatever is called for. It can be almost anything.

j) Deadlines are now coming up rather quickly. Another submission of final draft to Macy's. If there are any last-minute problems they need to respond to us within a few days of receiving the script. The script also has to go into mimeo [mimeograph copies for distribution to production personnel] and be ready for production meetings. Last-minute changes will have to be added afterward and inserted into the script by production staff. One needs to keep careful records of such changes to make sure everyone has the same final script.

k) A copy of the duplicated final script is sent [to on-air talent]. . . . Another copy must also go to NBC Compliance and Practices. They need to review it carefully. There's a good relationship here, too. I will warn them if I feel there are any problems coming up, possible product conflicts or doubtful tie-ins. They will notify me of any problems or changes they have. This [the changes] must also be included into all talent's scripts.

l) By now we're into final talent script readings and rehearsal. From here on it's like any other live network special. More than a little crazy, but at least you don't have to go into the editing room after it's all over. During the show itself I work right next to [the talent] helping with last-minute changes and trying to troubleshoot the various last-minute problems as best I can. . . .

There are other elements [involved in writing for special events] such as timing a script and special writing for stars. . . . Having a strong production background is certainly invaluable when you're writing this sort of a live event. A computer with a good word processing program is a wonderful help too.[1]

Academy Awards

The annual Academy Awards telecast is a premium special event and one of a growing number of annual awards presentations shown on local and national television outlets. The writer's preparations for this kind of program parallel those needed for other types of special events, such as parades, banquets, beauty pageants, and telethons. Live coverage of such special events has become commonplace at the local and national levels.

Figure 10.6 is one page from the thirteen-page rundown sheet used to produce "The 54th Annual Academy Awards" telecast on ABC-TV. Standard program information is included in each rundown sheet: program segment number and description, script page number in parentheses, segment length, and cumulative, or program running, time. In the column labeled "DESCR.," the abbreviation "VTPB WINNER" indicates a videotape playback of the winner of that particular category.

Figure 10.7 shows the "as broadcast" script of program segment 43, the documentary short subject award. These "as broadcast" scripts are not usually released to the general public. The script pages for each awards presentation display the same page format or layout: the program segment number is provided at the top center of the page, enclosed in parentheses; the script page number is at the top right; the program segment is identified just

	ITEM	PAGE	DESCR.	TIME	CUM TIME	
	43. AWARD #8 DOCUMENTARY SHORT SUBJECT (Richard Benjamin, Paula Prentiss)					
	a. TALK	(88)		1:04	1:23:40	
	b. NOMINATIONS & PRESEN- TATION OF AWARD		VTPB WINNER			
	c. WINNER ACCEPTANCE	(89)		1:30	1:25:10	
	44. AWARD #9 DOCUMENTARY FEATURE (Richard Benjamin, Paula Prentiss)					
	b. NOMINATIONS & PRESEN- TATION OF AWARD	(91)	VTPB WINNER	1:10	1:26:20	
	c. WINNER ACCEPTANCE	(92)		1:33	1:27:53	
	45. INTRO PERFORMANCE #4: SONG #3 - "ENDLESS LOVE" (Johnny Carson)	(94)		0:37	1:28:30	
	46. PERFORMANCE #4: SONG #3 - "ENDLESS LOVE" (Diana Ross, Lionel Richie)	(95)		3:15	1:31:45	
****	47. COMMERCIAL #8 (Orchestra plays to house)	(99)		1:32	1:33:17	
****	48. LEAD-IN STATION BREAK (Announcer (V.O.)) (VTPB)	(100)	VTPB	:16	1:33:33	
****	49. MID NET ID	(101)		:31	1:34:04	
****	50. MID-STATION BREAK #2 (Black)	(101)		1:14	1:35:18	
	51. REJOIN (No Announce)	(102)	VTPB	0:12	1:35:30	
	ACT VI					
	51a. FILM BUMPER #4	(103)	VTPB	0:10	1:35:40	
	52. INTRO DEBRA WINGER & PAUL WILLIAMS (Johnny Carson)	(104)		0:37	1:36:17	

Figure 10.6
One page from the rundown sheet used to produce the telecast of "The 54th Annual
Academy Awards."
Courtesy of Academy of Motion Picture Arts and Sciences.

Figure 10.7
"As broadcast" script
pages for one
segment from the
telecast of "The 54th
Annual Academy
Awards."
*Courtesy of Academy of
Motion Picture Arts and
Sciences.*

<u>AWARD #8 - DOCUMENTARY</u>
<u>SHORT SUBJECT</u>
(Richard Benjamin, Paula Prentiss)

<u>AWARD #8 - DOCUMENTARY</u>
<u>SHORT SUBJECT</u>

PAULA PRENTISS
Thank You. We have the privilege of
announcing the Documentary Film
Awards.

RICHARD BENJAMIN
The nominees for Documentary Short
Subjects are...

(1-13-11-1)   "Americas in Transition,"   C #42
              <u>Obie Benz</u>, Producer.

PAULA PRENTISS
(1-13-1-1)   "Close Harmony," <u>Nigel Noble</u>,
              Producer.

RICHARD BENJAMIN
(1-13-9-1)   "Journey for Survival," <u>Dick Young</u>,
              Producer.

PAULA PRENTISS
(1-13-3-1)   "See What I Say," <u>Linda Chapman</u>,
(1-13-5-1)   <u>Pam LeBlanc</u> and <u>Freddie Stevens</u>,
(1-13-7-1)   Producers.

RICHARD BENJAMIN
(1-13-13-1)   "Urge to Build," <u>Roland Halle</u> and
(1-13-15-1)   <u>John Hoover</u>, Producers.

              And the winner, Paula?
PAULA PRENTISS

(OPENS ENVELOPE)

Figure 10.7 *(continued)*

AWARD #8 - DOCUMENTARY
SHORT SUBJECT
(CONT'D)

PAULA PRENTISS (CONT'D)

And the winner is, the winner is
"Close Harmony," Nigel Noble,
Producer.

MUSIC: WINNER PLAYON

APPLAUSE

(NOBLE ENTERS)

NIGEL NOBLE

When the limousine pulled up in front of the
theatre, my son said, "You mean I have to
get out in front of all those people." I
feel exactly the same way.
I would like to thank the Academy for this
honor. I also would like to thank the
children of Brooklyn Friends School, the
Senior Citizens of the Cancer Center for Senior
Citizens in Brooklyn and the dynamic music
teacher who brought these two groups together,..
Arlene Simmons.
My crew - Ken Van Sickle, Kit Whitmore, Steve
Gurbson, Tom Houghton, Maggie Travis. Wonderful,
wonderful people who devoted themselves to the
film. And Jim Morris, who did such a marvelous
job editing the film - in China now - the American
film industry needs him back. And I would like to
thank Ruth Cogstein and Lee Berry for their
support.

(MORE)

Figure 10.7 *(continued)*

(43)   90.

<u>AWARD #8 - DOCUMENTARY</u>
<u>SHORT SUBJECT</u>
(CONT'D)

NIGEL NOBLE (CONT'D)
And I would like to thank the National
Council of Jewish Women, Brooklyn Section -
who made this film possible. My wife,
Jane, for supporting the idea and my cheering
section in the balcony, David, Benjamin
and Zachery. Thank you very much.

MUSIC: WINNER PLAYOFF

                                    <u>APPLAUSE</u>

(INTO: AWARD #9 - DOCUMENTARY FEATURE)

as on the rundown sheet and written in FULL CAPS and underlined; the
presenter or introducer is indicated in parentheses just under the identification of the segment and again in FULL CAPS in the center of the script
page; staging and production notes are written in FULL CAPS and enclosed
in parentheses or underlined. The presenter's comments are brief and pertinent to the award being presented. The excitement and anticipation of the
moment are heightened by showing excerpts from each nominee's work as
each is named. The recipient's comments are also brief and help maintain
the quick pace and even flow of the program. Obviously the writer cannot
control all of the comments made during such broadcasts, but as much prescripted material as possible should be generated.

Most radio and television programs are aimed at general audiences who share common tastes and preferences and who have money to spend on a variety of advertised products and services. There are special groups within this general audience, however, with unique needs, problems, and concerns that are not always fulfilled in general audience programs.

Some might believe that it is unrealistic to expect to find programs that address these special audiences regularly. The proliferation of cable systems, however, and the development of such technologies as videodisc and home computer learning and information centers provide an opportunity to "narrowcast" to such special audiences as shut-ins, the elderly, the retired or unemployed, the infirm, the hearing impaired, abused children, drug users, and various ethnic groups. Often women and teen-agers also find that their special needs and concerns are neglected and that their interests have been stereotyped as shallow so that only a limited range of program types is believed to appeal to them. This range is often narrowed to provocative programs, soap operas, and cooking and exercise shows. For these and many other special audiences, much of radio and television programming is unrealistic, stereotypical, and often denigrating.

The electronic media command attention and can realize the goals and objectives of most general and special audiences. The process begins when there is a commitment to do something about the situation. Commitment is the result of an attitude acquired through knowledge and understanding. It is beneficial not only to know but to experience the needs and concerns of special audience groups. Cultivate this kind of sensitivity as an individual, in a personal way, and as a writer, in a professional way.

As a writer, you can take several steps to improve the treatment of special audiences in the scripts you write:

a. *Avoid stereotypes.* They are unrealistic and an unnecessary writing shortcut.
b. *Avoid insensitivities and affronts* to the needs, problems, and concerns of special audiences.
c. *Present the interests of special audiences in programs intended for general audiences.* Without sermonizing, bring the message of special audiences into the consciousness of general audiences. Offer new alternatives and perspectives.
d. Use your writing to *relate the positive and unique contributions and activities of special audience groups.* Stress their community awareness and involvement.
e. *Project a positive attitude.* Show the diverse success achieved by such groups through concentrated effort and determination. Present a strong, consistent, positive, uplifting spirit worthy of imitation.

Special Audiences

f. *Stress the individual as well as the group.* Show how self-awareness, a sense of personal dignity and self-respect, and individual problem solving can have a lasting, positive impact. Demonstrate how this positive attitude can improve the visibility and treatment of special audiences in electronic media programs.

g. *Provide subject matter that addresses special audience concerns and problems.* Make the content, language, style, and manner of presentation appropriate for the intended audience.

h. *Relate contemporary developments to the interests, concerns, attitudes, feelings, and motivations of special audiences.*

All types of programs and scripting forms can be used to reach special audiences. Basic scripting formats do not vary; however, the skill, style, and sensitivity of the writer is important if special audience programming is to be worthwhile and effective. Review, in chapter 8, the description of the KUSA-TV public affairs series entitled ''Making a Difference Today.'' Notice how a combination of program and scripting formats is used to present to a general audience the concerns of ethnic groups.

The needs of special audiences can be fulfilled through the electronic media, but it is necessary to change the way these special needs and concerns are now addressed. That change begins once an individual recognizes that a problem exists and specific steps are taken to rectify the situation. It requires a high level of personal and professional dedication and determination to offer pertinent, quality programming despite ratings or financial consequences. Once the process begins, it is the writer who is in a primary position to make positive, enduring contributions to present uplifting programming for special audiences.

Religious Programs

Religion is a dominant influence in society. Nationwide surveys continue to document strong church affiliation despite declines in attendance.

A large portion of current religious programming is of the fundamentalist variety. Mainline churches acknowledge the success of these fundamentalist groups in raising funds and staying on-the-air with their messages. There have been efforts at combining forces in production and distribution facilities so that programs of all faiths can be offered at the local level and nationwide through syndication, network, cable, and satellite distribution systems.

Religious programming is designed for specific audiences and purposes. Among these are children, youth, married or single adults, divorcees, peer groups, social and moral issues, interpersonal relationships and concerns within the family or workplace, human values and freedoms, and essential religious beliefs and principles. The goal of a religious program may be one or more of the following: entertainment, information, persuasion, inspiration. Such programming may be produced by a particular denomination and then offered to target audiences either via local stations, networks, and cable systems or via nonbroadcast systems, such as videocassette distribution centers. These same distribution outlets might also produce the programs with the assistance, endorsement, and underwriting of a particular religious group.

In an effort to make religious programming as attractive and acceptable as possible, virtually all forms of programming and scripting are used. These include spot announcements, talk programs and interviews, religious news reports, magazine and feature programs and segments, the telecast of religious services and sermons, music and variety programs, editorials and commentaries, documentaries and investigative reports, instructional material, cartoons, dramas, and comedies. All of these forms of programming are used to present a religious message in a relevant, contemporary setting, with the hope that the audience will accept the message and act on its implications. Religious dramas, for example, portray contemporary, real-life situations and problems in which religious solutions are offered. The scripting formats described elsewhere in this book can be used to develop a variety of religious program material. The scripting format selected depends on the type of script and program developed.

The following techniques and suggestions can help you develop effective religious program material:

a. *Use the strongest possible writing techniques* to make the content and style of religious programming attractive, interesting, thought provoking, and acceptable. Except for special dedicated program services distributed via cable systems, the majority of religious programming is offered outside of prime broadcast airtime. This makes your job as a writer even more difficult and challenging as you attempt to reach a special audience with effective religious program material.

b. *Identify and remember your audience and objective.* What are you trying to say? To whom? Keep these objectives firmly in mind as you write.

c. *Prepare script material in which relevant contemporary concerns are fused with a strong but subtle display of religious spirit and insight.* Make an effort to break through the distractions, frustrations, and day-to-day concerns of most listeners and viewers and offer a clear, effective, and practical religious solution. Effective religious program material relates contemporary life-styles and basic human appeals and values to a target audience.

d. *Become conscious of the religious significance of everyday events.* Be sensitive to the application of religious principles to contemporary concerns.

e. *Be aware of current religious issues and interests* through regular professional and religious contacts and reading.

    f. If writing script material for a particular denomination, *be aware of specific beliefs, principles, and preferences.*

    g. *A deep, abiding religious spirit should permeate your work as a writer of religious program material.*

Except for the level of financial contributions made by the audience to help sustain such programs, the impact of religious programming is difficult to determine in terms of the lives affected and changes made in social interaction. The style and form of religious programming continue to evolve to respond to contemporary demands.

Marketing strategies and technological developments have become part of the mix of religion and electronic media. For example, videocassettes of previous religious services or special observances or behind-the-scene tours could be offered to regular donors to a religious organization. Donors who have been especially generous might receive a "video letter," with a special message from a favorite televangelist. Marketing and religion have become intertwined.

Children's Programs

The mass media, particularly television, have been scrutinized over the years in an effort to determine their impact on consumers, especially on children. More studies and surveys have focused on this audience group than perhaps all others combined. Although the results of such research are important and should influence, to a degree, a writer's work, the reporting and analysis of such research results are not within the scope of this book. See the suggested readings in Appendix A for pertinent research studies.

Some television stations have demonstrated a long-term commitment to the production of high-quality local children's programs. This commitment preceded the guidelines and regulations now imposed by the FCC for children's programs (review chapter 1).

Locally produced children's series have used a variety of program and scripting formats. Magazine formats, dramatic episodes, and even game shows have been used to produce material that entertains as well as informs young viewers. (Figure 3.2 showed a rundown sheet for a program from the popular and long-running children's series "The Bozo Show," seen in over 30 percent of U.S. households on superstation WGN-TV in Chicago.)

Characteristics of Children

Identify the basic characteristics of children under twelve years old and use this information when designing and writing specific kinds of children's programs:

    a. *Vulnerability.* Most children willingly trust and depend on those in positions of authority. This pristine vulnerability provides you with an opportunity to mold youngsters in a positive manner.

    b. *Impressionability.* Children imitate what they see and hear from parents and peers. A child begins as an empty reservoir of human experiences but is soon filled with specific attitudes, concepts, priorities, and life-style preferences.

c. *Need for a protective environment.* Most children learn and react within a sheltered environment. A child's needs are fulfilled as concepts, ideas, and morals are developed within a close-knit group.

d. *Simplistic notions.* For most children, life's complex problems and concerns are resolved simply and directly. Initially children display a degree of naïveté about what they see and hear in the world. This simplistic approach erodes as the child matures and begins understanding and accepting the complexities of life. One of the principal complaints about children's television programming is its unrealistic, misleading, and simplistic approach to human situations. It is usually difficult for a child, and even a young adult, to accept the fact that all of life's problems cannot be resolved in sixty minutes divided into four acts and interrupted periodically by commercials. Separating reality from fiction, and even program content from commercials, is a giant mental leap for most children.

e. *Short attention/interest span.* For children, the world is so vast, with so many interesting things to see and do, that they have only a short attention span. It is important to capture the child's attention and then present information and concepts quickly and effectively to enhance the child's retention.

f. *Fondness for repetition and uniformity.* A child, like most adults, appreciates a degree of repetition. It helps us learn and reinforces basic concepts and ideas. Knowing what will happen next is often reassuring. A consistent structure in program segments allows children to anticipate program content and, thus, to develop a sense of uniformity. This should increase the chances that the children will participate more fully in the presentation.

g. *Imaginative spirit.* The desire for uniformity and predictability is tempered with a free, uncluttered, imaginative spirit. Children create entire make-believe worlds—complete with sinister characters, unbeatable heroes, and villainous plots and schemes. It can be a wondrous time of life, probably never fully recaptured because of the world's complexities, except perhaps later in life when an adult views the world vicariously through a child.

h. *Curiosity.* Although younger children soon develop an egocentric attitude, in later years this attitude eventually matures into an almost insatiable curiosity about the world, its people, its objects, and its processes. This curiosity is shaped and developed by home, school, and peer group environments.

i. *Love of humor and involvement.* Most children enjoy various levels of humor. They like to experience happy, exhilarating events and people. They laugh at clichéd comedic pratfalls. They quickly become involved in chase scenes and imaginative mystery and adventure situations to which they can relate. They often verbalize rhetorical questions asked in school or on television. They sing the lyrics of commercial jingles after seeing a particular announcement many times. They may clap their hands, dance around the room, sing, or perform other activities that allow them to participate fully in what is presented.

Children have many other characteristics. If your ambition is to write children's programs, you should reinforce your background and information about children through formal instruction, as well as extensive observation and reflection. You will face a difficult challenge in attempting to capture the mind and spirit of a child, but it is a challenge that must be accepted if worthwhile children's programs are to be written.

Approaches

Children's television programs feature a wide range of content and scripting formats. There are a few live-action series produced for children. Superhero and science fiction animated programs dominate Saturday morning commercial television. Children's programming uses many other formats—including newscasts, variety and game shows, dramas, comedies, and spot announcements. The scripting format for each is the same as described and illustrated elsewhere in this book, but to adjust for content and style of presentation requires some adaptation of these basic scripting forms.

Remember that children's media habits and life-styles have changed dramatically since children's radio and television programs were first introduced. Children can now select from a variety of media channels, as well as other activities. Be aware of these changes when you develop and write children's program material.

When you write children's programs, strive to provide engaging and uplifting script material. The child's environment includes the mass media, particularly television, and children learn from their environment. Recognition by television legitimizes the status of particular groups, individuals, issues, and concerns in society. Eventually you may have to resolve the dilemma of providing commercially acceptable script material while sustaining a personal and professional sense of ethics and responsibility. Meaningful, realistic, and engaging script material should be your goal.

Writing Techniques and Suggestions

To write quality scripts for children's programs, you must learn to apply the characteristics of children creatively to each writing project to reach this special impressionable young audience in a meaningful and memorable way. The following suggestions can help you achieve these objectives:

a. *Be imaginative.* Expand your creative horizons by generating innovative and stimulating scripting and production techniques. To a certain extent, become childlike in your approach and perspective.

b. *Enhance realism.* Children tend to relate to what they see and hear in their own environment, circumstances, and personalities. Characters and situations are more believable and effective if the audience (children included) can identify with these elements.

c. *Relate the known to the unknown.* Introduce new concepts, information, and attitudes by connecting them to real or easily imagined situations and characters. Most children, though, are doggedly logical, so avoid disturbing a child's logical sensibilities with improbable situations, dialogue, and actions that are not clearly and reasonably established and developed. Extensive research and testing may be necessary to achieve this objective consistently.

d. *Use a simple, direct, cohesive program structure and writing style.* This should provide the opportunity to vary the content and pace of the program, and still make it a consistent, interesting, and meaningful experience. Keep word choices and sentence structure simple and direct. Children tend to disregard information that is belabored and unnecessarily complex. Use simple but natural language in an entertaining way.

e. *Respect your audience.* Children are more perceptive and intelligent than most adults believe. Children quickly reject programs and personalities that tend to patronize them. Also, do not perpetuate stereotypes. Observe and reflect life as it is, in all of its variations.

f. *Stress self-worth.* It is important for a child to know and appreciate the value and importance of each individual. Respect for others leads to self-respect and strong personal moral development.

g. *Engender confidence.* It is important for every child to know that certain skills and pieces of information can be learned and that it is possible to succeed.

h. *Provide action.* Make something significant and interesting happen. Children tend to be visually oriented and stimulated. In your scripts, capitalize on this characteristic. Make the action clear, simple, meaningful, and progressive so that the action builds to a climax.

i. *Encourage involvement.* Children tend to get caught up in the action of a program, especially dramas, in which interesting, well-developed characters are involved in a swift-moving plot full of intrigue and suspense. Involvement is intensified when the audience shares a critical piece of information not known to characters in the drama.

j. *Watch the violence.* Use it cautiously and only when necessary to reflect important, real-life situations and values.

k. *Avoid undue emphasis on romance.* Such situations generally hold no interest for younger children and often embarrass them. When such situations occur, most children become anxious to return to the main story line or to move on to the next program segment.

l. *Promote a positive, creative, and developmental spirit.* Try to enlighten and entertain rather than confuse or bore your young audience. Provide constructive entertainment. Sustain positive standards and values of conduct, morals, ethics, behavior, and language. Strive for high literary quality.

"Sesame Street"

One of the outstanding children's program series provided by Children's Television Workshop is "Sesame Street." This award-winning series has helped children adjust to different situations and experiences, develop positive values and attitudes, and establish healthy curiosity about the world. The programs tackle contemporary themes and such issues as death, adoption, sibling rivalry, and race relations, using a teach-while-entertaining approach to reach two-to-five-year-old viewers in more than eighty countries.

The scripting process for "Sesame Street" is unique. For each program segment, a writer is first given an assignment sheet with specific educational goals. After the first draft of each segment is written, the head writer for the series reviews the material and discusses the necessary revisions with the writer. The head writer then discusses the script with the research department to ensure the educational goals are properly implemented in the script. Final revisions are made based on this conversation. This script is then written in its final form.[2]

Figure 10.8 shows the suggestions made for rewriting a program segment featuring muppet character Grover dressed as a professor and two muppet lumberjacks ("A.M. Lumber Jacks"). The educational goal of this segment is to teach the child the value of listening. Notice how the change to a Lumber *Jill* helps the young girls in the audience identify with the muppet character and, thus, be more likely to feel that the information on listening applies to girls as well as to boys. The word change early in the segment from ". . . anything" to ". . . many important and fun things" reinforces the educational goal and sets up the situation that develops later. By eliminating the brief reference to why the diseased tree is being removed, the tree-cutting action can start that much sooner. Prof. Grover's lines are changed to emphasize the importance of listening carefully. The action and audience involvement in this segment intensify as Grover finally remembers to apply the principles of effective listening to his immediate situation and narrowly escapes injury.

Animation

Animation techniques are used in many different kinds of productions and programs. Advertising clients often use animated television commercials to present their messages effectively. Animation may be incorporated into informational, educational, training, and public relations presentations by businesses, institutions, and government agencies. Television music and variety

Any day of the week.

TELLY: That's amazing! I can fly! *He's some teacher isn't he, Maria?*

~~WOMAN ON PHONE: Would you like to fly first class?~~
MARIA: He certainly is.
~~TELLY: Wow!~~

~~MARIA REACTS~~

MUSIC BUTTON

FADE
- -
3...PROF. GROVER LISTENS (LISTENING)

SCENIC: MEADOW, WITH LARGE TREE
TALENT: PROF. GROVER, A.M. LUMBER
JACKS✓ *Jill* *2 man*
PROPS: MUPPET ~~CHAIN~~ SAW.
WARDROBE: CAP AND GOWN FOR GROVER.
EFX:
SFX: CHAIN SAW, TREE CRASH.

OPEN TO PROF. GROVER IN A MEADOW.
BEHIND HIM IS A LARGE OAK TREE.

PROF. GROVER: Good day. Professor
Grover here, and today, we're going to
talk about listening....

ENTER 2 A.M. LUMBER JACKS

PROF. GROVER: Listening is very
important. Because if you do not
listen, you will not hear ~~anything~~ *many important and fun things.*
FIRST LUMBER JACK: This it, ~~Pete~~ *Jill*?
SECOND LUMBER ~~JACK~~ *Jill*: Yeah. ~~Too bad.~~ *This is one we gotta cut down.*

Nice lookin' tree.

Figure 10.8
Suggested rewrite
comments on a
segment from
"Sesame Street."
Broken lines across
the pages indicate
original script pages.
*Script material
courtesy of Children's
Television Workshop
© 1991 Children's
Television Workshop.
Jim Henson's Sesame
Street Muppets
© 1991 Jim Henson
Productions, Inc.*

Figure 10.8 (continued)

FIRST LUMBER JACK: Well, ~~when they got~~ let's get started.
~~diseased, they gotta go.~~

THEY START ~~TO READY THE~~ SAW with a man saw.

SHOW #1787 J.B. R/W 6/16/82 Page 4

PROF. GROVER: For example, if you did
not listen, you would not have heard how
to get to Sesame Street. ~~So, as you can
see, listening is a very good way to
pick up information, and learn things.~~

continue to saw

THE LUMBER JACKS ~~GET THE SAW STARTED.~~
GROVER IS OBLIVIOUS.

PROF. GROVER: ~~Listening is also a lot
of fun, too. Like when you listen to a
joke...~~

If you did not listen you
would also not know
that I am Professor
Grover and today I am
talking about listening
Ha Ha.

THE LUMBER JACKS START TO CUT THE TREE.
GROVER IS OBLIVIOUS.

PROF. GROVER: ~~Or, when you listen to
music.~~ Now, there's one more thing
about listening that is very, very
important. Listening is a very SAFE
thing to do. Because if you're
listening, you can hear things around
you ~~like automobiles, and bicycles, and
your mommy calling.~~

warnings about
that might be
dangerous like

bicycle horns honking for you to
get out of the way
safe. Bicycle horn
Grover: Like that.
(Grover steps out of the way as a
riderless bicycle passes through)
Grover: (Does a take) ~~Did you
see that? There was nobody
riding on that bicycle~~ or
automobile horns
safe. Puts horn
Grover: Like that one.
(Grover steps out of the way as
a driverless car passes through.)

LUMBER JACKS: Timber!

(has not heard lumber jacks)

PROF. GROVER: ...or someone yelling
"Timber!", which means a tree is about
to fall.

get out of the way
because

LUMBER JACKS: Timber!! (They run out and
the tree begins to sway.)

PROF. GROVER: So remember, for
information, fun, and safety, open your
ears and listen. Timber? Timber!? Did someone say timber?

310

Figure 10.8 (*continued*)

(o*ff*)

LUMBER JACKS: Timber!!!

TREE FALLS PROF. GROVER JUMPS CLEAR
JUST IN TIME.

AFTER A MOMENT, PROF. GROVER RISES
THROUGH THE BRANCHES.

PROF. GROVER: Class dismissed.

GROVER FAINTS OVER BACKWARDS.

FADE

----

specials, newscasts, children's shows, and many other dissimilar types of programs have used recorded animated program segments or elements. Many art films, theatrical short subjects, and feature-length motion pictures are produced using animation techniques. The majority of children's programming on Saturday morning commercial network television uses animation production techniques despite inroads made on loyal viewers by cable channels, videocassettes, and video games.

There are several reasons animation is considered an effective presentation tool:

a. It offers a human or real-life element that appeals to the emotions of the audience.

b. Characters tend to become acceptable, lovable, and entertaining when shown in animated form.

c. Animation does not share the physical limitations of other media; thus, it allows animated figures to defy the laws of time, space, and often reason and still be accepted by the audience—who suspend reality and temporarily accept the fantasy of an animated world.

d. Animation helps simplify and explain complex structures and processes, such as how a human heart works, the parts of an automobile engine, or the various stages in the formation of human life; concepts and ideas can be isolated, dissected, reassembled, and reviewed through the innovative techniques of animation.

e. Although production costs remain relatively high for quality animation work, this presentation form is financially competitive with other available formats—for example, live-action and narration.

f. It has longevity: animated programs and segments tend to avoid the perishability faced by most programs; engaging animated characters and situations can communicate an idea or emotion in a universal and timeless manner.[3]

Approaches

When you write an animation script, anticipate every visual and aural detail. Once production begins, it is too late to add new script ideas or production concepts. The cost and complexity of animation preclude this luxury.

An animation project normally begins with an idea for a story line, a character, or a situation. The idea might be original or adapted from another medium, such as books, comic books, comic strips, silent films, theatrical plays, or magazine articles. A story treatment is developed, especially for longer, more complex animated projects. It is helpful to outline the story idea and include key action and plot points, characters, situations, action, dialogue, music, and sound effects. A rough storyboard can then be prepared to visualize the various sequences and arrange them into a logical progression. Dialogue is then written, recorded, and plotted on *barsheets,* which visually display the sound track, later matched with the animated pictures. Background music and narration can be added later. From the storyboard sketches and the script, camera shots, special visual effects, transitions, and movements are plotted on *exposure sheets,* which are a visual display of the action to be filmed once the animated material has been prepared for shooting.

For a Saturday morning animated series, a one-page idea or premise statement for each episode is prepared to obtain approval from the network or cable system that airs the series. Once the initial idea has been approved, a ten-to-twelve-page outline or treatment is written. The story editor for the series works with the program's director, the storyboard artist, and the writer to create and refine the storyboard and script that eventually are used to produce the animated program.

The script page format used for animation projects is similar to live-action formats. In animated projects, however, *two* pages of script are required to provide approximately one minute of screen time. Animation particularly calls for this two-to-one ratio because, as a predominantly visual medium, it requires the writer to develop a director's eye and to indicate when to move the camera, what to show, and how to present the characters and situations effectively. The animation script, more than other script forms, requires the writer to provide many more production details.

Writing Techniques and Suggestions

In addition to the suggestions already provided, several others should assist you when you are working on animated projects:

a. *Let animated humor grow naturally* out of inherently logical situations and characters.
b. *Clearly delineate each animated character* to provide recognizable contrast, consistency, predictability, and believability in all situations.
c. *Develop concepts that extend beyond human limits and abilities.*
d. *Suggest rather than show blatant violence* in animated projects. This approach avoids potential censorship and content clearance problems.

e. *Avoid including harmful actions* in the script that could be duplicated by audience members.

f. *Avoid including material that might unduly date the script.* Make your script fresh and universal in anticipation of multiple reruns over an extended period of time.

"Thundarr the Barbarian"

This series, originally produced by Ruby-Spears Productions, Inc., won critical acclaim and captured a large audience of both children and adults when it first aired. The opening narration sequence (see figure 10.9) provides a quick, vivid, and enticing introduction to the characters and setting for the series.

In the pilot episode for the series, entitled ''Secret of the Black Pearl'' (storyboard by Dick Sebast and script by Steve Gerber), Thundarr, Ariel, and Ookla rescue Tyronn, courier of the Black Pearl, from a swarming tribe of Groundlings (hairy mutant man-rats with burning red eyes). Because of his weakened condition, Tyronn asks them to take the magical Black Pearl to the humans who dwell in the Ruins of Manhatt (the ruins of the borough of Manhattan). They accept the challenge. Meanwhile, the chieftain of the Groundlings is given a command by Wizard Gemini—destroy Thundarr and recover the Black Pearl or the Groundlings will pay a terrible price.

The Groundlings attack on motorcycles, swinging laser-firing metal clubs. Thundarr soundly defeats the Groundlings and their chieftain. The Wizard Gemini vows to recapture the pearl and crush Thundarr.

Gemini's knights capture Ariel while she, Thundarr, and Ookla are exploring the Ruins of Manhatt. The knights threaten to kill her unless Thundarr gives them the Black Pearl.

As Act II begins, Thundarr discovers that the Black Pearl protects its holder from magical attacks. Thundarr and Ookla defeat Gemini's knights and steal their twentieth-century helicopter. The human dwellers of Manhatt show themselves and agree to welcome Thundarr and his allies as friends. Meanwhile, Ariel remains a captive in Gemini's stronghold as the Wizard waits for Thundarr's attempted rescue.

Just as Thundarr is about to present the Black Pearl to the Manhatt humans and to tell them of its magical powers, Gemini appears against a background of rolling black clouds and jagged lightning bolts, crashing thunder, and lightning slicing across the sky. The humans refuse to release the magical pearl despite the fatal consequences. Gemini's sorcerous blasts strike the Statue of Liberty. The aged metal giant shudders and then moves its limbs, fully animate. The statue's torch blazes with a sorcerous flame, which spurts like a Roman candle at Thundarr and the Manhattanites. The final battle begins (see figures 10.10 and 10.11).

The intense battle ends as Thundarr remembers the magical powers of the Black Pearl and hurls the gem at the statue. As the pearl strikes the statue, the blue flame at the center of the pearl spreads over and then engulfs the metal giant. Gemini, standing at the base of the statue, suddenly writhes in the mystical energy of the blue flame. Gradually Gemini disappears and with him the imminent danger to the Manhatt humans.

Figure 10.9
Opening narration
sequence for the
"Thundarr the
Barbarian" series.
*Courtesy of
Hanna-Barbera
Productions, Inc.*

The year is 1994 -- from out of space comes a runaway planet, hurtling between the earth and moon -- unleashing cosmic destruction!

(VISUAL: EARTH AND MOON SEEN FROM SPACE. RUNAWAY PLANET PASSES BETWEEN THEM. MOON CRACKS IN TWO. RUNAWAY PLANET SHATTERS. PUSH IN ON EARTH.)

Man's civilization is cast into ruin!

(VISUAL: ON EARTH. TIDAL WAVES, EARTHQUAKES, VOLCANIC ACTIVITY DESTROYS CITIES, RESHAPES THE FACE OF THE GLOBE.)

2,000 years later, earth is reborn! A strange new world rises from the old -- a world of savagery and super-science, a world of sorcery and slavery!

(VISUAL: ACTION SHOTS OF NEW EARTH. IN RAPID-FIRE SUCCESSION - THE MUTANT JUNGLES, MARSHLANDS, FORESTS AND THEIR STRANGE NEW CREATURES, THEN ONE OF THE SORCERERS' CITADELS WITH ITS ENSLAVED HUMANITY.)

But one man bursts his bonds and dares to fight for justice!

(VISUAL: THUNDARR, LITERALLY PULLING APART THE SHACKLES AND CHAINS THAT BIND HIM WITH HIS BARE HANDS.)

With his companions, OOKLA THE MOK and the PRINCESS ARIEL, he pits his strength, courage, and his fabulous SUNSWORD against the wizards' tyranny and the forces of evil! He is -- THUNDARR THE BARBARIAN!

(VISUAL: ACTION SHOTS OF THUNDARR, OOKLA, AND ARIEL. THUNDARR FIGHTING WITH SUNSWORD. ARIEL CASTING SPELLS, OOKLA RIPPING THROUGH A WALL. THUNDARR ON HORSEBACK, IN ACROBATIC ACTION, ETC.)

A celebration follows. Thundarr is melancholy because he had to destroy the pearl to save their lives. In the closing sequence, Thundarr draws his Sunsword, lifts it forward in a "charge" position, and shouts "Onward! A world of wonders lies before us!"

This episode of "Thundarr the Barbarian," as well as many other animated program series and projects, illustrates the magic and wonder of animation. Animation provides you with still another creative outlet. However, quality animation work requires skilled, professional specialists working with patient exactitude over an extended period of time.

THE STATUE

aims its torch downward. SHOT WIDENS as its sorcerous flame
SPURTS like a Roman candle at Thundarr and the Manhattanites!

ARIEL

gestures magically. A SILVERY BURST flashes from her palms,
hurtling UP AND OUT OF FRAME.

WIDE SHOT - THE RUINS

As Ariel's magical burst and the statue's spurting flame
COLLIDE IN A MAGICAL EXPLOSION over the heads of the humans,
each neutralizing the other!

TIGHT ON THE STATUE

About to launch another burst, it REACTS to the FWASSSH of
Thundarr's Sunsword, and looks down. CAMERA PANS DOWN the
Statue's body to its feet, where Thundarr, the pearl in
one hand, the sword in the other, is HACKING AWAY at its
metal gown.

                    THUNDARR
                 (shouting)
            It's still a thing of metal!
            It's not alive! How can it
            move?!

OOKLA

snatches a length of twisted metal out of the muck and comes
running toward the Statue. CAMERA TRACKING.

                    OOKLA
            (MOK GROWL: "Smash first, ask
             questions later!")

SHOT WIDENS as he dashes past Thundarr, leaps, and gloms
onto the Statue's copper form! CAMERA TRACKS as he begins
a strange climb up the Statue's body and OUT OF FRAME.

ANGLE THE STATUE'S HEAD

As Ookla climbs UP INTO FRAME, over the Statue's chin...and
lips...over its nose...and brow...onto its noggin. PUSH IN
as Ookla wields the length of metal like a club and WHAPS
the Statue repeatedly on the noodle! SFX: WHACKAWHACKA-
WHACKAWHAKA!!!

                    OOKLA
            (MIGHTY MOK ROAR)

Figure 10.10
Full-script excerpt
from the
"Thundarr the
Barbarian"
episode entitled
"Secret of the
Black Pearl."
*Courtesy of
Hanna-Barbera
Productions, Inc.*

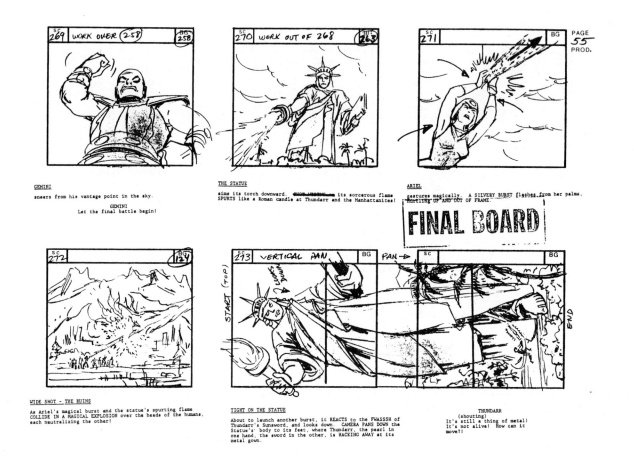

GEMINI
sneers from his vantage point in the sky.
GEMINI
Let the final battle begin!

THE STATUE
aims its torch downward. ~~SHOB LOOSING~~ its sorcerous flame
SPURTS like a Roman candle at Thundarr and the Manhattanites!

ARIEL
gestures magically. A SILVERY BURST flashes from her palms,
hurtling UP AND OUT OF FRAME.

WIDE SHOT - THE RUINS
As Ariel's magical burst and the statue's spurting flame
COLLIDE IN A MAGICAL EXPLOSION over the heads of the humans,
each neutralizing the other!

TIGHT ON THE STATUE
About to launch another burst, it REACTS to the FWASSSH of
Thundarr's Sunsword, and looks down. CAMERA PANS DOWN the
Statue's body to its feet, where Thundarr, the pearl in
one hand, the sword in the other, is HACKING AWAY at its
metal gown.

THUNDARR
(shouting)
It's still a thing of metal!
It's not alive! How can it
move?!

Figure 10.11
Storyboard for the full-script excerpt shown in figure 10.10.
Courtesy of Hanna-Barbera Productions, Inc.

Game Shows

A game show involves a participant competing with others or alone against another contestant or group of contestants, working against time, under an established set of rules, to perform a specific skill in hopes of winning money, prizes, merchandise, or prestige. It is a contest in which the rules of the game are laid out beforehand and then the participants simply join in the action.

Game shows are an important part of commercial television networks' daytime schedule and often form the basis for local station programming during access time, just after the early evening newscast and before prime-time network programming begins. Game show series are produced for network television use only, syndication only, or sometimes for both network and syndication use. Some local stations also produce game show

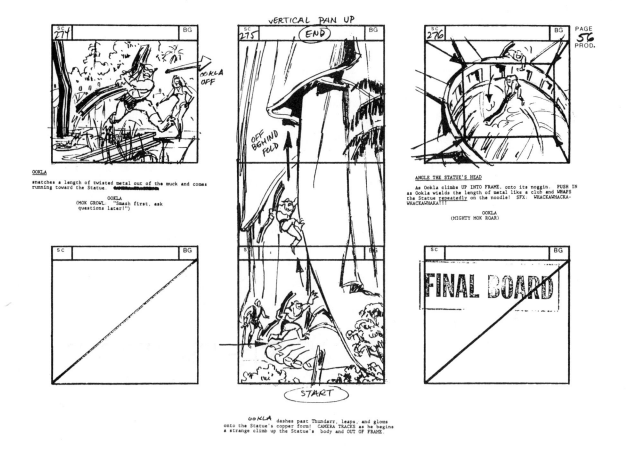

Figure 10.11 (*continued*)

series, often in association with state lotteries. Lottery ticket purchasers then become television game show contestants. A game show format is also an effective approach for instructional and corporate presentations.

Although it may appear to be easy, developing a strong game show series is difficult and extremely competitive. Most of the game show series now on television are produced by a handful of production companies. The precision and efficiency observed in long-running game show series come only after careful and thoughtful planning and development.

Approaches

The concept for the game show series comes first. Then the structure and rules of the game are developed in a master script for the series. In most cases, the fundamental concept remains constant throughout the life of the series, but variations or adaptations may be added during successive years to enliven and freshen the original concept. Most game show details are finalized after the program has been pitched in a proposal and the program idea initially accepted. This process may require months and sometimes years before the game show "sees the light of day."

The idea for a game show must be developed, tried, improved, adjusted, refined, and polished to produce a combination of elements that work consistently and effectively. Every detail must be considered: the precise rules of the game, with all possible variations and alternatives; the logistics of handling tie games and interrupted games carried over from the previous show; the format and timing of each program segment; the pace and tempo to be established and maintained in each program; production quality and technical requirements; the selection and use of contestants as well as the host or M.C.; the amount and type of participation desired by the in-studio and at-home audiences; the amount and type of prizes and promotional items to be awarded; and, most important, the marketability of the game show series.

Game show proposals may be written but generally are presented in a verbal pitch to a production company representative; to a packager, who pulls together the various components necessary to produce the show; or occasionally to a network representative. Whether presented in written or verbal form, the proposal is a hard-sell, practical description of the basic program series concept. The proposal must generate excitement for the concept and anticipate basic questions and details about the game show series. See chapter 13 for a description of the techniques used by writers to make effective verbal pitches for projects.

Most often, the writer is involved in writing only the rundown or routine sheet for a game show. The concept for the series is developed by the packager or production company. Writers who regularly work on game show development function as both writer and producer and, thus, do not have to separate writing and producing activities. Also, staff writers, employed by the game show production company, may be involved in the evolution of the master script, as well as the material needed for individual programs.

A minimal amount of writing is required for a continuing game show series. These programs are games and, to all intents and purposes, do not require what traditionally might be regarded as "writing." The key writing activity is the development of the master script for the series.

Writing Techniques and Suggestions

As the game show concept evolves, a writer can help develop a master script for the series. This basic document provides a blueprint to ensure consistency among programs in the series yet allows for the spontaneity necessary for each program. The master script is revised and refined throughout the development process and even after the series is on-the-air. Material for individual programs is prepared by other writers or production assistants, using the parameters and requirements established in the master script.

The master script details, in either a semi-script or show format, such program elements as the opening, closing, introduction and interviewing of contestants, statement of the game rules and categories, transitions between segments, introductions to commercial breaks, announcement of winners and losers, and essential stage directions for getting the host or M.C. and contestants on and off the set.

Although the standard semi-script or show format script form is used (review chapter 3), the master script for a game show is written so that specific kinds of information are included: each program segment must be clearly identified on each script page; succinctly written material must be provided for each segment; a modified two-column television format is used, in which the left column is kept blank for directorial and production notations, whereas the right column contains audio, video, and talent directions written in FULL CAPS and enclosed in parentheses plus the words read by the program talent written in regular upper- and lowercase letters; key words relating to crucial game rules and requiring emphasis are underlined; and, throughout the script, blanks should be provided, as appropriate, to help customize each program in the series.

"The $100,000 Pyramid"

John Davidson hosts "The $100,000 Pyramid," a Bob Stewart production that won an Emmy Award during its network run. Orbis Communications, a division of Carolco, syndicates this series.

The rules of the game remain essentially the same as when Dick Clark first hosted this popular series. On "The $100,000 Pyramid," celebrities work as co-contestants to provide clues to a subject or phrase. The prize money at stake increases as the game progresses and builds to a climactic "big board" segment. A special set area heightens the intensity and excitement of this big money segment. A tournament is held every seven weeks within a twenty-one-week production cycle. The three players who reach the top of the "Pyramid" in the least amount of time return for the $100,000 tournament, in which contestants play off until someone wins $100,000.

Figure 10.12 is the rundown sheet for the show. Notice how each major segment is identified and both segment and continuous program running times are indicated to ensure proper pacing and flow when the program is recorded. The rundown sheet is prepared as a parallel document to the series master script.

Figure 10.13 is the master script page for the opening to segment number 3 of "The $100,000 Pyramid." It illustrates the special scripting techniques described earlier for writing an effective master script for a game show series.

"THE $100,000 PYRAMID"

RUNDOWN

	SEGMENT TIME	RUNNING TIME
1. OPENING - INTERVIEWS - GAME #1		8:10
2. COMMERCIAL BREAK	(1:03)	9:10
3. BIG BOARD #1 ($10,000 TRY)	(2:00)	11:20
4. COMMERCIAL BREAK	(2:05)	13:25
5. GAME #2	(7:00)	20:25
6. COMMERCIAL BREAK	(2:26)	22:50
7. BIG BOARD #2 ($10,000/$25,000 TRY)	(2:00)	25:35
8. COMMERCIAL BREAK	(1:03)	26:20
9. CLOSING - A. GOODBYE	(:35)	
B. PLUGS	(:50)	
C. DISCLAIMERS	(:10)	
D. CREDITS	(:20)	28:22

Figure 10.12
Rundown sheet for "The $100,000 Pyramid."
Courtesy of Bob Stewart Productions, Inc.

Figure 10.13
Master script page for the opening to segment 3 indicated in the rundown sheet in figure 10.12.
Courtesy of Bob Stewart Productions, Inc.

John: (OUT OF COMMERCIAL)

CONTESTANT. You're going for
$_____. To win it all,
you must name the six subjects on
the Pyramid in less than 60 seconds.

CELEBRITY. You're only allowed
to give a LIST of the things that
fit the subject. If you use your
hands to describe _____ or give
a clue -- or mention part of the
subject, you'll hear this sound:

(BUZZER)

Which means you give up the chance
to win the $_____.

You have one minute to win $_____.
-- Here's the first subject....GO!

This chapter examined special situations that you may encounter as a writer of material used by the electronic media. For each specialty, there was a discussion of the approaches used by professional writers and a description or illustration of useful writing and scripting techniques. Although each writing situation is different, there is a noticeable overlap in the writer's approach to the preparation of diverse scripts, as well as to the final writing and presentation of the script material.

Each situation offers unique creative opportunities to develop special writing skills. The experienced writer should find such opportunities interesting enough to pursue under certain circumstances. The novice writer should find these opportunities challenging and should look forward to working on these kinds of scripts after mastering basic writing skills and scripting formats. Some writers work in these specialized areas exclusively. They continue to refine their writing talent and strive to become proficient in their writing craft. Other writers diversify their efforts and use the special writing techniques and approaches outlined for various kinds of writing.

The information in this chapter points up the need to identify the specific writing requirements of a situation; to acquire the necessary writing skills; to integrate the successes and failures of past writing experiences with each new undertaking; and to approach each new writing opportunity with confidence, enthusiasm, and a strong creative spirit willing to explore a new writing outlet.

Summary

Suggested Exercises and Projects

1. Write a television or radio full-script (length to be determined) for one of the following compilation programs: (a) a musical year-in-review for one of the current radio format designations; (b) a world and national news year-in-review; (c) a sports year-in-review for one team or for one sport at the college or professional level; (d) an entertainment industry year-in-review.

2. Design a thirteen-week radio or television magazine feature program series. The subjects featured in the series may include any of the following: consumerism, home repairs, personal finances and investments, crime prevention, health and medicine, nostalgia, religion, news or sports personalities or events, agriculture, children, entertainment news items and personalities, and issues related to specific and identifiable minority or ethnic groups. Submit the following material: (a) a brief prospectus for the thirteen-program series (title; suggested program length, adjacencies, and day/time of the shows; purpose, justification or need, and marketability of the series); (b) a routine sheet for the series; (c) a brief description of the content of each segment of each program in the series; (d) the full-script for the first program in the series.

3. One of the commercial television network morning news and information programs will be producing a two-hour show in your area. The program producer would like to review your ideas for

two segments for this special telecast. Each segment should be three to four minutes long. At least one segment must focus on a significant local historical event, person, organization, or building. The other segment could be designed as a live interview on a local issue or an expanded news, sports, or feature story that highlights an interesting event, location, or personality closely associated with your geographical area. Prepare a six-to-ten-sentence paragraph describing the contents of each segment. Then write a full-script for one of the stories or a semi-script for one of the interviews you have developed.

4. Submit the rundown sheet for a radio or television compilation or magazine program you have monitored. Critique the program based on the discussion in this chapter.

5. Prepare a routine sheet and appropriate filler material for the live radio or television broadcast of one of the following special events: the next major athletic event in your community; a news conference or speech by the governor of your state; election night coverage for the next scheduled statewide election; a one-night telethon for a local nonprofit, charitable organization; a special local or statewide awards or building dedication program; a local sports or auto show.

6. Analyze a "Sesame Street" program segment that explores one aspect of race relations—for example, self-esteem, beauty, skin color, cultural heritage, stereotypes, or discrimination. Describe the content of the segment. Analyze the approach used to reach a target audience with a specific message and a desired result.

7. Watch several programs in one of the following series: "The Bozo Show," "Sesame Street," "3-2-1 Contact," "The Electric Company," "Reading Rainbow," and "Square One TV." Report your observations on writing and production style and techniques; story lines, characters, or talent presented; program diversity and pacing; and entertainment/information value. Provide the rundown sheet for one of the monitored programs.

8. Watch at least two hours of Saturday morning commercial network children's programming. Report your observations on the same topics listed in exercise 7 but for the entire block of Saturday morning programs viewed.

9. Compare and contrast the children's programs viewed in exercises 7 and 8.

10. Individually or as a member of a writing team, prepare a rundown or routine sheet for a new half-hour children's television program. Then write the full-script for this program.

11. Write a full-script for a current Saturday morning commercial television network animated children's program series.

12. Write the full-script and, if possible, provide a preliminary storyboard for a one-to-three-minute animated segment to be used in a television program series aimed at children seven to ten years old. Then show how the script can be adjusted for use in a series aimed at children three to six or ten to twelve years old.

13. Write the full-script and, if possible, provide a preliminary storyboard for a five-to-fifteen-minute animated art film or short subject.

14. Use a popular Sunday newspaper comic strip as a storyboard. Write the full-script for a three-to-five-minute animated or live-action sequence based on this storyboard. Then create other short sequences, in full-script form, for the same comic strip. Use the scripting form shown in figures 10.9 and 10.10.

15. Watch two different television network or syndicated game show series. Critique each program using the suggestions and techniques contained in this chapter.

16. Develop a game show concept based on or patterned after one of the popular arcade or home video computer games or a popular card or board game. The two-to-five-page proposal for your half-hour television game show series should include information about the title of the series; the rules of the game, with all possible variations and categories; the format or order of events to be followed in each program in the series; the approximate timing of each principal segment; the recommended characteristics of the program host or M.C. to be selected; the selection and use of contestants; the types of prizes to be awarded; the technical requirements and tentative production schedule for the series; and a brief description of why your game show is entertaining, marketable, and distinctive from other current television game show series.

17. Individually or as a member of a writing team, prepare the rundown sheet and then the master script in semi-script form for the pilot program in the game show series developed in exercise 16.

Notes

1. Barry Downes, personal communication.
2. Summary of a portion of a letter to the author from Arlene Sherman, associate producer, "Sesame Street."
3. Paul da Silva, *The World of Animation* (Rochester, NY: Eastman Kodak Co., 1979), 35, 99–110.

Chapter

Instructional and Corporate Presentations

11

A vital and growing area of the telecommunications industry is the design and production of instructional, educational, industrial, and corporate presentations. Many diverse groups and organizations use various media to inform, train, persuade, and even entertain specific target audiences.

Government agencies and educational institutions long have recognized the importance of quality audiovisual material for instruction and education. Business and industry have enhanced the technological capabilities to design, write, produce, and deliver worthwhile material to train employees, upgrade skills, and present complex material in an interesting, well-organized manner. "Corporate Video" and "Professional Video Specialist" have begun to replace the more restrictive "nonbroadcast," "ITV," and "A-V Specialist" designations. Private companies, corporations, professional and special interest organizations, trade associations, medical and health service groups, religious organizations, and independent production companies are generating a large quantity and generally a high quality of material for instructional, educational, industrial, and corporate applications.

The scripts and processes described in this chapter have two applications: corporate clients and instructional clients. Corporate clients need a variety of presentations, some for employee orientation and training and others for "internal" employee news and promotional information. Still others offer "external" consumer messages that tell potential customers about company activities and try to persuade them to purchase or use the company's products or services. Corporate clients also must exploit marketing and sales opportunities and need presentations that present a strong, positive company image for such situations as trade shows, short point-of-purchase presentations, and in-store demonstrations. Instructional applications include telecourses, in-class presentations, interactive educational systems, and instructional videocassettes focused on educational objectives.

Each of these two broad applications can be further delineated into more specific content categories. For example, internal corporate presentations providing employee news and promotional information could include several kinds of material, such as company news, employee profiles, updates on internal forms and procedures, current issues and policy statements, reports on positive programs and projects, introductions of new product lines, historical company vignettes and employee profiles, illustrations of effective sales techniques, applications of new technology within a company, and demonstrations of equipment installation and repair, as well as job safety.

Many of the presentational forms discussed in this book could incorporate instructional objectives into their program design. This would include newscasts, dramas, talk shows, magazine programs, documentaries, and investigative reports. Such terms as "industrial or corporate video," "educational program," or "instructional presentation" refer to the context in which certain kinds of presentations are used. Many forms of media are used in these kinds of presentations. The most common are transparencies, slides, filmstrips, audiotapes, videotapes, motion picture films, multimedia presentations, and various kinds of print material. Each form requires specialized writing skills and presentational techniques.

Startling technological developments and the efficient use of established writing and production processes have expanded the available media, presentational options, and creative alternatives that writers and producers can consider. For example, advertisers can sponsor a program or series of programs specifically designed to match audience profiles, product lineups, and merchandising objectives. Infomercials, sometimes called long-form television advertising, showcase video, or direct-response television, have launched entire cable networks, reaching millions of viewers worldwide. Infomercials can be used to solidify an advertiser's public image or awareness level, explain a charitable organization's mission and expenditures, or showcase a celebrity endorsing a company or institution and the quality of its work. The delivery of such presentations can be accomplished on videocassettes that are rented, purchased, or leased by individual viewers or companies, or delivery can be achieved via satellite, direct to home or office downlinks, or through cable systems.

Satellite-based business television (BTV) networks have become increasingly popular. BTVs use technical innovations and improvements to impart information quickly to many sites and provide a means of avoiding the high cost of executive travel. Persons at different locations can be linked interactively with two-way video and audio. Graphics material and data can be included as well. The facsimile machine has made the exchange of hard copy information as simple and as immediate as a telephone call.

BTVs are a cost-efficient method of bringing company news to employees on a daily basis, providing in-store music and data on product availability, announcing results of important business meetings, and relaying training materials that can be used by management, sales, and service personnel immediately or at a later time from a growing company video training library. For example, interactive satellite videoconferences are used throughout the year to reach J.C. Penney store buyers, who can review merchandise and purchase specific items for a particular outlet based on that store's sales record, geographical preferences, and priorities. In addition, J.C. Penney works with local United Way coordinators to provide a videoconference on a topic or an issue of concern. Preproduced material, such as a documentary segment or dramatic vignettes, is used for the first portion of a two-hour teleconference. The rest of the time is spent in individual and group conferences with local residents at J.C. Penney stores.[1]

Although training uses dominate such dedicated, satellite-delivered communications systems, late-breaking business news can also be included. For example, a CEO can explain to employees throughout the company system the impact of a recent bankruptcy court ruling or federal law. Advertising dollars continue to fund programming for narrowcast networks and services emerging to reach large audiences, including potential customers. Several industries have begun to use subscription-based private BTV networks. These include financial and insurance companies, computer firms, retail operations, manufacturing companies, automotive dealerships, law enforcement agencies, fire and emergency units, government agencies, healthcare groups, and professional security companies.

A communications brokerage operation is an alternative to a company-owned and -operated interactive satellite system dedicated to distributing only one company or institution's material. Brokerage operations can form an ad hoc network, temporarily linking various sites to a central distribution system for a one-time-only occasion. Some brokerage firms not only arrange for satellite distribution time and facilities but can also work with institutions to develop, coordinate, write, and produce material for internal or external use. This might include video news releases, as well as live one-on-one interviews with newsmakers, customized for each marketing area and application.

Such presentational formats as infomercials, direct-response television channels, business television networks, interactive satellite and computer systems, and video news releases have emerged as critical vehicles for corporate and instructional presentations. They represent a new wave of technological innovations that can make such messages even more effective in the future.

Opportunities for both entry-level and experienced media writers in the instructional and corporate sectors continue to increase and diversify. Projects are interesting to design and produce, salary and working conditions are excellent, and the writing and production challenges are endless. Job opportunities in this field are discussed in chapter 13.

This chapter will focus on the visual media, specifically motion pictures and videotapes. Neither audio-only nor audiotape with slides is used extensively for contemporary instructional and corporate productions. The design and use of slides, filmstrips, multimedia presentations, and print material require special skills and procedures that are beyond the scope of this book; however, some of the suggested readings in Appendix A touch on writing for these media. If you are assigned to write a slide presentation, review the techniques already explained for writing narration and designing storyboards. These two elements are combined in a slide presentation. Storyboards and photoboards were discussed in chapter 3 and shown in figures 4.4, 4.6, 4.13, 4.15, and 10.11. Writing effective narration for a variety of presentations was discussed in chapter 7 and shown in figures 4.13, 5.15, 7.2, 10.9, 11.3, and 11.4.

The emphasis of this chapter will be on the role and function of writers in the preparation of script material for instructional and corporate motion picture film and videotape presentations. The basic design process for these types of presentations will be outlined. There will also be an emphasis on the process used to establish and accomplish specific goals and objectives to reach an identified audience with an effective, organized message, using available resources. The scripting process used for such presentations will be traced. The chapter will focus on how to apply standard scripting steps to the preparation of such material. There will be constant reminders that writers need to become involved early in the planning and development of such projects. Case studies, profiles, and examples at the end of this chapter will illustrate the principles and techniques discussed. Once you understand the essential steps in the design and scripting processes, you can better adapt to emerging technologies and use a variety of production options.

The Design and Scripting Processes

The design and scripting processes to be described apply most directly to independent production companies. In-house production units follow essentially the same processes but often modify, condense, or even bypass some of the steps outlined. A large share of the presentations prepared for industrial, corporate, educational, and instructional purposes are produced by in-house production units. Each kind of situation and application requires some adjustment. With some modification, the standard writing and production techniques already described and illustrated in this book are used for these special kinds of programs and presentations.

Become actively involved in these early stages of project development. The decisions you make will determine how you mold and shape the presentation exactly to specifications. Be aware of how these important decisions are made and what concepts and strategies are accepted and rejected. You can then use the most effective scripting approaches and techniques to complete the project.

Contact the Client

A client may approach a production company or an independent producer to design a presentation. The client's selection usually is based on the quality of previous work or perhaps the reputation of the individuals or company involved. In some situations, the production company or independent producer may bid on a project already formulated by the client or may generate the initial idea for a presentation and then approach the client to secure acceptance of the idea and funding for further development.

In-house production units have only one client—the company, organization, institution, or agency that employs them. In this situation, the initial idea for a presentation may come from the production unit or from a particular individual or division with the organization. Often regular contact is maintained to ensure the systematic development of worthwhile proposals and projects.

The client often senses when something is wrong—for example, with personnel or equipment assembly procedures—and tries to identify the trouble and pinpoint the possible causes. The production company is contacted if the client believes that a specific kind of presentation might help identify and solve the problem clearly and decisively.

A crucial stage in the development of a presentation, consulting the client, will lay the foundation and set the course for the rest of the design and scripting process. It must be a cooperative effort between representatives from the production unit and the client. If at all possible, you, as the writer, should be involved in these discussions. The ideas and comments that come from these meetings will help guide you later on.

Consult the Client

Several important decisions must be made at this point about the goals and objectives, intended audience, organization of the content, resources available, presentation design, media to be used, budget, timetables and deadlines, and approval points.

The client needs to identify the problem to be tackled or the objective to be worked toward. What is the communications task to be accomplished? What should the viewer get from this presentation? What should be the result after this presentation is seen? What should the viewer know, feel, or be able to do after the presentation?

Goals and Objectives

The client also has to determine if a specific kind of media presentation can help solve that problem or achieve that objective. Would regular meetings or a change in a particular written form solve the problem quicker and more directly than a video presentation? How important is the solution of this problem or the attainment of this objective to the overall goal or success of this client? A new video presentation is not always the answer to every instructional or corporate problem. Careful consideration of alternatives now can save time and energy later and also produce the right solution for the problem or objective that has been identified.

If a new video presentation is to be designed, scripted, and produced, it might be useful to identify its general goal first—information, instruction, training, enrichment, inspiration, motivation, persuasion, or entertainment. These general goals often overlap and fuse. However, it is best to select only one primary goal for the presentation.

The general goal should be refined into a specific statement of behavioral objectives or strategies. These objectives should be placed in written form and approved by the client *before* scriptwriting begins. This will help the writer select, organize, and present the material effectively. This procedure will also ensure the accountability of the script and the resultant presentation.

Behavior objectives can be grouped into three primary categories, or "domains":

a. *Cognitive.* Concepts and information are presented to convey knowledge and stimulate learning. Examples include the orientation of new students or employees, an overview of a company's or an institution's goals and projects, and the history or geography of a particular country.

b. *Affective.* In this case, thoughts, feelings, emotions, attitudes, values, and certain actions are stimulated or motivated in a certain direction. Examples include convincing students to discontinue the use of harmful drugs, improving employee morale, and accepting the reality of cancer treatment.

c. *Psychomotor.* Specific skills and procedures are presented. Examples include presentations on how to use a drill press, how to fill out an income tax form correctly, and how to grip a tennis racket properly.

Three components are included in an effective statement of behavioral objectives—action, condition, and standard. It is necessary to determine what someone must do (action) under what circumstances (condition) with what degree of accuracy or skill (standard).

A few examples should help illustrate how a variety of behavioral objectives can be formulated for the same topic. See figure 11.1. You will need to specify a behavioral objective in order to prepare script material at a later stage of development.

Not all projects can be based on stringent behavioral objectives. Many topics are abstract and elusive when it comes to identifying and measuring behavioral objectives. However, the effort involved in formulating such objectives in clear, simple, specific, and straightforward language will help you crystallize ideas and will provide a sound basis for writing the script and producing the presentation.

Intended Audience

During this preliminary meeting with the client, identify the target audience for the presentation. To whom will the presentation be directed? Preliminary information may have to be gathered to determine such items as the intended audience's educational level, background, interests, priorities, current knowledge and attitudes about the client or subject, learning requirements, language and visualization usage, and gender or racial orientation, if that is a consideration for this particular presentation.

Collect and analyze both life-style (psychographic) and statistical (demographic) audience information. This is the same type of information included in copy rationales prepared before the writing and production of commercials and announcements (review chapter 4). Virtually all material written and

A presentation on a new employee group insurance plan

Cognitive Objective. After viewing this presentation, employees will be able to compare and contrast the old and the new group insurance plans.

Affective Objective. After viewing this presentation, employees will be motivated to sign up for the new group insurance plan.

Psychomotor Objective. After viewing this presentation, employees will be able to fill out the necessary forms to activate the new group insurance plan coverage.

A presentation on new technology and equipment in a company

Cognitive Objective. After seeing this presentation, viewers will be able to list the new technology and equipment available to company employees.

Affective Objective. After seeing this presentation, viewers will be motivated to accept the new technology and equipment available to improve job productivity.

Psychomotor Objective. After seeing this presentation, viewers will be able to enter inventory information into the company's computer system.

A presentation on musical notations

Cognitive Objective. After seeing this presentation, students will be able to identify correctly the symbols used for bass and treble clefs, sharps, flats, and natural signs.

Affective Objective. After viewing this presentation, students will be motivated to appreciate the precision used in making basic musical notations.

Psychomotor Objective. After seeing this presentation, students will be able to write, in proper form, the musical notation symbols for bass and treble clefs, sharps, flats, and natural signs.

Figure 11.1
Three principal types of behavioral objectives prepared for various topics.

produced for the electronic media uses as a reference a wide range of audience information. This helps you better design presentations to reach a target group with a specific message and a desired result.

In addition, it would be helpful to determine why the intended audience would watch the presentation. Will viewing be required or voluntary? Will viewing the presentation be considered crucial to personal or professional development and fulfillment? Can the target audience really solve the problem or achieve the identified objective? The more you know about the intended audience, the more effectively you can write and present the material to meet specific behavioral objectives.

Determine what will be included in the presentation. List the primary and secondary points to be made. The goals and objectives statement should guide the selection and treatment of each primary idea. Limit each presentation to only two or three major points. If more emerge at this stage, consider redirecting or restructuring the presentation. It is better to present a few ideas well than to try to cram too much information into a single presentation. At a later developmental stage, you will need to expand the major points identified in this preliminary meeting with the client.

Organization of the Content

**Resources
Available**

At this same client conference, identify the available resources relating to the project. These resources might include access to archival material; pertinent research data gathered by the client or by outside sources; the services of a technical adviser, content specialist, or program consultant; assistance from a research assistant or a typist; and other material, programs, and presentations available to the client and relating to the project under development. The resources may be either extensive or limited. They could include people, facilities, equipment, information, and services.

**Presentation
Design**

An important strategy task involves deciding how to present the material. Should it be arranged into a single presentation or a series of presentations? What should be the length of the presentation(s)? Should the presentation(s) be designed for individualized instruction or for small- or large-group use, or at home or work, in school, in a social or business environment? What is the projected ''life'' of this presentation? Should themes or items, such as slogans, logos, or graphics, be included? Are there any goals or objectives that this presentation should work toward? Although writers generally do not decide how such material will be used in a presentation unless they also serve as producer or designer, it is important that writers understand the various criteria used to make that kind of decision. Information about the presentation's design and structure will help you shape the material exactly to specifications. This information is usually described in the treatment, which is discussed later in this chapter.

Media to Be Used

Each medium has distinct attributes that present such elements as motion, color, images, sound, and detail with varying degrees of success. (Review chapter 2.) Match the capabilities of each medium with the objectives of the presentation. Writers and production designers must determine which medium, given the available time, budget, and resources, will produce the desired results most efficiently and economically. Such choices will influence the remainder of the production process.

At one time, slide and transparency presentations dominated audiovisual production in both the instructional and corporate sectors. They provided inexpensive presentations that could be carefully planned and monitored. Most production companies that now produce material for corporate and instructional markets use slides with other media, such as computer-generated graphics or animated simulations offered on videodiscs. Videotape is now the dominant medium used to produce material for most instructional and corporate clients, including those in food preparation, automotive assembly, fashion merchandising, and financial services.

It has become a common practice for writers and producers to use a mixed media approach for instructional and corporate presentations. An interactive satellite presentation, for example, can be followed by off-line training or educational components for hands-on activities at computers or videodisc units. This multimedia approach reinforces the value of the original presentation and enriches the participation of each audience member.

Electronic systems are becoming readily available to interconnect a personal computer, touchscreen monitor, and videotape or videodisc player. The program user can touch a screen and begin or end a presentation; select an option for additional graphics, data, or exercises; answer questions; or access supplementary material of various kinds. This type of integrated system is useful for instructional as well as corporate applications—for instance, to select point-of-purchase presentations at trade shows or exhibitions.

By the year 2000, interactive voice technologies are expected to dominate this field. This will require more skills and a greater depth of understanding of multimedia design and scripting approaches from video managers, producers, *and* writers.

Budget

Even at this preliminary stage, it is necessary to have an estimated budget in mind so that you and the production unit can operate at a realistic level of development. Some clients already have a budget in hand for each project. A budget or several versions of a budget may have to be devised before further development of the project can continue. Formal approval of the project's budget generally comes at a later stage of development.

Be aware of the budgeting process and of the final budget for each project. Many writers function in a hyphenated role, such as writer-producer or writer-director. Knowing the budget for a project allows you to anticipate constraints and to control more effectively the eventual shape and quality of the final product. This will help you meet project specifications and expectations.

The availability and even the source of funds may cause certain writing and production limitations. Very effective and creative presentations, however, have been written and produced on relatively low budgets. Determine production capabilities and the budget before preparing the proposal, outline, treatment, and subsequent versions of the production script.

Timetables and Deadlines

Tentative deadlines should be established for each major step in the design and scripting process. These can be formalized later, when a written bid or proposal is submitted for the client's approval. Consider all the factors relating to the project before trying to establish realistic deadlines that satisfy the needs of the client, the production company, and you.

Approval Points

At several points or stages during the development process, the client may exercise approval rights. Identifying those approval points with the client and placing them into the formal contract, bid, or proposal will help ensure that everyone involved in the project is communicating properly on a regular basis and that satisfactory progress is being made. The approval points might include the final budget, each major stage of scripting development (for example, treatment, sequence outline, first and subsequent drafts of the full-script), the selection and use of graphics and on-camera talent (voice and picture), the use of locations and production sites, and the final edited version of the presentation. Other approval points may be needed in particular instances.

Using numerous approval points slows the development process. More people get involved in clearing or approving such items as content, policy, format, security, and usage. Determine who will ultimately own the rights to duplicate and show the finished presentation. This may help identify the key people who should be involved at each approval point.

Prepare the Proposal

The production and creative staff, including the writer, discuss and evaluate the determinations made during the client consultation. A proposal, sometimes called a "bid," is then prepared for presentation to the client.

The proposal is formulated based on the information supplied by the client and the capabilities and interests of those preparing the proposal. The proposal may be for any combination of further steps in development— budget, goals and objectives, treatments, full-script, production of the finished program or presentation, post-production evaluation, and the like. For example, the proposal may be made to develop only a goals and objectives statement for use in supplemental material, or it could be made to develop only the final script for the presentation. A full service unit prepares a complete proposal detailing goals and objectives, costs, timetables and deadlines, approval points, promotion, evaluation, the skeletal outline of the presentation, and special needs, objectives, and concepts related to the presentation.

The proposal, written in a concise and direct manner, should reflect the primary concerns of the client. Even for in-house clients, it is important that a proposal be written in the style and language the client expects to see. It must reflect a special interest in and an insight into the client's needs and expectations. When structuring the proposal, ask yourself what the people reading the proposal will want to know. More than likely their primary interest will be the results they can anticipate from their investment. Thus, you should list the results or benefits of the project in the first section of the proposal. Present the remaining information in a decreasing order of importance. An effective proposal clearly delineates the client's primary concerns and interests. It should also show the client the quantitative and qualitative benefits to be derived from the presentation.

Review the Proposal/Prepare the Contract

The client reviews the proposal and may reject it, request changes, or accept it as written. If the client rejects the proposal, you may either have to abandon the project or prepare a new proposal after further consultation with the client. If the client requests changes, the proposal may be adjusted and resubmitted to the client for approval.

If the client accepts the proposal, a formal contract is prepared. The contract becomes a legally binding document and details such items as costs, approval points, timetables and deadlines, policies and procedures to be followed, general responsibilities of all parties, and control of the rights to the finished program or presentation. In-house projects do not require a formal contract, but a statement may be drawn to clarify the responsibilities and expectations of the in-house units involved.

If you have been involved in the early stages of development, you know the requirements of the project. Otherwise you should be briefed thoroughly about the client's requirements, interests, and concerns. The specific information contained in the proposal and the contract now requires review and evaluation from the scriptwriter's perspective.

The scripting process described may not apply in all cases; however, this description should familiarize you with how the majority of such programs and presentations come together. Each step in the planning and scripting process should lead to an ever-increasing focus on the objectives and nature of the presentation. Each step requires you and the production team to identify and assess available options, select the best options, and then commit time and resources to a specific action. Each action should lead to the next step in the preparation of the presentation. (Review chapter 3 for details about these scripting steps.)

As quickly as possible, you must become thoroughly familiar with the subject of the project. This involves using traditional research methods, as well as tapping the available resources identified earlier in the client consultation. This is the first phase of script development.

Technical advisers, content specialists, and program consultants are valuable resources for such presentations. They can fill in information gaps, update your research and information, help interpret complex or confusing details and specialized terminology, and, often, refer you to other experts with even more specialized interests, information, and backgrounds. These resource people usually are thoroughly familiar with the subject matter, but they are not writers and often are not able to think visually in terms of what a writer needs. Work with these resource people to refine the main points and goals of the presentation, clarify ambiguities, identify material that needs special emphasis or treatment, and organize the subject matter into an attractive and effective arrangement. Alternative methods of presenting the material should be discussed. Attention should be focused not only on the technical information, but on the precise wording, sequence of ideas, and visualization techniques. All too often, resource people concentrate only on the technical information and neglect to respond to other important components of the presentation.

Field research may be appropriate. Get into the subject by becoming part of the environment you will write about. Talk to those who eventually will see the presentation. Scout locations that might be used in the script and later in production. Placing yourself in such an environment might call to your attention a unique camera angle, a distinctive sound, or an interesting person or image to include in the script.

Continue to do research throughout the writing process and maintain contact with the client or the client's representative to obtain specific facts or details as you assemble the script. Do not allow lack of information to be the reason for a poor script. Determine what you need, and then go find it right away.

Prepare Script Material

Complete Research

Prepare the Treatment

For the kinds of presentations under consideration in this chapter, the treatment is an efficient way for the client to review the content and to recommend changes in concepts and approaches. It is more efficient and less costly to make changes during this early developmental stage than to disrupt production later, when objections to the organization or visualization of the material cause unnecessary turmoil and delays. Take the time to rewrite the treatment to bring the idea into harmony with the client's needs and wishes.

Contents   As indicated in chapter 3, a treatment is a concise statement of the content of a program or presentation that explains what is planned and how it will be presented. The treatment is your statement of the purpose of the presentation, a list of the client's information priorities, and a condensed narrative of the envisioned final presentation. The treatment should be written by the person who eventually will write the final shooting script. The treatment is not a simplified shooting script, however. Much of the treatment should explain *why* the material is being handled a certain way.

The treatment for an instructional or corporate presentation generally contains four separate elements: *background information* that summarizes who the audience is, the format for the presentation, how the presentation will be used, and any other combined efforts that need to be identified and coordinated; *a statement of objectives* that indicates the attitudes, actions, or thoughts that should result from seeing the presentation; *a list of strategies* that notes the underlying ideas and approaches that will shape the script and will help determine the scripting and production techniques to be used to meet the stated objectives; and *a description of the creative approach to be used* for the opening, closing, structure, transitions, content, number of locations or sets needed, graphics, people and objects that will be seen or heard, and so forth.

Presentational Approach   The treatment needs to indicate the presentational approach that will be used. Many of the successful presentational formats described elsewhere in this book are used for corporate and instructional presentations. The once standard "talking heads" approach has been supplanted by newscasts, magazine programs, documentaries using archival material and host-narrators, reenactments, product demonstrations, role-playing exercises, dramas, simulated game shows, humor, puppets, and animation. The writer is no longer confined by a limited range of presentational approaches. The approach must reflect the appropriate level of visual and aural language. It must not only be interesting but high-powered to capture the increasing intensity and sophistication of today's audiences.

Almost any type of program or presentation form can be used in various contexts. For example, a television drama or documentary that examines the causes and consequences of child abuse could be useful for a sociology or criminal justice class studying this subject or a community service organization beginning to train new volunteers for self-help activities in this area. A talk program featuring leaders from major industrial nations may be the initial stimulus for further discussion of current issues and developments by political science or international relations students or perhaps executives from an import/export business assembled at sites throughout the world. Live satellite teleconferences are an example of a contemporary corporate and instructional application that has enhanced or expanded traditional presentational forms. The term "special events" now includes such activities as plant openings and the introduction of new product lines at crucial national and international trade shows. Even game shows and magazine programs can help fulfill the special requirements of institutions and corporations. Music videos can enliven instructional or corporate presentations. However, for these specific applications, a music video must display a logical sequence of scenes that develops a theme, conveys a message, tells a story, and moves to a recognizable conclusion. (Music videos were discussed in chapter 9.)

The nature of the project determines the presentational approach and design to be used. A drama might work best to create suspense, sustain interest, and convey attitudes and concepts about important issues. Role-playing segments could be considered when trying to illustrate techniques sales personnel can use to overcome customer objections to new product lines. Narration, with clear, sharp graphics and close-ups of a demonstration, would be ideal for training workers to operate particular pieces of equipment or to follow specific production steps. Perhaps an on-camera "wrong-way/right-way" approach would help change common mistakes into more efficient and less dangerous work habits. A combination of presentational formats works well. For example, begin with an on-camera host introducing the presentation, move to a narration of instructional material with graphics and animated segments, add a role-playing segment illustrating how new techniques can be used, and conclude with the on-camera host noting the impact expected from the presentation.

Many instructional designers recognize humor as an effective way to help someone accept and remember information, assess attitudes, and alleviate some of the fear and anxiety associated with learning new skills. If you decide to use humor in an instructional or corporate presentation,

    a. *As the basis of the humor, use material familiar to your target audience.*

    b. *Create characters that will develop humorous situations naturally and effectively.*

    c. *Start with what is believable and build characters and situations on that basis.*

    d. *Set up the basic premise, carry the body of the scene to its conclusion quickly and logically, and close with one punch line or situation.*

    e. *Choose the comedic texture, approach, and style to be used* (whether it's broad or subtle humor), *and then remain consistent* in the development of this humorous perspective.

    f. *Base the development of humor on the instructional or training points to be made or the objectives to be accomplished.* If the audience appreciates and remembers the humor, they will very likely remember the serious point.

Humor can be a risky presentational format for corporate and instructional presentations. Clients tend to shy away from humor that they suspect makes light of an important subject. Some subjects and clients are off limits to humor under most circumstances. This includes life insurance, home security systems, and automobile safety. Humor is also subjective. What you find humorous is not necessarily funny to someone else, especially someone who controls production development funds in an institutional environment. Experts in writing, producing, and performing are needed to make humor work effectively; however, experts are not readily available in tightly budgeted productions such as these.

The presentational approach selected and described in the treatment must be the *best* available to accomplish the objectives identified in initial client meetings. Often script ideas and approaches described in the treatment evolve from key phrases taken from these client meetings. From these sessions, central characters are shaped, themes are forged, and even presentational titles are determined.

Organizational Approach The organizational approach must arrange the content into logical sequences. These sequences must progressively increase interest and provide the proper emphasis on important points. In a single-concept instructional presentation, for example, the beginning must peak audience interest and curiosity, establish the nature and importance of the subject, and hint at how it will be developed. The middle portion needs to develop the subject in an ascending order of importance, interest, intensity, and impact so that the audience moves through the subject matter logically, clearly, naturally, and memorably. The conclusion should reestablish the main points of the presentation, interpret information and form conclusions as necessary, and provide a final thought or image to ensure the impact and memorability of the presentation.

The following is a three-step process many writers of such material find useful as they develop each sequence in a presentation:

1. *Isolate the essential idea* of the sequence. In one sentence, write the one point you want to communicate.
2. *Envision the specific images* that illustrate this essential idea. Note the particular mental pictures that would help explain or describe the central point of the sequence.
3. *Write the words* to be used in narration, role-playing scenes, dialogue, and so on. These words should supplement the visuals and underscore the significance of what is seen.

This three-step process should help you develop a pattern of sequential development. Each sequence should be constructed simply and logically and should interlock with the surrounding sequences. If designed in this manner, all sequences should help build a presentation that is strong, memorable, meaningful, and effective. Also, this design process eliminates the need for an official step or sequence outline.

Several checkpoints or criteria should guide you, the client, and the production staff as you evaluate the treatment. Does the treatment provide a clear, concise image of the finished presentation? Is the subject presented clearly, simply, directly, and in the manner desired by the client? Is the eventual presentation likely to spark and sustain interest? Will it stimulate and involve the audience and motivate them to think and react creatively? Will it motivate them to want to learn more about the subject? Will it be memorable and eventually produce measurable, tangible results? Is the treatment realistic in its content development and production implications? The development and evaluation of the treatment should bring all parties involved in the project to mutually acceptable terms.

Evaluate the Treatment

If the treatment is prepared properly, a step or sequence outline may not be necessary. This optional, intermediate scripting step may be needed, however, if the presentation is extraordinarily complex, if the content requires even more refinement, or if the client requires it.

Prepare and Evaluate the Step or Sequence Outline

The step or sequence outline describes the approach or "image" that will be sustained in the presentation. Additionally, attention is given, in narrative form, to the specific content of the sequences, the tone, the pace and rhythm of sound and picture, the specific scenes or settings to be used, the characters to be emphasized, the camera shots to be included, and other details that will ensure that the "vision" of the project will be captured in the final presentation.

All of your work and preparation lead to the writing of the shooting script. At that point, you have considered thousands of possibilities for presenting the subject. The treatment and sequence outline steps should have helped you focus and crystallize the presentation. Now get even closer to the subject, try various scripting techniques, and adjust and fine tune each shot and sequence—all in an effort to find the best way to present the material to the target audience.

Write the Shooting Script

A schedule for writing the final shooting script can be established once the nature of the presentation and the deadlines are known. Approval points can be identified for each step in the writing process.

The following timetable works well when you are trying to write the final shooting script for a corporate or instructional presentation: a treatment is prepared about one week after the initial meeting with the client; a step or sequence outline or the rough draft of the shooting script is written about ten days after the treatment is approved; a draft of the final script comes about one week later; and corrections, if any, follow a few days later. It is common for a writer to be scripting projects simultaneously. Be sure that project timetables do not interfere. If you adhere to your timetable and deadlines, clients are more likely to adhere to theirs.

The shooting script can be written in any of the standard scripting forms described and illustrated in chapter 3. In practically all situations, a full-script is prepared. In some circumstances, however, a semi-script or show format may be appropriate. For example, a semi-script or show format might be appropriate for segments that include interviews, panel discussions, or role-playing exercises. Use the script form that is most appropriate for the kind of segment or presentation planned and that meets or exceeds the requirements of the project and the client. Remember that script formats differ markedly from organization to organization. Use the script format required by the company that employs you.

Evaluate the Shooting Script

The evaluation of the shooting script is an important approval point for the client, as well as for the writer and production team. The client needs to determine whether the script meets or exceeds expectations, and if each of the primary objectives identified and finally approved during the initial consultation and in the preliminary scripting stages has been realized in the shooting script.

Some writers find that a client can visualize a presentation better if the writer and producer read the scripted narration aloud or walk the client through the project and describe how key segments or scenes will be handled. Sometimes a storyboard (illustrated in chapters 4 and 10) can help describe how a complicated process will be shown. Even slides, photographs, computer-generated graphics, and personally produced videotape segments can help a client understand and visualize each crucial sequence. This type of activity helps you, as a writer, select the best method of presenting material and helps you convince a stubborn client or production supervisor that the presentational approaches you have chosen are the best for the project under development. Some writers have used this verbal, or "pitch," presentation technique *before* writing the treatment. If done at this stage of development, several approaches can be suggested or illustrated and the most viable approach selected. This can save writers and producers valuable preparation time and effort. Pitches are discussed more fully in chapter 13.

The production team needs to determine the technical requirements and feasibility of the presentation. Thus, you should remember to use standard production terminology in proper form to ensure clear understanding of what is to be seen and heard.

If changes in the shooting script are required, one responsible person, preferably the producer, should synthesize the comments made by the client or the production team, present these comments to the writing team, and help rework the shooting script into acceptable form. You should be told why a specific change is needed. Adjustments in one part of the script usually necessitate changes in other parts. If all parties involved in the project have approved the treatment or sequence outline, the changes requested at this point should be minor and should not disturb the overall approach used in the script. Nevertheless, be prepared to rewrite the script as often as necessary to refine and polish it, to give it continuity, and to make it worthy of enthusiastic acceptance by the client and ready for production.

Begin Production

Strictly speaking, the writer's work is finished once the shooting script has been approved for production, unless the writer also serves as producer or director of these kinds of presentations. Combining these functions is common practice, especially for in-house production units, where the writer's job often continues through the production, editing, screening, and approval phases of a production.

Production of the script involves specific steps and procedures that require detailed explanation and illustration. For this kind of information, consult the appropriate readings in Appendix A. Basic production processes and techniques were outlined in chapter 2.

Approve and Evaluate the Presentation

The screening of the finished presentation is an essential approval point for the client. Changes made at this juncture are costly—in time and money. If all other developmental stages have gone well and received client approval, the screening of the finished presentation should provide only pleasant surprises for all involved.

The evaluation process should extend beyond cursory approval by the client. The presentation should be analyzed critically to assess how well it fulfilled the communications task identified earlier in the design process. The client should determine the cost effectiveness of the presentation, as well as the increased level of productivity and the certainty of attitude changes. The production team should scrutinize audience response to specific visual and aural techniques. The writer should assess how well essential concepts and information were understood and accepted by the audience.

The *results* of the presentation need to be determined. Various techniques can be used—questionnaires, surveys, pretests, posttests, and field tests of the presentation—before it is widely distributed. This kind of evaluation should provide additional insight into the most efficient and effective means to convey messages in various situations.

Profiles

A few examples will help illustrate how the design and scripting approaches described can be applied in various instructional and corporate presentation situations.

"High Feather"

The "High Feather" series of ten thirty-minute programs is

> designed to assist children [aged eight to fourteen] in developing sound
> nutritional habits while making them aware of nutrition-related health
> problems. The programs, dramatic in nature, follow a group of children
> through their daily activities at summer camp. Each episode contains nutrition
> information to enlighten young viewers while they are entertained. The
> continuing cast of characters is representative of the population in many
> towns, cities and states. . . . High Feather demonstrates that dieting practices
> affect the way one looks and feels, and the way one behaves and learns.[2]

Nutrition topics in the series include sugar and its effects, comparative shopping, wilderness diets, balanced low-cost meals, teenage drinking, ethnic foods, and the importance of fruits and vegetables. The series, and individual programs from the series, won a number of awards for production excellence from such organizations as the American Academy of Pediatrics, Action for Children's Television, the Information Film Producers of America, and the New York Chapter of the Academy of Television Arts and Sciences.

Kroyt-Brandt Productions, Inc. was hired by the New York State Education Department to produce the series. Yanna Kroyt Brandt explained how the series was developed:

> Initially, there [was] a series of meetings with a group of five nutrition consultants and myself as executive producer, the producer, and associate producer. We asked them to make a list of 100 nutrition issues they felt were important to get across. Out of those hundred in discussion we developed those issues which everyone felt were the most important.
>
> At this point the producer, associate producer, and I sat down in a series of meetings and discussed various series ideas. After arriving at a series concept and leading characters we all felt were viable, we then developed story lines for each show in the series. Each story line was coupled with a series of nutrition education objectives. We then met again with our nutrition consultants and went over concepts.
>
> An educational researcher also worked with us on creating goals and objectives for each program that could be tested. At this point the story lines and character descriptions and educational goals were sent to the writers.
>
> The scripts were gone over for dramatic value and educational goals both by us and the consultants. Most of the scripts went through at least three drafts.[3]

An excellent teacher's guide was prepared for the series to help teachers plan nutrition activities that help shape positive attitudes, develop abilities, and increase knowledge. The guide also provides learning objectives for each program in the series, background information on nutrition topics, a cookbook, and a resource index of pertinent booklets, filmstrips, guides, and posters.

In "Swifty," the third program in the series, everyone at camp is preparing for a race. Tom ("Swifty") joins in reluctantly. After a few mishaps, he learns much about self-image, diet, exercise, and teamwork. The objectives of the "Swifty" episode are

To help students:

1. analyze how they feel about themselves (their body, diet, and exercise habits).
2. realize that people of varied cultures, upbringing, and geographic location have varied eating patterns.
3. recognize the importance of eating a nutritious breakfast.
4. recognize the value of a regular exercise program in maintaining optimum health.[4]

The opening scenes from the "Swifty" episode, written by Alan Seeger, are shown in figure 11.2.

Figure 11.2 illustrates a very common instructional application. This script is one part of an educational series developed from specific educational objectives and aimed at a target audience. Another instructional/educational television scripting example was shown in figure 10.8.

FADE IN:

1. EXT. PATH TO BOYS' BUNK.
DOMINGO RAMOS is running along the path towards the
bunks.

2. EXT. BOYS' BUNK
STAN LIPTON, LEO BARTLETT, CARL KERN and BRUNO BONOMO
are lounging on the porch.

DOMINGO comes running down the path, shouting to Stan
and Leo as he approaches.

> DOMINGO
> Come on, Hawks. Let's put it on.
> Got to meet the girls in five.

Domingo springs up and enters the cabin.

> Carl
> Who are the Hawks?

> STAN
> Our Olympic Day Team.

> CARL
> We're the Tigers.

3. INT. BOYS' CABIN.
TOM PAGE, a rather pudgy camper, is sitting on his
bunk reading a rock magazine. His cassette recorder is
playing and he is munching on a bag of potato chips.
DOMINGO enters.

> DOMINGO
> Come on, Tom. All Hawks to the
> practice field.

> TOM
> I'm no Hawk.

Figure 11.2
Full-script for the
opening scenes from
the "Swifty" episode.
*Courtesy of Alan
Seeger, Yanna Kroyt
Brandt, Dr. Bernarr
Cooper, and the New
York State Education
Department.*

Figure 11.2 (*continued*)

                              DOMINGO
              You sit at our table, don't you?
              We're all Hawks there...the girls
              and us. Let's go. Have to start
              practicing if the Hawks are going to
              win.

                                TOM
                I never won anything in my life.

                              DOMINGO
                         I'll teach you.

Domingo runs out the door with Tom following somewhat
unenthusiastically.

4. EXT. BOYS' CABIN.
   DOMINGO runs from the cabin, jumps from the porch, and
   runs off down the path. STAN and LEO follow on his
   heels. TOM hurries from the cabin and looks for his
   friends. CARL and BRUNO laugh.

5. EXT. PATH TO FIELD.
   DOMINGO, STAN and LEO come trotting down the path.
   SUZANNE FREESTONE, ANN CAMPBELL, LESLIE REYNOLDS and
   CATHY EHLERS are jogging along an intersecting path.
   The two groups meet and run off together happily.

   As the group disappears from view, TOM appears,
   running awkwardly after his friends.

6. EXT. MESS HALL.
   Sitting on the steps are NAT SHAPIRO, BOBBY RAINWATER
   and BONNIE CONSTANZA. To the left of the steps are
   several vending machines.

   DOMINGO and SUZANNE come running down the path...past
   the Hall. ANN, LEO, CATHY, STAN and LESLIE follow.

   NAT, BOBBY and BONNIE cheer the runners on
   sarcastically.

                              BONNIE
                Hey, don't strain yourselves.

Figure 11.2 *(continued)*

                    NAT
        We got a kitchen table that runs faster
        than that. Betcha the Hawks are gonna
        lay an egg.

As the runners vanish from view, TOM huffs and puffs
into view. He's obviously pooped and his trot slows to
a walk and then, when he reaches the vending machines,
he comes to a complete stop.

                 BONNIE
              (teasing Tom)
        Hey, one of the Hawks got lost.

                 BOBBY
        That's Swifty..."Swifty" Hawk.

Tom ignores the taunting and buys himself a coke and a
candy bar from the vending machine.

                    NAT
        What'cha doing, Swifty? Getting a
        little quick energy?

Tom jogs off down the path toward the practice field.
He juggles the soda and candy, attempting to consume
them as he hurries to catch up with the others.

                    NAT
        Go ahead, go with your little Hawks,
        Swifty. C'mon, run Swifty, c'mon.

7. EXT. HAWKS ON THE PRACTICE FIELD.
   DOMINGO holds up a mimeographed sheet and seems to
   have taken charge of the group.

"Merck Focus"

Corporate video news and news magazine programs have become an essential part of many companies' employee communications efforts. Such programs can efficiently present several pertinent contemporary topics in a visually interesting manner. The programs can be tailored to the requirements of corporate and industrial audiences. For example, newscasts produced for employees at Federal Express and A. L. Williams (an Atlanta-based insurance company) are done in easily digestible, five-to-eight-minute packages and run during major shift changes and meal breaks. "FedEx Overnight" is beamed every morning at 5:30 central time to 1,100 sites, where a decoder unscrambles the signal and activates a videocassette recorder, which records the program, then automatically plays it continuously throughout the day.

At a meeting in November 1980, executives at Merck & Co., Inc., a major pharmaceutical firm, decided to produce a television magazine program for its seventeen thousand employees based in the United States. The objectives of the program were to foster a feeling of unity among employees in a diverse company; to improve employees' conceptions of company benefits;

to inform employees about company activities (for example, new plant additions, new products, and pertinent legislation affecting the company); to enhance employee understanding of the various facets of the company's operations, departments, and divisions; to show company involvement in community affairs; and to present information useful to each employee. It was decided to make this a regular program that focused on the employees and their interests, humanized top management, and concentrated on lower and middle management employees. At least one of the three or four segments in each thirteen-minute program was to include humorous material.[5]

Besides establishing goals, objectives, and content guidelines for the program, company executives also formulated a timetable and budget and determined a flexible delivery system for the program. They also identified the criteria for selecting on-camera talent, approval points, promotion activities, and evaluation steps. It was a thoughtful and efficient plan, well conceived and well executed.

Although the first few programs were produced entirely outside the company, a combination of outside professionals supervised by an in-house corporate video department producer and assistant now package the programs. A permanent staff of company employees is used for narrating program segments. Merck employees were also involved in naming the program. More than 800 submissions were received before "Merck Focus" was selected for the program and "TeleVisionMerck" was chosen for a Merck video network. "Merck Focus" is now seen on cable television on the Cable Network of New Jersey (the interconnect of all New Jersey cable systems) and on a system in Pennsylvania near a major plant.

Figure 11.3 is the script for one of the "Merck Focus" programs, which won top awards from the International Television Association, a nonprofit organization for professional video communicators. The script demonstrates how effective a magazine program format can be for corporate and industrial presentations. The segments display good pacing, flow, and entertainment value and provide the type of material that fulfills the program objectives listed earlier. Figure 11.3 illustrates a common corporate or business communication application. *Merck Focus* is an internal employee news and promotional information magazine series seen both at work and at home.

Maturity Broadcast News

Video news releases (VNRs) can be handled by brokerage companies or directly by institutions and corporate clients. VNRs are used often by instructional and corporate groups to relay information to an external audience—consumers. A VNR may be a late-breaking news story or a feature item that concerns a particular organization. It generally includes additional b-roll, sound bites, and graphics that can be used by television stations to localize or customize stories. Non-English scripts and narration can also be prepared and then distributed via satellite. Review chapter 5 for an explanation of standard scripting formats and techniques that can be used to produce effective VNRs.

((FADE UP ON ANNOUNCER, TINA DOUGHERTY, STANDING OUTDOORS. MUSIC HELD UNDER BACKGROUND.))

TD: Welcome to Merck Focus.

((CUT TO SEGMENT OF ARLENE FRANK. TITLE: PROFESSIONAL REPRESENTATIVE))

TD (VO): In this program, we'll look at a day in the life of one very unusual professional sales representative.

((CUT TO SEGMENT OF MERCK PEOPLE. TITLE: MERCK PEOPLE))

TD (VO): We'll hear our fellow employees and find out if one of them has said the secret word.

((CUT TO SEGMENT OF JAPAN STORY. TITLE: NEW LABORATORY))

TD (VO): And we'll travel halfway around the world to Japan, for the dedication ceremony of a new research laboratory.

((CUT BACK TO TINA DOUGHERTY))

TD: I'm your moderator, Tina Dougherty. And those are the stories we'll cover in this edition of Merck Focus.

TD: Our first story starts in New York City.

((FADE UP MUSIC. LOGO/TITLE. MUSIC UNDER AND OUT))

((CUT TO LONG SHOT OF ARLENE FRANK WALKING UP BLOCK. INCLUDE TRAFFIC AND SOUND.))

TD (VO): This is bustling Manhattan, with its apartment buildings and brownstones. This is the place where Arlene Frank, an MSD Professional Sales Representative comes every day to conduct business.

But the noise of New York doesn't distract her. At eighteen she lost most of her hearing and became legally deaf.

There are many important jobs at Merck, and a Professional Representative is one of them. They're the people who bring our products to

---

Figure 11.3
Script for one of the "Merck Focus" programs.
Courtesy of Jeffrey M. Goldstein, Merck & Co., Inc.

physicians. Representatives explain how Merck products may benefit their patients as well as inform them of possible adverse reactions.

Arlene tries to see about seven doctors and three pharmacists each day.

((CUT TO INSIDE OF DOCTOR'S OFFICE))

TD (VO): One of the most difficult parts of the job is the waiting. Arlene is an active woman and sitting isn't one of her favorite activities. But when it happens, she can catch up on her business reading and get ready for her presentation.

Before you can become a Professional Representative, you have to go through an extensive training program. You learn about Merck products and associated diseases. Arlene concentrates on knowing her products very well. Her objective is to find out the physician's concerns. Then she can gear her talk directly to the points that interest him.

((NURSE WALKS IN AND MOTIONS THAT THE DOCTOR WILL SEE HER NOW))

She lipreads the doctors in order to understand them, and lip reading forces direct eye contact.

((CUT TO APARTMENT, AF SETTING UP VU-PHONE))

TD (VO): Arlene is in frequent contact with her District Manager, Paul Cottone. The phone system they use is a telephone typewriter for the deaf called the Vu-phone. It's a valuable tool because it allows her to hear with her eyes.

((CUT TO PAUL COTTONE AT HIS VU-PHONE. ON IT READS: "HOW ARE YOU? I'M GOING TO PUT YOU IN THE MACHINE."))

Figure 11.3 (*continued*)

PC (VO): Arlene, like most of our Professional Representatives, does an outstanding job. It's a tough job, requiring both physical and mental stamina. But she gives it her all. We're really glad she's on our team.

((CUT TO AF AT VU-PHONE. ON IT READS: "I FINALLY GOT TO SEE SEVEN DOCTORS AND I ALSO GOT AN ORDER FOR FIFTY VIALS OF PNEUMOVAX."))

((CUT TO PC TYPING ON VU-PHONE. WE SEE HIM TYPE "LOOKS LIKE WE'RE GOING TO MAKE PLAN FOR THE QUARTER."))

((CUT TO TD ON CAMERA))

TD: A lot of you have told us that you like our new added feature of the "secret word," so we're going to do it again! We have one rule and it's quite easy: The first person who says the secret word, wins the prize.

((CUT TO DUCK WITH WORD IN MOUTH))

TD (VO): It's a common word, something you'd hear every day. Today, the secret word is SAILING.

((CUT TO MERCK PEOPLE))

TD (VO): We asked two questions. The first was "What do you think is a good investment for the future?"

Our second question was "Do you have a hobby?"

((CUT TO TD ON CAMERA))

TD: Our congratulations to Betty Posner for saying the secret word and winning two tickets to The Valley Forge Music Fair. Next time it might be your turn to say the secret word on Merck People.

For our last story, we go to Japan.

Figure 11.3 (continued)

((CUT TO FOOTAGE OF NEW LAB))	TD (VO): Recently, senior officers of Merck traveled to Menuma, Japan, 45 minutes northwest of Tokyo. There they took part in the dedication ceremony of our newest research lab.
((CUT TO EXTERIOR OF LAB))	Japan is the second largest pharmaceutical market in the world. In Japan, we are part of a joint venture with the Banyu Pharmaceutical Company, known as Nippon Merck-Banyu Co., Ltd.
((CUT TO HUSKEL EKAIREB SPEAKING AT CEREMONY))	
	The new laboratory is vital to the introduction of new products into Japan. The Japanese government requires extensive testing and often requires the company to replicate the findings of animal and clinical tests elsewhere in the world. So under strict controls, our products are analyzed and tested.
((SHOTS OF LAB TECHNICIAN))	The guests at the dedication saw a laboratory with some of the most modern technical equipment in operation. At a cost of $15,000,000, it's a sign of Merck's determination to be a leader in all of its worldwide markets.
((CUT TO ELECTRON MICROSCOPE))	Of course, a serious occasion will have its lighter moments too. At a reception following the dedication ceremony, there was the traditional opening of the barrel of sake.
((CUT TO SHOTS OF RECEPTION, CLOSE-UPS OF WOMEN IN KIMONO, AND BREAKING OF BARREL))	Sometimes our company officers don't know the amount of power they have!

Figure 11.3 (*continued*)

```
((CUT TO TD ON CAMERA))                    TD: This will be our last edition of
                                           Merck Focus until the Fall. We hope
                                           you've enjoyed them and we look for-
                                           ward to seeing you again in Sep-
                                           tember.

((ALL SHOTS FROM CEREMONY, JAPANESE        We'll close with the actual dedica-
MUSIC THROUGHOUT: WASHING OF HANDS,        tion ceremony of the laboratory in
HORAN OFFERS GIFTS, TRUCK SHOT OF          Menuma, Japan. It's an event full of
MSD OFFICERS, OFFERING OF SAKE.            custom and tradition -- a Shinto
EXTERIORS: GLOVES AND SCISSORS GIVEN       ceremony with symbols of nature and
TO HORAN AND JAPANESE OFFICERS,            ancestry.
CUTTING OF RIBBON AND RELEASE OF
DOVES.))

((FREEZE ON LAST FRAME. FADE TO
BLACK.))
```

Figure 11.3 (*continued*)

The television news service of the American Association of Retired Persons (AARP) is one of the most successful in the United States. Twice each week, stories important to older Americans are distributed by Medialink, a satellite communications brokerage firm that sends satellite feed times and script information on a special newswire and handles the details associated with distribution of these VNRs.

According to Medialink tracking surveys, Maturity Broadcast News stories have been viewed on local newscasts by more than 80 million people. Most of the stories are health and consumer related, but occasionally a feature is offered.

Figure 11.4 is a video news release prepared by Maturity Broadcast News and fed on the newswire mentioned previously. The format of this VNR is typical of those offered by other companies and organizations. Notice the distribution information at the top of figure 11.4. A suggested anchor lead-in encourages efficient processing and newsroom use. The words to be seen on the screen and heard on the tape during sound-on-tape (SOT) segments are provided on the script. The VNR in figure 11.4 also contains other elements: a suggested anchor tag read by the local newscaster to conclude the report, the video elements provided for this VNR, and the name of the person to contact if more details are needed.

Figure 11.4 illustrates how corporate and business clients can design messages to reach an "external" audience, one that is not employed by the company or organization. A VNR can inform interested consumers about the products or services offered in the marketplace or about an issue that may be of direct concern to them and to the company or organization.

```
                    RE-FEED DATE:   THURSDAY 8/1/91
                    RE-FEED TIME:   1:30 - 2:00 PM EDT

                 SATELLITE COORDINATES:
                    C-BAND: WESTAR 5/CHANNEL 22/AUDIO 6.2 & 6.8
          +++++++++++++++++++++++++++++++++++++++++++++++++++++++++++++++++

          SCRIPT:

          Suggested Lead:  Many frail elderly and physically disabled people are
          institutionalized too early because they need some help in daily living.
          But, as Peter Hackes reports, there is an alternative.  A federally funded
          program that can help those live independently.

          VIDEO                             AUDIO

                                            ANNCR V/O: Congregate housing can make a
                                            major difference in the lives of the frail
                                            elderly and physically disabled.

          S/PAULINE GRAY                    SOT GRAY:  "IT IS INDEPENDENT LIVING AND IT
          PROGRAM DIRECTOR                  DOES MAKE THEM FEEL GOOD ABOUT THEMSELVES."
          CONGREGATE HOUSING SERVICES
          PROGRAM, BALTIMORE CITY

                                            ANNCR V/O: The Congregate Housing Services
                                            Program is an alternative for people who
                                            might otherwise be put in a nursing home.
                                            The program provides affordable housing,
                                            usually an apartment, where residents live
                                            unsupervised but with help near by.

          S/PAULINE GRAY                    SOT GRAY:  "IT'S A GREAT BENEFIT BECAUSE YOU
                                            DO HAVE SOMEONE THERE WITH YOU AT ALL TIMES
                                            ... NOT SUPERVISION ... BUT THERE IS SOMEONE
                                            THERE DURING THE DAY TO MONITOR THEM."

                                            ANNCR V/O: Loretta Neal lives under The
                                            Congregate Housing Services Program at
                                            Primrose Place in Baltimore.

          S/LORETTA NEAL                    SOT NEAL:  "MOST PEOPLE GET SICK WHEN THEY'RE
          PROGRAM PARTICIPANT               OLDER.  I'VE BEEN SICK MOST OF MY LIFE.  AND
                                            I WAS TRYING TO RELEASE MY FAMILY FROM DOING
                                            SO MUCH WORK."

                                            ANNCR V/O: The federally funded program
                                            provides housekeeping and laundry services,
                                            personal care and three meals a day.  And if
                                            they can't get downstairs for a meal, food is
                                            brought to them.

          S/REBA WONDER                     SOT WONDER:  "I LOVE MY APARTMENT ... I LOVE
          PROGRAM PARTICIPANT               EVERYTHING THAT'S IN HERE."

                                            ANNCR V/O: Reba Wonder has lived at Primrose
                                            Place for six years.  She has had several
                                            knee surgeries and has a very tough time
                                            waling.  She's grateful for the independence
                                            that congregate housing has given her.

          S/REBA WONDER                     SOT WONDER:  "IF IT WASN'T FOR CONGREGATE ...
                                            MORE THAN LIKELY I WOULD BE IN A NURSING
                                            HOME."

                                            ANNCR V/O: I'm Peter Hackes reporting.

          Anchor Tag:  The Congregate Housing Services Program is funded by the
          Department of Housing and Urban Development.  The Senate has approved more
          funds for the program.  Final action by Congress is expected in the fall.

          Format:  2 Packages
                   SOTs
                   B-roll

          Produced by the American Association of Retired Persons

          FOR STORY INFORMATION, CONTACT:
          Ken Vest, AARP, 202-434-2576
```

Summary

This chapter examined how writers can design and prepare script material for instructional and corporate motion picture film and videotape presentations. It is important to participate actively in the design and scripting process so that specific objectives can be identified, agreed on, and then included in the final script. The standard script development process traced in chapter 3 can be used to generate material for such presentations. Writers and all others involved in such projects must rigorously evaluate each step in the design and scripting process. This kind of critical evaluation should result in insight about techniques that will produce even more effective presentations.

A bright future is predicted for these kinds of presentations. The optimism is based on developing technology. New transmission technologies are eliminating the costly and wasteful restrictions of conventional broadcast and nonbroadcast communications practices, thus permitting faster, more convenient, reliable, and more effective communications capabilities. Electronic mail, computer-based graphics and instructional systems, interactive cable systems, videodiscs, videocassette recorders, word processors, videotext, teletext, digital audio, and satellite teleconferencing have expanded the potential delivery system capabilities. As these and other delivery systems become even more accepted, the result is expected to be a savings in time and money, an increase in accessibility to material, a noticeable sense of unity in the presentation of such material, a more accurate and more efficient measurement of learning capabilities, and increased human productivity and interaction. The refinement of these delivery systems should expand the capability to present such material to individuals, as well as to small or large groups for various purposes in a variety of settings—in the home, at school, and in the work environment.

Suggested Exercises and Projects

1. Using the criteria described in this chapter, evaluate the effectiveness of three video presentations from your local library or media center, or evaluate three lessons from a telecourse offered for academic credit. Each presentation must concern instructional or corporate topics.

2. Obtain authorization from a nearby company, agency, or institution that regularly produces in-house corporate or instructional presentations to monitor the entire process involved in planning, designing, writing, producing, distributing, and evaluating one program or presentation. Maintain a logbook or diary of your observations and experiences. Accumulate written material used in the project. Note the changes and adjustments made at various stages of development. Report on your experiences.

3. A local department store needs a ten-to-fifteen-minute orientation presentation for new employees hired as general clerks. The store management wants to instill a sense of company pride in the employees and to show the basic skills required for these multifaceted jobs. These skills include stocking merchandise, using the cash register, handling credit card purchases, and completing an annual store inventory. Provide a *specific,* one-sentence statement of cognitive *or* psychomotor behavioral objectives for this presentation.

4. Write a one-page treatment for a presentation based on *one* of the following statements of objectives:

    a. After viewing this presentation, preschool children will be able to write on paper, in proper form, the numbers one through twenty.

    b. After viewing this presentation, field sales representatives of this company will be able to list on paper ten positive steps to increase sales of the new product line.

    c. On completion of this orientation program, nurses in this hospital will be able to correctly fill out standard inventory forms for medications issued to patients.

    d. After seeing this presentation, new cooks hired by this restaurant will be able to prepare properly the fifteen standard sandwiches offered to customers.

    e. After viewing this presentation, the assembly line factory workers of this company will be able to demonstrate the standard cardiopulmonary resuscitation techniques and procedures.

    f. After seeing this presentation, each employee will be able to list five steps the company has taken to improve employee morale.

5. In a few months, there will be a national conference of professional convention organizers, people who recommend locations for various kinds of business and trade association meetings. Prepare a one-page treatment for a two-to-four-minute videotape presentation promoting the merits of the nearest large city. This presentation would be used as a point-of-purchase video, shown continuously on large-screen monitors in a booth hosted by employees from this city's convention and visitors bureau.

6. After preparing the material specified in exercise 4 *or* 5, present a short (two-to-three-minute) oral presentation to a group serving as prospective clients for the presentation you have designed. During your presentation, fully explain one or two key sequences described in your treatment. Present the kind of material

suggested earlier for inclusion in the step or sequence outline. If possible, videotape your presentation and then evaluate its effectiveness.

7. Write a treatment and then a full-script for a fifteen-minute slide or videotape presentation that explains the goals and projects of an organization to which you belong. The target could be current or potential members of the organization or the general public.

8. For a course you are now taking or one that you have completed recently, write a treatment and then a full-script for a ten-to-fifteen minute instructional video module or segment focusing on one topic included in this course.

9. You have decided to start a video production service for amateur high school athletes interested in promoting their skills and abilities. These athletes hope to secure scholarship offers from colleges and universities. You intend to produce eight-to-twelve-minute videotape presentations customized for each athlete to use in contacts with recruiters. These recruiters often do not have travel time or funds to see athletes in remote locations or those who excel at sports other than football and basketball. Prepare a one-page treatment describing the content and structure you would recommend for such presentations. This treatment would be sent to high school athletes and coaches to encourage them to consider your new video production service. Be sure to select a good name for your company.

10. Prepare a full-script for a presentation based on the annual stockholders' report of a national company or organization.

11. Prepare a treatment and then the full-script for a series of short video presentations. There must be at least five presentations, each three to five minutes long. These presentations should show the basic skills and procedures associated with *one* of the following jobs:
    a. Cook at a local restaurant
    b. Waitress or waiter at a local restaurant
    c. Assembly line worker
    d. Poolside lifeguard
    e. Summer camp counselor
    f. Clerk in a convenience food store

12. Follow the steps, procedures, techniques, and recommendations contained in this chapter and design and write one presentation that would be appropriate for use by an area or a local business or company, school, nonprofit organization, hospital, or government agency. Determine the presentations' objectives, target audience, expected results, length (at least fifteen minutes), medium, uses, and so forth. Prepare a treatment and then the full-script.

13. Prepare a rundown sheet for a stand-alone, sixty-minute interactive satellite teleconference session for *one* of the following:
    a. A machine tool manufacturing company that wants to show new sales techniques to management and sales personnel assembled at sites nationwide
    b. A Colorado ski resort trying to entice prospective visitors who are gathered in motels and hotels in the South, Southeast, and Southwest
    c. A series of interviews with a well-known sports or entertainment celebrity who will respond to questions from reporters gathered in television studios in ten large cities throughout the country

Notes

1. Peg Slater, personal communication, 4 March 1991, Dallas, TX.
2. Rebecca Grimshaw Gardner, *High Feather Teacher Guide* (Albany, NY: New York State Education Department and The University of the State of New York, 1981), iii, v.
3. Yanna Kroyt Brandt, personal communication, 17 November 1982.
4. Gardner, p. 14.
5. Summarized from a Merck & Co., Inc., meeting agenda on internal video, 10 November 1980.

Dramas and Comedies

12

D ramatic principles are universal. They apply equally to dramas and comedies written for the stage and to those written for theatrical motion pictures, radio, and television. However, special techniques must be used when constructing a serious drama or devising a light comedy. The medium will also influence your approach.

This chapter will focus on the basic dramatic principles, with the understanding that they encompass both drama and comedy and that special techniques are used to apply these principles to various writing situations. The principles of writing dramas and comedies can be applied to many situations, including writing spot announcements, dramatic reenactments, role-playing exercises in instructional or corporate presentations, animation, and children's programs.

Unfortunately, the genius and inspiration needed for effective dramatic writing cannot be taught in a single chapter in a book such as this. Many years of training and practice are necessary to acquire the background and to perfect the skills needed by the successful dramatist. Many of the works listed in Appendix A focus on these special writing skills. What can be presented in this chapter are the basic principles of dramatic writing, the various steps used in generating dramatic script material, and the application of dramatic principles to specific writing situations. The emphasis will be on the fundamentals of dramatic writing for the electronic media, especially television.

Because of the length and nature of dramatic and comedic scripts, only excerpts from various kinds of dramas and comedies will be presented in this chapter to help you understand the basic principles and concepts and to cultivate dramatic insight and intuition. Because it is the scripting format used most often for dramas and comedies, review the standard one-column, full-script formats described and illustrated in chapter 3. Examine the application of these scripting formats to specific writing situations. Review figures 3.7, 3.8, 10.9, 10.10, and 11.2.

Sources of Dramas and Comedies

Ideas for dramas and comedies may come from any number of sources. The primary sources are incidents or situations, themes, settings, and characters. Although the original spark of a dramatic idea may originate from any one or a combination of these sources, you still must explore, expand, and focus that source. Relate it to other dramatic elements. Completely and consistently integrate the various elements into a strong and versatile premise for further dramatic development. Otherwise, the drama will fail to heighten and suspend reality for an audience.

The best ideas for dramas are those drawn from your personal experiences, observations, and consciousness. Ideas come from what you see, hear, read, and experience. It might be an emotion. It could be a word or phrase or even a piece of music that continues to ring with meaning long after it is heard. It could be a facial expression, a gesture, or even a mood that lingers in your consciousness. It might be a person or situation that makes you very angry, happy, melancholy, and so forth. It must be something that moves you emotionally and that you care about deeply.

Explore your curiosities, creative inclinations, and intuitions. Cultivate a sensitivity to the routine and mundane incidents of life so that you are able to recognize and then extract the essence of an important moment. Creatively filter these experiences and observations to extract the germ of a story idea. Prolific playwright Neil Simon indicates that story ideas "come from your own experiences, the sum total of who you are. Your brain, your personality is used as a filter so there is a little bit of you in everything you write."[1]

The more knowledgeable you are about the subject, the more enlightening and engaging the story can be. Your extra efforts in researching an unfamiliar subject and becoming engrossed in the mood and feelings of the settings, theme, and characters will pay dividends when you write the script. The reality and authenticity of each scene will shine through.

The story ideas, no matter what their source, are only the beginning of the dramatic writing process. Eventually these ideas must be expanded and crystallized so that the reality they reflect is compressed and rearranged to heighten the drama and intensify audience involvement. Transpose and condense your original source of inspiration into a vibrant, intense, and meaningful drama, with specific characters, concrete settings, and meaningful dialogue. Devote more time and energy to the planning and writing of the drama than to an analysis of how or why an idea was selected and developed.

Principal Elements of Drama

It is important to recognize and know how to use the principal elements, or components, of a drama. Each element fulfills a unique function, which, when combined with the other dramatic elements, produces a unity that is a mark of dramatic excellence. The elements within a drama must relate thoroughly and completely to each other to achieve a unity of action and impression for the audience.

The theme is the central idea of the drama, the moral of the story, the word **Theme** or phrase that best describes the central issue or problem posed by the dramatist. It is the underlying message, truth, conclusion, or thesis expressed by the writer in the specific terms of the script through the story and characters. The theme is the audience's intellectual conclusions about the drama based on the emotions displayed in the characters, dialogue, setting, plot, and story line.

An unlimited number of themes can be explored through a drama. Some dramatists reflect a wide range of themes in their work, whereas others explore the intricacies of a central theme in practically all their dramas. Eleanor Perry is perhaps most noted for dealing with the subjects of human disintegration and mental illness, as explored in her screenplays *David and Lisa* and *Diary of a Mad Housewife*. As a film writer, Carl Foreman, who endured the constraints and harsh realities of blacklisting in the early 1950s, concerned himself primarily with one major theme: individuals' struggles against the often hostile pressure of their environment. This theme is reflected in many of his screenplays—*Champion, The Men, High Noon, Guns of Navarone,* and *Bridge over the River Kwai.*

The themes expressed through dramas can range from the social and cultural, to the personal and interpersonal, to the philosophical and even the metaphysical. Paddy Chayefsky's teleplay and later screenplay entitled *Marty* explores the theme of self-image and self-realization through the character of a New York City butcher who comes to realize that he is not as ugly and undesirable as he had imagined or had been told by his friends and relatives. Tourist dollars is the theme used by Peter Benchley in *Jaws;* after brutal attacks on tourists by a great white shark, a police chief faces opposition from the mayor and townspeople when he tries to close a seaside resort's beaches just as a critical tourist season approaches. The motion picture *Grand Canyon* explored the futility of violence. *Shining Through* examined the need for human trust.

A theme is best expressed as an inseparable part of the fabric of the drama rather than as a blatant message that you impose on the script. The theme should be implicit in the characters and actions you have created. You should express the theme through the story rather than the other way around. If the story intrigues the audience, the theme will emerge—naturally, effectively, and memorably. The theme may serve as a point of departure as you write the script, but the story and its structure must dominate, providing bits of insight into the theme as the story progresses and characters develop. The theme should emerge and take shape for the audience through thoughtful and insightful reflection on the actions the central characters take to resolve their problems.

Some dramatists devise the theme before beginning the writing process. Others prefer to concentrate on constructing the drama and to allow the theme to take shape as the writing process continues. Once the theme is clearly focused, however, make certain that all dramatic elements contribute to the effective revelation of the theme. Nothing should remain in the drama that is extraneous to, inconsistent with, or detractive from the theme.

Taking the time to focus and limit the nature and scope of the theme will help you construct a plot involving strong emotional concerns that are important to the audience. The higher this level of emotional involvement, the more easily the audience will understand the theme, embrace its meanings, and individually act on its implications.

Setting

Setting indicates environment, backdrop, time, place, or locale. This dramatic concept can be broadly applied. Setting can be a particular country, region of a country, culture, era, life-style, neighborhood, socioeconomic group, time of day, holiday, time of year, and even type of physical environment—for instance, dusty, sandy, rainy, snowy, wet, dry.

The setting helps establish the mood, tone, and atmosphere of the drama. By identifying the particular surroundings in a drama you can refine script details and ultimately provide those extra insights that are unobtrusive but still important for total emotional involvement by the audience. The judicious selection and use of a dramatic setting help reinforce the theme, advance the action or plot of the story, and reveal characterizations convincingly and naturally.

A distinctive setting is an integral part of such television drama and comedy series as "Roots," "M*A*S*H," "Cheers," "Night Court," "Major Dad," "I'll Fly Away," and "Northern Exposure." Motion pictures that exemplify this dramatic element include *Dances with Wolves, New Jack City, Robin Hood: Prince of Thieves, Rocky, The Godfather,* the *Star Wars* trilogy, and the *Star Trek* series of adventures. Some dramas indicate, by their titles, their backdrop—for instance *Out of Africa, Havana,* and *Airport.*

Premise

The construction and eventual writing of a good drama begins with a good story; however, not all stories make good dramas. A worthwhile drama must actively involve the audience, who need to become emotionally absorbed in the action and reaction of identifiable characters to a set of progressively extenuating crises that test the characters' emotions and motivations. Each component must be present if a story is to be considered worthwhile as an engaging drama. When creating a drama or comedy, begin with a broad overview of the story and then progressively elaborate on the details with each succeeding step in the writing process until the story has blossomed into a finished script. The first step in the dramatic writing process is the formulation of the premise.

The premise is the basic story idea told in the fewest possible words from beginning to end. It tells what the story is about and presents the time and setting of the story. A complete premise statement describes who the central character, or protagonist, is; the protagonist's main goal or motivation; the conflict that develops between the protagonist and an opposing force; the principal complications or problems that provide actions, reactions, and progressive involvement; and the ways in which the main conflict will be resolved. The premise eventually might be reduced to one or two short sentences, as in the description of programs found in your local television listings, called a *log line*. The premise has also been labeled the synopsis, concept, and story line. Maybe the following could be the premise statement for the successful motion picture comedy *Tootsie:* an out-of-work actor successfully impersonates a woman, attains great success as an actress, and, as a man pretending to be a woman, simultaneously struggles to resolve relationships with others.

It is important to formulate a precise but complete premise statement. By doing so, you can begin to construct the essential dramatic conflict-development-resolution structure and point the way to later story development through the script. Only after you have identified the main character's major conflict can you develop the direction and tone of the story.

The premise helps shape the "spine" of the drama, which unifies and integrates all the story elements. Each moment, scene, sequence, act, piece of dialogue, and action in the script must be a part of this basic spine. Once formed, the premise provides the basis for constructing the story into effective dramatic form, eliminating extraneous elements, and developing those elements that will enlarge the premise. Unless you set up everything at this early stage, unnecessary complications and confusion will develop later when the script is written.

Dramatists use various techniques to devise the premise. Some search for even a tentative, or working, title for the drama. This helps capture the spirit and meaning of the story; for example, while the rest of his family travels to Europe at Christmas, a precocious boy is inadvertently left behind and faces the hazards of surviving *Home Alone*. Other writers select an incident, a general theme, a setting, or a character and then expand and refine that element through creative rearrangement; for example, a teenager is transported twenty years back in time, when his future parents were his age and he was not yet born—*Back to the Future*. Alfred Hitchcock's *The Birds* evolved out of a startling incident or situation: a small town is suddenly invaded by birds of all descriptions; as the townspeople struggle for survival against the birds, the drama intensifies through Hitchcock's unique style of character and plot development and sense of the macabre. Many writers use a variation of the "What would happen if . . . " approach. For example, what would happen if the residents of a rest home were to stumble into a scheme to retrieve items left behind by an alien force, material needed for life-sustaining systems by the *present* group of friendly aliens (*Cocoon*)? What would happen if a woman were to pretend to be a man pretending to be a woman, as in *Victor/Victoria?* Use this or a similar brainstorming technique if it helps you mold a basic story into a concise premise that displays solid dramatic developmental potential.

Once the premise is firmly in mind, a treatment can be developed more easily. The treatment will help you organize, expand, strengthen, and clarify the story premise. In the treatment, you can focus on the all-important plot and story line and the action of motivated characters. The treatment will help you check the quality of the story structure you envision and verify that each dramatic element captures the story's entire flow of action and features compelling conflict that eventually is resolved in a meaningful and dramatic climax. The treatment evolves from the premise. Review figures 3.1 and 3.7 for examples of a treatment and corresponding script for the same dramatic episode.

Plot

With the premise firmly established, you are in a better position to construct the plot. Experienced writers often formulate both the premise and plot simultaneously. Until the principles of dramatic writing are firmly in hand, however, it is best to separate the two steps.

There is a difference between premise and plot. A premise tells *what* happens. A plot tells *why* it happens. A premise tells the sequence of events, the chronological order of the story. A plot arranges the events of a story into a pattern that shows their relationships. A plot connects the events of a story to create a progressive intensity and involvement for the audience through action instigated by characters in a predetermined structure.

Plot is story construction, the blueprint on which the story is built. It constructs the protagonist's plan of action to reach a certain objective. It organizes the premise or story so that the central character confronts a problem that develops into an inevitable conflict with a strong opposing force. This force complicates the situation and presses the conflict into a major crisis that must be resolved by the protagonist in a final, climatic scene. As the protagonist struggles to achieve a predetermined goal, problems or complications develop. The protagonist must make decisions. Each decision produces a change in the situation, which causes even more urgent decisions to be made. This involves the protagonist even more deeply as the struggle progressively worsens. This is the kind of plot progression that produces conflict, suspense, intrigue, emotional involvement, and meaningful action. All are important components of strong dramatic structure.

The plot serves as the framework from which characters, events, and circumstances emerge and join in a conflict. It helps the audience participate mentally and emotionally in the drama as they anticipate events and developments. Devising a plot means building a structure, constructing a story. It means planning. This is the heart of the dramatist's work. Dramatic writing must evolve from this sense of structure and unity.

Following is one method you can use to examine the quality of the dramatic structure in the scripts you write. Read the first few pages of your script until the essential conflict is fully developed. Then skip to the closing scenes. Notice the final climax. Now move *backwards* in the script. Examine the plot, characters, settings, and other elements of dramatic structure. This approach will help you identify and use a variety of strategies when developing dramatic material. You will also gain a new perspective on the interaction of the dramatic "puzzle parts" of the plot as you unravel them from the end to the beginning of the drama.

Several approaches can be recommended for constructing the plot. Each approach works better for some dramatists than for others. Many writers use a combination of approaches or vary their approaches with the nature of the writing project and the premise. **Approaches**

One approach is to list the major problems to be faced by the protagonist and increase the frequency and intensity of these crisis points as the drama progresses until they culminate in the final confrontation and climax. Another approach is to identify the climax to be reached and then work backwards to ensure that each character's motivations and actions are completely logical and build progressively along the spine of the premise. Other writers prefer to set up the principal characters, the major problems they will face, and the crucial conflict that develops and then let the various dramatic elements interact to form the climax in a unique and creative manner. Playwright Neil Simon outlines the story in his mind, using only a few lines to describe the characters or setting. Then he lets the story take on a life of its own under his loose control. He has a basic plan when he writes, but he likes to be as surprised as the audience about what finally happens.[2]

The plot must be divided into three separate but related parts, or acts. However, this structure may not coincide with the unique commercial requirements of the electronic media, especially television. To accommodate the multiple commercial breaks needed within an hour, provide a dramatic high point and a natural pause in the progression of the plot. These commercial breaks may have to be artificially induced in the plot structure but should always be an outgrowth of the basic three-act plot framework. **Plot Structure**

The following is how the standard plot is structured into three acts:

Act I. The protagonist is introduced, establishes an objective or a goal, and faces a problem that develops into a conflict with an opposing force. The conflict intensifies as the protagonist attempts to solve the problem but fails.

Act II. The conflict deepens as the protagonist struggles to overcome the opposing force. Unexpected complications cause the problem to worsen, the protagonist's decisions to become more difficult, and the consequences to become more foreboding. A crisis is reached when the protagonist realizes that, unless the problem and conflict are resolved, disaster will result.

Act III. The protagonist takes extreme steps to alleviate the problem and the conflict, but instead they become even more insoluble. The protagonist makes one final, decisive choice that causes the conflict to come to a head and the problem to require a final resolution in the climax.

The plot must be organized into this basic framework. Each dramatic unit or element is a vital link in the plot chain, forming a definite pattern for the entire screenplay or teleplay. Each element must serve a specific function. Each scene must advance the plot; reveal character traits; develop conflict; and present specific crises, sometimes referred to as dramatic "beats," that grow naturally out of the plot. The scenes within a sequence must reveal even larger parts of the plot puzzle. The sequences within each act must provide a sense of unity and cohesion that heightens the audience's successful involvement in the plot and story line.

Plot Patterns

You can use various plot patterns and still remain within the basic framework of the standard plot structure outlined in the previous section. These plot patterns help you arrange or construct a story to heighten dramatic action, intensity, emotional impact, continuity, unity, and credibility. Use the plot pattern that helps you tell best the story you have devised.

The most common plot pattern is a simple, direct chronological arrangement. If the story is complex, however, or traces intricate biographical details, it could begin as the climax is forming and then, through the flashback technique, jump back in time to show the earlier complications that led up to the climax and then move on to the resolution of the main conflict. A multiple, or simultaneous, plot pattern presents different characters involved in separate plots, all linked to an underlying story line that is resolved at the end of the drama. It is difficult to sustain interest and continuity as the presentation alternates between the various story lines. The multiple, or simultaneous, plot pattern is evident in the motion picture *Fried Green Tomatoes* and in the television series "Northern Exposure." Under certain circumstances, you might use a combination of patterns to help develop the main plot.

Point of Departure

You must determine the point of departure, the point at which the story and the plot begin. This starting point is not arbitrary. It is determined by the nature of the story and how you want to unravel the plot. A story may be told in any number of ways. The plot pattern and the point of departure you use indicate the way you plan to tell a particular story.

The point of departure could be a startling or an intense action that upsets or alters an established balance of forces, as in *Raiders of the Lost Ark*. It could show a character already embroiled in a critical situation, as in *Star Wars*. It could present an unusual, perhaps confusing setting or character, as in science fiction dramas.

Whatever the point of departure, it must capture an important and critical moment in the drama. It must quickly establish the characters, story line, and emerging conflict. It should lay the foundation for the rest of the drama, signal the plot pattern to be used, and begin to establish the mood, tone, and pace of the plot.

Conflict

A primary component of compelling dramatic action is conflict, which is an opposition between two strong, incompatible forces. Conflict initiates the plot and develops the basic premise. Conflict is formed as the protagonist's goals are thwarted by an opposing force who places obstacles in the path.

The conflict between the protagonist and the opposing force must be drawn clearly, sharply, and deeply for the audience if you hope to justify the eventual resolution of the conflict in the climax.

The intensity of the conflict is determined by the nature and strength of the opposing forces. The audience must perceive that the main conflict involves crucial life and death issues and situations and believable characters struggling to survive. The more significant and threatening the conflict, the more the drama engages the audience's attention, interest, and involvement. Although one kind of conflict will dominate the plot, the protagonist will face and have to resolve any number of combined or related conflicts or confrontations that increase in intensity as the plot progresses.

In simplified form, dramatic conflicts can be categorized as the following:

a. *Individual versus individual.* Variations of this type of conflict are individual versus group and group versus group. Examples include the struggle between opposing athletes as they approach a crucial contest, as in *Chariots of Fire* and *Rocky;* the conflict between a forthright district attorney who battles the secretiveness of various people to unravel the details of a suspected conspiracy in a presidential assassination, as in *JFK;* and the struggle for power and control between two crime syndicates, as in *The Godfather.*

b. *Individual versus self.* Two or more opposing courses of action force a central character to make a final choice. Examples include a character's struggle to overcome dependence on Valium, as in the teleplay "I'm Dancing as Fast as I Can"; an ordinary hero's choice between the harsh responsibilities of the frontier military and the touching humanity of a Sioux tribe in the Dakota territory, as in *Dances with Wolves;* and the dilemma faced by a superhuman character who must choose between the love of a woman and the pledge to protect Earth from intergalactic archcriminals, as in *Superman II.*

c. *Individual versus systems and rules.* The protagonist may oppose established rules and restrictions imposed by organizations and systems. For example, *One Flew over the Cuckoo's Nest* is a study in conflict between an individual and a system that is supposed to help mentally ill patients. The plot of the motion picture *JFK* could also be viewed as a conflict between an individual and a system that imposes rules and presents roadblocks as a district attorney fights to gain access to documents and witnesses that will reveal who he thinks planned and completed a presidential assassination.

d. *Individual versus fate.* This kind of conflict could force a central character to face the wrath of nature or an unknown entity, as in *Predator, Alien, Terminator,* and *RoboCop.*

Several techniques can be suggested for developing strong and meaningful conflict in a drama:

a. *Clearly delineate characters* who have recognizable needs and goals and the capacity to overcome the complications presented.
b. *Place these characters into situations that are emotionally charged and that generate suspense, intrigue, and life-threatening danger.*
c. *Create in the audience a sense of urgent anticipation, concern, and curiosity about the problems faced by characters.*
d. *Heighten the conflict as the plot moves closer to the climax.* Make the audience emotionally cry out for the final resolution of the conflict.

Exposition

Another important component of plot development is exposition, or back story, which helps the audience understand and appreciate the protagonist's situation and the impact of current developments. It brings in other story details that fill in the gaps so the audience's emotional involvement can be intensified. Exposition helps give the plot greater significance and depth and makes events and characters more vivid and compelling.

Exposition should be woven into the fabric of the plot and revealed as a natural part of the characters' actions and dialogue. Exposition is needed at the beginning of the story but should not be given all at once. It should be imparted briefly, interestingly, and without undue distraction throughout the drama. It should fit naturally into the action of the plot and story line. Make the character giving this background information want to give it to a particular character who needs to receive it at that point in the plot. Make the audience need to have this background information to be temporarily satisfied emotionally. In effect, motivate exposition. Make it part of the protagonist's immediate problem. For example, in *The Empire Strikes Back,* Luke Skywalker learns that he is Darth Vader's son. This is not revealed earlier in the movie, when Luke is studying under Yoda at Dagobah or when Luke first confronts Darth Vader in battle. It happens in the final moments of an intense battle, when Darth is standing over Luke, who is hanging by only a few fingernails above a deep pit. This shocking revelation adds to Luke's absolute distress and intensifies the conflict between Luke and Darth.

Various devices can be used for dramatic exposition. Dialogue is used most often. On occasion, a reflective monologue might be effective. Exposition could be given by a narrator or by titles on the screen. A flashback sequence is another alternative; there is the danger, however, that, if prolonged, the flashback might temporarily slow the momentum of the plot, thus diminishing emotional involvement. In most dramatic and comedic television series, initial exposition is accomplished through a montage review of important characters and past developments during the opening credits, or even through the lyrics of the series theme song. Select the method in which exposition is presented based on the nature of the dramatic situation.

An important tool for plot development is preparation. It involves the technique of ''planting,'' or foreshadowing, later story and character developments so that they are believable and acceptable to the audience. Foreshadowing subtly prepares the audience through action or dialogue for what is to come so that, in retrospect, the audience can realize that the outcome was inevitable, that it could not have been otherwise, given the characters and circumstances established in the plot.

The audience and some dramatists often overlook subtle techniques of foreshadowing. It might be a brief, leering glance by a character that hints at a future romantic indiscretion. The twinge of a leg muscle during training could signal the eventual defeat of an athlete in a climactic marathon race. Foreshadowing is done throughout the progression of the plot so that the climax seems logical and, thus, acceptable to the audience.

Preparation

The climax is the final part of the drama, in which the conflict presented at the beginning of the story is finally resolved. The protagonist resolves the main conflict, which has progressively worsened throughout the story, and in the process makes a new discovery about himself or herself or about life in general. Both plot and character development culminate in the climax, reaching their peak at the same time. As they come together, the theme should emerge, since it is this new discovery by the protagonist that best reveals the theme of the story. The nature of the eventual resolution of the conflict in the climax must interrelate with the nature and capacity of the protagonist. This is revealed through characterization, which is discussed later in this chapter.

Climax

A subplot is a story line related to the main plot. It contains the same components as the main plot, conflict-development-resolution, but involves characters and situations in a different kind of conflict on a different level. Subplots add variety and interest, as well as reinforce the main plot. The number and use of subplots increase as a larger, more complex dramatic framework is formulated. Subplots should be identified and developed as part of the main story line; however, it should be possible to remove all subplot elements from a drama without disturbing the fabric of the main plot.

Subplots

The dramatist needs to recognize the importance and function of characters. For many in the audience, characters are the most interesting and memorable dramatic element. We are easily attracted to characters because of a natural desire to share their victories and defeats, to love or hate them, to embrace or reject them. Character development helps shape and reveal the story and plot and vice versa. In effect, they become fused, each influencing the other.

Each dramatic character must be shaped by a unique set of values and beliefs that determines what each character feels, thinks, says, and does. This uniform set of traits, revealed best in response to critical situations, determines identifiable goals that must be made clear to the audience. The goals or objectives of each character heighten the conflict, which moves the plot to its climax.

Characters

Components   Create and develop characters so that they fulfill the necessary dramatic functions. The following components of character delineation should be kept in mind:

a. *Characters must be based on reality.* Each character, especially central characters, should have a full, rich, and complete background and dimensionality. Nevertheless, only the essential portion of each character's background should be revealed in the dramatic script. All characters, to be accepted by the audience, must be credible. Thus, there should be a certain degree of vulnerability and uncertainty built into them. "Real" characters are not stereotyped. If turned upside down, a stereotype can be an interesting dramatic vehicle. Otherwise stereotypes should be avoided. For example, the character Lily in the television dramatic series "I'll Fly Away" is intelligent, caring, especially sensitive to the needs of children regardless of skin color, and forthright; she acts on her deep convictions and dispels the negative stereotypical characteristics of black women in 1950s America.

b. *Characters must be consistent.* Based on both revealed and concealed experiences, as well as the exigencies of the plot, each character must display traits that motivate actions that are logical and natural throughout the course of the drama. A character must act a certain way at a given point in the plot because of who or what that character is or is destined to become.

c. *Characters must develop or change.* Consistency should not mean stagnation. The dynamics of the plot require that each character develop or change and that this development be motivated by a unique set of traits and characteristics that has been logically and firmly established. Without progressive development in the plot and characters, you cannot hope to continually involve the audience.

d. *Characters must be distinguishable from each other.* Each character must be an individual, clearly identifiable by the audience. Although characters may be similar, they cannot be identical. Develop a point of view for each main character. Learn to see characters as *they* see themselves, rather than as you, the writer, see them. To do otherwise would be cheating the audience, who expect a rich, full, and varied set of characters.

e. *Characters must attract interest and involvement.* This is crucial to the potential success of the drama. Interest and involvement lead to caring about characters, wondering how they will cope with other characters and the constraints of the conflict. The audience will not necessarily like each character but should be interested and involved in his or her plight.

f. *Characters must have enough depth and dimension* to sustain the impact of the conflict, to struggle convincingly to resolve the conflict, and to move the plot and story line along to its appropriate resolution. Each character, especially central characters, must be multidimensional, flexible, versatile, and able to reflect a rich array of emotions and attitudes. There should be enough complexity and dimension to allow the audience to project their own interpretations of each character and to engender a certain measure of mystery and intrigue about each character. It is important to let the characters grow and expand to fill the void created by the plot's major problem and the resultant conflict.

g. *Characters must interrelate dynamically.* Interrelationships reveal how characters feel about themselves and about others, what they want, what they know and don't know, their emotions, their values, and their motives. It is this kind of information that brings a character to life and provides the proper environment and motivation for plot and character development.

h. *Characters must be goal centered.* Each character, especially the protagonist, must have a clear sense of direction throughout the drama. Each must have an identifiable goal or objective based on the attitudes and motivations displayed through the plot and story line.

Make use of several techniques to create and develop effective characters for a drama or comedy and to achieve the goals or components of character delineation just discussed:

Techniques

a. *Determine character goals and motivations.* Carefully analyze each major character. Briefly sketch fictional biographies of the principal characters to get a better feel for their emotional dimensions and motivations. Determine their predominant goals, values, attitudes, interests, and priorities. Determine how each character thinks, feels, acts, and reacts in each kind of scripted situation. In effect, get to know your characters well. Some writers develop a written character sketch or description for principal characters. This helps identify a character's primary problem or motivation, explains that character's function or role in the story, and points to particular physical characteristics that will help delineate each main character in the story.

b. *Emphasize key characteristics.* Characters must be dramatically heightened and condensed interpretations of reality. You might create a composite character, someone in the story who is constructed from several bits of reality from your own experience. You might combine a somber facial expression and a sordid family background here, an odd, penetrating laugh and a swaggering walk there. Select two or three primary characteristics for each character that are important and appropriate for the plot and story line. Emphasize and expand these dominant traits throughout the drama by revealing various dimensions in a number of situations.

c. *Place characters within the plot.* Characters are the primary movers of the plot. Their actions cause the plot to move to a climax. Plot and characterization must fuse to form a unified impression for the audience.

d. *Provide characterization through action.* The values and motivations of a character are best revealed by the instinctive and spontaneous manner in which that character reacts to emergency situations that impinge on the character's existence. Action is crucial to plot development. It is through action, reaction, and interrelationships that each character is brought to life for the audience and plays an important role in reaching the climax of the drama. Each character's actions must be compelled, either by the character's emotional drives or by an external force. Continually ask yourself, what would this character *do* in this situation? Explore the possibilities and then select an action that is based on established traits, that fulfills the needs of the plot, and that keeps the characters interesting for the audience.

Many dramatists evolve a central character and then let the plot or action develop out of the nature of this character. Examples of dramas in which the story, theme, dialogue, plot, and situations are formed more strongly by the characters than by any other dramatic element include *Dances with Wolves, Robin Hood: Prince of Thieves, The Rocketeer, Thelma and Louise,* the *Indiana Jones* trilogy, *The Boston Strangler, Patton, Bonnie and Clyde, Butch Cassidy and the Sundance Kid, Gandhi,* and *Tootsie.*

The creation and development of characters are interesting aspects of the dramatist's craft. Once the plot has been constructed, the writer paints in color and dimension and adds meaning and impact to the drama through rich, vivid characterizations. For many writers, the characters in a drama become real people—close, personal friends. In many cases, the writer struggles, along with the characters, to find the appropriate solution to the perplexing conflict that must be resolved. In the process, the characters, and the writer, make intriguing discoveries about themselves.

Dialogue

Dialogue is the words spoken by characters in a drama or comedy. It is an important dramatic element, since dialogue must be coordinated with the characters' actions and movements. Because screenplays and teleplays tend to emphasize visual elements, appropriate dialogue functions and techniques often are neglected or overlooked.

Dialogue serves several important functions in a drama:

a. *Provide insight into the scope and nature of the character speaking;* what a character says reveals his or her motivations, intentions, goals, priorities, feelings, emotions, and concerns; dialogue also reflects a character's personality nuances, education, life-style, and social standing

b. *Differentiate one character from another*

c. *Indicate a character's relationships with other characters*

d. *Provide the information necessary for the audience to understand and become progressively involved emotionally in the plot and story line*

e. *Link the words spoken by each character to the action and forward movement of the plot;* dialogue helps reveal the subtle shifts in a character's perceptions and attitudes that evolve as the plot develops; effective dialogue makes these changes believable in the audience's mind; plot is structure and movement realized through action, what characters do *and* say

f. *Unveil the theme;* each piece of dialogue, if written effectively, provides extra insight into the nuances of the theme

g. *Enrich the setting;* careful word selection can help reproduce the language and dramatic environment of an earlier time—for example, the 1940s in "Homefront" and *A League of Their Own* or the 1950s South in "I'll Fly Away."

h. *Create the rhythm, tempo, pace, and flow desired by the dramatist;* dialogue is an essential tool for creating and controlling the audience's perception of the mood and atmosphere of the drama

i. *Present refined language usage;* this would include unspoken implications, innuendoes, double entendres, and opposite meanings; a convenient term for such dialogue is "subtext"

To achieve the functions listed above, several techniques and approaches are recommended:

a. *Provide dialogue that compresses, concentrates, and distills the essence of real-life conversation.* Dialogue should reflect reality efficiently, directly, and economically by providing words that directly address those matters that are important to the plot and story line.

b. *Use natural pauses, hesitations, restatements, interruptions, incomplete phrases, and sentences to reflect natural conversation.*

c. *Create dialogue that matches the nature and intensity of the situation.* Some situations require more dialogue than others. Determine the goal of each character at every point in the plot and use this determination as a springboard to write appropriate dialogue.

d. *Make certain the dialogue is consistent with already established character traits.* Dialogue can help the audience begin to accept subtle changes in a character's attitudes and motivations, but this must be based on traits already revealed through previous action and dialogue.

e. *Listen to your characters.* Get in touch with them. Notice their distinctive speech patterns, vocabulary, sentence construction patterns, idiomatic expressions, and accents. Close familiarity with the characters in a drama allows you to let the characters seem to write their own dialogue, naturally and almost effortlessly.

f. *Take steps to reflect accurately the speech patterns of certain occupations, geographic regions, and periods of time.* Immerse yourself in the environment of characters that require special treatment. Then have someone familiar with each kind of character review and test your dialogue for authenticity, believability, and acceptability by the audience.

g. *Write leanly.* Use only enough words to advance the dramatic development of the story, plot, and characters. Five or six lines of dialogue, written within the space of the standard dialogue column width, should be sufficient. The use of more than six lines of uninterrupted dialogue should be reserved for special situations.

h. *Avoid providing too many dialogue interpretation notations in the script.* Provide motivated interaction between characters in each scripted situation. That should be sufficient for performer interpretation. Usually, an intelligent performer, under creative and sensitive direction, will properly interpret dialogue.

i. *Control pace and rhythm through dialogue.* Short, almost staccato dialogue tends to increase the tempo of a scene and the involvement of the audience. However, vary the length and frequency of the dialogue to provide variety and sustain interest.

j. *Whenever possible, substitute strong visualization for dialogue.* Powerful, meaningful pictures are better than distracting, ambiguous dialogue. Pictures provide more intense and lasting images.

k. *Choose words carefully* to provide both the explicit and the more important implicit meanings.

l. *Read the dialogue aloud.* Listen critically to the content, meanings, and implications of what each character says.

"L.A. Law"   Figure 12.1 shows the first few script pages from an "L.A. Law" episode entitled "He's a Crowd," written by David E. Kelley, executive producer of the series. Notice how the dialogue heightens the tension of the courtroom setting and intensifies the predicament of Edmonson, the character answering questions on the stand. Edmonson provides back story so that viewers can better understand his multiple personality disorder. Notice, too, the punch

L.A. LAW

"He's A Crowd"

FADE IN

1   INT. CRIMINAL COURT - DAY   1

The gallery is packed. Kuzak has GREG EDMONSON, forties, on the stand. ADA ZOEY CLEMMONS, late twenties, sits at the prosecuter's table. JUDGE MARY HARCOURT presides.

> **EDMONSON**
> It started when I was a teenager.
> I thought I was just hearing voices
> from people I didn't know or even
> see. I saw all kinds of doctors,
> but none of them could help.

> **KUZAK**
> How did they diagnose you?

> **EDMONSON**
> As a schizophrenic or a repressive
> psychotic, or just plain crazy.
> Finally, thirteen years ago, they
> discovered it was Multiple
> Personality Disorder.

> **KUZAK**
> How many personalities do you have?

> **EDMONSON**
> Originally, they brought out
> seventeen through the hypnosis.
> Through treatment, they've
> extinguished all but four.

> **KUZAK**
> Mr. Edmonson, I'd like for you to
> describe these four personalities
> for the court.

> **EDMONSON**
> Okay. Ninety-five percent of the
> time, I'm just me, Greg Edmonson.
> I went to college, where I studied
> musicology. I play the piano and
> the violin and I've worked for
> twelve years in a music store,
> tuning string instruments.

> **KUZAK**
> What about the others?

(CONTINUED)

Figure 12.1

Full-script for the first four pages in an "L.A. Law" episode.
Courtesy of Twentieth Century Fox Television and David E. Kelley.

1   CONTINUED: 1

                          EDMONSON
              There's Maxine. She's a midwife,
              in her fifties, she's been extremely
              latent for the last two years or
              so.

                          KUZAK
              Meaning she doesn't come out much?

                          EDMONSON
              Right. There's Allen Witt. He's
              the teacher. Intellectual,
              extremely well read, also a little
              arrogant. Then there's Sean.
              Angry. Psychotic. The reason I'm
              sitting here right now.

                          KUZAK
              Did Sean come out the night of
              August 9th, 1990?

                          EDMONSON
              I believe he did.

                          KUZAK
              Could you tell us what happened?

                          EDMONSON
              I was with my fiance, Sherril
              Eustis, having dinner at her place.
              Something was obviously bothering
              her, but I had no idea what. Then,
              to my shock, after dinner, she broke
              off our engagement.

                          KUZAK
              You didn't see this coming?

                          EDMONSON
              No. We'd talked out my problem so
              many times before, and I thought   *
              she'd accepted it.

                          KUZAK
              Sherril knew about your different
              personalities.

                          EDMONSON
              Oh yes, she'd <u>met</u> them all. In
              fact, intellectually, I think she
              was more intrigued by Allen than
              she was me.
                          (MORE)

                                             (CONTINUED)

              _____

Figure 12.1 (continued)

1   CONTINUED: (2)   1

                              EDMONSON (Cont'd)   *
                    Anyway, yes, she knew about my
                    illness and it wasn't an obstacle.
                    And then all of a sudden... she says
                    she can't be married to me.

                              KUZAK
                    How did you respond?

                              EDMONSON
                    I was devastated. I got very upset,
                    and I raised my voice. Then... the
                    next thing I remember... was seeing
                    her on the floor. Her um...
                         (this is difficult)
                    Her neck was all twisted. She'd
                    been strangled and... there was a
                    puncture mark on her throat and
                    there was blood everywhere.

                              KUZAK
                    She was dead.

                              EDMONSON
                    Yes.

                              KUZAK
                    What'd you do then?

                              EDMONSON
                    I called the police.

                              KUZAK
                    Mr. Edmonson. Do you know how
                    Sherril was killed?

                              EDMONSON
                    It had to be Sean. He comes out
                    sometimes when I get upset and...
                    Nobody else could've done something
                    like that. It was Sean.

                              KUZAK
                    I have nothing further.

          Kuzak returns. Clemmons rises.

                              CLEMMONS
                    Just before Sherril Eustis was
                    killed, she broke off her engagement
                    with you, right?

                                                      (CONTINUED)

_____

Figure 12.1 (*continued*)

1   CONTINUED: (3)   1

                            EDMONSON
                    Yes.

                            CLEMMONS
                    And just so we're clear.
                            (pointing)
                    These are the hands right here that
                    snapped her neck.

                            EDMONSON
                    Yes.

                            CLEMMONS
                    That's the thumb right there on your
                    left hand that punctured her throat.

                            EDMONSON
                    Yes.

                            CLEMMONS
                    And you're in here now, asking this
                    jury to set you free.

                            EDMONSON
                    I couldn't have done this. I loved
                    Sherril Eustis, Ms. Clemmons, she
                    was everything to me.

                            CLEMMONS
                    Exactly. And the very last thing
                    she did in life... was break your
                    heart.

            Off Edmonson, we

                                        SMASH CUT TO:

            MAIN TITLES

2   INT. CONFERENCE ROOM - DAY   2

            Staff meeting. Everybody getting settled. The room is
            jammed. Roxannne sits next to Brackman, under

                            BRACKMAN
                    Alright people, good turn out.
                    Let's begin. Roxanne?

                            ROXANNE
                    First up, People versus Edmonson.

                            BECKER
                    Hold on. Why is Roxanne here?

                                        (CONTINUED)

_____

Figure 12.1 (continued)

provided by Edmonson's short bursts of dialogue and how that helps illustrate the kind of character he is. Edmonson's testimony intensifies as the scene progresses. It becomes more difficult for him to talk about his situation. His character evolves, even within this first scene. Clemmons, the prosecutor, challenges Edmonson's testimony and provides an intense high point on which to conclude the prologue and begin the main story, after opening credits.

Principal Elements of Comedy

Humor and laughter are intensely personal experiences. The forms of humor are so diverse and the art of writing creative comedy so complex and intricate that it is difficult to provide universal concepts and techniques for all possible writing situations. The writer of comic material must develop a sense of timing and humor and must cultivate and nurture special kinds of skills to provide a unique perspective on the human condition. Successful comedy writers are grounded in sound dramatic principles and display a special instinct for the exaggeration of everyday human values, traits, mannerisms, and situations. No matter how well one understands the process of creating humor, it is the writer's skill, insight, experience, and comic instinct that determine the ultimate success of situation comedies, comic monologues, and comedy sketches in variety programs.

Nature of Comedy

Wit, comedy, and humor—terms used interchangeably by most writers—refer to forms of presentations that generally produce laughter and enduring pleasure for most audiences. What is funny? How does a writer know what will work in a given situation? The answer lies in the development of a sixth sense about the nature of comedy and the kind of stimuli that will compel an audience to respond in a certain way. The desired result could be a subtle, knowing, satirical response or a broad, obvious, raucous spurt of laughter. The writer must know the kind of response needed in a given situation and then create material to elicit that response from the audience.

Comedy implies different things to different people. Most agree that it reveals our basic human pretensions and absurdities in a pleasant, although often exaggerated way. Comedy unveils our common foibles and sensitivities. It is often impolite and even sacrilegious to established mores and traditions. It provides vicarious release from traditional restraints and constrictions, such as religion, authority figures, and patriotic representations. It allows us to share a few moments with a fellow human being, who struggles, as we do, with life's daily problems. In the process of enjoying comedy, if it is successful, we learn something about ourselves, our priorities, and our problems.

Experienced writers who create comedy material regularly trust their instincts rather than abstract knowledge about the nature of comedy. They know what works in a given situation because of their experience. They have searched and probed, failed and succeeded enough in previous writing assignments to project the kind of comedic mood necessary for a given time and situation. Trying to dissect the nature of comedy only to determine what makes us laugh results in a clinical approach that produces a mechanical, almost "plastic," form of humor. Memorable and creative comedy evolves naturally out of a potentially humorous situation featuring recognizable comedic characters.

Sources of Comedy

There are three primary sources of comedy material: situations, characters, and dialogue. Each source interrelates with the others to produce the final comic effort. The viability of each source depends on your sensitivity and comedic outlook on current mores, standards, and topical developments. Also, working with a team of writers, as is often done for situation comedy series, provides a sounding board for the development and refinement of noteworthy comedy. The "sources" of comedy expand when a group of writers works on a single project. A comedic idea suggested by one writer is enhanced by another until refinement is completed.

Situations

Many situations can be interpreted and presented in a humorous way. The family members and friends in the television comedy series "Evening Shade" and "Home Improvement" often cause perplexing situations to develop. These situations generate humor as the crises are resolved. Basil Fawlty, in the fine British comedy series "Fawlty Towers," often endures the inevitable consequences of his own false perceptions about various people and circumstances in and around his problem-laden hotel.

Another kind of situation with potentially humorous consequences involves reversed roles, in which one character takes over another character's life-style. Reversed expectations could also result from situations in which stereotypes based on age, sex, occupation, and so forth are turned upside down. For example, the audience might find it humorous if a kindly looking senior citizen, who moves more slowly than a turtle, suddenly were to unleash intricate karate moves against a mugger at a crowded bus stop.

Some humor is bizarre and broad in approach. Much of slapstick comedy is based on situations involving physical humor—for instance, slipping on a banana peel, falling into a lake, or hanging onto the edge of a building ledge by a few fingers. These and other situations are potential sources of comedy if developed creatively. Some humor is effective because of its incongruity or unanticipated switch when the punch of the humor becomes evident.

Much of today's television humor relies less on slapstick comedy or one-liners and gags and more on parody and satire. In a parody, the style of a well-known work or character is ridiculed or imitated for comic effect. In a satire, human and social customs or habits are spoofed. Both parody and satire use something that is currently popular and take it to an illogical extreme, usually through the exaggeration of situations and characters.

Characters

Much of the comedy that we enjoy is based on the attractiveness of individual comedic characters. Such famous comics as Buster Keaton, Charles Chaplin, Red Skelton, Sid Caesar, Milton Berle, Dick Van Dyke, and

Lucille Ball used their innate comedic gestures, facial expressions, and mannerisms to produce laughter for millions. Their intuitive comedic talent have provided many pleasant and memorable hours of entertainment.

Successful television situation comedies feature strong, identifiable characters who energize situations with humor. "Cheers" generates humor from the interaction within the odd assortment of characters who frequent the bar. Conflict and humor evolve naturally from the ensemble of characters in "Murphy Brown" and "Designing Women." Much of the humor of "Saturday Night Live" comes from the unusual group of characters and characterizations seen on regular segments.

Dialogue

To write comedy well, you must have a special ability to handle words. Dialogue tends to "drive" the comedic plot. You will have to be prepared to use various techniques to insert humor into scripts, including puns, parodies, spoofs, satire, irony, retorts, double entendres, dialects, odd speech patterns and habits, and the misuse of standard English.

Characters and dialogue form the heart of television situation comedies. They distinguish this comedic form from others, such as stand-up comedy and skit-based comedy. Characters and dialogue invigorate a potentially comedic situation and move the plot forward to its natural and humorous conclusion.

Principles of Comedy Writing

Effective comedy writing must be based on the principal dramatic elements described earlier: theme, setting, premise, plot, characters, and dialogue. These elements are universal, although their application varies for serious drama and for light comedy.

Prepare the audience for the humor that unfolds. Establish the comic mood early to avoid confusing the audience.

Occasionally you can mix humor with serious drama by using a delicate, sensitive approach. Several successful situation comedy series consistently tackle contemporary issues and themes and provide a few lighter moments as the severity and ridiculousness of the situation is dramatized. Series that have used this approach include "M*A*S*H," "Evening Shade," "Murphy Brown," and "Designing Women." Sometimes a light approach to a serious subject provides a new perspective for viewers that they had not yet considered.

Humor must evolve naturally and spontaneously from situations, characters, and dialogue. Add fullness, richness, and meaning to situations by analyzing each available element and determine what can be manipulated to interject humor as a natural outgrowth of a recognizable situation. You can also explore the irony that results when two or more situations or ideas that are not usually connected suddenly are allowed to intersect. If the comedy is natural and realistic, the laughter will follow.

The spontaneous nature of comedy must be tempered with exaggeration or understatement to provide the incongruity, contrast, and often absurdity that forms the basis for much humor. Comedy has a special meaning and impact when the audience suspends reality and accepts, even momentarily, the exaggeration or understatement of characters and situations. Notice how this was done in the motion picture *Hook.*

Much of the success of humor rests with the audience's sense of superiority over the comedy and comic characters. Audiences tend to savor the misfortunes that overcome others. There is a certain amount of sadistic satisfaction in watching a comic character struggle to overcome slightly exaggerated circumstances. We tend to empathize with characters who face our problems in a unique, humorous way. There is a fine line between providing only sadistic relief for an audience and providing an opportunity to see ourselves through the actions and words of others and to learn an important life lesson from that experience.

Just as in serious drama, comedy must build to a climax. The punch line, which may be verbal, visual, or both, often includes a surprise twist that fits the comedic situation but also provides a new and unexpected resolution of the situation. The laughter is a result of twisting the audience's expectations. The humor may be enhanced by topping the punch line with yet another, more humorous punch line.

Delaying the punch line or climax is an effective technique. Just when audience members think they have accurately anticipated the next action or line of dialogue, the climax can be delayed to produce an even richer comic moment. For example, in the motion picture *What's Up, Doc?* during the climactic chase scene, workers are carrying an oversized piece of glass across the street. Suddenly they must precariously balance their precious cargo as they dodge rapidly approaching vehicles. The viewers expect the glass to break, eventually, but they don't know when or how. The obvious does not happen. The speeding vehicles do not crash through the sheet of glass, as the audience would expect. Instead, just when it appears that the large piece of glass is safe, the last possible vehicle roars by and hits a ladder that supports a worker hanging a sign over the street. It is this innocent worker who crashes through the glass, producing a hearty delayed response from the audience. The inevitable happens, but in a fresh, creative way, enriching the comic moment for the audience.

Any number of devices can be used in comic plots. For example, an established character in a series can repeat a visual or verbal comic bit any number of times, with predictable results. This becomes a kind of comic shorthand for the writer and the audience. Examples include the promiscuity of Blanche or the naïveté of Rose in "The Golden Girls," the fastidiousness of Charles Winchester III in "M*A*S*H," and the cynicism of "Murphy Brown." The devices used to heighten and pace comic plots are discovered and perfected through observation, study, and experience.

"Who's the Boss?"

For eight seasons, "Who's the Boss?" anchored ABC-TV's Tuesday night primetime lineup; 199 episodes were produced by Columbia Pictures Television. The series helped launch several successful comedy series, which followed its time slot. This Blake Hunter and Martin Cohan creation spawned a duplicate program called "The Upper Hand," which became a top-rated British television comedy series.

Figure 12.2 shows the script for the opening scene from an early program in the "Who's the Boss?" series. Notice how characters begin to establish their identities and personalities through clever but meaningful dialogue and how the viewer can begin to sense the principal outlines of the story that is about to unfold. Although this initial scene does not advance the story line in an obvious manner, the scene is still important. Without it, the characters, setting, and problem that will soon develop would be less than believable. Few sentences could be shortened or deleted without making a noticeable cut in the content of the scene. Notice how the dialogue contributes to characterization, especially for Tony, who displays the fastidiousness and optimistic attitude that are the hallmarks of his character in the series.

Figure 3.8 illustrated a different type of comedy writing—the fast-paced, exaggerated, broad, and satirical humor that has become the hallmark of the popular television variety/comedy series "Hee Haw." This popular television comedy-variety program uses the same scripting format as "Who's the Boss?" The one-column *three*-camera full-script format shown in figures 3.8 and 12.2 is sometimes called the "taped" situation comedy scripting format, since the program is taped before an audience using multiple studio cameras. Figure 12.1 illustrated the one-column *one*-camera full-script format used for practically all television dramas and some situation comedies that are "filmed" using a single motion picture camera in a controlled production environment without an audience. If you write a television situation comedy script, be sure to determine the scripting format you need to use. The same cautionary comment can be applied to scripting formats used to write television dramas.

Electronic Media Applications

Despite the inherent value of dramatic and comedic principles, they must still be applied to practical writing situations in the electronic media. Several challenges must be faced: working under severe deadline pressure, where large amounts of money are at stake; maneuvering character and plot development to accommodate spot announcement breaks; establishing characters, settings, and plots quickly and securely because of time and budget constraints; and enhancing an established character in a continuing series and yet not exploiting stereotypes. These are some of the realities that you need to consider when writing dramatic and comedic material for the electronic media.

Radio

Although now very few radio drama and comedy scripts are written regularly, the young dramatist should not neglect this medium. Radio has been called the "theater of the imagination," because the writer is limited only by the listener's engaging imagination and willingness to creatively accept enhanced and suspended reality. Radio drama and comedy

"Briefless Encounter"

Figure 12.2
Sample pages from
a one-column
three-camera
full-script written for
the television series
"Who's the Boss?"
*Courtesy of Blake
Hunter, Martin Cohan,
and Columbia Pictures
Television.*

ACT ONE

SCENE ONE

FADE IN:

INT. KITCHEN - MORNING

(TONY IS AT THE STOVE. JONATHAN AND SAMANTHA

ARE AT THE TABLE. ANGELA IS READING THE PAPER)

                    TONY

          Sure you don't want breakfast, Angela?

                    ANGELA

          I've got breakfast...Juice and coffee.

          Listen to this. The Soviet arsenal

          has us outnumbered by...

(TURNS PAGE)

          Tony, there seems to be a hole in this

          story.

                    TONY

          I couldn't help myself. When you can

          get twenty-nine cents off a giant

          bottle of Window bright, you gotta go

          for it.

                    ANGELA

          Well, at least when they drop the big

          one, we'll be able to see it.

(RISES)

          Tony, when you finish up here, could I

          see you for a minute upstairs?

Figure 12.2 (*continued*)

TONY

You bet.

ANGELA

Eat your breakfast, kids.

(ANGELA EXITS)

TONY

And now, the Great Micelli will
demonstrate a feat of skill and
dexterity never before attempted in
this kitchen.

(TONY FLIPS A PANCAKE IN THE AIR)

(SAMANTHA AND JONATHAN APPLAUD)

Thank you, thank you. Now, let's have
a moment of silence for all the
pancakes who bit the dust while I was
perfecting this trick.

SAMANTHA

May they rest in everlasting maple
syrup.

JONATHAN

You guys are weird.

TONY

Okay, who wants seconds?

SAMANTHA

I'll have some, Daddy.

(TONY CROSSES AND SERVES THEM SECONDS)

Figure 12.2 (*continued*)

3.

SCENE 1

```
                        TONY
            Eat up.  Remember, there are people

            going hungry on the Scarsdale diet.

    (HE CROSSES TO STOVE)

            Well, duty calls.

    (HE EXITS)


    INT. LIVING ROOM

    (AS TONY CROSSES THE LIVING ROOM HE SPOTS

    A SMUDGE ON THE TABLE AND RUBS IT WITH HIS

    SLEEVE, THEN BOUNDS UPSTAIRS)

    CUT TO:
```

offer an interesting challenge to the writer in that there are virtually no time and place unity restrictions, and radio programs can be produced relatively quickly and inexpensively.

Dramatizations are often used as the presentational framework in radio commercials. The application of dramatic and comedic principles to the design and writing of radio commercials is discussed in chapter 4.

The basic dramaturgical concepts and principles apply to radio as well as to the other dramatic and comedic media; however, in radio, for the most part, subplots are avoided. Characters and the central plot are established quickly and early. The plot may have to be artificially enhanced to incorporate all the necessary dramatic components and to accommodate time and commercial constraints. Characters must be vividly created in the listener's mind and imagination. The number of characters in each scene and throughout the drama or comedy should be limited to help the listener differentiate among the various voices. Characters should speak each other's names often to reinforce identification. Dialogue is especially important; it should delineate characters and reveal changes and progressions in locales and plot development. Narration, along with music and sound effects, are basic tools to mark transitions, entrances and exits, and beginnings and endings of scenes and acts and to punctuate special dramatic moments or developments. Narration is an effective tool for providing exposition. The narrator could be one of the characters or an informed source separated from the characters and action of the story.

Because only sound is used in radio dramas and comedies, you can more easily focus the attention of the listener and, thus, control the various dramatic elements and their impact. Other media tend to bombard the senses and scatter the intensity and focus of each dramatic element. Television and motion pictures do exercise some control over audience focus, but by using both picture and sound. In radio, the sound dominates and projects the whole impact of the drama or comedy.

Television

When applying dramaturgical concepts to the television medium, certain special considerations must be observed. Stories must be structured into 30-, 60-, and 120-minute lengths, with the end of each multiple act providing a dramatic high point and a natural pause in the story line just prior to each commercial break. The television dramatist works under severe production, budget, and time constraints. The nature of television viewing precludes audience interaction in a meaningful and shared experience, as in a stage play. The number of characters and settings is limited, especially in regular series, because of the smaller screen size, the more intimate nature of the medium, and time and financial constraints that require concentration on a limited number of dramatic elements.

Despite these limitations, the television medium allows the dramatist to reveal the inner nature and intimate details of vital, human characters; to explore sensitive, personal, and contemporary themes and issues; and to create visual effects and impressions that would be impossible or difficult to execute in any other medium.

Regular Series

Regular or continuing television series feature the same central characters in separate and complete stories or episodes. Because viewers already know the primary settings and the backgrounds of the central characters, limited exposition is necessary. Main characters and ongoing conflicts have been established. You can focus on character and plot development.

Each week's episode focuses on a particular complication and conflict and shows how the regular series characters react in that situation. Conflict must be established early to attract and hold the audience and to accelerate the development of the plot. The identity and individuality of the series must be sustained through each script.

Sometimes story lines continue from week-to-week. This allows plots to enlarge and "mature" over several episodes. Characterizations can be enriched. A continuing story line is a scripting strategy commonly used for ratings, or sweeps, periods, during which regular series are "hyped" or enhanced to increase the size of the viewing audience. Even though the story line is spread over several episodes, each episode must provide the audience with a complete and satisfying story. Each episode must reach a dramatic high point and provide a conclusion for a conflict established earlier. However, each episode must also entice viewers to return to the story line or plot in the next episode and see how the characters resolve the rest of the conflicts that have developed.

"Cumulative narrative" is another technique often used in regular television series. When stories are written to continue from week-to-week, viewers experience them as more probable, more "realistic" than conventional, self-contained episodes. The action in one episode can have consequences in a later episode or string of later episodes.

Cumulative narrative can be a dramatically powerful and strikingly economical technique. It can produce a level of familiarity and intimacy that would not be reached otherwise. Characters can "remember" events from the fictional past. The past can play an active, significant role in the current plots in the series. Exposition can be accomplished efficiently while characters continue to evolve and progress along with the plot. Cumulative narrative helps reinforce the fabric of the series and the main characters. Each event resonates with the harmonics of a hundred other events in the fictional past. Despite this cross-referencing among characters and plots, each week's program is distinct yet grafted onto the body of the series, its characters' pasts.

Regular series are produced in thirty- or sixty-minute episodes. A thirty-minute program is written in two acts of approximately equal length, with a total story time of approximately twenty-three minutes. There may be a short prologue or teaser before the first act begins. (Review figures 12.1 and 12.2.) This opening vignette helps set up the story line for the episode and often provides an opportunity to bring together an ensemble cast just before the opening titles and theme music. A short epilogue or coda (tag) may be used after the second act concludes. Commercial breaks are inserted between each script segment—prologue, Act I, Act II, epilogue.

A sixty-minute program is written in four acts, with a total story time of about fifty-two minutes. Although there are no strict lengths for each act, in most cases Act I is twelve to fourteen minutes long, Act II ten minutes, Act III twelve minutes, and Act IV about sixteen minutes. Prologue and epilogue segments may also be used, with approximately one to three minutes allocated for each. It should be emphasized that the standard three-act plot structure described earlier remains intact no matter how many breaks are required because of commercial considerations.

Preparing script material for a regular television series is a special kind of writing experience. The series idea must be accepted by the network or distribution company, a pilot program may be produced and reviewed, and a limited number of episodes are ordered for production, generally not more than twenty-two and often as few as six episodes. A complex organization is established within the production company that produces the series, with various supervisory positions created for reviewing script material. These include story editor, executive story consultant, creative consultant, and script supervisor. Most of these people write scripts for the series. Networks now tend to hire successful producers who can also write effective scripts. These producer-writers help sustain the quality of a series concept as numerous episodes are produced over several years. Generally, in late spring, after a series has been approved or renewed for a season's run, this small group of people consult each other for a concentrated period of time (eight to fifteen days) to determine the various story lines or premises for the season's episodes. Then they scatter and write the individual scripts. They reassemble, polish each other's scripts, and make final decisions about other tentative premises for the few remaining episodes.

The free-lance writer has limited opportunities to write for regular series. If a writer is known to series coordinators, a first-draft full-script may be ordered after the initial idea is verbally pitched and accepted. An unknown writer may be permitted to submit a treatment but then probably will not write the full-script, even if the story idea is accepted for production. Time and budget constraints allow a narrow margin for error. Thus, producers and script coordinators tend to use writers who are known to them and who have a proven record of writing experience.

A serial features a complex array of characters involved in larger-than-life emotional entanglements and situations that continue to embroil them in a never-ending plot and story line. It is the type of drama that works well in both daytime and nighttime program schedules, on open-circuit as well as on cable systems. The serial resembles the novel in its dramatic form, style, and approach.

Serials

The serial, a durable dramatic form, continues to attract large and loyal followings. Loyal viewers read about their favorite serials and serial characters in various national publications. People use home videocassette recorders to tape the daily episodes they miss and arrange their lunch hours around viewing a favorite serial.

A number of reasons have been advanced for the continued success of serials: they provide an emotional catharsis for the audience, who seek escape from the cares and problems of everyday life; they satisfy a natural human curiosity and interest in the problems of other people; and they are an acceptable way to consider such vital issues and concerns as abortion, alcoholism, child abuse, narcotics, marital infidelity, and political intrigue. The characters and situations in serials often become a very real part of the viewers' daily lives.

The characters in a serial must be the kind with whom the audience can identify. They should have backgrounds and experiences that audience members envy. How the characters earn their livings and where they reside are not as important to viewers as the problems they confront and the personalities they encounter. The problems must be of an infinite variety. Characters must face obstacles of the most difficult sort in a strong, emotional manner. Interesting characters produce good stories.

Because of the number and complexity of the characters involved, and because of the emphasis placed on characters in a serial, it might be helpful to formulate a family tree, displaying the genealogy of the characters, along with brief descriptions of each one and essential interrelationships among them. This should help you develop the serial and distinguish the various characters.

In a serial, you must create a clever web of interlocking relationships. One character's actions, motivations, and complications should affect the lives and activities of other central characters. A number of stories and plots must be presented simultaneously to sustain audience interest and suspense. Just when a climax appears imminent, when a perplexing problem is about to be resolved, move to another character and another situation and leave the audience to wonder what finally happens. At a later time, often at a later point of development, this first story can be resumed and further complicated, but never resolved completely, and so the construction of an effective serial continues. As indicated earlier, some regular series also present simultaneous multiple story lines within the same episode.

The plots in a serial require special attention. Cumulative narrative techniques, described earlier, are often used in serials. Because a serial is a continuing dramatic series, many subplots and main plots must be developed simultaneously. Plots for daytime serials should be outlined, divided, and subdivided into the installments for each day and each week. Plots should unfold slowly with careful repetition, without making the events seem insignificant. There should never be a final climax to any plot but, rather, continuing complications that approach the crisis point at the end of each day's episode and especially at the end of each week. "Lead-in" and "lead-out" techniques help establish these sometimes artificial crisis points. A lead-in can be used at the beginning of a day's episode to recap the current situation. A lead-out provides a suspenseful preview of the next episode. To accomplish the purposes of either the lead-in or lead-out, an off-screen narrator or serial character can be used while excerpts from the appropriate serial episode are shown.

The dialogue in a serial must be slower, more deliberate, and more repetitious than in real life. More emphasis is placed on the spoken word than on the visual image so that the viewer need not be riveted to the television screen to follow plot and character development. The viewer should be able to hear the serial while performing personal or household tasks.

The locale in a serial often is a small, unrecognizable town or a generic urban area. Because of the professional backgrounds and occupations of a majority of the characters, the settings generally are doctors' or lawyers' offices, as well as hospitals, courtrooms, restaurants, and socially acceptable rooms in a typical home. Many serials use outdoor as well as indoor settings.

The continuing nature of a serial, featuring a relatively large group of central characters, requires that the writer accommodate tight time and production schedules by working from established, predetermined plot and character patterns; anticipate real-life situations, such as illnesses, contract disputes, and the death or introduction of characters; and write honest dialogue and strong emotional scenes to create intriguing and suspenseful plots and characters. Serial writers need special skills and abilities and generally work in a writing team to provide the necessary script material for thirty- and sixty-minute programs each weekday. Writing for a dramatic serial requires a lot of talent. It also requires planning, foresight, and the ability to write material consistently and rapidly under often severe time limitations.

A made-for-TV movie is like a theatrical motion picture release. Both are generally produced by independent production companies or studios. Most made-for-TV movies are two hours long and require seven acts written in approximately 105 full-script pages.

Long Forms

A mini-series presents a complete story in several installments over several hours and spread over several days or even weeks. Mini-series generally are either adaptations of novels or plays or special material written on a grand scale for television use. They are considered solid audience builders during crucial sweeps periods. One of the earliest and most successful mini-series, "Roots," attracted unusually large audiences when ABC-TV first broadcast the programs in primetime on eight consecutive nights.

Even though long-form dramas provide a broad canvas for the dramatist, basic dramatic concepts and standard scripting processes must be followed. There still must be a solid story premise forged into the framework of a tightly structured plot that features opposing forces engaged in a strong conflict resolved in a climax. A mini-series, however, does provide an opportunity to present exposition slowly and carefully, explore characters in depth, and enrich plot complications and settings. Long-form dramas generally require the scripting process outlined in chapters 3 and 11: proposal, treatment, teleplay or screenplay, and production or shooting script.

Made-for-TV movies and mini-series often are adaptations of dramatic material from other media. Adaptations are made primarily from novels and stage plays, but also from magazine and newspaper articles, short stories, and even cartoons and comic strips. One of the attractions of an adaptation is that the audience is already sold on the quality of the original work. A major consideration for the adapter is how closely the adaptation should be based on the original work's characters, theme, mood, tone, plot, and settings.

Adaptations

The adapter's challenge is to transpose the original work to the new medium with as much fidelity, sensitivity, and skill as possible, making adjustments to accommodate special requirements. The unique characteristics of the new medium must be used to the fullest. It is best to retain the key elements and to capture the creative and artistic spark of the original work, and then skillfully transpose these elements to the new medium, allowing additional creative dimensions to emerge and be explored. Try to maintain the dramatic integrity of the original work. This is more difficult when long narrative passages must be transposed into engaging action and dialogue, or when a major character or event must be eliminated or formed into a composite because of time or production requirements.

Following are the steps recommended for writing adaptations:

1. Select an original work that, after creative development, will retain its original "personality" but still enjoy an enhanced sense of unity, meaning, and dramatic power because of the transposition to the new medium. Determine if the original work has enough potential and substance to endure the rigors of developing the property into an electronic media presentation. For example, can action and characters be added or deleted without disrupting the basic spine of the story? What adjustments may be needed for the main plot and the subplots? Can main characters be maintained in the adaptation? Are there strong visual possibilities? Notice how well the spine of the basic story remained intact but how subplots and characters were added when *Steel Magnolias* was adapted from a stage play to a motion picture.
2. Secure copyright clearance to use the original work.
3. Become thoroughly familiar with the original work as though it were your own. Clearly identify and critically analyze the plot, characters, dialogue, settings, theme, conflicts, exposition, and other major dramatic elements. Determine what will have to be done to transpose the original work effectively to the new medium. Carefully outline the story by scenes and sequences and then combine, change, eliminate, or add dramatic elements as needed to make the adaptation interesting, effective, and viable. Plan your changes and modifications as fastidiously as though you were developing an original drama.
4. Follow the standard scripting development process outlined earlier to focus and plan the adaptation.
5. Write the first and subsequent drafts of the adaptation script.
6. Evaluate the impact and effectiveness of the adaptation to the new medium.

If the original work needs to be lengthened, as in adaptations of a one-act play or a short story, carefully expand the number and type of characters and situations. Although the central conflict should be retained, you must add new crises and complications to further heighten the plot and story line. In effect, the original work must be expanded, but always in keeping with the essential spirit, style, and quality of the original work and always with the purpose of increasing the audience's emotional involvement in the story, the conflict, and the characters.

If the original work needs to be shortened, as in adaptations of a three-act stage play or a novel, you face a different kind of challenge. Each time a character is eliminated or a scene is dropped, the story line and plot are affected. Determine what realistically can be eliminated from the original work and still provide an effective presentation in the new medium. The cutting process can begin by eliminating all or most of the subplots, condensing crucial scenes and eliminating extraneous scenes, forming composite characters to represent various supporting characters, beginning the story at a later point of departure, and providing dialogue or strong visual sequences to replace lengthy narration or character introspections in the original work. Understanding the essential feeling and emotion of the original work will guide you when deciding what to eliminate and how to shorten the drama or comedy. If, after making all reasonable efforts to condense the original work, you determine that a disjointed, almost patchwork, adaptation will result, then it is time to rethink the process and consider using the flavor and emotion of the original work but creating an entirely new plot and story line. This decision places you outside the realm of adaptation and back into the creation of an original drama or comedy.

Docudramas

Docudramas present dramatized versions of real events and persons based on reenactment and fictional reconstructions. They are a hybrid presentation form that combines the background and content of the traditional documentary with the often more attractive and startling presentation form of the drama. The docudrama presents the audience with the sense of real events and persons reappearing in a contrived and manipulated presentation.

The docudrama offers several interesting challenges. Original events and persons must be presented in a believable way. Additional material may have to be created to fulfill dramatic requirements and to present a full and interesting story. There is an extra burden of creating and sustaining suspense and intrigue, since the audience usually knows the final outcome of the story. If the docudrama is based on well-known characters and events, you do not have the luxury of surprising the audience, as in an original drama. Your greatest challenge is to interpret reality in a creative and believable way and to provide a simple, direct, interesting, and dramatically sound story line. Television has been the primary medium for a number of memorable docudramas.

Although ethical questions are raised by the presentation of real events and persons in a fictional format, such as a docudrama, audiences continue to be drawn to these presentations. The ethical writer must be sure to take dramatic license only when necessary and that events and persons included in a docudrama have been verified through extensive research.

Scripting Development Checklist

For drama and comedy, the writing process begins with a story idea, or premise. This is expanded on in various kinds of written or verbal presentations—proposals, treatments, first and subsequent drafts of the teleplay or screenplay, and finally a shooting or production script. For lengthy dramas, a ten-to-twenty-page outline or summary leads to a more detailed treatment or sequence outline, and finally to a full-script for production. The script must be assessed at each stage of development and adjusted before progressing to the next level. Review chapters 3 and 11 for illustrations of the contents of the key scripting formats used in script development for dramas and comedies.

Following this scripting development process allows the novice dramatist to progressively examine key elements of the drama or comedy and to make adjustments at various preliminary stages rather than as the final draft script pages are written and when changes usually are more difficult and expensive to accomplish. Experienced writers may combine or bypass one or more of these creative stages.

As you prepare script material for a drama or comedy in progressively more specific forms, ask yourself a series of questions to test the value and quality of your work. Such questions summarize the dramatic principles discussed in this chapter. The following questions can be posed at each stage of scripting development.

General

Is there justification for everything that happens in the drama or comedy?

Is there consistent, internal logic in the story?

What elements should be added or subtracted to heighten and intensify plot and character development?

Theme and Setting

Does the theme emerge clearly and naturally through the characters' actions?

Are the settings established quickly and clearly, and are they dramatically relevant to and helpful in the development of the characters and plot?

Premise

From the premise, does a sense of the main story line begin to emerge and the central characters begin to take form?

Does the premise help determine or identify the evolution of the main characters?

From the established premise, can you imagine the jeopardy main characters will face and the conflicts that will develop between the characters?

Plot

Is the spine of the story reflected in the effective development and progression of the plot?

To heighten dramatic impact, are there scenes that could be eliminated, shortened, or added? What are these ''soft'' spots? How can they be improved?

Does each scene (sequence, act) have a beginning, middle, and end or climax; reveal character; join the conflict; and move the plot forward?

Does each scene build on the previous scene and lead logically, naturally, and effectively into the next scene?

Point of Departure

Does the story begin at the ideal point to engage the audience and heighten emotional involvement?

Does it begin at a crucial emotional moment that is clearly established as important to the protagonist and other central characters?

From whose point of view is the story presented—first-person narrator, third-person protagonist, or multiple viewpoints switching from one character to another throughout the story?

Conflict

Are the protagonist's goals clear and meaningful?

Are the protagonist's opposing forces clearly identified, sufficiently strong, and meaningfully important to frustrate the protagonist's goals?

Is the central conflict significant enough or sufficient to interest the audience?

Does the central conflict emerge clearly, progressively, and early enough to create anticipation and intrigue for the audience?

Does the conflict worsen as the plot develops?

Can you identify the crucial scene in which the conflict reaches its ultimate intensity and in which the protagonist is forced finally to resolve the conflict? How can the dramatic value of this scene be improved?

Climax

Is the climax reached at the end of the plot and not prematurely?

Is the climax clearly, logically, and naturally related to the crises and complications presented earlier? Is it on the ''spine'' of the story?

How can you intensify the climax, make it more compelling?

Exposition and Preparation

Is the backstory creatively and unobtrusively woven into the main fabric of the story line?

Is there too little or too much exposition?

Has there been sufficient and appropriate preparation early in the drama or comedy that permits the audience to clearly connect what is revealed later with what was presented earlier?

Are the exposition and preparation crucial to the progressive development of the plot and essential to forming and resolving the central conflict?

Subplots

How many subplots are there? Do they relate to the central plot?

Could the subplots be removed from the drama or comedy without serious loss to or deterioration of the ''spine'' of the story?

Are the subplots resolved effectively as the main plot is resolved?

Are there unnecessary incidents or meaningless subplots that do not advance the development of the main plot?

Characters

Is each character unique, believable, and consistently developed?

Is there meaningful motivation for the major actions of each character?

Are character interrelationships drawn clearly and compellingly?

Do all the characters concern themselves in some way with the central conflict and its resolution?

Do the characters lack empathy, or are they developed so that the audience will care about what happens to them?

Are there too may characters or characters that serve no significant purpose in the development of the plot, the central conflict, or the main characters?

Dialogue

Is the individuality of each character expressed through the dialogue?

Is the dialogue based on conversational speech, and does it reflect unique dialogue characteristics?

Would it be impossible to transfer the lines from one character to another character?

Is dialogue used effectively to present exposition and preparation and to move the plot along to the climax?

Audience

Why will the audience be attracted to this drama or comedy within the first five minutes?

What specific dramatic elements and techniques have you used to progressively sustain and heighten emotional involvement?

What specifically can be done to increase audience anxiety, anticipation, suspense, and intrigue?

Unity and Change

Are changes in mood, flow, pace, and tempo logically motivated and effectively executed?

Does the plot display structural unity?

What are the high and low points in the plot development?

Track the intensity level of the plot. Does it continually increase?

Are there scenes that need more evident conflict and action?

Are there too many intense moments that strain credibility and exhaust audience participation and involvement?

Practical Mechanics

Is the script material in proper professional form?

Is the script visually dynamic and descriptive?

Have only essential visual and aural notations been included to provide a meaningful perception of the drama or comedy?

Is the script realistically producible for the intended market (television series, made-for-TV movie, theatrical motion picture, etc.)?

Suggested Exercises and Projects

1. From your own background and experience, list three story ideas for each of the following sources of dramas and comedies: situations or incidents, themes, settings, characters. Explain why you believe each idea is the starting point for an effective drama or comedy script.

2. Prepare a treatment for a one-hour radio or television drama based on one of the following themes or backgrounds:
   a. World War II
   b. France in the 1920s
   c. Colonial America
   d. courage and pride
   e. self-preservation
   f. fear

3. Prepare a one-page treatment based on *one* of the following premises or log lines:
   a. After determining that she is pregnant, an unwed sixteen-year-old hitchhikes to Los Angeles to start a life on her own with her child.
   b. A forty-year-old woman decides to finish her college education after raising three children and surviving the shock of a recent divorce.
   c. A video game fanatic is drafted to help save the universe against intergalactic invaders that are difficult to detect with ordinary human skills.

4. Record one of the following presentations and then write a critique in which you analyze and evaluate its theme, setting, story premise, plot, characters, and dialogue based on the discussion and the script development checklist presented in this chapter: a television situation comedy series episode, a television drama series episode, a made-for-TV movie, a television mini-series episode, or a theatrical motion picture shown on television.

5. Describe four examples of both exposition and preparation that you have seen recently in television dramas and comedies. Briefly explain why each was either well or poorly handled by the writer.

6. In a one- or two-page narrative, provide a character sketch or profile that describes the principal traits, motivations, physical features, and dramatic functions of *one* of the following, and then indicate how you would reveal and develop these characteristics in a dramatic or comedy script:
   a. The Terminator
   b. Indiana Jones
   c. Captain Kirk (from ''Star Trek'')
   d. Rocky Balboa
   e. Mary Poppins
   f. The Teenage Mutant Ninja Turtles
   g. Blondie
   h. Napoleon
7. Write the full-script for a few scenes in which the traits described in exercise 6 are revealed and developed.
8. Evaluate the dialogue given to two characters in the *same* drama or comedy program that you watch and record (if possible). Comment on the dialogue's content, word choices, sentence structure, length, rhythm, and pacing. Focus on the dialogue and not necessarily on the performance of the actor or actress who delivered it.
9. After receiving permission, observe and, if possible, record a conversation in a natural social setting or situation. Based on this conversation, write a full-script for a dramatic or comedy scene in which you heighten the conversation by using meaningful and purposeful dialogue.
10. Write a treatment for an episode of a current regular television network drama or comedy series.
11. Write the full-script for the first few scenes in the episode outlined in exercise 10.
12. Watch all episodes of one daytime television serial for one week. Describe the plot and character developments in the week's programs. Follow the same process, but four weeks later. Compare both weeks' plot and character developments. Then, for this same serial, write the full-script for the first few scenes that you would expect to see the next week (week #5). Compare your script suggestions to what was *actually* done on-the-air.
13. Prepare a treatment for an original made-for-TV movie. Write the full-script for the first three to five scenes of this movie.
14. Write the full-script for a thirty-minute radio or television drama or comedy program adapted from a short story or one-act play.

15. Prepare the treatment for an adaptation of a novel to a television mini-series consisting of three two-hour episodes seen on consecutive nights. As you outline each episode, accommodate twelve minutes of commercials each hour, plus teasers, transitions, and tags. Indicate how you would develop the theme, setting, story line, plot, subplots, characters, and dialogue.

16. Prepare a treatment for a one-hour radio or television docudrama based on a significant and recent news event. Include the following in your treatment: your sources of research, the chronology of events, and the principal people involved.

17. Work with others in a team to create a four-to-six-minute dramatic or comedic sequence or segment for a television music/variety program or a corporate training presentation. Provide a one-page treatment, as well as the full-script for this sequence or segment. An oral pitch could be done to help explain your scripting ideas. If possible, produce on tape a rehearsal of the full-script, using team members as performers. Critique the script material.

Notes

1. Neil Simon, quoted from the PBS television series *Screenwriters/Word into Image,* 1982.
2. Simon.

Professional Writing Opportunities in the Electronic Media

13

T he telecommunications industry continues to expand and develop beyond even the most optimistic projections. This rapid technological development creates an even greater demand for writers who can meet or exceed the expectations and challenges of this burgeoning industry. No matter what technological changes occur in the future, writers with talent, initiative, commitment, and flexibility will always be in demand.

This chapter provides an overview of professional writing opportunities. The writing marketplace will be examined to identify the kinds of employment available, as well as the areas of specialization and the potential for income and advancement. Emphasis will be placed on how to market your writing talent—setting realistic and challenging goals, developing contacts, preparing effective résumés and script samples, handling personal job interviews and script conferences, pitching story ideas and projects, working with agents who can help market your creative efforts, and guilds and unions that enhance your professional writing development. The business aspects of writing will be examined, with particular attention to protecting your material and avoiding common legal problems associated with a writing career.

This discussion will provide essential information on writing career development. The works listed in Appendix A contain more complete discussions of various aspects of professional writing opportunities.

Before learning how to apply for professional writing opportunities, it would be useful to review the qualifications of the writer and the role and function of the writer in chapter 1. This review will help you assess your interests and abilities as a writer and to use these assessments when applying for writing jobs.

To succeed as a writer in today's competitive marketplace, you will need to know the categories of employment and the areas of specialization that can help you advance in your work and increase your income potential.

The Writing Marketplace

Categories of Employment

There are three employment categories of work as a writer in the electronic media:

a. *Staff writers.* Staff writers work in-house for weekly or monthly wages on projects assigned by a studio, broadcast facility, or production company.

b. *Free-lance writers.* Free-lance writers submit script material on speculation without assurance of pay, prior acceptance, or continued employment. Free-lancers must line up clients in advance and overlap projects to maintain their reputations, livelihoods, and sanity. A successful free-lance writer has had enough writing experience to handle a variety of writing assignments and to know the difficulties that may be encountered in the marketplace. Such a writer has productive work habits. A free-lance writer must work consistently well, often under extreme deadline pressure, to produce quality material on deadline and without direct supervision.

c. *Contract or commissioned writers.* These writers receive prior approval and guaranteed pay for work done on a specific project. Although contract writers do not enjoy the economic and employment stability of staff writers, they are on more solid ground than free-lancers, since signed contracts assure that commissioned writers receive payment for the work done, even if the script material is never used.

Many writers have abandoned the restrictive ''writer'' classification in favor of increasingly common hyphenated designations—writer-director, writer-producer, or even writer-producer-director. There are several reasons for this development. Writers who combine their primary function with another generally make more money; they can also exercise more control over the production of the scripts they write. Writers have often expressed frustration because, once their scripts are finished and turned over for production, their basic concepts can be altered considerably without any recourse. Writers serving in two or more functions, however, can make certain that the original ideas and emotions expressed in their scripts are brought to life just as they visualized. A writer can assume a combination of responsibilities only after many years of experience and only after some assurance that he or she is ready. These hyphenated designations, especially that of writer-producer, have caused television production costs to increase dramatically. This is particularly noticeable when teams of writer-producers create, sustain, and creatively control a hit situation comedy show week after week for network or off-network program distribution.

Areas of Specialization

There are many professional opportunities for writers working in the electronic media. Some require minimal writing experience, whereas others necessitate an extensive background in a very narrow writing specialty. These opportunities exist in various kinds of facilities and systems—local broadcast stations, production and program syndication companies, networks, cable systems, advertising agencies, private businesses and corporations, charitable and service enterprises, and governmental agencies.

What follows is a profile of the employment opportunities young writers should consider. Experienced writers can consider a broader range of writing options. If a particular writing specialty interests you, review the chapter in this book in which this writing specialty is examined in detail. Also read a few of the works listed for this specialty in Appendix A. The more you know about the special writing areas that interest you, the better you will be able to assess your professional writing options.

If you are interested in creating copy for commercials and public service announcements, consider such prospective employers as advertising agencies, broadcast stations, charitable and public service organizations, and governmental agencies. Advertising agency work is difficult, if not impossible, to find as a young writer. You will have a better chance if your background includes both print and broadcast copy work. As a young writer, it is more productive to work for a commercial retail client, a nonprofit organization, a newspaper, or a radio or television station before attempting to land a job at an advertising agency.

Advertising Copy

Practically all the prospective employers listed earlier require writers for various kinds of promotion and public relations material. Again, a solid background in writing for the print media is helpful, because it demonstrates flexibility and diversity to a prospective employer. In a broadcast station or network, writers generate promotional announcements for on-air programs but also are expected to handle news releases, design handbills or billboards, prepare sales presentations, conduct facility tours, and perform many other jobs. This kind of work requires someone with a wide-ranging background and diverse professional interests.

Promotion and Public Relations Work

There are numerous subspecialties within this classification: general news and sports writers and specialists in business, consumerism, agriculture, health, meteorology, and documentary and investigative reporting. Each requires a specialized educational background, as well as extensive writing experience. Most require production as well as writing and reporting experience. One way for the young writer to acquire the necessary experience is to work full- or part-time in a small commercial or noncommercial broadcast station or cable facility, perhaps as a reporter or newsroom intern on either a paid or an unpaid basis. Networks and production companies often need temporary assistants for special news, sports, or information-related projects; however, the competition for these jobs is fierce.

News-Sports-Information-Related Specialties

Industrial and Corporate Presentations

Many private companies and businesses maintain a staff of writers and production personnel to handle in-house sales and marketing presentations, training programs, promotional campaigns, and internal and external corporate communications. Experienced radio and television journalists prepare electronic news releases for corporations and other types of companies and organizations. The influx of these broadcast journalists is expected to produce noticeable effects on the types and quality of business-related material generated for electronic media newsrooms.

In this business-oriented environment, writers often serve a variety of functions because of staff shortages and the need to consolidate the production and decision-making processes. It would be beneficial to be familiar with basic management systems and techniques, as well as emerging technologies applied to corporate presentation situations. Generally an extensive business background is helpful but certainly not required for such writing-production positions. However, diverse writing background *is* necessary.

Experienced writers find this work interesting and challenging and discover that it can lead to even more responsible positions in middle and upper management within an organization. Staff positions are common. Free-lance and contract work preparing corporate media presentations is also available.

Educational and Instructional Opportunities

School systems, medical facilities, public radio and television stations and networks, production companies, governmental agencies, religious groups, and other kinds of organizations need writers for educational and instructional material. Although some staff writing positions are available, much of this kind of work is done on a free-lance or contract basis. Combined responsibilities are common.

Drama and Comedy Writing

Drama and comedy writing is not a specialty the young writer should contemplate before acquiring considerable experience, background, and training. It is a tough, demanding job because of the kinds of pressures the writer faces and the special kinds of writing skills required to succeed (see chapter 12). Because of the nature of the work, the writer eventually will have to obtain representation by a literary agent, join a guild or union, and consider relocating to a major production center, such as southern California.

Scripts for ongoing television series are written by experienced staff, free-lance, and contract writers. Most series scripts are staff written. Submitting unsolicited scripts on speculation is not the best route for the beginning writer to follow. The material will not be read because of time pressures and legal constraints, but also because similar story ideas may have been developed by writers whose talents are known by the series producer and who are available for the crucial phone calls, story conferences, and memos that are all part of this kind of writing work.

Instead of writing a speculative script for a series that may or may not be renewed next season, it would be best for the young writer to generate an original comedy or drama, perhaps for made-for-TV or mini-series development or for a pilot program. This kind of script allows young writers creative flexibility to demonstrate their ability to produce quality material without the requirement that they incorporate a cast of continuing characters or predetermined locations or situations in a tightly written, easily marketable script.

A small percentage of writers work on serials, generally on a contractual basis for a designated period of time. The writing team consists of one or two highly experienced head writers and four to ten dialogue writers. This is a very specialized writing area. It requires extensive dramatic writing experience and a firm grounding in dramatic techniques in order to withstand the pressures of daily deadlines. It is unlikely that a young writer will be involved in writing a serial until he or she has acquired substantial experience and has cultivated significant contacts within the writing community.

There is another approach you should consider to demonstrate your ability to write effective dramatic or comedic material. Show your mastery of dramatic principles when you write a spot announcement that uses a dramatized presentation format. You might also write a comedy sketch or segment for a music/variety or magazine program intended for general entertainment audiences or instructional/corporate presentations. Perhaps you could demonstrate your ability to heighten a dramatic situation or add effective humor in an animation or a role-playing segment for an instructional or a corporate script. All these are short writing assignments that require little time to complete, yet they effectively demonstrate your grasp of effective dramatic and comedic principles and techniques.

Other Opportunities

There are many other kinds of writing opportunities to consider. These require unique writing skills and combined responsibilities. Some of these opportunities include writing music and variety programs for radio or television stations, networks, and production and syndication companies; developing game shows for network or syndication use; preparing news- or sports-related special events coverage; writing treatments and scripts for animation projects, such as cartoons, theatrical motion picture features, and television series and commercials; and working as a writer-producer-host for a talk or magazine program produced by a local station, network, or independent production company. Positions of combined responsibilities generally require sound writing, production, and performance skills.

Each professional writing opportunity must be considered carefully. Determine what is available and then pursue the kind of work that interests you most and will lead to a predetermined writing goal or objective. Each assignment you take should sharpen your skills and perceptions and enhance your writing craft.

Income and Advancement

It is difficult to generalize about income and advancement potential. Much depends on your talent and initiative. A bright, talented writer can earn a lucrative wage and advance quickly to more prestigious and complex writing work. Other young writers struggle to remain in their first writing job.

Several factors can influence how much you earn and how quickly you advance to larger, more challenging writing projects: your personal and professional goals; the kind of writing you do—your specialty; the job titles and responsibilities you have had (entry-level, intermediate, experienced); your current geographic location and your willingness to relocate; the size of the cities and production companies where you have worked; the reputations of the companies that have employed you; the reputation and recognition of your previous work; and your professional flexibility and diversity, as well as your years of writing experience.

In general, the smaller the market or facility in which you work, the lower the wages and the more limited the chances for advancement. However, at a small station or production facility, you have more opportunities to write a wide range of material and, thus, to acquire broad writing experience. Generally television and motion picture work pays more than radio work.

Several sources can provide information about salaries and advancement opportunities. Many of the trade publications listed in Appendix B regularly report the results of national salary surveys. Most of these publications also include employment want-ads in the back of each issue. Many of the professional organizations listed in Appendix C offer placement services to members and, in some cases, nonmembers. Those now working in the industry are your best source of *local* salary and job placement information when you are just beginning your career in the electronic media. Other sources are suggested later in this chapter.

Marketing Your Writing Talent

Writing high-quality, marketable script material is important but only the first step on the road to becoming a professional writer. No matter how good your writing, others still must see your work and become convinced that you have the necessary skills and background to work as a professional writer. It is advisable to develop a strategy to market your writing talent. This strategy should involve setting realistic goals; making professional contacts; preparing sample script material and often a résumé; and surviving job interviews, sessions in which story ideas and projects are pitched, and script conferences in which the depth of your writing ability is explored. Some writers may need the services of an agent, a guild, or a union. Developing a marketing strategy for your writing talent requires thoughtful planning and persistent execution.

Goals and Timetables

Your professional goals should be set down in writing. They should include decisions on such matters as your geographic preferences and requirements, your writing specialties and interests, and your writing ambitions. You should reevaluate these goals periodically to reflect changes in your interests, opportunities, and employment patterns.

Devise a realistic timetable to accomplish each goal. How long do you plan to remain in the first writing job you have identified? How long in the second and third jobs? What kinds of professional developments would alter your timetable? What are your two-, five-, and ten-year career plans? How long will it take to reach your ultimate goals? You should thoughtfully consider these and other questions before developing your professional writing timetable.

Set realistic professional goals. Learn how to find information *locally* about writing job opportunities. With the help of a guidance counselor, an instructor, or a school placement service, prepare yourself for the job application process. Do not become discouraged when your initial job applications do not pay off with firm job offers for work that you really want to do for pay that is beyond your expectations. Be prepared to search long and hard for jobs that may actually *combine* writing work with other specialties, such as production, operations, or management. Be prepared to work long hours for very low pay. Unfortunately, writing work does not pay as well as other specialties. Too many young professionals share your enthusiasm for this special field. Employers generally have many applicants for a limited number of jobs, but that is why you must always try to be the best writer you can be. When you get that first job, learn as much as you can about *all* the departments around you. Explore new employment possibilities that you perhaps had not considered. When you feel you have learned as much as you can in your first job, take the steps necessary to find the next job and move forward in your career.

It is important for you to cultivate and maintain personal contacts within the telecommunications industry. Who you know and the kind of work you have done often will determine whether you get an assignment for a special program or whether you are added to the writing staff of a broadcast station or production company.

Contacts

There are several ways to establish contacts within the industry. Various kinds of media directories list the names of individuals and companies in various geographic areas that may be interested in your work; ask a reference librarian for assistance in locating and using such reference works as *Standard Directory of Advertising Agencies* (often called ''the Agency Red Book'') and companion works entitled *Standard Directory of Advertisers* and *Broadcasting & Cable Market Place.* Many organizations listed in Appendix C offer placement services that often prove beneficial, and Appendix B lists periodicals and trade press publications that can provide potential job contacts. Subscribe to the publications and participate in the professional associations that best match your writing objectives and interests, and respond to the job opportunities offered. Stay in touch with those with whom you have worked in the past; often they move to new, more responsible positions and could be of assistance to you. You might have friends or relatives who know influential people you need to contact. Literary agents are essential for some kinds of writing work.

Résumés

Although a discussion of the steps involved in preparing a professional résumé is beyond the scope of this book, numerous books and pamphlets are available that provide the basic information you need to prepare an effective professional résumé. Consult your local library, your university placement center, or a professional employment agency. When applying for many beginning writing jobs, especially at broadcast stations, networks, and production houses, a résumé is just as much a part of the application process as the presentation of writing samples.

Script Samples

The best way to get work as a writer is to write something to present to a prospective employer. If you have identified a specific writing career objective, prepare several samples of your creative work in this area. You can draw samples from previous work in writing classes, but retype the script material in proper form and do not include the comments made on the original scripts. You could create scripts for existing products, services, programs, or personalities, or you could invent your own within realistic limits. You might volunteer to write script material for a public service agency, a nonprofit group, or a local or state government agency. Work with them as a client, as though you are already a full-fledged professional writer. Do it on a speculation, nonpaying basis, if necessary.

Whatever script material you prepare, make certain it represents only your best work. Your scripts present you and your standards of professionalism to the prospective employer. The important thing is to demonstrate that you have the ability and resourcefulness to produce quality creative script material.

You may want to consider compiling script material into a portfolio with recent samples of your work. This is a common practice for writers of commercials, public service announcements, promotional copy, editorials, commentaries, corporate and instructional presentations, and news and sports copy. You could use acetate-covered black pages to display your work or place each script in a separate file folder, clearly labeled and briefly explained.

Interviews

Many staff writing positions require a personal interview before employment can be secured. Other kinds of writing jobs bypass this step until the new writer is already hired. In either case, knowing what employment interviews are supposed to accomplish and how to conduct yourself in such situations are important considerations. A more complete discussion of this subject is available from career counselors and various career planning books and pamphlets.

Employment interviews serve two primary purposes, each equally important: (1) to convey information about your qualifications that will convince the prospective employer to hire you for a specific job and (2) to uncover as much information as possible about the job opening and the person you would be working with so that you can determine whether this is the job for you and if the interviewer is the type of person for whom you can work happily, creatively, and productively.

Set up an interview with the individual responsible for hiring. Learn as much as possible about your prospective employer's needs, problems, interests, and concerns. Give some thought to how you would respond to specific questions you might be asked. Prepare to discuss your professional attitudes and standards.

Make the interview situation as pleasant and productive as possible. Once the interview begins, be alert for opportunities to discuss your professional background and interests. Talk about the quality and diversity of your writing. Indicate that you are interested in becoming an active part of a creative and challenging experience, that you have the qualifications needed to produce solid, professional script material. Diplomatically convince the interviewer that you can think creatively, that you can put these creative ideas in proper form on paper, that your scripts are commercially viable, that you are aware of the demands and pressures placed on the writer, and that you work well under these conditions. Respond to questions briefly and directly, but always fortify your answers with all the positive information about yourself and your work that you can muster. Cite specific examples of your successful past performance to illustrate your points. Try to use each question as a springboard to uncover more information about you and your writing experience. Remember not to oversell yourself or talk too much. Your goal should be to have a friendly discussion that provides a full understanding of your qualifications and of the duties included in the job offered. Be certain to ask specific questions about the job—duties, wages, standards, and so on.

After the interview, leave something behind—your business card (if you have one), your résumé, a writing sample—anything that can remind the employer about your visit and how to contact you. As you leave, express your appreciation for the interview. Follow up with a short note, thanking the interviewer for his or her time and consideration.

Maintain contact with the prospective employer. If a decision on an opening is still pending, phone or write the employer and provide additional information or comments that may have been overlooked or inadequately discussed in the interview. At the same time, stress your strong interest in the job and confidence in your ability to produce the caliber of script material needed. When looking for work, especially as a writer, persistence and tenacity are important to achieve success—a job.

Pitching

A pitch is a verbal, in-person presentation in which a writer describes script ideas and concepts in a condensed but positive manner to secure approval for a project. For an episodic television program, for example, the writer presents, in five or ten minutes, a compressed version of the story line, complete with a description of the major characters, main conflict, setting, resolution of the conflict, and so forth. A motion picture concept can be pitched in ten to twenty minutes, depending on how complex the story is. Pitches for concepts for program series or multiple-part productions require more time.

When

When or if you pitch script ideas depends on the type of project. For an episodic television series, the pitch usually occurs after submitting a script to the producer. Generally the producer has an in-house reader make an initial assessment of your script. If it passes this first review, the associate producer or story editor reads the script and then recommends your material to the series producer. If the producer likes what you have written, you are called in to pitch your story idea. Script ideas for feature motion pictures follow a similar set of review steps.

Proposals for program series generally begin as a verbal pitch. Game show proposals, for example, may be written but generally are first presented in a verbal pitch to a production company representative, a packager (who pulls together the various components needed to produce the show), or occasionally to a network programming representative, if the production company or packager generates the game show concept. A master script for the programs in the game show series may be written long after the pitch has been heard and the series approved and produced.

Some instructional or corporate presentations use a combination of written and verbal pitch approaches. Verbal pitches tend to supplement and follow the presentation of written script material.

Pitches are used practically every day in newsrooms across the country. In routine story idea sessions, assignment editors, producers, and news directors listen to ideas pitched by reporters and photographers, who try to convince those who make daily news assignments about the news value of stories they want to cover. Documentaries and investigative reports begin as ideas pitched in similar sessions. The financial and on-air time commitments needed for the completion of these kinds of projects hinge on the persuasiveness of reporters, photographers, writers, and producers who have to convince newsroom supervisors that a particular idea will result in a program or series of programs that will generate large audiences and enhance the reputation of the news operation.

Why

There are many reasons verbal pitches are used as a preliminary or replacement step for written script material, especially for dramatic and large-budget television or motion picture productions:

a. *In a pitch, listeners can achieve consensus on key concepts and interact with the writer* in a way that is not possible with sheets of paper.
b. *The collaborative nature of television and motion picture production requires agreement about the treatment of a subject.* This includes the tone, structure, and pace of a presentation.
c. *Pitches can be used to explore the practicality of an idea or a concept in terms of time and money.*
d. *Pitches can help determine if an idea meets or exceeds the audience needs* that have been identified and accepted.

e. *Producers want assurance that ideas can be stated in terms simplistic enough to be grasped by the target audience or be accepted by advertisers or backers for funding.*

f. *Pitches also help producers remain flexible in expressing preferences for script ideas and development.* Producers often fear that outright rejection of a script will preclude another opportunity to review a potentially viable script idea.

g. *Time constraints preclude many producers from reading, rather than hearing, about an idea.* Many producers simply prefer to hear about a script idea rather than read about it.

h. *The basic concepts of many programs and presentations can easily be expressed in a few sentences, so why not use a short pitch to outline the idea?*

Whatever the reasons, you must be prepared to pitch script ideas. The effectiveness of this verbal, personal presentation is just as important for the acceptance of an idea as the final written script. With practice, you can make the transition from writer to creative pitch presenter with a minimum of trauma.

How

Accepting the inevitability of occasionally pitching your ideas is the first step; preparing yourself and your pitch is the next. What steps should you take to prepare a pitch for one of your ideas? What would help make a pitch effective enough to secure a contract or commitment to write a script? How do you determine what to include and what to leave out of a pitch? How can you develop an accurate and a complete yet brief description of your idea and still express your commitment to and excitement about its viability?

The variations must always be considered; however, let's trace the steps normally used to pitch script ideas for screenplays and teleplays. With modification, this process can be applied to pitches for other types of writing projects. Following are the *steps to take to prepare a solid pitch* for teleplays and screenplays:

1. *Review your script idea carefully.* Identify its strengths and weaknesses. Be sure the story is well constructed and clear in your mind.

2. *List sequentially the important elements of your story.* Tell your story in only a few sentences.

3. *Put away the list for one day.* Now toss out the elements that are not absolutely essential to telling your story.

4. *Write or type your final list of key elements.* Use this list to prepare your pitch. Some writers find that ideas are placed firmly in mind when written on a page with a pencil or pen.

5. *Practice the pitch alone.* If possible, tape your pitch. Pay attention to the way your voice sounds and the way you look during your presentation.

6. *Find ways to make your pitch entertaining as well as informative.* Gesture. Stress a key scene or character: act out the parts of the major characters in one key scene.
7. *Try your pitch on someone.* Pitch the idea to those who have read the script as well as to those who haven't.
8. *Get feedback.* You need an honest appraisal not only of your performance but also of the quality of the story information you provided.
9. *Polish.* Refine your approach until you have developed an effective routine that will create a strong, positive feeling about your story idea. Practice enough to strengthen your pitch, but not so much that you become bored with your own story and convey that boredom in your pitch when it *really* counts.

Following are a few *suggestions that will help you deliver an effective pitch:*

a. *Know the marketplace.* Be aware of ideas and concepts currently receiving acceptance and funding.
b. *Know the preferences of the person or company representative* who will hear your pitch. Some projects are easier to sell than others. By doing your homework, you will know the ideas that are best to pitch and the approaches that are likely to secure a writing contract.
c. *Select key points* to pitch a specific idea to a specific person. Focus on one or two key elements. You might emphasize the story line, the characters, the setting, or the target audience.
d. *Identify and exploit the hook for your idea.* If your story is more of a character study, stress what makes that character interesting and be sure to tell what eventually happens to him or her. Maybe the setting should be emphasized to stress exotic locales.
e. *Demonstrate that your idea is feasible* and will produce the anticipated results.
f. *Make your pitch interesting while you do it and memorable after you have left.* Make your pitch vivid and colorful. Inject humor when appropriate. Practice becoming a good storyteller. To ensure that their pitches are delivered in a sincere and friendly manner, during a pitch some writers pretend they are telling a story to a friend.
g. *Put your full energy and enthusiasm into painting a vivid and compelling word picture.* Be animated in your facial expressions and gestures.
h. *Be loud enough to be easily heard.*
i. *Maintain solid eye contact.*
j. *Keep an open posture.* Avoid folding your arms or turning your back on the person hearing your pitch.

k. *Learn to adjust your pitch as you receive visual and verbal feedback.* Watch for subtle body language indications of how your pitch is being received. If you see signs of boredom, move quickly to recapture the lost attention by speeding things up or by changing your tone of voice or body position—anything to get back on track. If you see confusion, pause for a moment; maybe a question will eliminate the confusion.

l. During your pitch or after your presentation, *accept comments graciously and productively.* Be secure about the soundness of your original idea. Readily accept any changes that do not disrupt the key elements in your original concept. Suggest alternatives if the changes dilute the quality of your original idea. Build on the comments offered. Compromise on a few points, if necessary, to achieve your overall vision.

m. For corporate or instructional presentation pitches, especially, *consider using visual or aural material to help illustrate a particular look or sound* that is crucial to your concept. Potential clients for nonfiction productions appreciate the clarity provided by music or sound effects, photographs, slides, or graphics presented in a style you are considering. Be aware that you have less flexibility to adjust your ideas when you present such items during a pitch.

Despite your best efforts to convince someone that your idea is truly worthwhile and that you should be hired to write script material for this project, your idea may be rejected outright or perhaps a short time after your pitch. Be prepared to pitch at least three or four ideas, approaches, or projects you can explain easily and convincingly. Have enough ideas in mind to demonstrate your flexibility and versatility, but limit the number of ideas you present to show that you are confident about the quality of your work.

Your success as a writer will be determined not only by how well you write scripts, but also by how well you sell yourself and your material. Good pitching techniques can be learned and can even be enjoyable because you will be selling something you believe in: yourself and your scripts.

Script Conferences

After a story idea or project has been pitched and accepted for production, script conferences help refine the approach that will be used to write the final script. The key elements can be identified and a plan established to incorporate those elements in the final draft of the script.

Script conferences are sessions in which an attempt is made to improve the quality of a writer's work. They are a part of the marketing effort by writers of dramas, comedies, advertising copy, animation projects, editorials, and commentaries, as well as industrial, educational, instructional, and corporate presentations.

Ideally the person coordinating such sessions thoroughly understands the writing and production process; clearly knows what is needed and desirable; expresses views freely, clearly, and persuasively; and makes the necessary decisions about script changes within a reasonable amount of time. Unfortunately, this ideal person is not always in attendance.

At a script conference, follow these suggestions:

a. *Come prepared.* Know the script well. Anticipate questions and problems. Evaluate the material from as many perspectives as possible.
b. *Be ready to talk about the script.* People prefer to hear rather than read about a script idea or concept.
c. *Answer questions simply and directly.*
d. *Be prepared to make compromises and incorporate new ideas* that may not always turn out to be the best but often must be considered to gain acceptance and continued development of a script.
e. *Be a professional at all times,* no matter how inane the comments or questions.
f. *Keep the mood of the session light but productive.*
g. *Know when to stop.* Determine when major ideas and suggestions have been made and then make an obvious move to exit. Many writers have successfully developed what has been called the ''door knob'' technique—one final, fleeting, loosely constructed idea tossed out as the writer reaches the door to leave the room. Often these vaguely formed ideas are readily accepted, then enthusiastically developed, and eventually produced.

Agents

An agent is an intermediary between the writer and the prospective buyers of the script. An agent markets a writer's scripts or services and negotiates prices and contract terms. An agent relies on personal contacts, experience, and a thorough knowledge of current marketplace demands and trends to service writer clients. For the effort, an agent receives 10 percent of a writer's earnings. Literary agents, who should be bonded and licensed, are needed by writers of dramas and comedies, as well as major productions mounted by large broadcast facilities, networks, and syndication production companies.

If you need the services of an agent, write to a few agents whose names and addresses can be supplied by the Writers Guild of America (see Appendix C). Agents willing to represent young writers are indicated by an asterisk on the WGA list. If you know a professional writer who is willing to recommend you, obtain this endorsement and have this writer contact the prospective agent on your behalf. When writing to an unknown agent, introduce yourself. Briefly explain your writing interests and goals and stress that you are serious about writing as a professional career. In a few sentences, describe the script material you have prepared and request that a program material release form be sent so you can send your treatments, proposals, story ideas, or scripts. Include a self-addressed stamped envelope for the agent's response. If no response is received in about four weeks, write again and remind the agent about your previous correspondence. If there is still no response after a few months, try other agents. Be persistent.

Agents are looking for promising writing talent as well as marketable script material written in proper form. Agents tend to favor clients who will regularly provide solid money-makers. High-quality, productive writing clients enhance an agent's reputation and income.

Guilds and Unions

As your work in the electronic media takes you into larger production facilities and markets, you will find it necessary to consider union or guild membership if you wish regular employment. Whereas some criticize these organizations because of various regulations and restrictions, others welcome the specialization and protection afforded by such membership.

If you hope to write network or syndicated programs, an integral part of your work will involve submitting prospective script material for review, acceptance, and ultimate production. Information on how, when, and where to submit this material is provided by literary agents who represent your interests, through your informal associations with other writers, and through membership in a guild or union.

The acceptance of your script material may depend on your membership status in the appropriate guild or union. Essentially these groups are associations of individuals with similar interests and pursuits. Usually it is possible to have your script material reviewed by a potential employer even though you are not a member of a particular guild or union at the time of your initial submission. The use of a program material release form is recommended. Should your initial work have merit, you would be expected to join the appropriate guild or union. Once a member, you may be expected not to submit material to those who do not abide by the rules or regulations required by your guild or union membership. Adherence to this membership restriction allows the organization to protect its members and to provide a unified front when negotiating specific issues and concerns of the membership.

The largest radio-television-motion picture writers' guild in this country is the Writers Guild of America, Inc. with offices in Los Angeles and New York City. Among the *primary functions of the WGA* are

a. *To represent writers for the purpose of collective bargaining* in the motion picture, television, and radio industries
b. *To verify and administer individual writing contracts*
c. *To prepare market lists and other informational material and to assist members in writing for specific series or projects*
d. *To organize craft meetings and workshops* to improve members' writing skills

e. *To study and report on copyright, censorship, taxation, and other matters affecting Guild members*
f. *To undertake special projects* for Guild members, such as the maintenance of a pension fund, credit union, and group insurance plan

The *minimum requirements for admission to the WGA, west, Inc.* are that you have been employed within the past two years as a writer for screen, television, or radio or that you have sold original material to one of these media. In addition, you must have worked for signatories to WGA collective bargaining agreements. The initiation fee is $1500. Your membership application must be supported with a copy of your contract or other acceptable evidence of such employment or sale. WGA, west, Inc. has devised a schedule that itemizes the value or credit assigned to standard writing assignments. For example, two credits are assigned for each complete week of employment within the Guild's jurisdiction on a week-to-week basis, but eight credits are assigned for a screenplay for a short-subject theatrical motion picture. Twelve units must be accumulated before WGA, west, Inc. membership is granted.

The Writers Guild of America requires members and contracting companies to adhere to strict contract standards specified in the WGA's Theatrical and Television Basic Agreement. This document provides specific information on several items, including compensation rates, grievance and arbitration rules and procedures, pension and health contributions, nondiscrimination rights and policies, screen credits, and the extended rights of Guild members.

Information about the WGA is available from either Writers Guild of America, west, Inc., 8955 Beverly Boulevard, West Hollywood, CA 90048-2456 or Writers Guild of America, East, Inc., 555 West 57th Street, New York, NY 10019. The Guild can send information about membership requirements, the functions of the WGA, the manuscript registration service, the Television Market List—listing contact and submission information for current weekly primetime television program series and published monthly in the WGAw *Journal,* standard contract forms, minimum contract fees for WGA members, and agents currently subscribing to Guild regulations. Some of this information requires the payment of nominal fees.

The Business of Writing

A successful writer must also be effective in business. Many writers have their agents handle these business details and, thus, free themselves to concentrate on their writing. Others handle the business details themselves. They maintain tax and script submission records; check contract terms, even though agents are responsible for this; and take steps to protect their work. Legal and financial protection has become an increasingly important part of the writer's world.

A minimal amount of record keeping is needed. If you work as a free-lance or contract writer, keep track of your script submissions by noting the name or nature of the project, to whom the script material was sent, when a response was received, and what (if any) follow-up was done. For tax purposes, maintain a separate account to handle earnings and expenses. Financial record keeping should be accurate and complete and backed up with receipts, cancelled checks, deposit slips, sales tickets, and other documents. Check with an accountant or a tax consultant about other financial information related to the writing profession. **Keep Records**

Before you sign a contract, read it carefully. These written agreements specify what services you will provide, with what compensation, and within what period of time. Writers are often involved in step-deal contracts, which specify what payment is to be made at each script development stage. Generally there are provisions for stopping development at each stage if the script does not proceed according to expectations.

Take steps to protect your work. Your scripts are precious commodities. As a professional writer, they are your source of income, the results of your creative efforts. Make certain that what you write is copied, dated, clearly identified as your work, and (if appropriate) registered with either the WGA or the copyright office *before* you send it out for review. **Protect Your Work**

The WGA registration service is available to members and nonmembers. Registering your formats, outlines, synopses, story lines, and scripts with the WGA does not confer statutory protection but merely provides evidence of a writer's claim to authorship and of the date of its completion. To register script material with the WGA, write to either of the WGA addresses provided earlier. Request the appropriate form to be sent and ask to know the cost of registration before sending one copy of the script material prepared in standard copy form and accompanied by a check or money order for the registration fee.

More secure protection is obtained through formal copyright registration. Application for copyright registration is made on one of four forms corresponding to the nature of the work:

Class TX: Nondramatic Literary Works (includes advertising copy or scripts)
Class PA: Works of the Performing Arts (includes dramatic works, motion pictures, and other audiovisual works)
Class VA: Works of the Visual Arts (includes logos and photographs)
Class SR: Sound Recordings

The proper application form and additional information on copyright regulations may be obtained from the Register of Copyright, Copyright Office, Library of Congress, Washington, DC 20559 (202/287–9100).

Summary

Many exciting and challenging opportunities are available to the writer who has creative talent and who recognizes the need to market that talent. Take the steps necessary to create a demand for your services. Evaluate your background and skills and then determine where you want to be as a writer. Then go for it.

Write because you are enthusiastic about what you are doing and not because of the wages or prestige your writing might bring. Develop a commitment to yourself and to your audience that is reflected in the quality of the scripts you write. There are no shortcuts. It may be a difficult journey, but one that will provide a great deal of personal satisfaction, one that will contribute significantly to the improvement of the human condition.

Suggested Exercises and Projects

1. Identify five writing opportunities in the electronic media in your area. Contact one of these potential employers and determine the qualifications for an entry-level job. Report your findings.
2. Consult appropriate career literature and employment agencies to determine the recommended contents for a professional résumé. Prepare your typed résumé, stressing electronic media writing experience and goals.
3. Prepare a portfolio containing three to five samples of your writing. Write a generic cover letter to accompany your résumé and portfolio. This letter should explain the purpose and contents of each writing sample and then briefly outline your goals as a writer.
4. Team up with another person in a role-playing exercise. You are a writer applying for an entry-level job. The other person interviews you for the position. Agree on the type of job under consideration. Stress your positive writing abilities and potential. If possible, record the short interview. Critique your abilities as a job interview subject.
5. Follow the suggestions offered in this chapter and prepare, deliver, and then critique a four-to-eight-minute verbal pitch for a script or presentation you prepared for an earlier assignment. If possible, videotape your pitch.

Appendix A
Supplementary Reading

The following publications provide additional insights, techniques, and processes that writers working in the electronic media may find useful. The readings are arranged into categories that match the organization and content of the chapters in this book.

General

Barnouw, Erik. *Tube of Plenty: The Evolution of American Television.* 3d ed. New York: Oxford University Press, 1990.

Gross, Lynne Schafer. *The New Television Technologies.* 3d ed. Dubuque, IA: Wm. C. Brown, 1990.

Gross, Lynne Schafer. *Telecommunications: An Introduction to Electronic Media.* 4th ed. Dubuque, IA: Wm. C. Brown, 1992.

Hartwig, Robert L. *Basic TV Technology.* Stoneham, MA: Focal, 1989.

Head, Sydney W., and Sterling, Christopher H. *Broadcasting in America: A Survey of Electronic Media.* 6th ed. Boston: Houghton Mifflin, 1990.

Matelski, Marilyn J. *Daytime Television Programming.* Stoneham, MA: Focal, 1991.

Mirabito, Michael L., and Morgenstern, Barbara L. *The New Communications Technologies.* Stoneham, MA: Focal, 1990.

Sterling, Christopher, and Kittross, John M. *Stay Tuned: A Concise History of American Broadcasting.* 2d ed. Belmont, CA: Wadsworth, 1990.

Production Techniques and Processes

Adams, Michael H. *Single-Camera Video: The Creative Challenge.* Dubuque, IA: Wm. C. Brown, 1992.

Alten, Stanley R. *Audio in Media.* 3d ed. Belmont, CA: Wadsworth, 1990.

Burrows, Thomas D.; Wood, Donald N.; and Gross, Lynne Schafer. *Television Production: Disciplines and Techniques.* 5th ed. Dubuque, IA: Wm. C. Brown, 1992.

Gifford, F. *Tape.* 3d ed. Englewood, CO: Morton, 1987.

Lindheim, Richard D., and Blum, Richard A. *Inside Television Producing.* Stoneham, MA: Focal, 1991.

O'Donnell, Lewis B.; Benoit, Philip; and Hausman, Carl. *Modern Radio Production.* 3d ed. Belmont, CA: Wadsworth, 1993.

Oringel, Robert S. *Audio Control Handbook for Radio and Television Broadcasting.* 6th ed. Stoneham, MA: Focal, 1989.

Utz, Peter. *Video User's Handbook.* 4th ed. White Plains, NY: Knowledge Industry Publications, 1989.

Whittaker, Ron. *Video Field Production.* Mountain View, CA: Mayfield, 1989.

Zettl, Herbert. *Television Production Handbook.* 5th ed. Wadsworth: Belmont, CA, 1992.

Basic Writing Styles and Processes

Berger, Arthur Asa. *Scripts: Writing for Radio and Television.* Newbury Park, CA: Sage, 1990.

Coopersmith, Jerome. *Professional Writer's Teleplay/Screenplay Format.* rev. ed. New York: Writer's Guild of America, East, Inc., 1983.

Haag, Judith H. *The Complete Guide to Standard Script Formats: Part II, Taped Formats for Television.* Hollywood, CA: CMC, 1988.

Haag, Judith H., and Cole, Hillis R., Jr. *The Complete Guide to Standard Script Formats.* Hollywood, CA: CMC, 1980.

Hilliard, Robert L. *Writing for Television and Radio.* 5th ed. Belmont, CA: Wadsworth, 1991.

Kessler, Lauren, and McDonald, Duncan. *The Search: Information Gathering for the Mass Media.* Belmont, CA: Wadsworth, 1992.

Kessler, Lauren, and McDonald, Duncan. *When Words Collide: A Media Writer's Guide to Grammar and Style.* 3d ed. Belmont, CA: Wadsworth, 1992.

Lee, Robert, and Misiorowski, Robert. *Script Models: A Handbook for the Media Writer.* New York: Hastings House, 1978.

Rivers, William L. *Finding Facts: Interviewing, Observing, Using Reference Sources.* Englewood Cliffs, NJ: Prentice-Hall, 1975.

Rivers, William, and Work, Allison. *Writing for the Media.* Mountain View, CA: Mayfield, 1988.

Strunk, William, and White, E. B. *The Elements of Style.* 3d ed. New York: Macmillan, 1979.

Walters, Roger L. *Broadcast Writing: Principles and Practice.* New York: Random House, 1988.

Zinsser, William. *On Writing Well.* rev. ed. New York: Harper & Row, 1985.

Commercials and Announcements

Baldwin, Huntley. *How to CREATE Effective TV Commercials.* 2d ed. Lincolnwood, IL: NTC Business Books, 1989.

Bergendorff, Fred; Harrison, Charles; and Webster, Lance. *Broadcast Advertising and Promotion: A Handbook for TV, Radio and Cable.* New York: Hastings House, 1983.

Eastman, Susan Tyler, and Klein, Robert A. *Promotion & Marketing for Broadcasting & Cable.* 2d ed. Prospect Heights, IL: Waveland, 1991.

Hagerman, William L. *Broadcast Advertising Copywriting.* Stoneham, MA: Focal, 1989.

Meeske, Milan D., and Norris. R. C. *Copywriting for the Electronic Media: A Practical Guide.* 2d ed. Belmont, CA: Wadsworth, 1992.

Ogilvy, David. *Ogilvy on Advertising.* New York: Vintage, 1983.

Orlik, Peter B. *Broadcast/Cable Copywriting.* 4th ed. Boston: Allyn and Bacon, 1990.

News and Sports

Biagi, Shirley. *Newstalk II: State-of-the-Art Conversations with Today's Broadcast Journalists.* Belmont, CA: Wadsworth, 1987.

Bliss, Edward, Jr. *Now the News.* Washington, DC: RTNDA, 1991.

Hausman, Carl. *Crafting News for the Electronic Media: Writing, Reporting, and Production.* Belmont, CA: Wadsworth, 1992.

Hewitt, John. *Sequences: Strategies for Shooting News in the Real World.* Mountain View, CA: Mayfield, 1992.

Hitchcock, John R. *Sportscasting.* Stoneham, MA: Focal, 1991.

Kuralt, Charles. *On the Road with Charles Kuralt.* New York: G. P. Putnam, 1985.

Mayeux, Peter E. *Broadcast News Writing and Reporting.* Dubuque, IA: Wm. C. Brown, 1991.

National Association of Broadcasters. *Sports on Television: A New Ball Game for Broadcasters.* Washington, DC: NAB, 1990.

Stephens, Mitchell. *Broadcast News.* 3d ed. Fort Worth, TX: Harcourt Brace Jovanovich, 1993.

Whittemore, Hank. *CNN: The Inside Story: How a Band of Mavericks Changed the Face of Television News.* Boston: Little, Brown & Company, 1990.

Yoakam, Richard D., and Cremer, Charles F. *ENG: Television News and the New Technology.* 2d ed. New York: Random House, 1989.

Editorials and Commentaries/Documentaries and Investigative Reports

Barnouw, Erik. *Documentary: A History of the Non-Fiction Film.* 2d ed. New York: Oxford University Press, 1993.

Campbell, Richard. *60 Minutes and the News: A Mythology for Middle America.* Champaign, IL: University of Illinois Press, 1991.

Ellis, Jack C. *The Documentary Idea: A Critical History of English-Language Documentary Film and Video.* Englewood Cliffs, NJ: Prentice-Hall, 1989.

Osgood, Charles. *The Osgood Files.* New York: Putnam, 1991.

Williams, Paul N. *Investigative Reporting and Editing.* Englewood Cliffs, NJ: Prentice-Hall, 1978.

Interviews and Talk Programs

Biagi, Shirley. *Interviews That Work: A Practical Guide for Journalists.* 2d ed. Belmont, CA: Wadsworth, 1992.

Brady, John. *The Craft of Interviewing.* Cincinnati, OH: Writer's Digest Books, 1976.

King, Larry, with Yoffe, Emily. *Larry King by Larry King.* New York: Simon and Schuster, 1982.

Wallace, Mike, and Gates, Gary Paul. *Close Encounters.* New York: Berkley, 1985.

Walters, Barbara. *How to Talk with Practically Anybody About Practically Anything.* Garden City, NY: Doubleday, 1970.

Music and Variety Programs

Denisoff, R. Serge. *Inside MTV.* New Brunswick, NJ: Transaction Books, 1990.

Eastman, Susan Tyler; Head, Sydney W.; and Klein, Lewis. *Broadcast/Cable Programming: Strategies and Practices.* 4th ed. Belmont, CA: Wadsworth, 1993.

MacFarland, David T. *Contemporary Programming Strategies.* Hillsdale, NJ: Lawrence Erlbaum, 1990.

Specialized Writing Styles and Processes

Abelman, Robert, and Hoover, Stewart, eds. *Religious Television: Controversies and Conclusions.* Norwood, NJ: Ablex, 1990.

Bruce, Steve. *Pray TV: Televangelism in America.* New York: Routledge, 1991.

Hayward, Stan. *Scriptwriting for Animation.* New York: Hastings House, 1977.

Lesser, Gerald. *Children and Television: Lessons from "Sesame Street."* New York: Random House, 1974.

Liebert, Robert M., and Sprafkin, Joyce. *The Early Window: Effects of Television on Children and Youth.* 3d ed. Elmsford, NY: Pergamon, 1988.

Palmer, Edward L. *Television and America's Children: A Crisis of Neglect.* New York: Oxford University Press, 1990.

Schneider, Cy. *Children's Television: How It Works and Its Influence on Children.* Lincolnwood, IL: NTC Business Books, 1989.

Signorelli, Nancy, ed. *A Sourcebook on Children and Television.* Westport, CT: Greenwood, 1991.

Veciana-Suarez, Ana. *Hispanic Media: Impact & Influence.* Washington, DC: The Media Institute, 1990.

Instructional and Corporate Presentations

Corporation for Public Broadcasting. *Annual Report.* Washington, DC: CPB, annual.

DiZazzo, Ray. *Corporate Scriptwriting: A Professional's Guide.* Stoneham, MA: Focal, 1992.

DiZazzo, Ray. *Corporate Television: A Producer's Handbook.* Stoneham, MA: Focal, 1990.

Hausman, Carl. *Institutional Video: Planning, Budgeting, Production and Evaluation.* Belmont, CA: Wadsworth, 1991.

Iuppa, Nicholas V., with Anderson, Karl. *Advanced Interactive Video Design.* Stoneham, MA: Focal, 1988.

Matrazzo, Donna. *The Corporate Scriptwriting Book.* Emeryville, CA: CVD Bookshelf, 1989.

Morley, John. *Scriptwriting for High-Impact Videos: Imaginative Approaches to Delivering Factual Information.* Belmont, CA: Wadsworth, 1992.

Stokes, Judith Tereno. *The Business of Nonbroadcast Television.* White Plains, NY: Knowledge Industry Publications, 1988.

Dramas and Comedies

Alley, Robert S., and Brown, Irby B. *Murphy Brown: Anatomy of a Sitcom.* New York: Dell, 1990.

Armer, Alan A. *Writing the Screenplay: TV and Film.* 2d ed. Belmont, CA: Wadsworth, 1993.

Brady, Ben, and Lee, Lance. *The Understructure of Writing for Film and Television.* Austin: University of Texas Press, 1988.

Dmytryk, Edward. *On Screen Writing.* Stoneham, MA: Focal, 1985.

Egri, Lajos. *The Art of Dramatic Writing.* New York: Simon and Schuster, 1960.

Field, Syd. *Screenplay: The Foundations of Screenwriting.* rev. ed. New York: Dell, 1982.

Field, Syd. *The Screenwriter's Workbook.* New York: Dell, 1984.

Goldman, William. *Adventures in the Screen Trade: A Personal View of Hollywood and Screenwriting.* New York: Warner Books, 1983.

Gross, Edward. *Cheers: Where Everybody Knows Your Name.* Las Vegas, NV: Movie Publisher Services, 1991.

Idman, William, et al. *Word Into Image: Writers on Screenwriting.* Santa Monica, CA: American Film Foundation, 1981.

Miller, Pat B. *Script Supervising and Film Continuity.* Stoneham, MA: Focus, 1990.

Miller, William. *Screenwriting for Narrative Film & Television.* New York: Hastings House, 1990.

Portnoy, Kenneth. *Screen Adaptation: A Scriptwriting Handbook.* Stoneham, MA: Focal, 1991.

Rouverol, Jean. *Writing for Daytime Drama.* Stoneham, MA: Focal, 1992.

Thompson, Robert J. *Adventures on Prime Time: The Television Programs of Stephen J. Cannell.* New York: Praeger, 1990.

Vale, Eugene. *The Technique of Screenplay Writing.* New York: Simon and Schuster, 1986.

Wolff, Jurgen. *Successful Sitcom Writing.* New York: St. Martin's Press, 1988.

Wolper, David L., and Troupe, Quincy. *The Inside Story of TV's "Roots."* New York: Warner Books, 1978.

Careers

Corporation for Public Broadcasting. *Guide to Volunteer and Internship Programs in Public Broadcasting.* Washington, DC: CPB, 1988.

Gross, Lynne Schafer. *The Internship Experience.* Prospect Heights, IL: Waveland Press, 1988.

Jurek, Ken. *Careers in Video: Getting Ahead in Professional Television.* Emeryville, CA: CVD Bookshelf, 1989.

National Association of Broadcasters. *Careers in Television.* Washington, DC: National Association of Broadcasters, 1991.

Reed, Maxine K., and Reed, Robert M. *Career Opportunities in Television, Cable and Radio.* 3d ed. New York: Facts on File, 1990.

Stone, Vernon A. *Careers in Radio and Television News.* Washington, DC: RTNDA, 1990.

Appendix B
Selected Publications

Some of the following national publications are magazines or newsletters provided as part of professional association memberships (see Appendix C). Write to the publications that interest you to obtain current subscription information.

Advertising Age
Crain Communications Inc.
965 E. Jefferson
Detroit, MI 48207–9904
Weekly. Standard trade paper for advertising in all media.

Audio-Visual Communications
Media Horizons, Inc.
50 West 23rd St.
New York, NY 10010
Monthly. Publication offering hands-on advice for scripting and developing institutional presentations, especially training videos.

Billboard
Billboard Publications
One Astor Plaza
1515 Broadway
New York, NY 10036
Weekly. Trade paper for the music and recording industries.

BM/E (Broadcast Management/Engineering)
Broadband Information Bureau
401 Park Ave., South (6th Floor)
New York, NY 10016
Monthly. Technical and management-oriented publication covering broadcasting and cable.

Broadcasting & Cable
Broadcasting Publications, Inc.
1705 DeSales St., N.W.
Washington, DC 20036
Weekly. A primary news magazine of the electronic media, covering regulation, programming, technology, news, sales, and management systems.

Broadcasting and the Law
One S.E. Third Ave., Ste. 1450
Miami, FL 33131–1715
Bimonthly. Newsletter about rules and concerns that affect daily operation of the electronic media.

BusinessTV
TeleSpan Publishing Corporation
P. O. Box 6250
Altadena, CA 91001–9958
Quarterly. Magazine covering television for business use.

Cablevision
International Thomson Communications
600 S. Cherry St., Ste. 400
Denver, CO 80222
Biweekly. News magazine covering the issues, developments, and trends in the cable industry.

Cable World
Cable World Associates
1905 Sherman St., Ste. #1000
Denver, CO 80203
Weekly. Business news magazine that emphasizes technology, programming, and business aspects of the cable industry.

Cash Box
330 W. 58th St.
New York, NY 10019
Weekly. Popular music industry trade publication.

Channels
P. O. Box 6438
Duluth, MN 55806
Twenty-two issues each year. Business and management information, analysis, and perspective for television professionals.

Columbia Journalism Review
Graduate School of Journalism
700A Journalism Building
Columbia University
New York, NY 10027
　　Bimonthly. Journal featuring critical review of print and electronic news media.

Communicator
Radio-Television News Directors Association
1000 Connecticut Ave., N.W., Ste. 615
Washington, DC 20036
　　Monthly. Publication of the RTNDA emphasizing freedom of information and ethics issues, reporting, and news management.

Corporate Video Decisions
NBB Acquisitions Co., Inc.
401 Park Ave., South
New York, NY 10016
　　Monthly. Publication emphasizing emerging technologies and the application of video materials in an institutional, corporate setting.

Current
2311 18th St., N.W.
Washington, DC 20009
　　Biweekly. Newspaper of public radio and television, covering local and national issues and concerns.

Electronic Media
Crain Communications
740 Rush St.
Chicago, IL 60611–2590
　　Weekly. Primary news magazine of the electronic media, covering regulation, programming, news, sales, and management systems.

Emmy
Academy of Television Arts & Sciences
3500 W. Olive Ave., No. 700
Burbank, CA 91505–4268
　　Bimonthly. Publication covering matters of interest to members of the Academy of Television Arts & Sciences and the television industry.

FineLine: The Newsletter of Journalism Ethics
600 E. Main St., #103
Louisville, KY 40202–9723
　　Monthly. Newsletter that uses case studies to examine practical ethical situations from newsrooms across the country.

The Hollywood Reporter
6715 Sunset Blvd.
Hollywood, CA 90028
　　Weekdays. Entertainment industry newspaper.

The Independent
625 Broadway, 9th Floor
New York, NY 10012
　　Ten issues each year. Coverage of the work of independent producers in film and video fields.

Interact
International Interactive Communications Society (IICS)
P. O. Box 1862
Lake Oswego, OR 97035
　　Quarterly. Primary scholarly publication on interactive media.

Interactive World
Virgo Publishing, Inc.
13402 N. Scottsdale Rd., B-185
Scottsdale, AZ 85254
　　Monthly. Journal emphasizing interactive communications, especially FAX publishing, telemarketing, telephone and television services, and privacy concerns.

International Documentary
International Documentary Association
1551 S. Robertson Blvd. #201
Los Angeles, CA 90035
　　Monthly. Coverage of all aspects of documentary, nonfiction film and video.

International Television News
International Television Association
6311 N. O'Connor Rd., LB51
Irving, TX 75039
　　Ten issues each year. Official newsletter of the ITVA.

Journal of Broadcasting and Electronic Media
Broadcast Education Association
1771 N St., N.W.
Washington, DC 20036
　　Quarterly. Research journal on development, policy, economics, process, programming, technology, effects, and criticism of the electronic media.

Journal of Communication
School of Journalism
University of Maryland
College Park, MD 20740
　　Quarterly. Research journal providing contemporary perspectives on telecommunications, new technology, popular culture, and social issues.

PromoFax
6255 Sunset Blvd., Ste. 624
Los Angeles, CA 90028
   Weekly. Newsletter covering marketing and promotion, especially for emerging technologies.

The Quill
The Society of Professional Journalists
P. O. Box 77
16 S. Jackson
Greencastle, IN 46135
   Monthly. Publication of the Society of Professional Journalists that examines print and electronic journalism concerns and issues.

Radio and Records
1930 Century Park West
Los Angeles, CA 90067
   Weekly. Popular radio music industry publication featuring research, formats, and national programming and industry news.

Religious Broadcasting
National Religious Broadcasters, Inc.
299 Webro Rd.
Parsippany, NJ 07054
   Monthly. Publication emphasizing issues relevant to religious broadcasters.

Satellite Communications
P. O. Box 6218
Duluth, MN 55806–9918
   Monthly. International magazine for news, applications, and technology affecting the satellite industry.

T.H.E. (Technological Horizons in Education) Journal
150 El Camino Real, Ste. 112
Tustin, CA 92680–9833
   Monthly. Publication covering educational technology and design systems, especially emerging technologies and curriculum integration.

Television Digest
Warren Publishing
2115 Ward Ct. N.W.
Washington, DC 20037
   Weekly. Standard trade periodical emphasizing regulations and consumer electronics.

Television Quarterly
The National Academy of Television Arts & Sciences
111 W. 57th St., Ste. 1020
New York, NY 10019
   Quarterly. Publication featuring commentary and analysis of the television industry, especially the role of television in society and its relationship to new technology.

Variety
Variety, Inc.
475 Park Ave. South
New York, NY 10016
   Weekly and daily. Standard entertainment industry trade paper.

Videography
P.S.N. Publications
2 Park Ave., Ste. 1820
New York, NY 10016
   Monthly. Magazine of professional video production, technology, and applications to multimedia presentations.

Washington Journalism Review
2233 Wisconsin Ave., N.W., Ste. 442
Washington, DC 20007
   Ten issues per year. Publication featuring the analysis of the print and electronic news media, especially business and legal concerns.

WGAw Journal
Writers Guild of America, west
8955 Beverly Blvd.
Los Angeles, CA 90048
   Monthly. Publication for Writers Guild of America, west members, featuring activities of the Guild and its members plus the Television Market List, containing contact submission information on current weekly primetime television programs.

Writer's Digest
9933 Alliance Rd.
Cincinnati, OH 45242
   Monthly. Magazine featuring writing and marketing techniques for writers in all media.

Appendix C
Professional Associations

Listed in this appendix are many national and international groups that offer individual rather than only station or institutional memberships. Many offer student or associate memberships at reduced rates.

Contact the groups appropriate to your interests. Some groups offer a broad perspective of the electronic media, whereas others are more specialized. *Broadcasting & Cable Market Place* provides an annual update of listings for many of these national associations and professional societies.

Alpha Epsilon Rho (national honorary broadcasting society)
College of Journalism
University of South Carolina
Columbia, SC 29208
803/777–3324

American Meteorological Society
45 Beacon St.
Boston, MA 02108
617/227–2425

American Sportscasters Association
5 Beekman St., Ste. 814
New York, NY 10038
212/277–8080

American Women in Radio and Television Inc.
1101 Connecticut Ave., N. W., Ste. 700
Washington, DC 20036–4303
202/429–5102

Asian American Journalists Association
1765 Sutter St., Rm. 1000
San Francisco, CA 94115
415/346–2051

Association of Independent Video and Filmmakers
625 Broadway, 9th Floor
New York, NY 10012
212/473–3400

International Documentary Association
1551 S. Robertson Blvd. #201
Los Angeles, CA 90035
310/284–8422

International Interactive Communications Society (IICS)
P.O. Box 1862
Lake Oswego, OR 97035
503/649–2065

International Television Association (ITVA) (nonprofit organization serving the professional development needs of video communicators in nonbroadcast settings)
6311 N. O'Connor Rd., LB51
Irving, TX 75039
214/869–1112

Investigative Reporters and Editors, Inc. (IRE)
100 Neff Hall
School of Journalism
University of Missouri
Columbia, MO 65211
314/882–2042

The National Academy of Television Arts & Sciences
111 W. 57th St., Ste. 1020
New York, NY 10019
212/586–8424

National Association of Black Journalists (NABJ)
11600 Sunrise Valley Dr.
Reston, VA 22091
703/648–1270

National Association of Farm Broadcasters
26 E. Exchange Street
St. Paul, MN 55101
612/224–0508

National Association of Hispanic Journalists
529 14th St., N. W., Ste. 1193
Washington, DC 20045
202/662–7145

National Black Media Coalition
38 New York Ave., N. E.
Washington, DC 20002
202/387–8155

National Broadcast Editorial Association
6223 Executive Blvd.
Rockville, MD 20852
301/468–3959

National Federation of Press Women Inc.
P.O. Box 99
Blue Springs, MO 64013
816/229–1666

National Religious Broadcasters
299 Webro Rd.
Parsippany, NJ 07054
201/428–5400

Native American Journalists Association
School of Journalism and Mass Communication
University of Colorado
Campus Box 287
Boulder, CO 80309
303/492–7397

Promax International
(Promotion and Marketing Executives in the Electronic Media)
6255 Sunset Blvd., Ste. 624
Los Angeles, CA 90028
213/465–3777

Public Relations Society of America, Inc.
33 Irving Pl.
New York, NY 10003–2376
212/995–2230

Radio-Television News Directors Association
1000 Connecticut Ave., N. W., Ste. 615
Washington, DC 20036
202/659–6510

Society of Professional Journalists
Box 77
16 S. Jackson
Greencastle, IN 46135
317/653–3333

Society of Professional Videographers
P.O. Box 1933
Huntsville, AL 35807
205/534–3600

Women in Communications Inc.
2101 Wilson Blvd., Ste. 417
Arlington, VA 22201
703/528–4200

Writers Guild of America East Inc.
555 W. 57th St.
New York, NY 10023
212/245–6180

Writers Guild of America, west, Inc.
8955 Beverly Blvd.
West Hollywood, CA 90048
213/550–1000

Appendix D
Self-regulation Efforts: Program Standards and Practices and Codes of Ethics

The following information is provided to give you some notion of the nature, scope, and concerns of self-regulation efforts by networks, stations, telecommunications companies, and professional organizations. These guidelines reflect the efforts of those in the electronic media to provide the best programming possible. The guidelines included in this appendix were effective 1 December 1992 and do not reflect changes made since that date.

NBC TELEVISION NETWORK PROGRAM STANDARDS

I. INTRODUCTION

It is NBC's goal to provide programming that is consistent in quality, integrity, and entertainment value. To support that goal, NBC's Program Standards guidelines reflect an appreciation of fundamental elements of taste and propriety and an understanding of our viewers and their expectations.

NBC serves a vast national audience which mirrors the rich diversity of backgrounds, customs and tastes found across our country. This audience is composed ultimately of individuals, each of whom makes viewing selections and reacts to programs from his or her own unique perspective. NBC's Program Standards are designed to accommodate these diverse interests and sensitivities.

Our viewers have come to expect NBC to provide a wide selection of programs that present positive values, stimulate thought, and entertain without causing embarrassment or harm. By providing quality television entertainment which aims to meet these expectations, NBC best serves its audience, affiliated stations and advertisers. Therefore, Program Standards guidelines have been developed to provide a framework for writers, actors, directors and producers to continue to create innovative and entertaining programming which respects the sensibilities of our audience.

These Program Standards guidelines are general statements of principle. Their successful application to any particular program involves inherently subjective judgments. Additionally, the environment of current taste and sensitivity is constantly undergoing subtle shifts. Therefore, when Program Standards guidelines are implemented, each program is evaluated, taking into consideration such factors as intended or established audience, research information, viewer feedback, and time of day a particular program is intended for broadcast.

While these policies and standards apply to all programs, special standards have been developed for certain programs in recognition of the needs or sensitivities of their particular audiences. For example, there are special standards guidelines for Saturday morning children's programs.

Clearly these policies have evolved from our experience as conscientious broadcasters. NBC has a long tradition of responsible self-regulation and will continue to ensure that its programming reflects standards that merit the acceptance and trust of our viewers.

II. GUIDELINES FOR ENTERTAINMENT PROGRAMMING

This section sets forth a summary of NBC Program Standards policies with which all entertainment programming produced for telecast on the NBC Television Network must conform. Programs must meet with appropriate standards of taste and comply with all applicable governmental regulations.

A. SPECIFIC ISSUES

1. DRUGS AND ALCOHOL

Drug and alcohol abuse are among society's most serious social problems. NBC recognizes it has a duty to ensure that depictions of drug or alcohol consumption are presented in an appropriate and responsible manner.

All portrayals of alcohol consumption and/or use of legal or illegal drugs should be restricted to situations necessary to plot and/or character delineation. The use of illegal drugs and/or the abuse of legal drugs or alcohol is destructive behavior and shall not be shown as desirable, beneficial or as an effective problem-solver.

Drug and alcohol use should not be glamorized, and, when substance abuse is noted, attention should be directed to the adverse consequences of such abuse (e.g. the dangers of driving while intoxicated).

2. LANGUAGE

Language and dialogue must be judged generally acceptable to a mass audience and appropriate to a public medium. Coarse or vulgar language should be voided. Blasphemy and obscenity are unacceptable.

3. SEXUAL MATERIAL

Sexual scenes must be sensitively handled and contribute to plot or characterization. Gratuitous or overly explicit sexual action is unacceptable and the depiction of physical coercion intended to satisfy prurient interest is to be avoided. The depiction of the act of sexual intercourse in prohibited.

Particular care must be taken in scenes where sex is coupled with violence. Rape must be portrayed as an act of violence, not a sexual act.

In general, nudity is unacceptable. Partial nudity and degrees of undress shall not be used for prurient or exploitative purposes.

4. STEREOTYPES

Characters in NBC programs should reflect the wide diversity of our audience, keeping in mind the importance of dignity to every human being. Sensitivity is necessary in the presentation of material relating to age, sex, race, religion, sexual preference, ethnicity or national derivation to avoid demeaning stereotypes.

Special precautions must be taken to avoid portrayals and terminology which ridicule or patronize those who are physically or mentally disabled.

5. VIOLENCE

Explicit, excessive or gratuitous violence is to be avoided. Programs are not to glamorize violence and/or promote violence as the solution to problems. Depictions of violence in any form must be essential to the development of theme, plot or characterization. The intensity and frequency of violent acts must also be limited. While any act potentially can be imitated, special care must be taken so violent acts do not invite imitation.

Exceptional care must be taken where children are victims of or threatened by acts of violence.

B. GENERAL ISSUES

ADVISORIES

NBC will determine whether circumstances (subject matter, treatment, and time period) warrant the use of special audience advisories in programs and program promotions. The specific language and manner of presentation included in advisories must be approved by Program Standards.

ANIMALS

The use and handling of animals must conform to accepted standards of humane treatment.

CHARITIES

Solicitations within the body of an entertainment program for charities or other non-profit organizations are generally not permitted.

COMMERCIAL MENTIONS/SPONSOR REFERENCES

Extraneous commercial mentions or exposure of commercial names, products or trademarks included in program content are to be minimized and are subject to prior approval by NBC. Identification of, or references to, a program's sponsor other than previously accepted commercial announcements, billboards, and program titles must be specifically approved in advance by NBC.

CONTROVERSIAL TOPICS

Issues of social importance or controversy must be handled with care. A decision to present such subject matter in an entertainment program should include a determination that the particular program involved is appropriate for the presentation contemplated.

HYPNOSIS

Actual hypnosis techniques may not be demonstrated in detail.

INSTRUCTIONAL CRIMINAL BEHAVIOR

Scenes containing complete and accurate instructions in the use of illegal drugs, harmful devices or weapons, or describing imitable techniques for other illegal activities or evasion of apprehension are not permitted.

MISLEADING DRAMATIZATIONS, SIMULATIONS AND RECREATIONS

NBC programs may not be deceptive to the viewing public in any material respect. In cases where the audience might be misled, appropriate disclaimers are to be used. Programming purporting to present non-fictional material in a non-fictional manner must be accurate with respect to material facts or statements.

The use of techniques or language such as "we interrupt this program" which may cause viewers to believe an actual news report is being presented is not permitted.

PROFESSIONAL PROCEDURES

Dramatization or actual presentation of professional advice and procedures must be accurate and comply with recognized professional practices. When appropriate, Program Standards will assist in obtaining qualified consultants.

PROMOTIONAL ELEMENTS

Promotional elements such as "teasers" and "trailer", including "promos", must properly reflect the actual nature and content of the program. Certain material acceptable in the context of the program may not be appropriate for inclusion in promotional elements.

PSEUDO-SCIENCES

Program material should not promote belief in the efficacy of occultism, astrology, mind-reading or other pseudo-sciences.

SUBLIMINAL MESSAGES

Audio and video content which is inserted within the body of a program which attempts to convey information below the level of normal viewer awareness is prohibited.

C. SPECIAL FORMATS

1. PROGRAMS INTENDED TO BE VIEWED PRIMARILY BY CHILDREN

NBC recognizes its responsibility to young people and expects producers to be sensitive to their special needs. NBC encourages the presentation of educational and pro-social material and requires that producers avoid program content that would have an adverse effect on a child's behavior or development. NBC acknowledges the audience's expectation that children's programs will provide young viewers with a positive entertainment experience. Therefore, producers of children's programs should not only observe NBC's general standards guidelines, but should be particularly careful with respect to the following:

a. Characters should not be placed in situations that would provoke excessive or prolonged anxiety in children.

Catastrophe and jeopardy should not be so extreme as to frighten younger viewers. References to death and/or suicide should be handled with extreme caution.

b. Characters should reflect the ethnic and racial diversity of NBC's audience. While NBC encourages the inclusion of women, minorities, disabled persons and distinctive characters with whom viewers would personally identify (e.g. kids who wear glasses), derogatory stereotypes should be avoided.

c. Violence should not be depicted as glamorous or shown as an acceptable solution to problems. The negative consequences of violence should be stressed. To mitigate violence, action sequences should emphasize unrealistic settings, fantasy weapons, and superhuman feats.

d. Dangerous behavior which could prompt a child to place himself or others in jeopardy should not be shown. Special care should be taken with respect to depicting fire-making techniques or use of readily combustible materials, especially when such materials are readily available in the viewer's home. Depicting household items as weapons must also be avoided.

e. Characters should not engage in unlawful, anti-social or self-destructive behavior without suffering negative consequences for their actions. Whenever possible, protagonists should be shown following generally accepted rules of safety (e.g. wearing seatbelts).

f. Romantic storylines which include acts of affection are generally considered appropriate but should be handled with discretion. Language and storylines that are sexual in nature should be avoided.

g. Commercial products and references may only be included in programs with NBC's approval and must serve a valid entertainment purpose.

h. Children's programs on NBC are required to have Separator Devices before and after commercial messages.

2. FACT-BASED DRAMAS

NBC prohibits the broadcast of any deceptive or misleading programs or program material. This is especially true as regards fact-based dramas and presentations. Program Standards, in cooperation with the Law Department, reviews all such programs for accuracy and actuality.

3. THEATRICAL FILMS

Theatrical or other programs originally produced for another medium must be reviewed before broadcast and shall comply with all NBC Program Standards.

III. PRACTICES GUIDELINES
  A. PROCEDURES AND LEGAL REQUIREMENTS
    1. PAYOLA
       Section 507 of the Communications Act of 1934 generally prohibits the acceptance or payment of money, service or other valuable consideration for the inclusion of any person, matter or thing in a program unless disclosure is made before the broadcast to the broadcaster. Each violation of this statute carries personal criminal liability for fine or imprisonment or both.

       Pursuant to NBC policy and contractual provisions, any arrangements for such inclusion in a program to be broadcast by NBC must be approved by Department of Program Standards and Marketing Policy ("the Department") in advance.

    2. PACKAGER'S DISCLOSURE PROCEDURES
       NBC requires that each outside producer/packager complete and return to the Department a Packager's Disclosure Letter which requires specific agreement to and/or disclosure of the following:

       a. The requirement of Section 507 shall be included in each performer's contract.
       b. Disclosure of Payola/Plugola issues. Plugola involves the inclusion in a program of any person, matter or thing in which the packager or any employee of the packager has a direct or indirect financial interest.
       c. Disclosure of Production Assistance (i.e., tradeout arrangements) calling for broadcast credit or air exposure in consideration for furnishing props or other matter for use on or in connection with the program. The approval of Program Standards and Marketing Policy must be obtained and a written agreement setting forth the understandings of all the parties, including NBC, shall be executed.
       d. Any arrangement requiring a performer to pay the producer/packager or anyone in their employ anything of value in order to secure an appearance on a program produced for NBC must be approved in advance by the Department.
       e. No contest or promotion shall be undertaken on or in connection with any program without the Department's advance approval.

    3. SPONSORSHIP IDENTIFICATION
       Section 317 of the Communications Act requires that broadcasters make an appropriate on-air announcement when consideration is received by persons in the program production chain in exchange for including matter in a broadcast. NBC policy requires prior approval of Program Standards and Marketing Policy for any such arrangements. Placement and duration of any required sponsorship identification announcement will be determined by the Department.

    4. COMMERCIAL MATTER
       NBC reserves the right to limit and control the nature, form and duration of any and all "commercial matter" included within any program or broadcast produced for or presented over NBC or any of its broadcast facilities.

       "Commercial matter" includes any mention or exposure of any person, product, service, trademark, brand name or logo of a commercial nature which is identifiable within the broadcast, regardless of whether a charge has been made or value promised to or received by any person working on or in connection with the broadcast in exchange for its inclusion.

    5. PRODUCTION ASSISTANCE
       NBC policy rigorously controls the acceptance of production assistance. Generally, packager/producers are encouraged to buy or rent whatever services or property are required for use in connection with a program they are producing. However, in certain circumstances, and with the prior approval of Program Standards and Marketing Policy, some kinds of production assistance can be utilized in connection with programs produced by NBC or presented over its facilities.

    6. PRODUCTION ASSISTANCE PROMOTIONAL ANNOUNCEMENTS
       Audio and video announcements describing the supplier of goods and services furnished to a program to defray or offset production costs which go beyond simple disclosure of the receipt of such services or property as may be required by Section 317 of the Communications Act are generally not permissible on programs broadcast over the facilities of the NBC Television Network.

       Inclusion of such announcements in syndicated programming must be specifically negotiated as part of the program acquisition agreement.

  B. SPECIAL FORMATS
    1. GAME AND AUDIENCE PARTICIPATION PROGRAMS
       Federal law (Section 508 of the Communications Act) and NBC policy prohibit any person from unfairly influencing or attempting to influence the results of a game or quiz show or

contest. "Quiz rigging," which is a federal crime, includes supplying a contestant with secret and special assistance which will affect the outcome of a game or quiz show; inducing a contestant not to utilize his knowledge or skill in a game or quiz show; or engaging in any conduct whatsoever for the purpose of improperly affecting the outcome of a game show, quiz show or contest. Each violation is subject to a fine of not more than $10,000 or imprisonment for not more than one year or both.

In addition, NBC requires that all game or quiz shows presented over its facilities shall be conducted fairly, honestly, and in the manner they are described to the viewing public and that they not be misleading in any material respect.

NBC's commitment to broadcast any game show shall be subject to Program Standards and Marketing Policy's review and approval of all details of the game format and security procedures.

A list of donors of all prizes identified on a game show shall be displayed in the 317 announcement at the conclusion of such program regardless of whether the announcement is legally required by Section 317. This announcement shall be in a form approved by the Department.

2. CONTEST, AWARD AND PAGEANT PROGRAMS

Prior to the broadcast of any contest, award or pageant program or any segment of a program containing a contest or award element, the producer must demonstrate the bona fides of such contests and/or awards. In addition, the entry, judging, balloting and security procedures utilized must be fair, honest and effective and that the script language describing the contest or award must not be deceptive or misleading to the audience.

3. PRODUCT OR PROGRAM PROMOTIONAL CONTESTS

Producers shall submit to the Department for review and approval in advance the particulars of contests or contest announcements concerning programs broadcast over any NBC facility.

4. NON-FICTION PROGRAMS

NBC policy prohibits the broadcast of any deceptive or misleading programming or program material. This is especially true with respect to the production of programs which purport to treat subjects in a non-fictional manner.

This includes programs which present opinions or commentary, programs which are essentially documentary in nature or reportorial programs which purport to depict real people or events in a non-fiction context, and non-fiction nature programs.

The inclusion in such program of any staged, recreated, reenacted or dramatized segments or elements may require an appropriate in-program disclosure in order to make certain that what is presented is not misleading to the public. The Department shall determine the necessity of and approve the content, placement and manner of presentation of all such disclosures.

5. PARADES

NBC policy requires that television coverage of parades shall avoid unreasonable displays of identifiable commercial advertising or promotion during parade coverage. References and descriptions of commercial sponsors of parades or participating floats, bands or other parade elements shall be limited, reasonably related to program content and subject to the approval of NBC.

6. SPORTS PROGRAMMING

In addition to the general NBC policies and procedures directed toward the honesty and integrity of Sports programming, NBC has adopted a set of Sports Policy Guidelines which governs the broadcast of all sports programming over the facilities of NBC. The guidelines establish certain procedures to be followed in the general areas of (a) event legitimacy, (b) program promotion, and (c) commercial considerations.

These policies are detailed in the NBC Sports Policy Guidelines manual available from the Program Standards and Marketing Policy Department.

C. REGULATORY AND POLICY GUIDELINES "PRE-RECORDED" ANNOUNCEMENTS

Pursuant to FCC regulations and NBC policy, any program which contains taped, filmed or recorded material and which 1) makes an affirmative attempt to create the impression that it is "live" or occurring simultaneously with the broadcast or 2) which by its nature makes time of special significance shall announce at the beginning of the program that it contains recorded material or shall identify at the time of its inclusion in the broadcast any recorded material within the program which may otherwise appear to be "live."

PROGRAM PROMOTIONAL MATERIAL

Broadcast and non-broadcast advertising and promotion for programs to be presented over the facilities of NBC may not be false, misleading or deceptive with respect to the nature or character of the program to be presented. Promotional copy must be accurate in all material respects.

Such advertising and promotion shall also comply with NBC policy regarding references and/or exposure of commercial names, logos, and/or products.

POLITICAL BROADCAST RULES

During political campaign periods, no person who is a legally qualified candidate for public office may appear in programming to be presented over the facilities of NBC unless approved by Program Marketing and Administration prior to broadcast. This prohibition extends to the picture and/or the voice of any person who may be a legally qualified candidate at the time of the broadcast. This shall not apply to programs specifically exempted from the "equal opportunity" provision of federal law.

FAIRNESS CONSIDERATIONS AND PERSONAL ATTACKS

Entertainment programming produced for NBC containing discussions of controversial issues of public importance should include legitimate contrasting views on those issues. Federal regulation also provides for certain "reply" rights arising out of the broadcast of attacks against the honesty, character, integrity or other personal qualities of any identifiable person or group made during any discussion of a controversial issue of public importance. Any program element which may contain such a discussion should be brought to the attention of Program Standards and Marketing Policy Department.

BROADCAST OF TELEPHONE CONVERSATIONS

The FCC has enacted specific rules to be followed whenever a telephone conversation is to be broadcast or recorded for broadcast. Any program element involving the broadcast or recording of telephone conversations must be reviewed and approved in advance by Program Standards and Marketing Policy.

NBC policy prohibits the use of audience paid telephone call-in systems in programming presented over the facilities of the NBC Television Network unless such a program element has the prior approval of the Department and the NBC program executive responsible for the broadcast and conforms with the requirements of NBC Program Standards and Marketing Policy Directive #15.

IV. PROGRAM CREDIT RULES

Production credits for all programs must be submitted in writing to the NBC Program Production Department for approval before they are included in any program. In order to be acceptable to NBC, credits must always pertain to persons or entities actively involved in the production of the program.

1. Time and Content Limits for Production Credits

All credits which appear at the beginning or the end of a program (except for opening program titles, episode titles, starring and co-starring credits) are counted in determining the total time allowable by NBC as described below. In addition to limited program titles and star listing, credits at the opening of the program should not exceed 10 seconds, and may include only Executive Producer, Producer, Creator, Writer and Director. In the event a program supplier wishes to accord credit for a program contribution other than those above (e.g. Composer) such contributor may be included in the opening of the program provided that one of the previously enumerated contributors is deleted from the opening and placed in the closing credits. No opening credits, titles or star listing may be repeated in the closing credits.

A. Programs 90 Minutes or Less

In programs of 90 minutes in length or less, credits may not exceed 40 seconds.

B. Programs Longer Than 90 Minutes

In programs longer than 90 minutes, credits may not exceed 60 seconds. Credits at the opening of "made-for-television" feature films two hours in length or longer may, in addition to the credits specified in paragraph #1, include Director of Photography, Art Director and Film Editor.

C. Special Class

The following program formats may use a maximum of 80 seconds for credits:

1. Award or Variety programs two hours in length or longer;
2. Movies/Miniseries three hours in length or longer;
3. Programs two hours in length or longer involving two or more production units in different locations.

D. Production Company Tags

Production company tags which must be included in the foregoing time limitations are limited to 3 and shall not exceed a combined total of 6 seconds.

2. Stripped Programs

On programs telecast two or more times a week, credits may be given once weekly on average. Where credits are required by collective bargaining agreements for such programs, the terms of those agreements shall prevail.

3. Production Assistance Credits

Credits which include the name of a commercial entity are generally prohibited. Credits including the names of organizations, trademarks, products, or brand names given in exchange for property, service or other consideration furnished for use in connection with a program are not permitted without prior approval by the Program Marketing Department. Such broadcast credits requiring approval include:

a. wardrobe,
b. travel arrangements and/or hotel accommodations,
c. props or any other type of production assistance,
d. work or services performed by sub-contractors, and
e. courtesy acknowledgments.

4. Credit Lettering

All credit lettering must be readable and placed over a contrasting background. Other than production company tags, no logo or logo-typeface is permitted.

V. NBC PROGRAM PRACTICES DIRECTIVES AND POLICY GUIDELINES

The following is a listing of policy directives governing a variety of subjects, some of which are touched upon in this manual. These directives are available from the Program Standards and Marketing Policy Department upon request.

Directive #1 - Payola
Directive #2 - Kickbacks
Directive #3 - Quiz Rigging
Directive #4 - Contests
Directive #5 - Commercial Matter
Directive #6 - Sponsorship Identification
Directive #7 - Merchandise Prizes
Directive #8 - Wardrobe Credits
Directive #9 - Identification of Taped, Filmed or Recorded Materials
Directive #10 - NBC Policy and Guidelines for Nature Documentaries
Directive #11 - Production Assistance Promotional Announcements for NBC Produced Programs
Directive #15 - Use of Audience-Paid Telephone Systems

Other NBC Policy Sources
NBC Sports Policy Guidelines
NBC Stations Legal, Policies, Practices and Procedures Manual
NBC News Policy
NBC Production Manual
NBC Financial Policies and Procedures
NBC Alcohol Policy
"Where NBC Stands"
Courtesy of the NBC TV Network.

CBS TELEVISION NETWORK PROGRAM STANDARDS

Foreword

The CBS Television Network has been dedicated since its inception to presenting the American television viewing public with entertainment and other programs of the highest calibre and standards. Over the years, this commitment has developed into an extensive case history of program-by-program judgments as to what constitutes material suitable for broadcast on CBS. Although these broadcast standards were never published in concise written form, generations of Program Practices editors have conscientiously applied and refined them. Our broadcast standards tell an interesting and important story about the CBS sense of public and corporate responsibility toward its viewers. That story is reflected in this publication of PROGRAM STANDARDS for the CBS TELEVISION NETWORK.

Introduction

In order to understand the CBS Program Standards and the process by which they are applied, it is necessary to understand certain characteristics of our medium, our industry and CBS.

First, we exist for, and ultimately succeed or fail by, how well we serve the needs and interests of our viewing public. This public is vast, incredibly diverse and, we believe, both knowledgeable and discriminating.

Second, we are built on human creativity—our business is not derived from material resources but from people who strive to further human expression and development.

Third, we are a dynamic medium, never static but constantly evolving as the society we serve evolves around us.

Finally, we operate in an intensely competitive environment—the most advanced and prolific media marketplace in the world. To survive, we must search for new and rewarding ways to respond to our viewing public.

In this environment program standards must not only articulate important principles of responsibility to our audiences, they must do so in a manner which does not inhibit the responsiveness, dynamism, creativity and innovation of the programs we are to present.

There is no way to feed a television program into a computer and determine whether it meets appropriate standards for the "typical television viewer." Indeed, there is no "typical viewer." Each year CBS broadcasts over 6000 hours of programs to a vast audience of widely divergent backgrounds and interests. Every viewer brings a slightly different perspective to each program he or she watches. It would be impossible to anticipate and address in one set of standards each and every potential viewer reaction to that which we broadcast. Our standards address the "mass audience" that watches us, recognizing that, in the final analysis, it is the individual viewer that establishes his or her own standards, for it is in their power simply to change channels or turn us off.

The standards to which entertainment programs broadcast on the CBS Television Network are held are enunciated here. But is must be constantly appreciated that program review is ultimately a subjective and personal process of skilled and caring individuals—writers, producers, directors, actors, programming management, Program Practices editors and viewers—interacting among themselves

General Standards

A CBS television program is a guest in the home. It is expected to entertain and enlighten but not to offend or advocate. CBS entertainment programs are intended to conform to generally accepted boundaries of public taste and decorum, although as those boundaries change over time, programs will strive to be contemporary. In pursuing these goals, CBS takes into account the suitability of the time period in which a particular program is to be broadcast and the corresponding differences in audience composition and expectation.

Language

The language in a broadcast must be appropriate to a public medium and generally considered to be acceptable by a mass audience. Coarse or potentially offensive language is generally avoided and if permitted for important dramatic reasons cannot be employed flippantly or exploitatively. Blasphemy and obscenity are not acceptable for broadcast.

Nudity and Sexuality

If consonant with prevailing societal standards, used for legitimate dramatic or historical purposes and not perceived as exploiting the body for prurient interests, certain degrees of undress are acceptable.

The depiction of sexual intercourse is unacceptable for broadcast. Scenes or dialogue involving sexually oriented material necessary for reasons of plot or character development must be presented with good taste and sensitivity and cannot be gratuitous or exploitative.

Characterizations

Creative imperatives of the script will dictate the behavior and mannerisms of all characters. Character portrayals must be carefully crafted and sensitive to current ethnic, religious, sexual and other prominent social concerns and unacceptable stereotypes. Care is also to be exercised when depicting characters subject to physical or mental disabilities to ensure that such persons are not demeaned.

Accuracy and Misapprehension

A CBS television program must be what it purports to be.

Programs or scenes containing elements whose technical accuracy is important to maintaining public confidence in the integrity of a profession or institution must strive to be accurate in all material regards. Consultation with qualified advisors is encouraged.

Presentations which could convey the misapprehension that a dramatized or prerecorded event is occurring "live" or in the form of spontaneous news coverage of a contemporary event are not permitted. Use of words such as "bulletin" or devices such as a "horizontal crawl" are unacceptable and reserved solely for the use of CBS News.

In any case where it may be unclear on its face what a broadcast purports to be, appropriate viewer advisories will be considered.

Violence

As a component of human experience, the dramatic depiction of violence is permitted. Here, violence is defined as "the use of physical force against persons, or the articulated, explicit threat of physical force to compel particular behavior on the part of a person." Accidents and incidents of comic violence are not included in this definition. Any depiction of violence must be relevant to plot and/or character development. It should not be gratuitous, excessive or glamorized. Violence should not be used exploitatively to entice or shock an audience. The intensity and frequency of violent incidents should be consciously reviewed to assure adherence to the foregoing standards. The use or portrayals of animals shall conform to accepted standards of humane treatment.

Substance Abuse

Character portrayals and scenes depicting the consumption of alcohol, drugs, cigarettes and similar substances must be thoughtfully considered, essential to plot and role development and not glamorized. When the line is crossed between normal, responsible consumption of a particular substance and abuse, the distinction must be clear and the adverse consequences of abuse specifically noted and explored.

Children and Television

Children watch television throughout the day, throughout the week. Parental supervision and interaction is the best means by which to ensure that children do not watch or are not confused or distressed by programs which are intended for an adult audience and which may contain mature themes and scenes. In certain cases CBS will broadcast and include in the promotional material for a particular program viewer advisories intended to alert parents to the need for special attention.

Programs intended for the child audience are reviewed with special care and, in some areas, according to different and perhaps more rigorous standards:

Role Modeling. Protagonists, "heroes," should exemplify the most positive elements of social and personal codes of conduct such as honesty, fairness, compassion and respect for authority. Attitudinally, such characters should show respect for important societal institutions, concern for distinguishing right from wrong, and commitments to such ideals as justice, ethics and humanity. Characters which represent unacceptable social and personal conduct need not be avoided but must be clearly portrayed as undesirable.

Violence. Violence should not be portrayed as a socially acceptable means of conflict resolution. It should not be glorified, made to seem fascinating, amusing or palatable. While villains may exhibit some violent behavior, this action should not be imitable, horrific or extended in its presentation. Acts which carry the potential for violence should be clearly set in the realm of fantasy. Human beings should not be severely harmed or killed.

Jeopardy and Peril. While a certain amount of jeopardy may be appropriate in a particular program, characters should not be placed in circumstances that provoke excessive or prolonged anxiety, or suggest gratuitous psychological pain. Characters should not be placed in hopeless situations and those in peril should be presented with ways to overcome their predicaments.

Responsible Social Practices. Whenever appropriate, socially responsible attitudes and practices should be favorably portrayed and reinforced. When socially inappropriate or irresponsible behavior is portrayed, it should be disparaged and discouraged.

Commercialization. Program content and commercial messages must be clearly distinct. (See CBS TELEVISION NETWORK ADVERTISING GUIDELINES.)

Dramas Based on Fact

The artistic device of combining elements of fact with elements of fiction to produce a condensed dramatic whole is a long-standing and widely accepted one. It is found in literature, the theater and cinema. It is equally appropriate to television.

There are many program forms which combine elements of fact and fiction. They can be placed along a continuum which begins with pure and unequivocal fact at one end and ends with pure fiction at the other. On this continuum are found programs based on legend, those adapted from specific autobiographies, those based on particular biographies or histories, and, finally, teleplays derived from original research.

A viewer who is aware of what kind of program is being presented is capable of evaluating the program in the light of his or her own knowledge and experience, taking into consideration the professed limitations and idiosyncracies of that program form and the material upon which it is based. Accordingly, the program and its promotional material should represent clearly to the viewer its genre and frame of reference. In some cases, viewer advisories which label or categorize the nature of the program or the material upon which it is based, or present any other information that may be pertinent to a full viewer understanding of the program may be helpful and will be used when appropriate.

Dramas based on fact adapted for television from another published source, and so denominated, must faithfully represent, in all material regards, the plot and characterizations of the original work. The nature of further review by Program Practices will depend upon the type of literary work involved, its subject matter and the background of the author. This review will seek to ensure proper viewer appreciation of the program according to the standards articulated above.

The original television drama based on fact, sometimes referred to as the "docudrama," is a particularly challenging program form. Its material factual components should be accurate and cannot be changed merely to enhance dramatic value. Fictionalized elements consistent with the events being presented may amplify or enhance the story, so long as they do not materially alter or distort history. Any presentation of a significant controversy should be done in a fair and balanced way. To ensure the achievement of these standards and thereby the integrity of this program form, the following guidelines are generally applicable.

- Unsubstantiated elements may be included only if they do not distort the material factual elements of the historical record.

- Omissions of historical information which materially distort the perception of historical events are not acceptable.

- Editing or condensation in the portrayal of historical events should maintain the accuracy or value of those events. Distortions of time, changes in the sequence of events or composite events which materially alter the historical record are to be avoided.

- All characters, including composite characters, based on real persons must accurately reflect those persons in reality and their actual roles and behavior in any significant events in which they are portrayed. Thus, in a composite character based on real persons, each of the characteristics and actions ascribed to the composite character(s) must be properly derived from the characteristics and actions of a real person or persons involved in those events. Composite or fictional characters used in roles essential to development of the main plot(s) must be carefully reviewed to ensure that their fictional or representative nature does not undermine in any material way the overall accuracy of the historical events portrayed.

- Care should be exercised in the employment of production techniques, such as casting, character and dialogue interpretation which have the potential to alter or distort the historical record.

These guidelines are applicable to all dramas based on fact. Any program project involving very sensitive themes or events which occurred in or are presently surrounded by a highly charged atmosphere or which is to be broadcast in close time proximity to the actual events upon which it is based is to be evaluated with great caution.

Theatrical Films

Standards for programs created for television are applicable to films originally created for theatrical release and subsequently broadcast on the CBS Television Network. Application of these standards to theatrical films will take into account the frequent inability to make changes for television in the film during its production and the limited ability to excise material after a film is complete without unacceptably altering its nature and creative integrity.

Game Shows

CBS has adopted and continuously refines rules and procedures to ensure that game shows are conducted honestly, fairly and as they appear to the public. These procedures guard against contestant access to information which could jeopardize the fairness and integrity of the game. Steps are taken to ensure that no contestant is placed in advantageous or disadvantageous circumstances outside the game competition itself. Disruptions that necessitate editing of the broadcast must be disclosed. All programs must conform to Sections 317, 507 and 508 of the Communications Act of 1934.

Promotional Materials

All promotional material must accurately and tastefully reflect the content of the program to which it refers. Program material not cleared for broadcast cannot be included in the promotional material for that program. Certain elements, while acceptable in the context of the program, may not be suitable for inclusion in promotional materials. On-air promotion will be scheduled to ensure that it is appropriate to the program in which it is placed.

Procedures

Selection or creation of entertainment programs for broadcast on the CBS Television Network is the responsibility of the CBS Entertainment Division. Some programs are wholly produced by the Division. Most programs are produced for the Division by independent producers and production companies and licensed to CBS for telecast. The Program Practices Department reviews all of these programs for compliance with our

PROGRAM STANDARDS. Program Practices is not a part of the CBS Entertainment Division or the CBS Television Network but a completely separate and independent staff function of the CBS/Broadcast Group.

A television program begins with a spark of imagination in the mind of its creator. It takes form over a period of time through the collaboration of many people. Program Practices editors are involved in this process from the very outset and follow a program through all stages of its maturation to final approval of the completed project.

In many cases, the CBS PROGRAM STANDARDS are clear and easily applied by the producers themselves with minimal guidance from our editors. In other cases—those involving novel themes or particularly sensitive subjects or program elements—more complex and sophisticated judgments must be made about the applicability of and compliance with the STANDARDS. Here, the involvement of Program Practices editors will be more extensive. Thus, the timing and extent of program review is determined on a program-by-program basis.

Generally, an editor's observations on program compliance are offered at the concept, outline, script, rough-cut and final cut stages. At the script stage, an editor will issue detailed, often page-by-page, scene-by-scene or line-by-line, notes. Such notes might range from requested dialogue or scene staging changes to directorial cautions on the execution of a particular scene. Often alternative approaches to problem areas are discussed with the creative team. This interaction between the Program Practices editor and the creative team continues through the program's completion.

When advisable, qualified experts may be consulted to provide the information necessary to ensure accurate or appropriate portrayals. This is particularly true in the area of children's television where child psychologists are frequently consulted.

Original dramas based on fact are a unique and challenging program form and review procedures are structured accordingly. Most are produced by independent producers outside of CBS. The producer is expected to undertake extensive and reliable research into the factual elements of the drama and should have the ability and resources to do so. In applying the original drama based on fact standards, Program Practices will test the producer's research through an evaluation of that research and independent cross-checking, at times involving original research by Program Practices and, when appropriate, specifically including personal interviews of real persons portrayed in the program. The nature and magnitude of original CBS research and the process of factual verification will vary from project to project. Projects will also be reviewed by the CBS Law Department and the nature and extent of that review will be tailored to the particular program.

Postscript

As noted at the outset, television is a dynamic medium. The PROGRAM STANDARDS articulated here express the principles embodied in and the standards to which programs broadcast on the CBS Television Network are held. But these standards cannot be immutable. For the ultimate principle to which we subscribe is that the viewer and society at large set the standards of acceptability. As cultural and social views change over time we must be prepared to respond.

CBS Program Standards provided courtesy of CBS/Broadcast Group.

CAPITAL CITIES/ABC, INC. DEPARTMENT OF BROADCAST STANDARDS AND PRACTICES PROGRAM STANDARDS

Preamble

These Program Standards set forth the procedures and criteria which apply to review by the Broadcast Standards and Practices Department for programming produced for telecast on behalf of ABC Entertainment for telecast over the ABC Television Network.

Written standards cannot cover the entire universe of situations and must, therefore, be worded broadly. These Program Standards are not intended to inhibit creativity and will be applied with flexibility, taking into consideration context and character. Each program will be evaluated on its own merits with due consideration for its creative integrity.

Advisories

When appropriate, Capital Cities/ABC televises audio and video advisory announcements in certain entertainment programs containing sensitive material (e.g., violence, certain adult themes) to afford viewers the opportunity to exercise discretion and, in particular, for parents to exercise discretion with regard to young viewers. The content and placement of advisories will be determined by the Broadcast Standards and Practices Department.

Advisory announcements, when made, are intended to describe the general content and nature of the program in order to facilitate viewer evaluation of the program, and, in particular, parental evaluation of the program's suitability for young viewers.

These advisories are also included in print advertising and in on-air promotional material.

Alcohol Beverage Consumption

The portrayal of alcohol usage should be de-emphasized. When depicted, it must be consistent with, and necessary to, plot and character development. Over-indulgence should be discouraged as it is not an acceptable mode of behavior, and care should be exercised to avoid glamorization or promotion of alcoholic beverages.

Animals

The use of animals should conform to accepted standards of humane treatment.

Appeals/Solicitation of Funds

Absent special public interest considerations, no solicitation of funds may be made in any program.

Broadcast Tickets

Broadcast tickets may be offered over the air only after clearance with Broadcast Standards and Practices.

Children: Programs Intended Primarily for Their Viewing

In the course of a child's development, numerous social factors and forces, including television, affect the ability of the child to make the transition to adult society. Thus children's programming must strive to entertain and engage the imaginations of young viewers.

Programs designed for children should be appropriate to the audience's age and stage of development. The child's training and experience during the formative years should include positive sets of values which will allow the child to become a responsible adult, capable of coping with the challenges of maturity.

Children should also be exposed at the appropriate times to a reasonable range of the realities which exist in the world sufficient to help them make the transition to adulthood.

Because children also watch programs designed primarily for adults, this factor may be taken into account in the presentation of material in programs where children may constitute a substantial segment of the audience.

Clearance of Program Titles and Promotional Slogans

All titles of prospective programs (and recurring program segments) and all promotional slogans (including promotions for Capital Cities/ABC services) must be referred to Capital Cities/ABC Literary Rights as far in advance of broadcast as possible in order that a title search may be made. No title or slogan may be used on the air without clearance by Literary Rights.

Contests

A contest is a plan in which a prize is offered or awarded to the public based upon chance, diligence, knowledge or skill. Contest information may be broadcast within programs, provided that the contest offers a fair opportunity for all contestants to win, does not constitute a lottery (either as broadcast or conducted), and complies with all applicable law. All broadcast copy, Official Rules, and any additional supporting material must be submitted to Broadcast Standards and Practices or Legal for review.

In most instances, contest copy must disclose the following terms:

1. How to enter or participate;
2. Eligibility restrictions;
3. Entry deadlines;
4. The extent, nature, and value of prizes;
5. Time and means of selection of winners;
6. Tie-breaking procedures;
7. Means of identifying participating outlets (if relevant);
8. Clear sponsorship identification.

Copyright, Literary and Music Rights, Rights of Privacy

Capital Cities/ABC reserves the right to require evidence of the right to use specific musical or literary material as well as photographs, paintings, maps and films or other works and documents.

1. Music Clearance

   For music clearance, at least seven business days prior to broadcast time, Capital Cities/ABC requires the submission of written lists in duplicate showing the correct titles, the names of composers and publishers and the composer's and publisher's performing rights affiliation such as ASCAP or BMI, and copyright owners of any and all musical numbers to be used whether the use is vocal or instrumental, live or by records and if records, the label and artist. If lyrics other than as published are to be used, then such lyrics must be submitted in writing. Any music used in connection with commercial copy, directly or as lead-in or background, must be so cleared. In the case of unpublished manuscripts, lead sheets of the melody line (including lyrics, if any, together with performance permission from the copyright owner) must be submitted seven days before program use. No changes may be made thereafter without the approval of Capital Cities/ABC's Music Rights Department.

   For television programs, Capital Cities/ABC also requires the submission of a brief description of the program for which music has been cleared, whether "filmed" "live" or "taped" including a description of the backdrop, scenery and costumes, if any. The manner in which each composition is used should also be specified, i.e., whether a composition is to be presented "live" or by "prerecording" or any combination thereof, whether vocal or instrumental and to what extent the composition is connected or interwoven with the dramatic portion of the program. For purposes of describing the use, the standard industry conventions of "visual vocal", "visual instrumental", "visual dance", "background instrumental", or "background vocal" should be used. For films, Capital Cities/ABC requires the submission of the title, the name of the producer and distributor and a cue sheet listing the music numbers in the film.

   The submission to Capital Cities/ABC must be made at least seven days prior to the broadcast of a "live" show or the "taping" or "filming" of all other programs.

2. Literary Materials
   a. Outside Productions

      For programs produced by anyone other than Capital Cities/ABC, the producer is obligated to obtain, in writing, all necessary licenses and releases.

   b. In-House Productions

      For programs produced by Capital Cities/ABC, the producers must be aware that the Copyright Law includes within its scope non-dramatic literary works. Since it is imperative that the necessary clearances be obtained each time a use of a poem, novel, short story, or any other literary material is contemplated on a program, Capital Cities requires copies of all written permissions be sent to the Literary Rights Division approximately one month in advance of date of production.

3. Photographs and Films
   a. Outside Productions

      For programs produced by anyone other than Capital Cities/ABC, the producer is obligated to obtain in writing all necessary licenses and releases.

   b. In-House Productions

      In the majority of circumstances, the copyright owner's permission is required before using photographs or copyrighted programs or program material belonging to others. Whenever such material, that is, anything other than material prepared by ABC personnel, is to be used, Capital Cities/ABC should ascertain that the person supplying such material for broadcast on television has the right to grant Capital Cities/ABC a license to use the material provided.

      Whenever the name or likeness of a real person is to be used on a program in more than an incidental way, it may be necessary to obtain a release in writing from that person. This may even apply to public figures, and in some instances, deceased public figures. It may also apply to use of a person's face in a crowd shot, if such a crowd shot emphasizes the actions or presence of one individual. If more than an incidental use of someone is contemplated, check with Broadcast Standards and Practices or the Legal Department.

Credits

Producers must submit their program credits to Capital Cities/ABC's Program Administration and to Broadcast Standards and Practices for clearance prior to broadcast.

Criminal Activities (See Also "Violence")

Criminal activities, when depicted, must be consistent with and reasonably related to plot and character development. The presentation of such activities as acceptable behavior should be avoided. The treatment of criminal activities should attempt to convey their social and human consequences.

The presentation of techniques of crime in such detail as to be instructional or invite imitation shall be avoided.

Displays or Samplings for Studio Audience

Any plans for displays, samples or materials intended for distribution in Capital Cities/ABC studios or on its premises must be discussed with the Company at least a week prior to the broadcast in connection with which they are to be used. Capital Cities/ABC reserves the right to reject such plans in any case.

Dramatic Programming Containing Factual Elements

The following guidelines set forth standards for dramatic programs (often called "docudramas"), that contain elements that are based on actual events or on the lives or actions of actual persons, living or dead. The range of programs falling within this category is broad, and the guidelines are of necessity, therefore, general. The degree of substantiation required will vary on a project-by-project basis. Actual requirements in each case will be established by Broadcast Standards and Practices and the Legal Department. With respect to each project, our goal is to ensure needed levels of accuracy without unduly burdening those who are responsible for a project's creation, development and presentation.

1. Procedures

    When any project falling within these guidelines is placed into development, the producer is expected to provide:
    a. A written summary of the actual persons or events to be portrayed, highlighting dates and participants;
    b. A description of the ways in which the proposed script is intended or expected to depart from the actual events, including any proposed name and/or locale changes;
    c. The source for the depiction of any actual person (individual or composite) in the script;
    d. Copies of key substantiation materials: books, articles, interviews, medical records, etc., accompanied by a bibliography of corroborating sources;
    e. If the story involves court proceedings:
    —a list of the relevant individuals who testified or participated;
    —trial transcripts and appellate decisions;
    —information regarding the existence of any ongoing or related litigation, and the current status of such litigation;
    f. Any releases that have been secured, and a list of those which are forthcoming;

    g. The identity of key individuals who are not cooperating;
    h. If based on a book or articles, documentation regarding any existing or settled claims. The producer shall also advise of any present or past actions relating to a source used as a basis for a project;
    i. Names and credentials of any consultants the producer is using or considering;

    Broadcast Standards and Practices also reserves the right to interview individuals, or require producers to interview individuals, who are relevant to the project.

2. Documentation Procedures

    At the development stage, the producer will be informed by Broadcast Standards and Practices of the degree to which the script for the program must be annotated. Before the script will be approved, the producer will be expected to provide an annotated version, complying with those requirements.

    Typically, the producer will be expected to provide specific support (from books, articles, interviews, tapes, transcripts, etc.) corroborating each element that is based upon actual events, that depicts the actions of an actual person, or that characterizes such a person. Where available, specific quotations from books, statistical reports, interviews and the like should be used to corroborate dialogue, events or dates. The degree to which a script must ultimately be annotated (including the number of sources which may be required to substantiate a particular scene) will depend upon legal requirements, the nature of the project, and the degree to which fictionalization may otherwise be disclosed to the viewing audience.

    After receipt of an annotated script, Broadcast Standards and Practices will issue a detailed preliminary report responsive to the documentation materials. It will issue revised documentation reports as necessary on the basis of the producer's response. Approval for the project will not be given until all required documentation annotations have been provided to Broadcast Standards and Practices.

3. Guidelines

    The following standards apply to programs falling within these guidelines. They are not all-inclusive; additional requirements may be imposed on a case-by-case basis.
    a. Composite/Fictitious Characters
        i. It is permissible to create composite characters (i.e., characters who are based on two or more actual individuals). However, fictitious characters, other than incidental characters who have little or no bearing on the basic plot, should not be included in programming that is intended to be a recreation of actual, past or current events in dramatic form.

ii. In any case where a project will use composite characters, the annotated script should indicate the specific characters who have been used to create the composite. All dialogue and actions by composite characters throughout the script must be related to, and consistent with the actions and behavior of, the actual characters on which they are based.

b. Chronology

i. The chronology of significant actual events portrayed should be substantially accurate, and supportive evidence to this effect must be submitted in the annotated script. Telescoping may be employed so long as the compression does not misrepresent actual events.

ii. Where relevant to accuracy, passages of time must be clearly indicated, either in dialogue, by supers, dissolves, or other visual techniques.

c. Characterization and Attitudes

i. Personal characteristics, attitudes and the demeanor of actual persons portrayed must be consistent with corroborating evidence as to the actual characteristics of these persons.

ii. Created dialogue must be consistent with the actions, values, attitudes, and personalities of the actual figures being portrayed.

d. Representative Events

Fictionalized or compressed representations of actual events must be reasonably consistent with the historical record regarding them. For example, although a conversation between actual persons on a specific matter may not be capable of documentation, depictions of such conversations may be acceptable if they accurately characterize the individuals portrayed and their specific attitudes at the time in which the scene is depicted, and if they are consistent with available evidence regarding their actions and thoughts.

e. Controversial Subject Matter

Depending upon the nature of the issues involved, contrasting viewpoints may be required in programs that deal with controversial subjects.

f. Name Changes in Factual Recreations

Actual names and locales should generally be used in programs that are intended to be recreation of actual events. However, for legal reasons, the changing of a character's name or a given locale may be required by Broadcast Standards and Practices or the Legal Department.

4. Disclaimers and Advisories for Programs Subject to These Guidelines

Programs falling within these guidelines will be clearly and prominently identified for the viewing audience at the beginning of the telecast. The substance of that identification and its mode of presentation will be determined by Broadcast Standards and Practices and the Legal Department.

The following are for the purpose of general illustration and are not intended to foreclose use of other forms of disclosure which ABC may require:

Sample/Representative Disclaimers

—"The following is a recreation of [the event or story]. The action is based upon court records, eyewitness accounts, reportage, personal interviews, investigative reports, official documents, etc." [optional—"The names we use are real with the exception of certain composite characters who have been given fictitious names]."

—"The following is a dramatization of the life of [name] based on the book by [name] and other sources. Some composite characters and time compression have been used for dramatic purposes."

—"The following dramatization of the life of [name] is based on the recollections of [name] as described in his/her book [name]."

—"This story was inspired by/based upon the life and deeds of [name]. This motion picture is not an attempt to reproduce actual events, although it is suggested by them. The producer intends no more than to present a dramatic story."

—"Although the following film is fictionalized, it was inspired/suggested by real people and events."

Drug Use and Abuse

The use of illegal drugs or the abuse of legal drugs shall not be encouraged or shown as socially acceptable or desirable. When depicted, such use must be consistent with and reasonably related to plot and character development. Care should be exercised to avoid glamorization or promotion of drug usage. The portrayal of cigarette smoking shall be de-emphasized.

Emergency Situations

The terms "Flash" or "Bulletin" are terms reserved for special news exclusively and may not be used for any other purpose.

The horizontal crawl is exclusively for news usage.

The "Standby" slide and explanations accompanying the slide, as for instance, "Due to conditions beyond our control" or terms of similar connotation, are reserved for actual emergencies and may not be used for any other purpose.

Feature Films

Feature films initially produced by others for theatrical release and intended for Capital Cities/ABC Television exhibition are screened prior to acquisition by Capital Cities/ABC to determine whether they require deletions or are completely unacceptable. Relevant parties will be provided with a deletion report to enable them to appropriately edit the film. The edited versions are viewed prior to telecast to ensure compliance with Broadcast Standards and Practices directives.

Fictitious Call Letters

In order to protect the identity of AM, FM, and television stations and to prevent any possibility of confusion or misunderstanding, the use of station call letters that may be necessary to the plot or action of the program must be cleared with Broadcast Standards and Practices.

Financial and Investment Advice

Financial and investment advice will not be permitted except when it conforms with law and recognized ethical and professional standards.

Gambling

The broadcasting of information which could be expected to encourage illegal gambling on the part of the general public or which might otherwise aid the interests of or be useful to gamblers will not be permitted.

The use of gambling devices or scenes reasonably related to the development of plot or as appropriate background is acceptable only when presented with discretion and in moderation, and in a manner which would not encourage or foster betting.

Sports programs involving on-the-scene betting considered legally acceptable must observe federal, state, and local laws as they relate to the broadcasting of such events.

Game Shows and Audience Participation Shows

Quiz and similar programs that are presented as contests of knowledge, information, skill or luck and in which prizes are awarded must, in fact, be genuine contests; and the results must not be controlled by collusion with or between contestants, or by any other action which will favor one contestant against any other.

Prior to the taping of such programs, a "bible" must be prepared in which are set forth the rules and regulations of the program, eligibility standards for participants, security measures, and other safeguards which may be required, including those specified in Sections 507 and 508 of the Communications Act.

Game show pilot programs are not acceptable for telecast. Participants on pilot shows may not appear on a program taped for broadcast from the same series but may appear on other Capital Cities/ABC game shows provided they meet all necessary eligibility requirements.

Except as provided below, no Capital Cities/ABC contestant may appear in any audience participation/game show competition more than once in any one (1) year period or more than twice in any five (5) year period. Appearance on a nonbroadcast pilot shall not be counted as competition provided no prizes were awarded. An appearance on a game show where personality or other subjective qualifications are the basis for selection, e.g., The Dating Game, shall not be counted as an appearance. Nothing in the foregoing provision shall preclude reappearances on network programs for the purpose of "Championship" or "Alumni" competitions.

Giveaways/Prizes (See Also "Contests")

All giveaways/prizes must be approved by Capital Cities/ABC, and the Company reserves the right to limit or reject the use of giveaways on any program. The length and content of any material which describes any prize or award shall be subject to the approval of Capital Cities/ABC. If part of a contest, any such giveaway shall comply with the foregoing guidelines on contests.

Government Regulations

All material broadcast must conform to all applicable governmental laws, rules, regulations and announced policies.

Guest Appearances and Gratuitous Plugs

Talent/guests appearing on an interview program may identify and discuss their current interest (book, movie, etc.). Any other casual references to (or props of) a product or service other than their own by trade name or language sufficiently descriptive to identify it are unacceptable.

Human Relationships

The presentation of marriage, the family, interpersonal relationships, and other material dealing with sexuality shall not be treated exploitatively or irresponsibly, but with sensitivity.

Hypnosis

To avoid adverse effects upon the viewing audience, hypnosis should not be presented in a purposeful demonstration with extended technique. Hypnosis should not be ridiculed or presented as a game to be played.

Legislation or Litigation

Comment on or discussion of current or proposed legislation or pending litigation will be permitted only on political, news commentary, discussion, public affairs, or similar programs. Comment on or discussion of pending litigation must be within the bounds of fair comment.

Live Programs or Others for Which Scripts Cannot Be Prepared Prior to Broadcast

Live, live-on-tape quiz and audience participation programs in the entertainment field for which scripts cannot be prepared before broadcast are subject to the same Capital Cities/ABC policies and standards as are programs with written scripts. The Capital Cities/ABC designated representative assigned to the program will be responsible for enforcing all applicable policies on such programs.

All material used in pre-broadcast performances or "warm-ups" shall conform to ABC policies and standards. The designated Capital Cities/ABC representative will be responsible for enforcing such policies.

Lyrics

The lyrics of all songs to be incorporated in a program must be submitted to and be approved by Broadcast Standards and Practices prior to their use.

Misrepresentation

No program should be presented in a manner which through artifice or simulation would mislead the audience as to any material fact.

Non-fiction Programming

Non-fiction programming by definition is intended to represent facts, events and opinions. To promote accuracy in the presentation of facts, it is long-settled Capital Cities/ABC policy not to broadcast any non-fiction programming in which any scene or sequence appears in any manner to be what it, in fact, is not.

This policy must be clearly and affirmatively communicated to any individual associated with the production of non-fiction programming. It must constitute an essential element of any program bible.

Obscene, Indecent, or Profane Material

Obscene, indecent, or profane material is unacceptable. Determinations involving interpretation of the foregoing require consideration of context and scheduling.

Physical and Mental Infirmities

Physical handicaps, developmental disabilities and deformities should not be ridiculed or exploited for humorous effect. Material which is dependent upon such conditions should be presented in good taste as a matter of respect for those individuals who suffer from similar infirmities.

Point-to-Point Communications

Absent an emergency situation, a broadcasting station may not broadcast a message intended primarily for a specific individual and not intended to be received by the public. A message may, however, be addressed to a particular person if it is an integral part of the format of the program and is clearly understandable to the general public.

Product Identification/Use of Products As Props

The identification of products (or services) by brand name or the use of brand-name products as props should be kept to a minimum and must be specifically approved in each case by Broadcast Standards and Practices. Approval will be given only when the product reference or prop is important to sustaining the dramatic and production values of the program. Acceptance of consideration (in the form of money, goods, services or anything else of value) in return for product identification or prop use is prohibited. Capital Cities/ABC employees and outside production companies and their employees are required to inform Broadcast Standards and Practices whenever they become aware that consideration has been offered or accepted for any product identification or prop use. Failure to disclose the acceptance of such consideration may result in a violation of FCC regulations.

Professional Advice

Legal, medical and other professional advice, diagnosis, and treatment will not be permitted except when it conforms with law and recognized ethical and professional standards.

Promotions and Program Introduction

Promotional announcements and program "teasers" must properly reflect the actual nature and content of the program.

Pseudo-sciences

Programs based on or pertaining to fortune-telling, occultism, astrology, phrenology, palm-reading, numerology, mind-reading, character-reading, and the like are unacceptable if they encourage people to regard such activities as methodical analyses with a basis in exact science.

Race, Religion, Color, Age, National Origin and Sex

Capital Cities/ABC will accept no program whose effect misrepresents, ridicules, or attacks an individual or group on the basis of age, color, national origin, race, religion, or sex. Special sensitivity should be exercised in dealing with these concerns.

Safety

Special consideration should be given to the possible consequences of depicting unsafe acts. Potentially unsafe behavior should generally be avoided especially in programming intended for children's viewing.

Sexuality

The depictions of emotional and physical interpersonal relationships are essential elements of comedic and dramatic programming. In a changing society issues of human sexuality portrayed with sensitivity are appropriate programming fare.

Sensitive themes, however, cannot be treated in sensational or exploitative ways. Gratuitous sexual references, implicit or explicit, are prohibited.

In making programming decisions relating to human sexuality, Capital Cities/ABC's Department of Broadcast Standards and Practices considers many contextual factors. These include, but are not limited to, day part, audience demographics, program genre, prosocial value and audience expectations.

Subliminal Perception

Any technique which attempts to convey information to the viewer by transmitting messages below the threshold of normal awareness is not permitted.

Submissions Required in Entertainment Program Development

All entertainment programming, including Specials, Series Programming, Mini-Series and Novels for Television, Motion Pictures for Television, Pilots, and Promotion Featurettes, intended for broadcast over the facilities of Capital Cities/ABC, Inc., must be submitted to the Department of Broadcast Standards and Practices for review and approval at each stage of development and production. These include, but are not limited to, story idea, outline storyboard, all published script drafts and revised pages thereto, 35mm or videotape rough cut and 35mm answer print.

Talent Performances

Producers of Capital Cities/ABC may not obtain reimbursement for talent fees from record companies, the talent itself, their agents or managers, or others without prior approval of Broadcast Standards and Practices.

Telephone Numbers and Locales

To avoid prank calls the fictitious exchange "555" should be used. The use of any other number requires telephone company confirmation that the number is fictitious.

Telethons

Absent special public interest considerations, no telethons may be broadcast. All telethons must be approved by Broadcast Standards and Practices.

Violence

The use of violence for the sake of violence is prohibited. While a storyline or plot development may call for the use of force the amount and the manner of portrayal must be commensurate with a standard of reasonableness, with due regard for the principle that violence, or the use of force, as an appropriate means to an end is not to be emulated. Additionally, extreme caution must be observed in avoiding the portrayal of specific, detailed techniques involved in the use of weapons, the commission of crimes, and avoidance of detection.

Courtesy of Capital Cities/ABC, Inc.

RADIO-TELEVISION NEWS DIRECTORS ASSOCIATION CODE OF BROADCAST NEWS ETHICS

The responsibility of radio and television journalists is to gather and report information of importance and interest to the public accurately, honestly and impartially.

The members of the Radio-Television News Directors Association accept these standards and will:

1. Strive to present the source or nature of broadcast news material in a way that is balanced, accurate and fair.
   A. They will evaluate information solely on its merits as news, rejecting sensationalism or misleading emphasis in any form.
   B. They will guard against using audio or video material in a way that deceives the audience.
   C. They will not mislead the public by presenting as spontaneous news any material which is staged or rehearsed.
   D. They will identify people by race, creed, nationality or prior status only when it is relevant.
   E. They will clearly label opinion and commentary.
   F. They will promptly acknowledge and correct errors.
2. Strive to conduct themselves in a manner that protects them from conflicts of interest, real or perceived. They will decline gifts or favors which would influence or appear to influence their judgments.
3. Respect the dignity, privacy and well-being of people with whom they deal.
4. Recognize the need to protect confidential sources. They will promise confidentiality only with the intention of keeping that promise.
5. Respect everyone's right to a fair trial.
6. Broadcast the private transmissions of other broadcasters only with permission.
7. Actively encourage observance of this Code by all journalists, whether members of the Radio-Television News Directors Association or not.

Courtesy of the Radio-Television News Directors Association (RTNDA).

SOCIETY OF PROFESSIONAL JOURNALISTS CODE OF ETHICS

SOCIETY of Professional Journalists, believes the duty of journalists is to serve the truth.

We BELIEVE the agencies of mass communication are carriers of public discussion and information, acting on their Constitutional mandate and freedom to learn and report the facts.

We BELIEVE in public enlightenment as the forerunner of justice, and in our Constitutional role to seek the truth as part of the public's right to know the truth.

We BELIEVE those responsibilities carry obligations that require journalists to perform with intelligence, objectivity, accuracy, and fairness.

To these ends, we declare acceptance of the standards of practice here set forth:

I. Responsibility:

The public's right to know of events of public importance and interest is the overriding mission of the mass media. The purpose of distributing news and enlightened opinion is to serve the general welfare. Journalists who use their professional status as representatives of the public for selfish or other unworthy motives violate a high trust.

II. Freedom of the Press:

Freedom of the press is to be guarded as an inalienable right of people in a free society. It carries with it the freedom and the responsibility to discuss, question, and challenge actions and utterances of our government and of our public and private institutions. Journalists uphold the right to speak unpopular opinions and the privilege to agree with the majority.

III. Ethics:

Journalists must be free of obligation to any interest other than the public's right to know the truth.

1. Gifts, favors, free travel, special treatment or privileges can compromise the integrity of journalists and their employers. Nothing of value should be accepted.

2. Secondary employment, political involvement, holding public office, and service in community organizations should be avoided if it compromises the integrity of journalists and their employers. Journalists and their employers should conduct their personal lives in a manner that protects them from conflict of interest, real or apparent. Their responsibilities to the public are paramount. That is the nature of their profession.

3. So-called news communications from private sources should not be published or broadcast without substantiation of their claims to news values.

4. Journalists will seek news that serves the public interest, despite the obstacles. They will make constant efforts to assure that the public's business is conducted in public and that public records are open to public inspection.

5. Journalists acknowledge the newsman's ethic of protecting confidential sources of information.

6. Plagiarism is dishonest and unacceptable.

IV. Accuracy and Objectivity:

Good faith with the public is the foundation of all worthy journalism.

1. Truth is our ultimate goal.

2. Objectivity in reporting the news is another goal that serves as the mark of an experienced professional. It is a standard of performance toward which we strive. We honor those who achieve it.

3. There is no excuse for inaccuracies or lack of thoroughness.

4. Newspaper headlines should be fully warranted by the contents of the articles they accompany. Photographs and telecasts should give an accurate picture of an event and not highlight an incident out of context.

5. Sound practice makes clear distinction between news reports and expressions of opinion. News reports should be free of opinion or bias and represent all sides of an issue.

6. Partisanship in editorial comment that knowingly departs from the truth violates the spirit of American journalism.

7. Journalists recognize their responsibility for offering informed analysis, comment, and editorial opinion on public events and issues. They accept the obligation to present such material by individuals whose competence, experience, and judgment qualify them for it.

8. Special articles or presentations devoted to advocacy or the writer's own conclusions and interpretations should be labeled as such.

V. Fair Play:

Journalists at all times will show respect for the dignity, privacy, rights, and well-being of people encountered in the course of gathering and presenting the news.

1. The news media should not communicate unofficial charges affecting reputation or moral character without giving the accused a chance to reply.

2. The news media must guard against invading a person's right to privacy.

3. The media should not pander to morbid curiosity about details of vice and crime.

4. It is the duty of news media to make prompt and complete correction of their errors.

5. Journalists should be accountable to the public for their reports and the public should be encouraged to voice its grievances against the media. Open dialogue with our readers, viewers, and listeners should be fostered.

VI. Mutual Trust:

Adherence to this code is intended to preserve and strengthen the bond of mutual trust and respect between American journalists and the American people.

The Society shall—by programs of education and other means—encourage individual journalists to adhere to these tenets, and shall encourage journalistic publications and broadcasters to recognize their responsibility to frame codes of ethics in concert with their employees to serve as guidelines in furthering these goals.

Courtesy of the Society of Professional Journalists.

Index